ENVIRONMENTAL MANAGEMENT AND BUSINESS STRATEGY

Leadership Skills for the 21st Century

Bruce W. Piasecki
Rensselaer Polytechnic Institute

Kevin A. Fletcher
Rensselaer Polytechnic Institute

Frank J. Mendelson
Rensselaer Polytechnic Institute

JOHN WILEY & SONS

New York   Chichester   Weinheim   Brisbane   Singapore   Toronto

Acquisitions Editor	Ellen Ford
Marketing Manager	Tracy Guyton
Senior Production Editor	Kelly Tavares
Senior Designer	Laura Boucher

Photo of "Fallingwater" by Frank Llyod Wright, courtesy of Western Pennsylvania Conservancy/Fallingwater.

This book was set in Palatino by Matrix Publishing Services and printed and bound by Malloy Lithographing. The cover was printed by Phoenix Color.

This book is printed on acid-free paper. ♾

The paper in this book was manufactured by a mill whose forest management programs include sustained yield harvesting of its timberlands. Sustained yield harvesting principles ensure that the numbers of trees cut each year does not exceed the amount of new growth.

Library of Congress Cataloging in Publication Data:
Piasecki, Bruce, 1955-
    Environmental management and business strategy : leadership skills
for the 21st century / Bruce W. Piasecki, Kevin A. Fletcher, Frank J. Mendelson.
        p.   cm.
    Includes index.
    ISBN 0-471-16972-2 (pbk. : alk. paper)
    1. Industrial management—Environmental aspects.   I. Fletcher,
Kevin A.   II. Mendelson, Frank J.   III. Title.
HD30.255.P52   1999
658.4'08—dc21   98-28233
                                                                           CIP

Printed in the United States of America

10 9 8 7 6 5 4 3 2 1

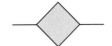

About the Authors

Bruce W. Piasecki has authored four books including Wiley's *Corporate Environmental Strategy: The Avalanche of Change Since Bhopal*. He is also president and founder of the American Hazard Control (AHC) Group, Inc. which since 1981 has provided business development advice on a range of environmental issues. In addition, he is Director of Rensselaer Polytechnic Institute's (RPI) Environmental Management & Policy program, a professor in the Lally School of Management & Technology, and Editor-in-Chief of *Corporate Environmental Strategy: The Journal of Environmental Leadership*.

Kevin A. Fletcher serves as a Managing Editor for *Corporate Environmental Strategy: The Journal of Environmental Leadership*. He has prior work experience with Bausch & Lomb, the National Environmental Policy Institute, and management consulting experience with the AHC Group. With a prior degree in biology from SUNY Geneseo, he is currently pursuing a Ph.D. in environmental management from RPI's Lally School of Management & Technology and serves as Director of Policy Initiatives and Press Relations for the AHC Group.

Frank J. Mendelson is the Assistant Director of the Environmental Management and Policy Program at Rensselaer Polytechnic Institute, and Executive Editor for the past five years of *Corporate Environmental Strategy: The Journal of Environmental Leadership*. He is an environmental management consultant, and Vice President of Client Relations with the AHC Group. He earned his Masters of Science in the Urban and Environmental Studies Program at RPI, and has over twenty years of experience in communications, management, and program operations.

Purpose Statement and General Introduction

It takes time, speed, and a readiness to accept work that is not yet proven to write effectively about real choices of consequence. The world of business strategy and environmental management is constantly changing and often reinventing itself. Furthermore, business strategies are often developed behind closed doors, and typically those who know intimately about the difficult choices involved in matching corporate goals with environmental initiatives either do not write or do not write much. That is why so many myths have developed around the relationship between business and the environment, most of which are simply inaccurate, and a few quite dangerous to real progress.

Over the last fifteen years, we have learned to cope with these realities by hitching our interests alongside some of those larger ships, escorting them into safe harbor. We do this as management consultants. We also do this as business educators at Rensselaer Polytechnic Institute. Finally, we do this as a group of a dozen editors at our quarterly practitioner journal—*Corporate Environmental Strategy: The Journal of Environmental Leadership.*

Time, quality, representative choice, reliable insight: these words suggest core elements of all successful strategies, whether we are examining issues of war, business, or the ever-gentle realm of publication.

The great thinkers of the quality revolution in business, such as Juran and Deming, often tried to boil down strategic choice as a function of time. Their work is useful, and on occasion brilliant, but seldom are such classics in business writing exactly right for environmental decision makers.

The classics in business writing since World War II have often taken too much of a mechanistic view of how business decisions are made, as if what works at a manufacturing site or on an engineer's design sheets is enough to represent the larger realm of strategic choice. At midlife, I have found that business strategists and environmental leaders are far more humanistic in their approach to key decisions. They involve publics, explain themselves when they are pressed with the right questions, and base their decisions on a wider range of concerns than just the "bottom line." This book is about the "top line," the skills needed to operate in the new world of corporate environmental strategy.

With this more humanistic spectrum of concerns in mind, we have organized our book around three classic global needs shared by both business strategists and environmental leaders: Achieving Compliance, Recognizing Business Opportunity, and Answering Public Expectations.

Every firm, in every nation across the globe, from Canada to Chile, must be concerned about these three realms in all the choices they make regarding their economy and their environment. We have worked hard to bring you some of the best and most representative cases in each of these broad categories.

AVOIDING HOGWASH AND OTHER MARKETING BUZZ

Anyone involved in management consulting knows how hard it is to get a business to publish its failures or missteps. In fact, most cases become rather "sanitized" before publication. This is because the very choice to focus on representative corporate cases opens you up to criticism. If you focus on Volvo, for example, as we do in this text, some critic will ask why you did not focus on General Motors' strategy to develop the electric car; others will note that Vice President Al Gore wants a supercar that averages over 80 miles per gallon. Readers, especially informed ones, will ask for far more than business will deliver. It doesn't matter that it is impossible to write the Al Gore supercar case right now because it does not really exist yet, or that the GM electric car case has been written, but cannot tell us much yet. Our culture is endlessly and deceptively fascinated with the new and promising.

This book is presented with several stories in its design, so readers can wander up and down the structure with different levels of sophistication. It pays to explain how this enables us to sidestep the usual hogwash. Some readers ask for information that does not exist yet, and will claim that anything about current business practice, no matter how innovative or progressive, is "nothing short of greenwash." Other readers will remain adamantly concrete. They will claim that what works for Volvo could not possibly work for the rest of the auto industry, or for their firm. My answer is harsh: I instruct our research team to ignore these anticipated critics. Instead, we have selected representative corporate cases that exist in reality, in the current realm of markets, government policy, and consumer choice. We have compiled these cases in such a way to allow us to fulfill three often-competing goals at once:

Primary Goal: To reach both experienced managers and newcomers to the field of business strategy at the same time.

Secondary Goal: To publish cases that respect the full range of management responsibilities, from basic civil laws of government to those facing competitors and customers.

Tertiary Goal: To mix our casework with an appealing conceptual narrative that enables readers to discover what is representative about the case, as we describe what made the case successful and consequential to the world of business, law, technology, and consumer behavior.

In order to achieve these competing goals, we have included sidebars and visual road signs such as charts and graphs. In another effort to help newcomers, we supply a set of questions at the end of each case. To challenge the seasoned reader, we add provocative parallels about failed competitors, or still unanswered questions, whenever possible.

THE BASIC ARCHITECTURE OF THIS BOOK

Neither business strategy nor solid business decision making has become an armchair science. Instead, this text remains littered with the evidence of struggle, failure, and false starts. Yet by the time it gets on the page, or before the public, and you are comfortably reading the case in your study or library, it all appears calm and clear. The truth behind all good strategy, or writing for that matter, is years of anxious preparation.

The construct of this book is contrived; it makes a ruin appear like a well-structured mansion. By allowing this transformation to occur, we can provide a dwelling place for new students of business, while we allow a thoughtful sanctuary for experienced executives seeking a few moments of calm to come in from the rain.

The most reliable way for the reader to imagine our purpose is to envision the construction of a mansion. This passage on the works of Frank Lloyd Wright may help you feel what the writer feels:

> The architecture of Frank Lloyd Wright (1867–1959) is marked by a richness of conception, unity of expression and fertility of invention that unerringly honor the fundamental laws of design while drawing strength and inspiration from a profound respect for American traditions, landscapes, and native materials.

"A richness of conception," "unity of expression," and the "fertility of invention," these three important phrases outline how a successful book composition, in its complex design choices and its overall architectonics, matches the choices of an architect. Over the last four years, we have spent more time stripping down the cases included in this book than embellishing them. Through the right case selection, less can be more. In building this book, we rely on the representative cases. It is your job to examine the uniqueness of each case.

Teaching is about the basic human desire to share a valuable, not-to-be-missed experience with others. This is not the same as exchanging chit-chat on a train ride to your job. Teaching is different, when it works, because it is about sharing the meaning of experience, not just its details. Thus, we have tried to make these teaching cases, not just state-of-the-art research cases.

PROFESSIONAL RESPONSIBILITIES IN STRATEGY AND ENVIRONMENT

What is Teaching?

The desire to share a valuable experience is a basic human desire, which is why there are so many natural teachers, from coaches of little league to the instructors of violin virtuosos. Although there is an element of presumption in teaching, good teaching shares the meaning of the experience not just its details.

Teaching is about lived experience. When it comes to the fields of environmental management and business strategy, it is often useful to embed the principles of teaching in actual cases so that the drama and the detail of the case carries the complexity of the situation for the reader or student. As in all good teaching, what matters in the end is the insight into how management works, not just the details.

What is Consulting?

Consulting is a complex business art. In the process of providing a client with a great deal of analysis and working knowledge, the consultant becomes a trusted advisor. In the end, what matters is the strength of the trust, not just the depth of the analysis or the density of the insight, because often the consultants are not around when their advice is best used. This puts a lot of pressure on the consultant in the early stages of working for the client, since the consultant's value decreases rapidly the more effective they are at the start.

While the consultant is always secretly serving as a model on how to solve some heavy corporate problems, he is also trying to change or improve the client's situation without any direct control over budgets, implementation, or direction.

Consulting on projects that involve a client's attempt to elevate the importance of environmental services within the firm in question is particularly risky, yet needed, as this century comes to a close. The world of consulting is a liquid stage: The consultant never knows how stable her footing can remain or exactly how high her advice can go up the corporate chain.

What is Sound Judgment?

We have designed this text to meet the needs of both teachers and environmental and business consultants because both realms rely heavily on the cultivation of sound judgment. A decision is sound when it profits not only the individual decision maker but also the larger society as well. Many of the cases in this book were selected because they involve sound judgments, decisions that allowed the company in question to position itself for a brighter or more profitable future.

What is Attentive Reading?

One of life's few controllable joys is reading. The most attentive readers are often successful consultants. They come into a new corporate setting and quickly read the signals of what is doable and what is not. In addition, executives who are known for their sound judgments are often also extensive readers. They can absorb huge amounts of material and are sometimes described as being a "quick read." Leadership in business strategy and environmental management is a rare commodity. Leaders have the will and knowledge to help shape the search for reliable answers. Acquiring these skills takes far more than attentive reading, but it is a good start in becoming a successful practitioner.

You Know Strategy When

- You cannot be deceived by popular cynicism or by the limits of the established convention.
- You accept how hard change is and know why people are tempted to remain entrenched in the old ways of doing business, yet are still ready to help people move forward.
- You mix the needs of functional management with surprise.
- You know the paradoxical nature of wrestling with internal constraints and external demands, and you can keep a sense of proportion.
- You are able to balance line functions, plant manager demands, management roles, and core business directions.
- You can shape stakeholder expectations.
- You strive for efficiency (i.e., through technological answers) and effectiveness (i.e., adhering to reliable indicators of customer satisfaction, legal adherence, and engineering savvy) simultaneously.
- You are able to learn from history, understand stakeholder interests (not merely positions), and create new solutions.
- You can go from plan to action (often the most difficult task).
- You know not only how to fight and win, but also when not to fight.

Reliable Signs of Leadership

- Many managers are good at analysis, the careful demarcation of a problem. The leader also knows what kinds of thinking should precede the next actions. The leader's analysis yields a prognosis and a set of actionable items that are worthy of the staff's sustained attention.
- Max DePree, in his two brilliant books on leadership, refers to "the bright red thread of resolve and commitment" that is woven into every fabric a leader weaves. It is nearly impossible to measure resolve and commitment of this kind, but everyone can notice the leader's resolve.
- Leaders, unlike every other professional's job description, are responsible for making the future of their organization promising. Many organizations have their top management tiers filled up with people capable of limiting that firm's liabilities, both public and legal. But true leaders do

more than protect assets; through strategic thinking they position the entire firm's future and make it promising.

- What makes it so difficult to define environmental leadership is that many of the old definitions of political or corporate leadership do not quite do it. While a great political leader may make the future of his or her party or nation prosperous, leaders for sustainable development have a task that is validated beyond their immediate organization. All leaders view leadership as tribal. Their self-crafted job description is about amassing extensive relationships, contracts, and credits. Leaders view their organization as a semipermeable cell that includes customers, citizens, government representatives, the press, potential allies, and distant colleagues.

- Leaders enable their deputies to do many things. Ever attentive to what is precious and so easily depleted about human capital, leaders polish results, nurture risk-taking, liberate good ideas, and enable people to capitalize on their past efforts, and they do so instinctively.

While the consulting world is built on a liquid stage, the realm of applied business decision making consists of relatively solid footing. We measure success by sales volume, profit margin, and power over consumer needs. Yet beneath these measures beats the vital heart of sound judgment. How do we, as readers and researchers, measure the soundness of those judgments? As the cases and reflections throughout this book illustrate, a decision is sound when it profits not only its host organization, but also the larger society that surrounds it. Eighty percent of this book's content is comprised of contributed pieces for good reason: The voices of the contributing authors are where much of the sound judgments reside. The following is an abstract checklist of the skill set you can deduce from these special cases:

Primary Skill: An astute sense of history gives you the wisdom to appreciate the complex standards of environmental regulations and programs. It gives you the strength to sift through the morass of past mistakes and present predicaments with a freshness capable of recognizing new solutions and opportunities.

Secondary Skill: An analytical ability to sort through present predicaments takes legal, economic, and technical teams and abilities; the leader must unite these complex professionals in a common direction.

Ultimate Skill: Management savvy to lead beyond basic competencies allows the leader to steer staff consistently; allows the organization to sidestep the usual costly traffic jams in court or in the court of public suspicion; and positions the organization for success in the future.

The power of this book resides in the distinct voices of those officials or executives whose names are attached to the contributed pieces. We have selected these pieces because of their established authority, and we have re-worked them to make sense to both practiced readers and newcomers to the fields of business strategy and environmental management. Our contributed authors can be thought of as serious independent researchers, since often their quest for a new product or a new corporate direction took them away from their industrial peers, apart from the realm of technical know-how and regulatory certainty. In short, they went out on a limb of innovation and did not fall off. In the beginning, these leaders had to keep their innovation secret for market reasons. As they grew the staff, capital, and distribution systems to deliver their proposed change and environmental improvement, they often remained with a small number of disciples, surrounded by pure and abstract questions, or glitches, still in need of resolution. Finally, they go public.

By calculating the lasting value of the selected articles, we have encouraged the researchers to sit back and explain their normally quiet moves. In a way, we have asked them to leave the inner sanctum of their innovations and explain themselves—the risks they took, the compromises they made, and their refusal to back down.

A FINAL CAVEAT TO CYNICS, SCHOLARS, AND PRACTITIONERS

In the end, what matters most in this field is the cultivation of future leaders. In the more established corporate disciplines of accounting and finance, companies know where to go to hire the best. Yet in the field of environmental management a hiring manager (or an eager student) must look long and hard to find educational programs that are training future leaders, rather than just entry-level functions.

Because of this serious gap in training, our world is in short supply of environmental leaders that can deliver on their promises. It is not enough to be good at winning in court, or shaving a few million dollars off a liability exposure or insurance premium. The hiring manager wants both basic competencies and leadership potential. Throughout this text, we have tried to remain honest to this dual demand.

We know that the first fifteen or twenty years of most environmental careers will be consumed by the many technical demands toward legal compliance. The duties of environmental managers will always concern environmental auditing, waste minimization, (TSDF) site selection, permitting hassles, safety requirements, recycling demands, hazardous materials identification, and paperwork. Yet we have chosen not to limit your exposure in this book to these common responsibilities, but to foster and mentor leaders as well.

Consider one of the best-paid clinical professions—the doctor. When we choose a doctor, we select the best not only for their diagnostic skills, but for their prognostic abilities—the leadership skills it takes to improve our general health, not just medicate a symptom. Similarly, the field of environmental management needs more prognostic abilities. It is no longer adequate to simply locate and describe a problem. We are expected to fix it and, in the process, make the firm more competitive. You can think of the overall logic of this book as a stairwell. The higher you go up the corporate stairwell, the more responsible you are for making the future of your organization promising.

Every corporation has a bottom line on what they will pay to achieve environmental compliance. But what is often missed is a sense of the firm's "top line," that level of strategic decision making that involves the right price, and the right staff at the right time. Our final warning is deceptively simple: Don't get fooled by the popular buzz about the vicious bottom line. Throughout history, leaders have learned how to march up the stairwell with a set of richer goals. It takes far more than cynical analysis, simple youthful arrogance, professional blame-throwing, or linear thinking; it takes leadership skills.

The cases in this book serve as a snapshot of the field, where everyday people—line workers, managers, and executives alike—are making the decisions that affect both their organization's effectiveness and competitive stature, and also determine our industrial world's sustainability. Our goal is to assist that discovery and help leaders—current and future ones alike—make sustainable enterprises work to sustain our world.

UNDERSTANDING THE LOGIC OF THE BOOK

We live in the age of environmental compliance and its complex demands. "Corporate environmentalism" has been historically defined through the laws and regulations created to protect the environment and the public (as signaled through the creation of the Environmental Protection Agency in 1970 here in the United States). As such, "Achieving Compliance" seems to be the most practical and intelligent way to begin this text.

In Part I, on compliance, we explore the complex skills and resources companies need to meet their fundamental legal requirements. Understanding that there are both internal and external components to compliance, we focus primarily on the internal aspects (i.e., management integration, measurement), leaving the bulk of the discussion of the external forces for Part III, "Answering Public Expectations."

In Parts II and III, we explore what is real and what is possible in business when it comes to strategic choices and the environment—truly the core of the book. The marriage of business strategy and environmental management is strange and new to most; but to the decision makers and companies presented in this text, this marriage is viewed as essential for business survival and competitiveness as we enter the next century.

Finally, in the concluding section we blend the role of leadership skills and leaders with the maps and road-signs developed from the entire book to give added direction. Leadership skills are a requirement for change in this field, a point emphasized in the words of those managing everyday business decisions of environmental consequence.

With each part of this book, more of the whole is captured and cultivated. Yet, we deliberately simplify the job at the start. Often the most difficult skill to master in research and writing is the ability to see both the microscopic view and the whole picture. In this text, we've tried to do just that while merely looking at the field of environmental management. Behind each selected topic are at least 10 more that could have been discussed. We have chosen to present the most tangible pieces of the field that we can in order to demonstrate the skills needed at the intersection of environmental management and business strategy.

To create a coherent structure that is both useful and representative, we have chosen each section of the text as a distinct room. We furnish each room with key elements of the topics under discussion—this structure allows the reader to cleanly and concisely gain a larger value from the otherwise complex, dynamic, and often contradictory field of practice.

These structural "pieces" of the text help to build the broader lessons on environmental management and business strategy from research, from experience, and most importantly, from the practitioners themselves.

Case Studies and Teaching Cases

We've chosen to include case studies to help identify what is "real" in environmental management. Business insiders know that decision making is a daily affair; as such, they offer the most enlightened view of strategic choices made on the environment. They view these case studies as both thoughtful and useful examples of environmental leadership. But what, exactly, is a useful case study? In his seminal book on case-writing, *Case Study Research*, Robert Yin presents five general guidelines for developing truly exemplary and useful cases.

First, the case study must be significant. Allowing practitioners to write about the corporate decision making they're experiencing leads to both discovery and a useful understanding of the field, rather than merely hypothesized relationships and theoretical connections. Second, the case study must be complete. Completeness is characterized by a clear presentation of the boundaries of the case, a mature and appropriate collection of evidence, and a realistic understanding of the resource and time constraints on developing the case. Third, the case study must consider alternative perspectives. Fourth, the exemplary case study judiciously and effectively presents the most compelling evidence so that the reader can reach an independent judgment regarding the merits of the analysis. Yet another goal is to present sufficient evidence to gain the reader's confidence in the knowledge presented in the piece, without getting bogged down in unnecessary detail. Finally, the case study must be composed in an engaging manner; that is, the report should be enjoyable. As Yin states, "a good manuscript is one that 'seduces' the eye. If you read such a manuscript, your eye will not want to leave the page but continue to read paragraph after paragraph, page after page, until exhaustion sets in. This type of seduction should be the goal in composing any case study report." This is a lofty goal, but one worthy of effort. We have found that most leaders, in practice, do this instinctively.

Based on our own experience and the insights presented above, we have included only representative cases throughout the text, each varying in size and depth. At the end of Parts I, II, and III, we have included a full-blown teaching case as a further means of adding value for the reader. We hope these longer, integrative cases fulfill all five of Yin's elements of successful case writing.

Each of these cases helps to make up a world of environmental management and business strategy that consists of actual choices, problems, and solutions. The lasting value of such case study doesn't lie in looking just at the progressive fringe of the world, although studies of the Body Shop or Patagonia do provide hopeful and valuable lessons for approaching sustainable development. For us, lasting value lies in studying the art and science of organizational learning—what it takes to change the petroleum industry, the auto industry, the utility world, or even the chemical industry for the better. These established industrial sectors with significant environmental liabilities are the strongest economic drivers; as such, they offer the most valuable lessons for environmental managers and strategists alike.

Topic Discussions

We have selected experts in the field—practitioners and researchers alike—to present information on the various tasks, roles, and responsibilities tied to corporate environmental strategy. This host of experts and grizzled veterans in the field help present a snapshot of their respective professions and their place within the broader scheme of corporate environmental strategy. Each has submitted to rigorous editing, allowing us to fit their experience into our overarching arguments.

In the spirit of presenting cases while avoiding an encyclopedic feel, we have included minicases and insights that serve as a surrogate to a more patiently laid-out presentation. As such, they are less rich than the larger cases but in many ways they stand on equal footing with them by offering concise lessons on management choice. These accompanying pieces offer additional facts or opinions and add weight and insight to the subject by presenting a different or alternative view. For instance, Ronald Van Epps and Susan Walter's piece, entitled "Why Are Environmental Performance Measures Necessary?", gives insight into measurement choices from the perspective of management consultants and the corporate clients they serve, while the accompanying World Resources Institute offers a perspective on this topic by one of the premier research-based Nongovernmental Organizations (NGOs).

Executive Spotlights

These supplements give the reader the direct perspectives of the organizational leaders operating at the busy crossroads of business and the environment. Each includes a biography that explains how the individual got to where he or she is today, as well as the opportunity to comment on corporate environmental strategy and sustainable development, both in terms of the organization and in broader terms. It is our hope that the voices of these men and women will provide readers with valuable insights and the tools needed to succeed in acting as a force for positive social change.

Follow-up Questions

Learning does not occur without sustained inquiry. As all of the contributed pieces present insights worthy of discovery, we have included questions and discussions that help frame these pieces so that these valuable insights are not lost on the new reader.

Suggestions for Further Reading

With this book, we look to both inform the reader on the state-of-the-art in environmental management and business strategy and to direct students toward their own specific areas of interest. Since the text itself cannot present all of the relevant information in the field without approaching a state of tedium, we have provided our choices for texts that can help satisfy the reader's continuing interest in a subject area. As with professional life, it is up to the reader to tease out the delicate components of a field or topic area that comprise his or her own interest.

Bruce W. Piasecki
Rensselaer Polytechnic Institute
Troy, New York
August 1998

Acknowledgments

The life of a book often spans across more years than it actually takes to write it. This book is no different. In many ways this text has its roots in the early 1990s with the creation and maturation of our quarterly practitioner's publication, *Corporate Environmental Strategy: The Journal of Environmental Leadership*. As such, the list of acknowledgments could be exhaustive to a fault in an effort to reflect over six years of editorial assistance developing pieces that now appear in their updated form in this book. In order to underline the value and contributions of Journal editors, student research assistants, and staff, let us point to this history and acknowledge the culmination of many years of editorial advice in these pages.

Many of the articles appearing in this text were originally published in *Corporate Environmental Strategy*. It is with thanks and appreciation that the following people contributed their time and energy in direction and editorial assistance over the past five years, most notably Rich Mansfield, publisher and co-founder of the Journal at PRI Publishing as well as Dixie Sipher Yonkers, first managing editor of the Journal. Others contributors to the editorial staff of the Journal over the years include: James Atkinson, David Rainey, Fred Williamson, Jeff Paules, Nancy Rose-Halse, Scott H. Shapleigh, Martin Charter, Joy Parisi, Elena Rose La Rocca, Michael Stevenson, Dawn M. Varacchi, Chao-tung Jorden Wen, Matthew Moustakas, Jennifer Ellefsen, James Harrison, Evangeline Casey, Gena Gallinger, Cori Fay Traub, Tucker Ruberti, Timothy Herbst, Deneen Hatmaker, Patricia Jackson, Sean McCandless, Camille Douglas, Thomas Lindberg and Tara Koch. There are more that could be included, and so we apologize for those not mentioned.

Just as the early life of a book is fluid, so too are the people involved in its development, especially in academia. Students enter RPI's Environmental Management & Policy program, lend their insights and perspective to the current range of research project, graduate, and then go on to influence the field as trained professionals. This means that many competent students have had a hand in fine-tuning this text.

Most specifically, in its early stages of development, we had valuable input from people like Scott Shapleigh, Tucker Ruberti, Jennifer Meyerson, Pete Weglinski, Amy Muska, Matt Moustakis, Dawn Varrachi, Michelle Peattie, and

Aurora Amores. In later iterations, Chris Renaud, Walt Tunneson, Tim Judge, David Hopkins, James Harrison, JoAnn Drost, Jennifer Ellefson, and Sri V. among others, added their valuable advice and editorial assistance.

We would also like to acknowledge the comments of the external reviewers that Wiley provided for us. This list includes:

- Helen S. Fine, Bridgewater State College
- Mark Starik, George Washington University
- Gordon Rands, Penn State University
- Vicki Milledge, University of Massachusetts, Boston
- Mark Cohen, Vanderbilt University
- Lucian Spataro, Ohio University
- Chris Stinson, University of Texas/Austin
- Marsha Haas, College of Charleston
- Ron Cheek, LaGrange College
- Virginia Gerde, Virginia Tech
- James Hershauer, Arizona State University
- Jane Humble, Arizona State University
- Bill Stevenson, Boston College
- William F. Wescott, A. D. Little Co
- Peter Reynolds, Northern Arizona University
- Anne T. Lawrence, San Jose State University

Along with the watchful eye of the reviewers chosen by John Wiley & Sons, we also called upon reviews and comments from some of our colleagues, including Rick Bunch, Darryl Banks, Tim Herbst, and Dick Johns. We also received direct and indirect feedback from the environmental managers, executives, and policy experts who have attended our Corporate Affiliates Event, held at the Rensselaer campus each year.

Of course, for their assistance and patience, our editor, Ellen Ford, and the Wiley staff must be wholeheartedly thanked as the folks who road-tested this vehicle and then pushed it down the road.

Contents

PART   1   ACHIEVING COMPLIANCE   1

Chapter 1   What Is Environmental Leadership?   3

Chapter 2   The Role of Upper Management   8

Balancing Corporate Environmental Responses with Business Needs   8
Hitting the Green Wall: Why Corporate Programs Get Stalled   10
Lessons from the Field: Thoughts on Environmental Management,
   Compliance, and Strategy   22

**Chapter 3   Establishing an Effective Environmental
                  Audit Program**   29

The Paradoxes of a Proactive Auditing Strategy: Environmental Auditing
   at WMX Technologies, Inc.   30
Lessons from the Field: The Basic Legal Elements in Audit Protection   40

Chapter 4   The Question of Measurement   47

Why Are Environmental Performance Measures Necessary?   61
Lessons from the Field: Environmental Measurement Feasibility   64

Integrative Case I: Going Green: The Niagara Mohawk Story   71
Suggestions for Further Reading   90

**PART   2   RECOGNIZING BUSINESS
                  OPPORTUNITIES**   93

Chapter 5   Defining Strategy in the "Age of Environmentalism"   95

Chapter 6 Environmental Accounting for Competitive Advantage 107

Aligning Financial Concerns and Goals with
Environmental Responsibilities 107
Greening the CFO: Implementing Environmental Accounting in
Industry 109

Chapter 7 Environmentally Driven New Product Development 121

Driving the Product Development Process 121
Leading Change in the Face of Product Elimination: ARCO's Choice in
Creating a Cleaner-Burning Gasoline 123

Chapter 8 Environmental Management Systems 137

From Plan to Action: Implementing Corporate Environmental Strategy 137
Converging Integrated New Product Development with Design for
the Environment 140
Leveraging Innovative Potential: Design for Environment at AT&T 151

Chapter 9 Management Information Systems and Environmental Management 164

The Wheel of Decision Making: Informing the Executive 164
Innovations in Environmental Information Management 166
Information Challenges at Anheuser-Busch 180

Integrative Case II: Volvo's Strategic Approach to
Environmental Management 192
Suggestions for Further Reading 207

PART 3 ANSWERING PUBLIC EXPECTATIONS 209

Chapter 10 The Public Face of Corporate Environmental Strategy 211

Chapter 11 Responding to Stakeholders 216

Responding to a New Social Charter: The Responsible Care® Initiative 216
Preempting the Crisis: Key Concepts in Anticipatory Issues
Management 226

Fixing Past Mistakes by Managing Expectations   243

A Prime in Alternative Dispute Resolution Approach and Terminology   250

When an Agreement Is Not Profitable: The Paint Industry and Its Search
for a National VOC Standard   254

Successful Voluntary Agreements: The Case of EPA and AFPA   263

Chapter 12   Public Disclosure and Environmental Reporting   273

Going Beyond Required Reporting and Financial Disclosure   273

Corporate Accountability: The Evolution of
Voluntary Environmental Reporting   279

Lessons from the Field: Practioner Insight on Environmental Reporting   295

Integrative Case III: Environmental Commitment at the
Southern Company   308

Suggestions for Further Reading   328

AFTERWORD: LEADERSHIP SKILLS FOR SUSTAINABLE DEVELOPMENT   329

APPENDICES AND ENDNOTES   339

INDEX   343

1

ACHIEVING COMPLIANCE

What Is Environmental Leadership?

Leadership is not something that is done to people, like fixing their teeth. Rather, it is what unlocks people's potential, challenges them to become better, calls them to task for the lies they have told themselves.
—Bill Bradley, former New Jersey Senator[1]

Have you ever noticed how seldom environmental leadership is defined clearly and intelligently? Business books abound with cases that explore what creates a leader within a private sector organization. Environmental books, on the other hand, typically emphasize wrongdoing, imminent doom, and identification and solution of technical problems. Seldom do these two traditions meet. Yet the increasing importance being attached to the qualities of leadership warrants looking at what distinguishes environmental leadership from other kinds of superior corporate performance.

Environmental leaders in the corporate arena face a challenging set of demands that differ from those faced by their corporate peers in other, more defined and established departments, such as finance, sales, and marketing. First, they must achieve regulatory compliance. Second, they must go beyond compliance to recognize business opportunities while taking on prudent business risks. Third, they must work skillfully with a wide range of external stakeholders, not all of them friendly. Environmental leaders, then, require an extraordinary range of knowledge, diplomatic and political talent, dispute-resolution abilities, basic business skills, and a humanism in their decision making that reaches beyond this quarter's balance sheet.

Although many of these skills are shared by political or corporate leaders, what's unique for environmental path-breakers is the *comprehensiveness* of their skills. A second special feature is the frequency with which environmental leaders must initiate and guide companywide change with limited staff and resources.

LEADERSHIP GOALS AND ENVIRONMENTAL BUSINESS NEEDS

The first goal of environmental leaders is to achieve compliance cost-effectively. Much has been written about the complexity of compliance, from the overlapping and often conflicting levels of government to the sheer volume of data that must be managed. To reach this goal, the leader must comprehend legal, engineering, and scientific needs, and make the goal understandable to others within the firm, especially the chief executive officer and product champions. Part I of this text is designed to delineate these many skills and requirements.

Yet compliance is merely the starting-point, not the finish line. Leaders also pursue a second goal: achieving compliance without extinguishing the spark for risk taking, innovation, and business advances. Here the leader achieves a productive balance between regulatory demands and business expectations. We dedicate Part II of this book to that complex cause.

The third goal of environmental leaders is to answer public expectations by satisfying key stakeholders. ARCO's pursuit of reformulated gasoline, Bristol Myers Squibb's development of its Herbal Essences line, and Monsanto's bold attempt to move into industrial products that allow sustainable development are all examples of how environmental leaders must operate in an increasingly public arena. Compliance might represent an expensive "three-foot hurdle" that all must jump, but new corporate product lines that are based on environmental considerations must scale the "nine-foot hurdle" of public expectations.

These three goals are never reached in isolation. The environmental leader figures out how to find and harness them all, not in a single person, perhaps, but in the team he or she leads. The leader serves as the example that such integration of skills and goals is not only possible but profitable.

PERSONAL LEADERSHIP SKILLS

There are nine basic skills that enable a leader to identify the right team and then jump the hurdles in record time. We explore each in this text at length, although they are summed up in Figure 1-1.

The first is the ability to find what works, not just what is right. Leaders seem to sidestep blame, instead stepping back to find what works, or better, to reveal what works best. Perhaps Bill Bradley's idea about the "unlocking" of potential starts here, since environmental leaders focus themselves and others on answers, not opinions and positions.

The second important skill is recognizing the power of affiliation. National Public Radio commentator Joel Makower once stated whimsically at a conference: "Remember, there is only one letter difference between networking and not working."[2] That letter spells the difference between creative sustained growth and institutional stagnation. In other words, there is little lasting value in a professional life without networking or affiliation building. Environmen-

1. Forget about blame—find out what works.

2. Build a broad and deep network of personal friendships, associations, and affiliations.

3. Cultivate risk, ambiguity, and uncertainty as sources of powerful change.

4. Select brilliant, reliable deputies.

5. Check your instincts against your clients' needs.

6. Replicate success, using lots of small steps to clear the top.

7. Make the future of the organization promising to everyone in it.

8. Acknowledge the importance of everyone's role.

9. Use stories and metaphors to reinforce the goals of the organization and a sense of belonging.

Figure 1-1 Top Personal Skills for Environmental Leaders

tal leaders seem to grasp this lesson intuitively. For instance, an effective environmental leader may spend a significant chunk of the week rediscovering the values latent in her network of personal affiliations, from old employers to new hires, from contact with regulators who once gave the firm a slap on the wrist to recent college graduates looking for a break. Leadership is about viewing environmental challenges as a route with a few good options, not a downward spiral toward dead ends.

A tolerance for productive ambiguity is the third skill. Suppose you are an environmental consulting firm and the overwhelming majority of your company's clients are petrochemical-based companies. Your leaders, sensing but not quite knowing that changes are in the wind, ask you to look into attracting clients from cosmetics and other low-volume, low-risk specialty manufacturing businesses. In eighteen short months, you acquire a whole new list of clients who make adhesives and other products with issues involving volatile organic compounds (VOCs). The Clean Air Act Amendments, it turns out, had suddenly prompted these new clients to act, and you were there to help them, capitalizing on your CAA and VOC expertise from the petroleum work.

How did your leaders move the company toward these new clients? The answer is not direct, but as Max DePree warns in his book on leadership, "People with vision inject ambiguity and risk and uncertainty in our lives."[3] Leader push their firms to find new opportunities in new places.

Leaders also persuade others to pursue the thrill of the chase. What enables them to survive on such high-altitude challenges? We may think we know that realistic changes are only incremental. But the leaders—such as ARCO, with its reformulated gas, or AT&T with its ozone-free electronics, or Patagonia, with its recycled plastic fibers—show how a tolerance for ambiguity can spawn radical, productive change (what the management buzz books call "quantum" change).

Leaders know how to select brilliant deputies—the fourth vital skill. Frank Friedman, senior vice president of Elf Atochem, said: "Too many companies still employ technicians rather than managers. I would rather have one swan than two turkeys working for me."[4] Selecting brilliant deputies allows leaders to maintain compliance as they pursue the further goals that compound value throughout the organization.

The fifth skill of environmental leaders is an ability to know what the client needs. This may seem obvious, but in practice it is rare. One extreme example is the Dutch government, which provides grants to radical environmental groups as early warnings of issues the government will eventually have to address. Corporate leaders, too, know that analytical problem-solving skills aren't sufficient; the right targets must be hit again and again, often before others even get ready to aim.

While many professionals seem preoccupied with their current tasks, a leader outsmarts the ceaseless pressures of competition by building on, or repeating, past successes—the sixth important skill. A look at a skills chain shows the value that compounds through this skill: Jumping a 15-foot hurdle seems impossible, but jumping 15 feet in three-foot increments gets you to the top of the stairs.

Too often in business the question of just how an action "adds value" arises. The real trick, as in accumulating wealth, is compound interest. The last three leadership skills compound the value of everyone in the organization. To do this, environmental leaders first make the future of their organization promising. They then develop an ability to take everyone seriously. And finally, they use "tribal" stories through which the millions of single actions by members of the organization, or "tribe," cohere into a meaningful message.

These related points are best illustrated through a famous story about Abraham Lincoln. During an early and critical phase of the Civil War, Lincoln was confronted by a Northern governor about his draft policy. The governor had hinted to the president's cabinet that he would not carry out the president's orders. On the right occasion, Lincoln told this story as he urged Secretary of War William Stanton to proceed with the draft:[5]

> The governor is like a boy I once saw at the launching of a ship. When everything was ready they picked out the boy and sent him under the ship to knock away the trigger and let her go. At the critical moment everything depended on the boy. He had to do the job well by a direct, vigorous blow, and then lie flat and keep still while the ship slid over him. The boy did everything right; but he yelled as if he were being murdered, from the time he got under the keel until he got out. I thought the skin was scraped off his back, but he wasn't hurt at all. The master of the yard told me that this boy was chosen for that job, that he did his work well, that he never had been hurt, but that he always squealed that way.

That's just the way with the governor. Make up your minds that he is not hurt, and that he is doing his work right, and pay no attention to his squealing. He only wants to make you understand how hard his task is, and that he is on hand performing it.

This parable, so typical of Lincoln, embodies many of the attributes of environmental leadership noted here. The ease and gracefulness of such a tale suggest better ways for Lincoln's deputies, the cabinet members, to replicate their successes. It tells them that their leader takes them and their staffs seriously and understands their roles, just as he understood the role of the squealing boy and the truculent governor; it compounds the values of organizational stability while endorsing creative productivity; and it positions them for complexities still ahead. The challenges faced by environmental leaders to make their organizations as productive as possible while meeting the demands of both regulators and the public are exceedingly complex.

When you read the following reflections on "Hitting the Green Wall" within today's compliance-bound firms, please keep the above Lincoln tale and the itemized list of skills in mind. It is the only known way out of the box. To achieve compliance is a vitally important first step. To get out of the box into adding business value is what will define leaders in the next century.

While few people possess the abilities of Abraham Lincoln, one of the greatest presidents in American history, the development of comprehensive, diverse, and personally exacting skills distinguishes today's environmental leader from others in the corporate tribe. As you read this book, keep this rough ratio in mind: Over 80 percent of your time may be consumed on achieving and keeping compliance, especially in our wild world of rapid mergers and acquisitions. Roughly 15 percent of your time will be spent recognizing business opportunity, especially if you care to escape the corporate dungeon of the "mindless functionary." That leaves less than 5 percent of your time for all the rest on public trust, initial messages, and stakeholder involvement.

Somehow, the leader lives on all three floors of corporate life at once, scaling the hurdles each day. In the first part of this book, where we assemble pieces on the difficulties of achieving compliance, please remember how demanding these additional requirements of leadership must be. It is hard to achieve compliance. It is ten times harder to make money while doing that, as you answer consumer and public needs and expectations. This takes real leadership.

NOTES

1. BILL BRADLEY, *Time Present, Time Past: A Memoir,* Knopf Publishing, New York, 1996.
2. Conversation with JOEL MAKOWER at Global Environmental Management Initiative conference, 1995.
3. MAX DEPREE, *Leadership Jazz,* Currency Doubleday, New York, 1992.
4. Keynote speech by FRANK FRIEDMAN at RPI's "Fifth Annual Corporate Affiliates" event coordinated by the Environmental Management & Policy program, June 1997.
5. DONALD PHILLIPS, *Lincoln on Leadership: Executive Strategies for Tough Times,* Warner Books, New York, 1995.

The Role of Upper Management

BALANCING CORPORATE ENVIRONMENTAL RESPONSES WITH BUSINESS NEEDS

Many of you who are reading this text may be practitioners—decision makers fighting to integrate regulatory compliance tasks with the arduous chores of money making and liability containment. So those of you in the trenches know this essential paradox of decision making—those who are great at it have very little time to explain or to even state the terms of their decisions. This makes describing the actual roles of upper management in environmental initiatives both a challenge and a thrill. A further difficulty heightens the significance of the chase. By 1998, most executives of consequence see environmental decisions as reshaping all aspects of their business functions—from acquisitions and facility operations to manufacturing, design, and distribution. Yet most corporate decision makers continue to respond to environmental choices in only a manufacturing or waste management context, subsequently limiting their management and strategic choices. Furthermore, when the decision makers in a firm eventually try to raise their environmental programs to the strategic level, creating opportunity and new product lines, they fall short.

Why do environmental strategists so often hit these earlier hurdles? The answers are explored at length by A. D. Little's Robert Shelton in his now classic essay, "Hitting the Green Wall: Why Corporate Programs Get Stalled." First published in *Corporate Environmental Strategy: The Journal of Environmental Leadership* in 1994,[1] this article has been used and cited by thousands of practitioners. An extended and updated version now follows.

In today's unsteady economic terrain, environmental controversies often have been misshaped as matters for technical or regulatory staff only. Yet to develop a reliable environmental strategy, corporate strategists now employ expert opinion, historical perspective, a measured sense of public expectations, political opinion polls, sheer instinct, and basic intuitions. They involve lawyers, MBAs, engineers, and more and more new product development staff, as shown in Figure 2–1. The once two-dimensional field of environmental management now includes the added dimension of strategic vision and other facets of business traditionally known as "MBA functions."

In *Corporate Environmental Strategy: The Avalanche of Change Since Bhopal*,[2] this "business reality" in environmental management led me to define corporate environmental strategy as the "lively confusion of corporate plans and accidents, profits and incidents, along with the simple miscalculations that are improved by resolve and panic." Yet, the strategic implications of environmental choice involve data management, shifts in measurements, communication training of senior management, and strategic advice on approaching insurers, to mention just a few instances of the immense new world of environmental measurement and performance metrics.

So just how large is this environmental market? This question is too often answered narrowly. The cost of environmental regulations alone is $125 billion worth of business per year in the United States. That is already equivalent to one-half of our textiles industry, or nearly one-third of our defense industry during the zenith of Cold War spending. Most experts now concede that the volume can be increased to $300 billion per year domestically by including the *actual* legal fees of environmentally driven liability containment efforts, such as the huge churning of funds over Superfund (stemming from the legal liabilities firms with the ownership of contaminated properties) or the legal positioning now resulting from the new Federal Facilities Compliance Act. To be completely inclusive, the actual cost of environmentally driven expenditures hovers now around $400 billion annually, since the final rough estimate of $100 billion comes from environmentally driven new product development. Entire books are devoted to this link between environment and new product devel-

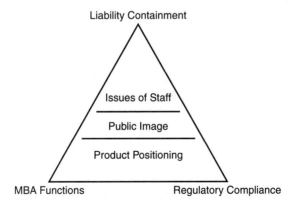

Figure 2–1   The Full Triangle of Environmental Management

opment. Taking these figures to an international scale, it is easy to see that the size of the environmental marketplace is staggering.[2]

Looking over this complete set of responsibilities—regulatory compliance, new product development, and liability containment—you can see why Harvard's Michael Porter finds "the environmental component the most exciting part of corporate strategy today, more critical to achieving advantage than costs, quality, and pricing."[3] This comment, made by Porter at the 1994 Global Environmental Management Initiative conference, avoids the issue of actual dollars spent by emphasizing, instead, the excitement of the field and its increasing linkages to competitive advantage.

Despite Porter's careful hedging on the actual size of these increasing expenditures, his 1994 announcement has become more accepted as we enter the next century. Environmental management has been elevated by corporate strategists, and when it works, has reached the same level of importance as the well-known agenda items of price, quality, and distribution.

NOTES

1. See Robert Shelton's "Hitting the Green Wall" *Corporate Environmental Strategy: The Journal of Environmental Leadership* (Elsevier Science, Inc.), Vol. 3, No. 2.
2. Piasecki, Bruce, *Corporate Environmental Strategy: The Avalanche of Change Since Bhopal,* John Wiley & Sons, Inc., New York, 1995.
3. From a speech given at the 1995 GEMI conference. Please also see Porter, Michael, and Claas van der Linde, "Green and Competitive: Ending the Stalemate," *Harvard Business Review,* September–October, 1995.

Hitting the Green Wall: Why Corporate Programs Get Stalled

Robert D. Shelton

Robert Shelton is director of Arthur D. Little, Inc., located in San Francisco. He is the firm's Global Champion for EH&S Strategy, specializing in the integration of environmental management into a company's business strategy, organization, and operations. Past clients have included ABB, Xerox, Hewlett-Packard, Bechtel, Sun Microsystems, Digital Equipment Corporation, S. C. Johnson, Weyerhaeuser, Apple Computer, Levi Straus & Co., Raychem, and Boeing. Shelton has spoken at the House of Commons, the Rio Earth Summit, the European Union's Workshop on Business and the Environment, and the Global Environmental Management Initiative (GEMI). Prior to joining Arthur D. Little, Shelton held management positions at Stanford Research Institute, Booz, Allen & Hamilton, and Envirotech.

Currently, Shelton is an adjunct professor of strategic environmental management at the University of California and participates as a board member of the Silicon Valley Environmental Partnership and the Environmental Business Cluster. The author would like to acknowledge the assistance of Ann Graham in the preparation of this piece.

In the late 1980s and early 1990s, companies adopted strategic environmental management initiatives because of the apparent competitive advantages that would accrue, including decreased manufacturing costs, faster time to market, increased clout with regulators, and increased market share. Strategic environmental management provided considerable advantages over the reactive, costly compliance, and "end-of-the-pipe" environmental management strategies that were dominant in the 1970s and early 1980s (i.e., attacking the pollution problem at facilities through air scrubber, wastewater treatment technologies, and other after-the-fact remedies). The stories of leaders such as 3M, Dow, and Du Pont that pioneered strategic environmental management and their early successes are well known by now to the business and environmental management communities.

However, a close inspection of the situation as we approach the end of this century indicates that everything is not going smoothly. While some companies are successfully moving forward with reliable strategic environmental management initiatives, others are repositioning or backing away from the broad proactive programs that they had adopted earlier. Why? Because they have hit the "Green Wall," as pictured in Figure 2–2.

The Green Wall is a point at which the overall organization refuses to move forward with its strategic environmental management program, and the environmental initiative stops dead in its tracks, as if it had hit a wall. Symptoms of hitting the Green Wall include negative or deferred decisions due to a lack of management support for the strategic environmental management concept and program; environmental, health, and safety (EH&S) programs that are lacking focus; and the inability to demonstrate to others in the organization attractive returns on further investments in the environmental programs. Examples of companies that have hit the Green Wall include:

- Apple Computer, which cut its award-winning Advanced (environmental) Technology Group as part of corporate downsizing;
- Warner Lambert, which is exiting the environmental packaging arena;
- ABB, which has positioned itself to sell off many environmental units and alter the internal Environmental Health & Safety (EH&S) role; and
- McDonalds, which is struggling with how to sell hamburgers on the basis of the environmental merits of the company.

Other companies are also bumping into the hard realities of the Green Wall. For example, the senior management of a major consumer products company recognized that although process-related environmental management investments and programs (i.e., pollution prevention) made sense and saved money, no one inside the company had been able to effectively demonstrate that significant product-related environmental changes were warranted. Likewise, a Fortune 500 company, a leader in strategic environmental management, found a significant lack of support for a proactive environmental strategy

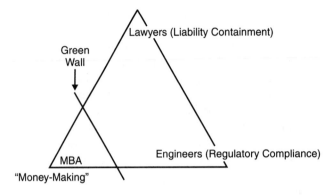

The core nature of business is sliced from the environmental decision-making process, leaving the two-dimensional way of compliance, which lacks any strategic vision.

Figure 2–2 Defining the "Green Wall"

among many of its product managers. These managers simply have not been convinced that the benefits justify the costs, despite notable successes in their company.

Such recent experiences demonstrate that the "Green Wall" poses a real threat to strategic environmental management programs. Leading companies are coming up directly against this problem, and it seems likely that other companies are doomed to face the same risks. As we enter the end of this century, it is safe to say that the problem will still be with us in the next.

In fact, many companies that are already pressing up against this wall may not know it. Companies that have hit the Green Wall are caught in the "one step forward, one step back" phenomenon in their environmental programs. Although individual program activities are moving forward (giving the impression of progress), others may stall, a phenomenon characterized by the lack of real progress which prevails across the portfolio of environmental programs.

WHY IT TAKES STRATEGIC THINKING TO SCALE THE GREEN WALL

Historically, traditional, compliance-oriented environmental management organizations have had difficulty finding an effective place in the business enterprise because environmental management is neither an operations nor a staff function. Accordingly, environmental management functions have been often difficult to integrate sufficiently with the business units for these functions, to become both effective and "businesslike" *and* sufficiently "corporate" and autonomous enough to provide the independent perspectives required for environmental quality assurance and enforcement.

The tension created by this dual role has been relieved somewhat through the adoption of strategic environmental management initiatives. The goal of such initiatives is greater integration of environmental management with the business functions. As a result, more effort is invested in identifying the bottom-line contributions that environmental management can make and in the collaborative work with the business units needed to achieve those contributions. Nevertheless, the tension between business and environmental issues in organizations continues to exist. As a result, there is an uneasy fit of strategic environmental management with the business functions and with the inability to convince doubting Thomases in the corporate structure that any of this "green stuff" really makes *business* sense. For many in the corporation, strategic environmental management lacks credibility, for reasons shown in Figure 2–3.

All of the factors in Figure 2–3 frustrate attempts to integrate environmental management with the business functions and to build a credible set of expectations regarding the potential contributions of the strategic environmental initiative. Not all of these factors can be readily addressed by the environmental team because they are facts of life in conducting business in today's corpora-

Figure 2–3   The Environmental Management Credibility Gap

Factors that have contributed to the credibility gap include:

- Corporate downsizing, which often throws environmental (and other) programs into tailspins
- Tight financial controls and increased scrutiny of the bottom-line contribution for all organizations in the company
- New management paradigms (i.e., reengineering, TQM) that distract management attention and reorient priorities
- Environmental strategies and programs that are too broad or try to do everything at once (thereby increasing costs and diluting payback) and do not fit well with the overall business strategy
- Unrealistically high expectations for potential benefits from strategic environmental management, resulting from overly aggressive sales jobs or cheerleading
- Early EH&S initiatives have picked the low-hanging fruit, removing the high-return/low-effort opportunities
- Creation of an environmental culture that is not congruent with the business culture of the company
- Poor communication between the environmental organization and the lines of business about the types and sources of competitive advantage that can be accrued

tions. But together they act to undermine the credibility of the environmental initiative.

Many skeptical business managers do not welcome environmental issues or environmental managers to the table when plans and budgets are being made; as a result, they effectively halt progress with the environmental management plan and implementation. Given the turmoil and change common in corporations today (e.g., reengineering, TQM), being left out of the inner circle of business managers is equivalent to being left out entirely. And being left out creates the foundation for the Green Wall.

THE WALL THAT ENVIRONMENTAL HEALTH AND SAFETY BUILT

Environmental managers are quick to blame the narrow-mindedness and recalcitrance of nonbelievers in the corporation for the lack of understanding of the value of environmental programs. One environmental manager lamented that "nobody else in the organization even understands what we do for it."

Nevertheless, the sad truth is that the Green Wall is created largely by the environmental management organization itself. Its players have not come to terms with the fundamental reality of the corporation. A company has a business culture that speaks a business language and it tends to discount or exclude those who do not share similar attributes. The environmental manager must be cognizant of this.

Environmental management programs that have hit the Green Wall have failed to fit in with the business culture of the corporation. Environmental managers have tended to expect other parts of the organization to accept them, and the unstated assumption by the environmental group has been that the overall organization would have to change to accommodate their environmental initiatives. Yet, the harsh reality is that the overall organization expects the environmental organization and initiatives to adapt to the business culture. This difference in viewpoint might not necessarily result in the creation of a Green Wall, if it weren't for two factors that environmental managers overlook: (1) the business culture has been around a lot longer and is firmly entrenched, and (2) the purse strings are held by the old guard.

SCALING THE WALL: EVIDENCE OF PROFITABILITY

Many environmental organizations assume that the value of their strategic environmental programs is obvious and significant. However, what is obvious to the environmental managers is frequently less clear to the business managers. Return on investment is still the most common business test of validity, and many hard-nosed managers have not seen business-oriented analyses and explanations of the costs and benefits of environmental initiatives. Therefore, they have not been convinced that strategic environmental management can or will help them.

One major electronics firm found that the engineering group did not appreciate the value of the environmental programs, and when push came to shove, the environmental programs were severely curtailed during a corporatewide restructuring. The company's engineering management and environmental management had not reached agreement regarding the benefits of the environmental function. No clear measure of its benefits to the business was available for engineering management to use in assessing its effectiveness. The strategic environmental group assumed that the benefits of its activities were evident and fully appreciated by engineering management. Communication was muddled, resulting in the creation of a Green Wall.

To make matters worse, when the message regarding the benefits of environmental management is delivered, it is often unintelligible to business managers because it is in "environmentalese." One senior manager said, "For the typical business executive, the messages that environmental managers deliver are as difficult to understand as those of the lawyers, and about as welcome."

Typical environmentalese includes lots of nonbusiness acronyms (e.g., ROD, BOD, NOD, EIR, LCA) that preclude all but environmental managers and EPA employees from understanding and serve to distance environmental managers from business managers. In addition, environmental managers tend to couch their analyses, logic, and lexicon around regulations and compliance issues even in strategic environmental management programs. Although their emphasis on bottom-line contributions has increased, strategic environmental managers have generally failed to adopt the business logic and lexicon used by business managers.

Only when the message is put in business terms and the environmentalese is dropped, as shown in Figure 2–4, can real communication begin. One vice president of environmental management of a pharmaceutical company was having trouble getting through to other managers in the corporation regarding the net contribution that the strategic environmental program was making, especially in the training arena. Up to that point, a lot of OSHA compliance language had been used that went over (or perhaps under) their heads. The business managers just did not seem to get it and were openly skeptical. So the vice president shifted away from environmentalese and adopted a business perspective. He said, "Lost time accidents to this group of employees typically cost you $100,000 per injured employee per year. The program has reduced our lost time accidents by two per year this year, and similar reductions are expected over the next three years. The investment was $25,000." The executives immediately understood what they were getting for their money, and they liked it.

Unfortunately, the business perspective is not used often enough by environmental management organizations. Too often, environmental logic is

Figure 2–4 The Language of Business and Environmentalese

Turning Environmentalese . . .	Into Business
Got the enforcement guys off our back	Net present value of avoided fines
Fewer fines than last year	Lost market share of fines as a percentage of industry fines
Spent millions on remediation	Decreased backlog of remediation, on time, on budget, and according to our strategy
Met new regulatory requirements and invested in pollution prevention	Return on investment for environmental capital investments
Created a matrix team of EH&S and Engineering	Leveraging of staff from engineering and operations to keep down the head count in the environmental group
Decentralized EH&S staff into operations	Embedded environmental function in operations with a net increase in value added and a decrease in overall costs
Created a Design for the Environment function	Added environmental issues that are important to our customers into the product development process
Added environmental features to our products	Improvement in time to market and increased share due to improvements in the Design for the Environment program

Source: Originally assembled by Robert Shelton for *Corporate Environmental Strategy: The Journal of Environmental Leadership.* Published by Elsevier Science.

couched in environmentalese, with the potential business benefits of strategic environmental initiatives misunderstood as a result. Following the example of the pharmaceutical company, translation of environmentalese into business logic and lexicon could lead to very interesting results.

Editor's Note: The following chart by Robert J. Kloepfer is provided by the authors to sum up in "ten strategic ways" how some firms outsmart the real constraints described so vividly by Robert Shelton. You can think of these as a map to get past the Green Wall within your organization.

ROADMAPS FOR THOSE LOST IN THE CORPORATE MAZE

There are examples of strategic environmental initiatives that have not been externalized by the business organization. One multibillion-dollar company epitomizes the mental and cultural shift required to outsmart the Green Wall.

Ten Strategic Elements of Strong Environmental Management Programs

Business Element	Steps for Integration
ORGANIZATION AND STAFFING	• Design functions to assure that EHS professionals are qualified and appropriately positioned. • Write formal job descriptions that clearly outline technical qualifications, duties, and responsibilities free from conflict. • Identify clear lines of authority, span of control, and anticipated interactions with corporate entities and support staff. • Commit to ongoing training and education of staff.
POLICIES AND PROCEDURES	• Write explicit policies and procedures that come from or have clear support from the top. • Define specific practices and indicate performance expectations and measures. • Be specific and appropriately configure for all levels of personnel. • Schedule periodic reviews/updates to account for changes in regulations, industry practices, and corporate goals.
PLANNING	• Integrate EHS concerns into business planning process and vice versa. • Consider environmental due diligence in acquisitions and divestitures of real property, early in transaction planning. • Consider environmental aspects early for R&D; capital project budgeting; and new product development to minimize cost and maximize efficiency. • Track emerging EHS issues for potential impact to operations and to facilitate appropriate response plans.
PROGRAM MANAGEMENT SYSTEMS	• Implement effective day-to-day program and project management systems. • Institute delivery systems and controls to assure facility compliance with regulations and operating goals. • Include personnel direction and performance; operation and maintenance of pollution control and safety equipment; and emergency response and accident investigation in system controls.
REVIEW AND EVALUATION	• Establish effective environmental audit programs to serve as a periodic check on conformance to regulations, good management practices, and corporate goals and objectives. • Assess "point-in-time" compliance status and the effectiveness of the management system. • Evaluate problems, analyze root causes, and work with management to make corrective actions. • Follow up on findings and recommendations, and repeat program periodically.

MANAGEMENT INFORMATION SYSTEMS	• Establish a formal MIS system that is well communicated and understood and regularly updated. • Allow the flow of environmental data up to the corporate and executive level, and down to the facility manager. • Give the corporate group and facility managers the ability to share the same knowledge about operations, problems, and priorities.
BUDGETING AND SCHEDULING	• Prioritize environmental programmatic needs along with other corporate endeavors. • Allow early input of environmental department needs when allocating funds for necessary expenditures. • Allow the environmental department to have executive level control of its budget, to avoid funding shortages. • Avoid using least-cost approaches rather than best-cost approaches to satisfy regulatory requirements. • Rank environmental needs to identify priorities and establish timeframe for meeting needs, to allow the opportunity for a range of options and voluntary management practices.
COMMUNICATION AND OUTREACH	• Establish a proactive community relations program to better control public and stakeholder perceptions about EHS issues. • Solicit input from concerned groups and permit joint decision making on sensitive issues to address community concerns. • Inform public about programs such as pollution prevention initiatives (i.e., by publishing an annual report). • Inform workers of corporate commitment to environmental management, to acquire "buy-in" by employees. • Disseminate formal, written crisis management plans that address specific areas (i.e., interaction with media and elected officials). • Establish an active government relations program to build relationships with key opinion leaders in advance of "crisis."
LEGAL AND REGULATORY SURVEILLANCE	• Track regulations, good management practices and trends for efficient compliance. • Comment on proposed regulations or rulemakings. • Assess potential operational and financial impacts of new regulatory initiatives and communicate to senior executives and lobbyists, to formulate a strategy for comment. • Analyze new regulations and communicate requirements to facility coordinators consistently and early on. • Monitor trends in case law, negotiated settlements, and other regulatory and legal interpretations.
RISK AND LOSS MANAGEMENT	• Develop a strong relationship between environmental and risk management staff.

- Identify environmental liabilities and assess exposure to unacceptable financial risk through joint efforts.
- Work together on insurance coverage review, acquisition support and design of environmental loss management programs.

Source: Robert J. Kloepfer, "Ten Steps That Integrate Environmental Management Functions," *Corporate Environmental Strategy,* Vol. 2, No. 4, Spring 1995: 65–68.

The company accomplished this by emphasizing its business strengths in its environmental programs. Its vice president of environmental management described it this way:

> We prided ourselves on selecting and growing the best managers. Our company was built upon a tradition of aggressive technical improvement of our products and processes, and we were the recognized innovators in our industry. We were organized to facilitate creative solutions and provided incentives to our employees to break away from the "traditional" and create the best. However, when it came to environmental management, we did not have the same approach. Our approach violated our culture and business strategy, and it left the environmental management organization outside of the business arena. So we changed the rules and said that the goal in environmental management was the same as in all the other areas of our business. Innovate and compete.

This company realigned its environmental activities with its business culture and has avoided the Green Wall. It made environmental considerations part of the responsibility of the product development groups (before it was called Design for the Environment) and was able to integrate environmental concerns into products and processes in a seamless manner. (Please see Parts II and III of this text for further examples.)

Design for the Environment (DFE) programs can exemplify the type of interactive environmental management that tears down or avoids the Green Wall. At its roots, Design for the Environment is a technology management activity whose goal is to align product development activities in order to capture external and internal environmental considerations. Environment is only one of the design criteria that must be integrated into the product. Since organization usually follows strategy, the DFE logic of a company must include the essential features of technology management (i.e., product management and development) and the overall business strategy of the company.

In many organizations (e.g., Xerox, Hewlett Packard, AT&T) DFE has integrated easily with the business units and the line operations because the DFE efforts have successfully been organized close to or inside the organizations that claim primary responsibility for the design function without compromising their need for independence. The environmental activities and the business

An Example of Avoiding the "Green Wall"

Sun Microsystems recently realigned its strategic environmental management programs to reflect the hard-nosed business priorities of its president, the competitive realities of its industry, and the innovative culture of the company. The result is a highly interactive environmental program that integrates Sun's overall business strategy, smarter, smaller, faster, into its environmental strategy. Sun credits this realignment with an overall increase in the bottom-line effectiveness of the environmental organization. Staff productivity increased, transaction costs decreased, and the environmental program met with less cultural resistance throughout the entire organization. For instance, Sun's engineering function internalized the packaging function, which had traditionally been in the environmental organization. Engineering was surprised at the added value that this function provided and immediately began to make plans to increase its size and activities. When packaging was part of the environmental shop, its value was heavily discounted and ignored, and a Green Wall could have resulted. Now, construction of a Green Wall is unlikely because both sides have too much to lose.

As this example shows, an interactive environmental strategy stresses innovative, tailored approaches that focus on developing a sustainable program within the corporate structure, including the management of technology, human resources, and financial resources.

activities are interactive and supportive. The result is that many companies have adopted aggressive DFE programs without creating the Green Wall.

TEARING DOWN THE GREEN WALL: OPTIONS FOR THE NEXT-CENTURY EXECUTIVE

There are two paths that strategic environmental management can follow, as shown in Figure 2–5. One builds a Green Wall; the other allows environmental management that is interactive and integrated into the business. Tearing down an existing Green Wall requires developing an environmental strategy, organization, operations, and culture that follow this second path. Determining which path to follow and steering the environmental organization down that path is the responsibility of the environmental management organization.

An integrated, interactive strategy requires:

- Making environmental management a business issue that complements the overall business strategy. (See the Kloepfer sidebar in this section.)
- Changing environmental communications within the company to reflect business logic and priorities, using clear, accepted business terms and

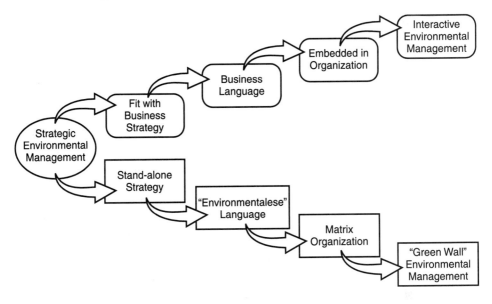

Figure 2–5   The Integrated Potential for Environmental Management

Source: Shelton in *Corporate Environmental Strategy: The Journal of Environmental Leadership.*

concepts, and avoiding the use of environmentalese. (See Part III of this text.)

- Creating and adopting metrics to measure the real costs and business benefits of the environmental management programs in all areas of the business in order to avoid the use of environmentalese to justify or promote programs. (See Parts I and II in this text.)

- Making environmental management part of the business organization, not just tacking it onto the organization via decentralization or the ubiquitous matrices that so many companies use, and actually embedding environmental management into operations similar to the successful DFE models. (This is reflected in Part II.)

- Radically changing the job descriptions and compensation of environmental managers to reflect the interactive and innovative realities of doing business and reinforcing the overall business culture.

These actions require that environmental management adopt the same attitudes, habits, and patterns of decision about running its shop as the rest of the company has about running theirs. If the company thrives on innovation and value-added products and processes, the environmental organization must prize those same values and measure itself accordingly. In all cases, the environmental managers must learn to think and talk like their business counterparts. To do otherwise is to send strong signals that the environmental organization is different and operates outside of the concerns and needs of the traditional businesses.

Strategic environmental management is an emerging, important concept that is evolving along with many other important business and management concepts in the 1990s. Its success depends, in great part, on its ability to avoid being separated and left out of the mainstream of the organization. In the early days of strategic environmental management, common wisdom dictated that success depended on the endorsement of the CEO, ensuring that the initiative would be taken seriously and actively included in all parts of the business. Today, at the end of this century, it is becoming apparent that the CEO's endorsement is not sufficient. The business organization must accept the environmental organization on its own merits, and environmental management must adopt an interactive strategy. Ultimately, this comprehensive strategy is the responsibility of the environmental management organization itself, although benefits accrue to the entire organization.[4]

NOTE

4. This piece first appeared as an article in *Corporate Environmental Strategy: The Journal of Environmental Leadership,* Vol. 3, No. 2, 1994. The views expressed and the models presented come as a result of research and consulting work at A. D. Little on issues of environmental management and business strategy.

Lessons from the Field: Thoughts on Environmental Management, Compliance, and Strategy

Frank Friedman

Frank Friedman is part of a small group that was present at the creation of environmental law in the late 1960s. After graduating from Columbia Law School, he joined the Lands Division of the Justice Department, handling an active natural resources litigation docket. He moved to Atlantic Richfield Corporation in 1970 when major companies began responding to the cleanup challenges presented by the new federal pollution control laws. Over the next 10 years, he became a recognized leader in the emerging fields of environmental law and management.

The former vice president for Health, Environment and Safety of Occidental Petroleum Corporation, Frank Friedman built and oversaw a large and sophisticated environmental management program covering facilities in the United States and overseas. He next became a partner, based in Los Angeles and Washington, D.C., with the Los Angeles law firm of McClintock, Weston, Benshoof, Rochefort, Rubalcava & MacCuish. In 1994, he became the senior vice president of Health, Environment and Safety and a member of the Executive Committee of Elf Atochem North America, a chemical company based in France which is one of the largest in the world.

The nature of environmental management over the last few decades has been defined by the regulatory structures and "laws of the land" that have evolved through the states, federal government, and worldwide. Fear of permit violations, fines, and criminal prosecution has comprised the history of corporate environmentalism. Up to this point, this strict adversarial framework has been effective in cleaning up our air sheds and waterways, but as we approach the next century a new vision described in this text is needed to drive environmental leadership. This new vision becomes especially relevant in light of a world economy that knows no boundaries.

Strictly stated, unless there is a business incentive, it is very difficult to establish environmental leadership. Terms like "integrating EH&S" and developing "sustainable business practices" only serve to remind our professional community of the importance of these business drivers. Balancing the needs of the world-at-large with the wants of the consuming public seems like a tall order for business, but with the right mindset it becomes second-nature to those companies willing to invest in this "beyond the law" thinking.

Despite the high-sounding rhetoric, compliance is still the major driver for most companies; yet, if companies understand the full implications, it is only one of a few significant drivers. Companies operate in a complex competitive environment, rich with threats and opportunities. Issues of cost, distribution, new product development, and even corporate image have always been of paramount importance to senior management. These core business concerns seemed to have been lost by these executives in the fray of environmental litigation and regulatory creation over the last twenty-five years. Throughout the environmental professionals' tenure, environmental problems have amounted to legal or technical management issues—not business decisions. At best, environmental issues were concerns of liability containment and risk minimization.

This misrepresentation of environmental management concerns has perpetuated internal staff uncertainties as well in many companies. Are environmental managers business managers, and are they part of senior management? Due to the entrenched nature of the corporate cultures, conflicts often arise between the legal staff and environmental management staff in companies. Who is running the environmental arm of the firm, and how should we fully measure such business and legal risks? These are the questions that the executives are asking in firms around the world.

The quandary continues as the paradox of this historical legal treatment of environmental problems clashes with the new "business model" of addressing environmental management concerns. The conflict between managers and lawyers is exhibited in Figures 2–6 and 2–7.

In the spirit of this change of regulatory emphasis, environmental departments should do more than merely serve as the corporate compliance department. The EH&S functions, as well as the overall mission, must be integrated as a part of general management. The problems and opportunities managed by an environmental staff transcend legal, technical, or business boundaries, and yet embrace them all.

Figure 2–6 A Tale of Two Perspectives—Environmental Managers and Legal Staff

Looking at the nature of managerial staff and legal staff in the corporation leads to important insights into the culture of underlying tension that often leads to what Robert Shelton has termed the "Green Wall."

Managers...	Lawyers...
• Want data—if you can measure it, you can manage it.	• Feel the more data you have, the more legal risk you have.
• Are programmed to act.	• Are programmed to be cautious.
• Want to ensure the bottom line.	• Want to ensure the legal line.

NEW ENVIRONMENTAL MANAGEMENT DRIVERS

There is often a blurred line as agencies begin to focus on management systems. The deluge of paperwork burdens, end-of-the-pipe malfunction management, and staff errors are being supplemented by EH&S staff concerns with management systems and refined audit protocols such as those evolving in the ISO 14000 standards (see the accompanying sidebar for a brief description of these new environmental standards). Agencies have difficulty focusing on the difference between management systems and audits. As such, these new ISO standards are a very real concern to environmental managers.

ISO 14000 is not a "magic bullet." A company can be in compliance with this new set of "environmental" ISO standards while still exhibiting poor regulatory compliance and weaknesses in internal accountability. While the ISO 14000 standards attempt to codify environmental management systems worldwide, the "devil is in the details" and, as such, professionals can't bet their companies on such standards. Likewise, the concern with unnecessary paperwork and details that may be counterproductive to established MIS systems add to the overall weakness of ISO 14000.

Then there is the question of managing data through intranets, the Internet, and MIS systems. There are a number of questions that arise from information management—both internal and external. Is the Internet a friend or foe? Where do the EPA, Internet, and environmental reporting fit when data can be

---

- Major increase in extremely complicated legislation and regulations
- Civil and criminal liability exposure
- Massive record-keeping and certification requirements increase possibilities of violation
- Enforcement priorities and "repeat" citations
- Audits and reporting—no good deed goes unpunished

Figure 2–7 External Forces to the Conflicting Cultures

What Are the ISO 14000 Standards?

The International Standards Organization (ISO), based in Switzerland, is an international organization whose members make up the national standards bodies of 111 countries. Founded in 1946 to voluntarily facilitate the efficient exchange of goods among countries, the ISO process involves consensus-based development of international standards so that, for instance, our electrical devices can be used worldwide.

In much the same way that the ISO 9000 standards developed a recognized process for assuring quality in manufacturing and service, the ISO 14000 standards serve to normalize environmental management systems throughout the world so that stakeholders have a sense of the types of environmental management systems companies use if they are ISO certified. In many ways a response to the Rio Conference in 1994, the ISO 14000 standards are being developed to include standards that address Environmental Management Systems, Environmental Performance Evaluation, Environmental Auditing, Life Cycle Assessment, Environmental Labeling, and Environmental Aspects in Product Standards.

Source: Tom Tibor and Ira Feldman, *ISO 14000: A Guide to the New Environmental Standards*, Irwin, Chicago, 1996.

so easily misrepresented online? And are there other exposures besides the Internet to be wary of?

Add to the information management issue the goal of total quality and the picture becomes even more complicated. Under a TQM regime, one goal should be to reduce and eliminate "just in case" reporting and look to track only the significant indicators of performance. Data management systems provide the necessary tool for this function but often are not used in this manner. Effective managers use the system to change the way the functions are done, not merely automating the existing data management functions.

IMPROVING THE "TOOLS OF THE TRADE": THE ROLE OF MIS

EH&S vulnerabilities must be reduced at the corporate, business, and facility levels. This requires a forward approach for the management of the EH&S risks and liabilities and the establishment of programs that assure compliance. Once again, compliance lays the groundwork for all other facets of the overall environmental strategy. Using management information systems effectively can enhance that existing groundwork and assure quality measurement for compliance. Information systems and environmental management should go hand-in-hand. Some of the benefits of MIS to EH&S professionals are shown in Figure 2–8.

- Improve regulatory compliance
- Contain and reduce EH&S costs
- Manage risks and liabilities
- Help support the EH&S activities at the plants
- Make addressing EH&S requirements an integral part of conducting business
- Make existing resources more productive
- Provide a common software which further integrates EH&S functions across business lines
- Provide a means to track and manage commitments, measure performance, and manage risks at all levels in the company
- Establish common EH&S data and structure to ensure compliance and to facilitate performance measurement and trend analysis
- Improve regulatory compliance documentation—crucial in an era of increased civil and criminal liability
- Help manage EH&S costs—a bottom line concern for any department
- Help manage risks more effectively—unless you have the data and assurance of the integrity of the data you can't manage risks
- Allow you to manage your environmental concerns—complying with government regulations is critical, but the government shouldn't be managing your company, especially in light of your intended strategic response to environmental threats and opportunities

Figure 2–8 What Correct Use of Information Systems Can Do

Another crucial part to managing data effectively in order to ensure compliance is the willingness to fix what is found. Like any change that occurs in a company, environmentally related change requires an understanding of the scope of the problems before implementing anything. Change equates to uncertainty in an organizational mindset, and as such, even though the problem has been diagnosed, corrective action requires a tempered realization of the conditions in the company: the existing management systems, staff concerns, resource constraints, and so on.

Management accountability has increased primarily because of the financial importance of environmental issues. An appropriate mantra for environmental professionals follows from this: If environmental issues are *managed,* the legal risks should be acceptable. One should follow the other, not vice versa.

CONCLUSION

So just what is environmental leadership? How much of what passes for environmental leadership today is the result of good corporate speechwriters rather than actual performance? How does the corporate community look to gain the public trust? How does the corporate community eliminate the crisis mentality of the agencies and public interest community?

These are the questions that professionals are asking in order to gain a handle on the nebulous notion of "environmental leadership." Yet, environmental leadership—on issues of compliance and beyond—must still reside in the actual decisions of business. Corporate environmental leaders should treat its many stakeholders as customers—direct customers, supplier and distributor chains, local communities, and regulators alike. This mindset frames the environmental leadership question in terms familiar to senior management and creates room for environmental personnel at the top levels of the firm's decision making. (Part III of this text offers a more extended discussion of this notion, under the business mantra: "Recognizing Business Opportunities").

A too-often used term—*paradigm shift*—is unfortunately appropriate here. Reframing environmental decisions in a traditional business decision model while acknowledging their unique dimensions of moral responsibility, efficiency, and sustainability is much different than seeking compliance first and "good deeds" second. Too many businesspeople are looking to be loved by the public. If we recognize the business incentives to far-sighted business and environmental management, we may gain at least some grudging and lasting admiration.[5]

NOTE

5. This piece came about as a result of Frank Friedman's keynote address at Rensselaer's Environmental Management and Policy Program "Corporate Affiliates" conference, June 23–24, 1997. The piece later was refined by Kevin Fletcher from Mr. Friedman's remarks for use in *Corporate Environmental Strategy: The Journal of Environmental Leadership.*

QUESTIONS FOR FURTHER THOUGHT

1. Shelton suggests that environmental management is "neither an operations or staff function." Do you agree? How could an environmental manager change how the function is perceived by upper management?

2. Why might the failure of an environmental manager to adequately demonstrate the economic benefits of strategic initiatives lead to the erection of the Green Wall?

3. Shelton observes that often there is an underlying tension between the EH&S department and other departments in the corporation. Where do you think this tension originates and how might it be managed or resolved?

4. Shelton suggests that environmental management is "neither an operations nor a staff function." Do you agree? How would you define environmental management? How might environmental management change how it is perceived within an organization in terms of its role toward the overall goals of the company?

5. Frank Friedman, in his book, *Practical Guide to Environmental Management*, notes that in "environmental management 'people skills' may be even more important than technical understanding" (p. 62). Do you think such skills are important for getting EH&S objectives to be considered?

6. How might a corporation's management style affect how well the EH&S department interacts with other branches of the organization? Would certain management systems, such as those structured after TQM principles, be more likely to integrate EH&S objectives?

7. Are there aspects to integrating environmental management into the core business structure other than those discussed in Shelton and the accompanying sidebar by Robert Kloepfer?

8. In a world dominated by the struggle to achieve compliance, what then, are the distinctive features of strategic environmental management?

CHAPTER

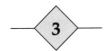

3

Establishing an Effective Environmental Audit Program

SELF-ASSESSMENT AS A MEANS TO FORESTALL ERROR

Too often companies have little sense of themselves when it comes to an understanding of their environmental liabilities. Of those firms that do possess such an awareness, few adequately look to contain and extinguish those liabilities systematically, and even fewer look to turn those liabilities into assets. This is a precarious situation.

The preceding two assertions can be derived from looking over the environmental crimes section of most states in most nations. The very real fear of heavy fines, lost reputation, and even jail time gets the attention of corporate leaders. Just look at the U.S. EPA's record of convictions and penalties for 1997. During that year, EPA's enforcement efforts set all-time records with 287 criminal cases referred to the Department of Justice and $169.3 million in fines assessed. With an additional 426 civil cases and $95.1 million in civil penalties, corporate executives understand that there is a real potential for civil and criminal prosecution.[1]

Likewise, the threat of becoming a headline in EPA press releases and the media adds to executive concerns. A sampling of EPA press release headlines illustrates this point: [2]

- "Five Plead Guilty to CFC Scheme"
- "Washington State Company and Founder Sentenced for Violating the Clean Water Act"
- "Maryland Company and Owner Sentenced for Clean Air Act, Clean Water Act Violations"

29

Similar headlines can be found in almost any paper in almost any country. Clearly, in most cases the missteps and resulting penalties are unintentional, and more importantly, avoidable. The only reliable way out of this "environmental gutter" of fines and penalties is a top-grade environmental audit program. In very simple terms, environmental audit programs are a means for firms to look very closely at their facilities, identify the potential for spills or accidents, assess management systems intended to address these problems, and even identify opportunities for reducing risks and related costs.

Frank Friedman, in his superb introductory text, *Practical Guide to Environmental Management*, provides the best comprehensive account of these corporate audit functions. In honor of Friedman's significant contribution to this field, we have chosen not to simply repeat his achievement. Instead, what follows attempts to supplement the prior work.

As we enter the next century, a majority of America's larger firms have significant audit programs, especially those with sizable liabilities such as utilities, chemical manufacturers, or petroleum exploration and refining multinationals. The next piece is a detailed case of how WMX, the world's largest waste management firm, improved its global environmental audit functions—from main street Hong Kong to Wall Street in Argentina. The great books on strategy, from Musashi's *The Book of Five Rings* to Sun Tzu's *The Art of War*, conclude that one of the best ways to forestall significant error is to audit your own faults. Environmental audits are an important start, a formal system at self-policing and an elaborate checklist to provide executive assurance. They even help in mergers and acquisitions. Environmental auditing is an effective tool for corporate self-assessment.

NOTES

1. EPA press release, "Enforcement Actions Increased in 1997," March 4, 1997.
2. Collected from three separate EPA press releases on March 2, 1997.

The Paradoxes of a Proactive Auditing Strategy: Environmental Auditing at WMX Technologies, Inc.

Eric R. Beaton

Eric R. Beaton serves as program coordinator for Energy Conservation with the Massachusetts Division of Energy Resources in Boston. His prior experience includes working with energy conservation programs for NorthEast Energy Services (NORESCO), Inc. and Conservation Services Group, Inc. He holds a Master's degree in Environmental Management and Policy from Rensselaer Polytechnic Institute in Troy, New York.

WMX Technologies, Inc., a $10 billion conglomerate, has embraced environmental auditing as an integral component of its corporate environmental management program. In providing services to its clients that include solid and hazardous waste services, clean air services, water and energy services, engineering, environmental consulting, and project management services, in addition to international waste services, the need to contain liability and risk is essential.

The importance of environmental auditing may be best expressed by WMX chairman Dean L. Buntrock and president Philip B. Rooney as stated in their 1992 letter to stockholders:

> There is one area, however, where excellence is essential, where performance is paramount. That is environmental compliance. That means meeting all of the requirements—and adhering to their spirit—no matter how burdensome or complicated. When your business is managing millions of tons of wastes and more than 25,000 separate waste streams under more than 500 different federal waste codes, that's not always easy.

But they are making good progress. According to Arthur D. Little, Inc., WMX's environmental management and audit systems "have consistently established the company as a leader not just of their own industry but among all industries."[3]

While companies are not required by law to conduct environmental audits, Buntrock and Rooney make clear that top management views environmental audits as a key which unlocks the door to superior environmental management. Environmental audits are commonly thought to only address compliance with environmental regulations. However, according to the U.S. Environmental Protection Agency's definition of environmental auditing:

> Environmental auditing is a systematic, documented, periodic, and objective review by regulated entities[4] of facility operations and practices related to meeting environmental requirements. Audits can be designed to accomplish any or all of the following: verify compliance with environmental requirements; evaluate the effectiveness of environmental management systems already in place; or assess risk from regulated and unregulated materials and practices.[5]

Thus, audit programs may also be defined and designed to account for environmental management systems and risk management issues. Although an audit structure may be successful while focusing on only one of the above three categories, a proactive audit program will address all three areas.

THE DEVELOPMENT OF ENVIRONMENTAL AUDITING AT WMX

Environmental auditing at WMX is a management practice which has evolved patiently over the past fifteen years. The impetus for developing both an audit program and department at WMX was primarily regulatory in nature. In order to ensure that WMX was meeting the ever-expanding and changing list of regulations, management adopted the process of auditing company facilities.

In 1983, the inaugural year of WMX's environmental audit program, twenty-three audits were conducted. By 1992, that number had risen to ninety-nine.[6] A philosophical change in the management of audits accompanied this dramatic increase, embodied by the transition from a reactive audit program to a more proactive program. WMX's management realized that environmental audits were not limited to mere regulatory compliance issues. Keith E. Kennedy, a former audit process manager at WMX Technologies, summed this change up as follows:

> There was a definite shift from compliance verification to management systems verification. With compliance verification, our auditors would review a facility's compliance by looking at each sentence in the site's requirement manual and verifying that it was being achieved. Thus, the auditors were not looking at the big picture. With management systems verification, our auditors examine the big picture. They examine a site's potential impact area such as air, water, waste storage, or disposal and address all related issues such as permits, monitoring processes, environmental, health, and safety issues, etc.[7]

In essence, audits may be used to bridge the transition from a focus on finding problems to a focus on confirming the absence of problems. This may be visualized as a series of three steps evolving over time from: (1) the identification of problems, to (2) the verification of compliance status, to (3) the confirmation of management systems effectiveness (Figure 3–1).[8]

This concept is reflected in WMX's environmental compliance hierarchy, which is depicted in the 1992 Annual Environmental Report (Figure 3–2). In this hierarchy, preventing compliance issues from arising is upper management's foremost desire. For those issues which do arise, WMX finds it favorable if fa-

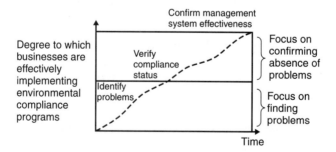

Figure 3–1   Evolution of Corporate Environmental Audit Programs

Source: International Chamber of Commerce, 1991.

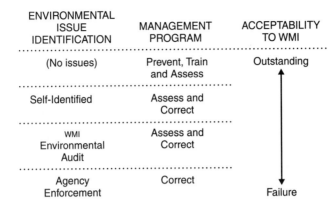

Figure 3–2 Environmental Compliance Hierarchy

cility management discovers its own problems and takes appropriate actions. Environmental auditing represents the third component of this hierarchy. The report explains, "The Environmental Audit Program provides a 'safety net' mechanism for detecting issues not identified by the facility." In essence, audits are designed to prevent the discovery of problems by the last and least desirable component of the hierarchy—regulatory agencies. In addition, when an audit occurs, it will foster the awareness of environmental issues as well as the prevention of future problems. Thus, preventative techniques will be implemented with the goal being the identification of no new compliance problems.

WMX'S AUDIT STRUCTURE

WMX's Environmental, Health, and Safety Audit Department is centralized and based at corporate headquarters in Oak Brook, Illinois. The corporate structure allows for direct access to the company's top management. In recent years, there have been eighteen auditors of whom two were managers and one a department director. The Director of Environmental Auditing reports to the Director of Environmental Compliance, who in turn reports to the Senior Vice President of Law and Compliance. Such a structure aids the management process by integrating the audit process with other compliance issues, as well as providing an assessment of established company objectives and not just individual department objectives.[9]

The EPA definition of environmental auditing demands that audits must be systematic, documented, periodic, and objective. The structure of WMX's audits is similar to other environmental audit programs that include pre-audit activities, on-site activities, and post-audit activities. The steps involved during these phases are represented in Figure 3–3.[10]

Kimberly Harms noted that "audits are conducted periodically on a set return interval. For example, hauling companies are audited every five years,

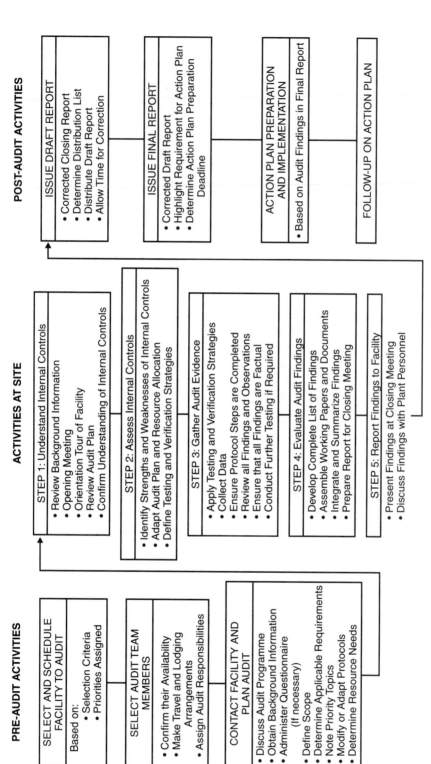

PRE-AUDIT ACTIVITIES

SELECT AND SCHEDULE
FACILITY TO AUDIT

Based on:
• Selection Criteria
• Priorities Assigned

SELECT AUDIT TEAM
MEMBERS

• Confirm their Availability
• Make Travel and Lodging
  Arrangements
• Assign Audit Responsibilities

CONTACT FACILITY AND
PLAN AUDIT

• Discuss Audit Programme
• Obtain Background Information
• Administer Questionnaire
  (If necessary)
• Define Scope
• Determine Applicable Requirements
• Note Priority Topics
• Modify or Adapt Protocols
• Determine Resource Needs

ACTIVITIES AT SITE

STEP 1: Understand Internal Controls

• Review Background Information
• Opening Meeting
• Orientation Tour of Facility
• Review Audit Plan
• Confirm Understanding of Internal Controls

STEP 2: Assess Internal Controls

• Identify Strengths and Weaknesses of Internal Controls
• Adapt Audit Plan and Resource Allocation
• Define Testing and Verification Strategies

STEP 3: Gather Audit Evidence

• Apply Testing and Verification Strategies
• Collect Data
• Ensure Protocol Steps are Completed
• Review all Findings and Observations
• Ensure that all Findings are Factual
• Conduct Further Testing if Required

STEP 4: Evaluate Audit Findings

• Develop Complete List of Findings
• Assemble Working Papers and Documents
• Integrate and Summarize Findings
• Prepare Report for Closing Meeting

STEP 5: Report Findings to Facility

• Present Findings at Closing Meeting
• Discuss Findings with Plant Personnel

POST-AUDIT ACTIVITIES

ISSUE DRAFT REPORT

• Corrected Closing Report
• Determine Distribution List
• Distribute Draft Report
• Allow Time for Correction

ISSUE FINAL REPORT

• Corrected Draft Report
• Highlight Requirement for Action Plan
• Determine Action Plan Preparation
  Deadline

ACTION PLAN PREPARATION
AND IMPLEMENTATION

• Based on Audit Findings in Final Report

FOLLOW-UP ON ACTION PLAN

Figure 3–3 Basic Steps of an Environmental Audit

Source: United Nations Environment Programme: Industry and Environment Office, 1990. Technical Report Series No. 2: *Environmental Auditing,* January 10–11, 1989.

landfills and transfer stations every three years, medical waste incinerators every two years, and hazardous waste facilities every year." The design choice implemented concerning the time interval between audits is significant when dealing with compliance issues. With the finite number of auditors, it is not possible for them to cover all of WMX's 450+ facilities annually or even biennially.[11] Thus, an effective management structure must address both the compliance needs and potential liabilities of individual facilities in a timely fashion.

While WMX's set return interval structure accounted for categorical risk (i.e., hazardous waste facilities were audited more frequently than municipal solid waste facilities), it did not account for the risk posed by each individual site within a specified category. Here, management had the foresight to "reengineer" the audit program's core structure:

Audits were conducted according to a "risk"-based schedule beginning in 1995. The risk-based approach means that audits are not scheduled according to a predetermined return frequency, as had been the case since the inception of the program. Instead, several risk factors are considered in establishing the audit schedule including:

- Complexity of the facility/operations;
- Complexity of the regulatory environment;
- Past compliance performance;
- Continuity of the facility's management team; and
- Elapsed time since the previous audit.[12]

This enhanced process creates a strategic shift that enables the audit staff to conduct audits in a manner that effectively reduces risk and liability. This results in a more efficient environmental management program at each individual site, which will prevent liability losses, reduce costs, foster profits, and elicit positive responses from both government agencies and the public.

The final element instrumental to environmental audits is that they remain objective. According to the standards set by the Environmental Auditing Roundtable, auditors must remain objective and independent of the audit site, free of conflict of interest, and not subject to internal or external pressures. For example, an auditor must base findings on observable, measurable, and verifiable evidence, while not allowing personal opinions or beliefs to influence the audit.[13]

WMX has designed a centralized structure to maintain objectivity in its audits. When asked why WMX favors a centralized structure rather than a decentralized structure, Kimberly Harms explains, "It really depends on what management sees as being of utmost importance. We [WMX] believe that we can retain a greater degree of independence as a centralized unit. Sure this leads to higher travel expenses, but it also results in a greater degree of consistency between audit studies of different facilities."

WMX considers consistency between audits a critical aspect of the process. As a centralized unit, the Audit Department Director or other top management may expect a polished format. In addition, if reports are not consistent, a centralized structure facilitates corrective actions. If audits are conducted by individual facilities, the reports may not be as consistent. Thus, upper management may have a difficult time delineating potential problems and recommending changes. There are both advantages and disadvantages to WMX's method of assuring independence. The present structure, however, appears to yield the greatest objectivity while remaining consistent for use by WMX's management.

WMX'S AUDIT PROCESS

An audit team may consist of two to six individuals depending on the site to be audited. According to Kimberly Harms, a solid waste landfill typically requires three auditors for five days, a transfer station or recycling facility may require two auditors for two or three days, while a hazardous waste facility may require five or six auditors for up to two weeks. Again, it is worth noting that more complex, higher-risk facilities warrant more auditors, as well as greater time and cost commitments.

In addition, WMX has addressed the issue of the audit staff's ability and competence, as this is paramount to the success of the audit process. The company recently considered the consequences of its hiring practices in terms of prospective environmental auditors. In fact, management changed its focus because it felt that a different route might enhance the quality of the audit process as well as alleviate the potential for negative consequences. As summarized by Kimberly Harms:

> Until about four to five years ago, we [WMX] hired many of our new auditors right out of college. Now we prefer that an individual has roughly two years' experience in environmental issues or at the very least a Master's degree without any experience. While we seek external candidates who possess engineering degrees or environmental degrees with a strong technical emphasis, we also look to hire internally from divisions involving operations and engineering.

Management realized that the auditors are the heart and soul of the audit process. In an effort to achieve excellence proactively, management felt that more experienced or highly educated individuals would be able to conduct a more critical and thorough audit. WMX also utilizes a training program to develop both the auditing skills and regulatory expertise of its new auditors. Auditors must successfully complete internal training modules as well as certification exercises. This is necessary to ensure that auditors are fully qualified to conduct audits according to WMX's internal standards.

WMX's environmental audit process is systematic. It involves a pre-audit, an on-site audit, and a post-audit. The pre-audit period usually encompasses the entire week preceding the audit. During this time, the audit team develops a working knowledge of the particular facility to be audited. Typically, the team will brief themselves on issues ranging from permits and operations to federal, state, and company environmental compliance requirements. The pre-audit phase is critical in enabling the audit team to thoroughly understand the workings and regulations surrounding the site.

After the pre-audit phase, the team travels to the site. Once on-site, WMX's audit team utilizes facility inspections, document reviews, and management interviews in an attempt to evaluate the site's compliance status and management systems. It is important to realize that the process and goals of on-site auditing differ greatly from a mere inspection that focuses on checklists. In reality, WMX does not conduct its audits solely by checklists. The auditors certainly inspect the facility, but they also address management issues. Interviewing site management and reviewing site documents enables WMX to understand the managerial practices of those operating its facilities. It is important, however, not to let audits become sterile. Each site audit is unique and thus requires an individualized approach. In addition, audits are a time in which decisions need to be made concerning the long-term management of the individual site. Audits that address the larger issues of a site offer the greatest benefit to WMX. For example, an audit that uncovers the "root cause" of an adverse effect will ultimately force management to examine alternatives before a similar adverse issue arises.

Identifying the "root cause" of a compliance and/or management systems issue has poised WMX to achieve environmental excellence. This has been accomplished via a proactive shift from compliance auditing to management systems auditing. To emphasize this shift, Roig and Schneider use the example of a 55-gallon drum which is missing its label:

> In our experience, the facility will often respond by labeling the offending drum and, perhaps, telling the person in charge of the main accumulation area that "the label needs to be put on the drums." This action corrects the problem with the existing drum, but would it solve the problem for the next drum or for drums generated six months from now? By contrast, let's examine the potential root causes behind the drum's missing label:
>
> - The site environmental coordinator doesn't understand the details of labeling regulations.
> - The site environmental coordinator understands the regulations, but has not communicated these requirements to the operator of the storage area, either verbally or in writing.
> - The site has developed a labeling procedure for drums and communicated it, but the label supply had run out.
> - The label had been put on the drum, but the label was not waterproof and fell off after exposure to rainfall.[14]

In a pre-1995 process improvement study conducted by WMX benchmarking eight other companies, WMX was found to spend 20 percent of its verification activities on management systems verification and 80 percent on compliance verification. When WMX's management realized that environmental excellence may be attained via "root cause" analysis, a shift in focus occurred. Emily Barton, an environmental auditor with WMX, estimated that the new audit process focuses more like 60 percent on management systems evaluation and 40 percent on compliance verification.[15] This is a key shift in focus—an essential shift if environmental excellence is to be attained.

The post-audit is the final phase of the process. This is the phase where the audit team reports its findings to site management. The report indicates the compliance status of the facility as well as highlights any deficiencies. Kimberly Harms noted that if there were substantial or significant issues found during the audit, and an audit manager was not present as part of the audit team, a manager would travel to the site in order to participate in the post-audit meetings with facility management. This scenario illustrates the commitment WMX has toward ensuring compliance and maintaining effective management systems.

WMX's CEO and president helped this shift toward a more proactive audit approach by proclaiming that corrective actions for imperfections discovered through audits are essential. If audits exist, but recommendations are not adopted in a timely manner, or never adopted at all, the purpose of the audit is defeated. WMX wants to avoid any misconceptions that the company is auditing merely to impress the public. Followers and researchers of the environmental audit movement have recognized these misconceptions:

> Environmental audits are being carried out by many large companies and some far-sighted smaller ones. Although it is possible to use them cynically, simply to try to improve a company's environmental image, this is not an approach that I would recommend because pressure groups are very keen to identify these companies. It would be better to not have an environmental audit if your management is not prepared to adopt even the less radical recommendations.[16]

The above passage illustrates a situation which WMX successfully avoided through implementation of the Compliance Action Reporting System (CARS)—a personal computer (PC) based software package. This process applies to the response required of a facility at which infractions were discovered during an audit. As Emily Barton stated, "issues identified by the audit department are entered into CARS for tracking, and we follow up thirty days after the audit to see that they've [site management] developed an appropriate corrective and preventative action plan to resolve the issue." Thus, the tracking system monitors sensitive issues and assures that corrective actions will be quickly taken. Implementation of corrective actions is enforced by the environmental manager of each of the nine Waste Management, Inc. regions. This ensures that each issue in CARS is resolved before it is documented as being finalized. This method enables WMX to reduce the company's potential liabilities and costs associated with penalties. This approach also aids government regulators because corrective action will occur before it reaches a level at which government must become involved. Finally, this will significantly reduce negative reactions from public pressure groups claiming that WMX's audits are only a facade and do not elicit change.

Currently, WMX voluntarily reports several compliance violations in its annual environmental report. If regulations dictate that a specific issue be reported, WMX will act accordingly and report the environmental infraction. Keith Kennedy also notes that individual states are currently developing and implementing audit privilege legislation. Such legislation may indemnify or lessen liability penalties for a firm which voluntarily discloses environmental violations to the appropriate regulatory agency before the regulatory agency uncovers them itself.

The changes that WMX has made in its environmental audit program have poised the company to achieve environmental excellence in a most effective fashion. By enacting change such as the conversion from a set return to a risk-based audit structure, the transition in focus from compliance verification to management systems evaluation, and the implementation of CARS, the corporation has firmly established its ability to move beyond compliance. While the structure and process of environmental auditing will continue to evolve and progress toward excellence, WMX's audit program serves as a proactive and successful model for other companies to emulate in this complex age of corporate environmental strategy.

NOTES

3. WMX Technologies, Inc., *Annual Report 1992,* Oak Brook, Illinois, Corporate and Public Affairs Department.

4. "Regulated entities" include private firms and public agencies with facilities subject to environmental regulation. Public agencies can include federal, state, or local agencies as well as special-purpose organizations such as regional sewage commissions.

5. Federal Register, 1986, *Environmental Protection Agency: Environmental Auditing Policy Statement,* Vol. 51, No. 131, July 9, 1986.

6. WMX Technologies, Inc., *1992 Annual Environmental Report,* Oak Brook, Illinois, Corporate and Public Affairs Department.

7. Kennedy, Keith E., Audit Process Manager/WMX Technologies, Inc., Oak Brook, Illinois. Phone Interviews by Eric R. Beaton, 3-16-94 and 3-31-94.

8. International Chamber of Commerce, 1991, *Evolution of Corporate Environmental Audit Programs* (graph).

9. Kennedy, Keith E., Audit Process Manager/WMX Technologies, Inc., Oak Brook, Illinois. Phone Interview by Eric R. Beaton, 8-31-95.

10. United Nations Environment Programme: Industry and Environment Office, 1990, *Technical Report Series No. 2: Environmental Auditing,* United Nations Publishing, Paris, France, January 10–11, 1989.

11. WMX Technologies, Inc., *Process Improvement Study (Draft Charts)*—internal document. Furnished by Kimberly A. Harms.

12. Nagy, John S., Robert G. Newport, and Keith E. Kennedy, 1995, *Environmental Audit Re-Engineering: From Compliance Verification to Management System Evaluation,* WMX Technologies, Inc.

13. Environmental Auditing Roundtable, Inc., 1993, *Standards for Performance of Environmental, Health, and Safety Audits,* Morristown, NJ, February 1993.

14. Willig, John T., 1995, *Auditing for Environmental Quality Leadership,* John Wiley & Sons, Inc., New York. (Chapter 16 case study entitled "Audits and Root Cause Analysis," by Randy A. Roig and Peter Schneider.)

15. Barton, Emily, Environmental Auditor/WMX Technologies, Inc., Oak Brook, Illinois. Phone Interview by Eric R. Beaton, 5-4-95.

16. Smith, Dr. P. R. J., 1992, "Benefits of Environmental Audits," *Chemistry in Britain,* Vol. 28: 227, March 1992.

Lessons from the Field: The Basic Legal Elements in Audit Protection

Alicia K. Raddatz

Alicia K. Raddatz is an Environmental, Health and Safety Administrator at Morton International, Inc., where one of her duties is to perform environmental audits.

Environmental auditing is an increasing practice among corporations, both in the United States and worldwide. As far back as 1994 a survey, completed by Price Waterhouse, found that nearly 75 percent of the worldwide companies surveyed conducted environmental audits.[17] The survey showed that over 90 percent of those who conduct audits do so for good business or assurance reasons, or because they seek to be proactive in their environmental management. However, perceived fears of involuntary disclosure continue to restrict both the extent of the audit and its use as a management tool within the company. According to Robert Ruddock, senior vice president of Energy and Environment Programs for the Associated Industries of Massachusetts, one common reason companies do not conduct environmental audits is the fear that government officials, environmental advocacy groups, or competitors will request a copy of the audit report.[18]

In addition, a company can be charged with a *knowing and willful* violation of the law in the United States if the issues in the audit report remain uncorrected. Even if a company immediately corrected a problem identified in the audit, it can be fined for the days of noncompliance based on information documented in the audit report. Since most fines are calculated using the number of days of noncompliance, the outside organization can simply count the number of days between the date of the audit and the date a copy of the report was obtained and multiply that number by $25,000 (the standard penalty per day). The risk of monetary penalties and the loss of confidential business information are real disincentives in the practice of environmental auditing.

The U.S. Environmental Protection Agency has repeatedly stated it will not "routinely" request environmental audit reports, but that lack of certainty forces the regulated community to limit and protect its internal auditing procedures. A second environmental survey completed by Price Waterhouse in March 1995 found that 9 percent of the respondents had had their audit reports involuntarily discovered or disclosed, and an additional 12 percent said that results of audits voluntarily disclosed to regulators had been used against them in enforcement proceedings.[19]

The loss of confidential business information to nongovernmental organizations (NGOs) is equally important. An NGO can obtain access to an audit report if the audit report has been made a public document, thereby making it available under the Freedom of Information Act. The government is not required to inform the company that their audit report has been requested or honor any prior confidentiality claims made by the company. In addition, under certain circumstances, courts have allowed audit reports to be given to private groups.

The Price Waterhouse survey of March 1995 stated that outside parties had attempted to obtain information from an environmental audit from 25 percent of the respondents and that those efforts had been successful in 15 percent of those cases. Almost half of all the respondents to the survey had some audit security issues. Therefore the fear of audit results either becoming public or being used against the company are founded.

To address these concerns, five approaches to protecting information obtained in an environmental audit are possible: the vague audit report, attorney-client privilege, work product doctrine, self-evaluation privilege, and legislated audit privilege.

THE VAGUE AUDIT REPORT APPROACH

This seemingly ineffective approach is used quite often by companies conducting environmental audits. The theory is that a company can't be prosecuted for something that can't be understood by regulators. Vague audit reports use a variety of vague descriptions of compliance deficiencies to protect the audit results. For example, "All drums of hazardous waste must be properly labeled" could mean that one or more drums of waste were unlabeled or mislabeled, or it could mean that everything was fine, but the facility just needed a reminder that proper labeling was required by law. A drawback to this approach is that the vague description of the deficiency gives too little information. As such, the person who must correct the deficiency must be told *in person* exactly what the problem was and how to remedy the situation.

Although this approach does baffle regulators, it also can baffle the company's own compliance people. Therefore, unless a company is prepared to relate audit issues through face-to-face discussions with the personnel responsible for any corrective actions, this approach should be avoided.

ATTORNEY-CLIENT PRIVILEGE

Approximately 43 percent of companies that conduct environmental audits protect the results of those audits using attorney-client privilege or work product doctrine.[20] An attorney-client privilege stamp gives a company a ready answer when an outside organization requests a copy of their audit report. However, this approach involves the use of an attorney, who adds cost to the audit process. In addition, this method, like the next two approaches to be discussed, invariably would have to be confirmed in a court of law if contested by an outside organization, and trials cost a great deal of money.

The attorney-client privilege is used to protect information that a client shares with his or her attorney in order to obtain legal advice. This privilege facilitates open communication between the attorney and the client. In order for an audit report to be considered attorney-client privileged information, the entire audit process must be managed by an attorney, and the sole purpose of the audit must be for obtaining legal advice. In addition, all documents related to the audit, including audit checklists and follow-up memos, must be marked "Attorney/Client Privilege."

The attorney-client privilege is a well-recognized mechanism for protecting confidentiality. This privilege has been used successfully for environmental audits on at least one occasion. In *Olen Properties, Inc. v. Sheldahl, Inc.* (DC C. Calif., No. 91-6446-WDK, 4/12/94), the judge found that an audit conducted by a company was not discoverable in a private cost-recovery action to assess liability in a Superfund case. In this case, the audit report met the criteria for attorney-client privilege established in 1950, which requires that the information was gathered in order to obtain "(i) an opinion of law or (ii) legal services or (iii) assistance in some legal proceeding."[21] The *Olen* decision is important because it proves that environmental audit reports are protected even if there is no current or threatened litigation, as long as the audit was overseen by an attorney.

However, using attorneys to manage an audit is expensive, especially if outside counsel must be hired. In addition, there may be problems with the focus of legal advice, and the privilege is, in general, narrowly construed and easily waived. Finally, dissemination of the audit report must be limited since the reason for the audit would be to obtain legal advice, and not for general environmental compliance. This restricted use of the audit report may hinder efforts to correct any identified problems at the facility manager's level.

WORK PRODUCT DOCTRINE

A second type of legal assistance commonly used to protect an audit report is work product doctrine, which protects the thought process and preparation of an attorney faced with possible litigation or enforcement proceedings. According to Raymond Buschmann, assistant general counsel at Morton International, Inc., to legitimately claim an audit as work product doctrine, the entire audit should be performed by an attorney. The drawback to this variation is obvious; most lawyers are not trained as auditors, and therefore would not be as effective at discovering compliance issues as trained environmental professionals. More importantly though, the majority of audits are not conducted in response to litigation, but to avoid it—unless, of course, it is already known or highly likely that serious compliance deficiencies will be found as a result of the audit.

Protection of audit documents via work product doctrine has been effective in at least one case. In *Olen*, discussed earlier, an environmental professional prepared notes regarding the audit which the plaintiff sought to discover. However, the judge agreed with the defendant that these notes had been prepared for use in the *Olen* trial, and therefore did not need to be produced. This confirms that only information gained in preparation of actual legal proceedings are protected by the work product doctrine. Therefore, like attorney-client privilege, work product doctrine is expensive, narrowly construed, and easily waived.

SELF-EVALUATION PRIVILEGE

This approach attempts to assert a company's right for a self-evaluative privilege, or self-critical analysis, and that these evaluations are confidential. The foundation of this privilege for environmental audit reports is based on self-evaluative privilege used in the contexts of other legal actions, such as malpractice lawsuits and affirmative action/employee discrimination lawsuits. This method was used successfully for an environmental audit in *Reichold Chemicals, Inc., v. Textron, Inc.* (DC N. Fla., No 92-30393-RV, 9/20/94). However, this approach can only be used when the company is reviewing a situation which has already occurred—in the case of *Reichold* an investigation into past groundwater contamination. Therefore, the modest protection of confidentiality under this variation does not extend to the principal goal of conducting environmental audits—assessing compliance and supporting practices that will help ensure compliance in the future.

LEGISLATED AUDIT PRIVILEGE

Given the obvious communication problems with the "vague audit report approach," and the costliness and narrow applicability of the other three approaches discussed so far, it is understandable that in the United States many states and the federal government have attempted to come forward with legislative relief on the issue of audit confidentiality. The official EPA position on these laws was outlined in its December 1995 "EPA Final Policy Statement on Voluntary Self-Policing and Self-Disclosure." This position stated that if violations are voluntarily disclosed and reported to the EPA, the penalty could be reduced. It did not, however, grant full immunity from any fines or penalties. The final position also did not recognize protection of audit findings from disclosure to the government or other parties.[22]

Despite such views that tend to place emphasis on enforcement agendas over legitimate confidentiality concerns, several states have passed an environmental audit privilege law. In addition, many other states and the federal government are considering or have considered similar legislation. State audit privilege laws can be separated into two types—audit privilege and audit privilege with voluntary disclosure. Audit privilege laws protect the audit report and any other information obtained as a result of the audit. This protection does not include any information required to be maintained on site by permits or regulations, such as quarterly wastewater discharge monitoring reports, annual toxic release inventory reports, or hazardous waste manifests. Government officials may obtain the privileged information through a hearing process if it can be proven that (1) the privilege was claimed for fraudulent reasons, (2) the company failed to file an *in-camera* review within so many days of a request for an audit; or (3) for criminal cases, the government official has a compelling need for the information and that information cannot be otherwise obtained.

By contrast, audit privilege with voluntary self-disclosure laws adds an additional clause. If a company performs a voluntary environmental audit, finds an area of noncompliance, corrects the noncompliance, and voluntarily reports the situation, that company is immune from certain penalties (administrative, civil, and in some states, criminal).[23]

SUMMARY

There are many methods to protect a voluntary environmental audit: writing vague audit reports, attorney-client privilege, work product doctrine, self-evaluation privilege, and legislated audit privilege. However, each of these methods is only suitable in certain cases, and each has its own drawbacks. A company wishing to perform an environmental audit should consider the following:

1. Does the company expect to find serious compliance deficiencies? If so, audit protection with an attorney's involvement should be strongly considered.

2. Does the budget for the audit allow for the participation of an attorney? Certain protective approaches require the participation of an attorney. If an attorney's participation was not planned, should the appropriate money be added to the budget?

3. Is the facility in a state with legislated environmental protection? If so, follow the directions of the law explicitly, especially as to how privileged documents must be marked. However, it must be understood that the privilege claim may still need to be proven in court.

4. What is the intent of the audit: to obtain an overview of the facility's current compliance status, to obtain legal advice, to prepare for enforcement action, or to research a past noncompliance situation? Depending on the intent, only certain protective approaches can be used.

5. Does the company have a policy of making audit findings public, such as with signatories of the CERES and Valdez Principles? If so, the vague audit report approach may work well.

In any event, it is in a company's best interest to find, correct, and in many cases report compliance deficiencies before the government or the public finds them. An environmental audit program is the most effective means to that end. Much of the legal and regulatory environment related to audit process, content, and disclosure is in a state of flux, with EPA's ever-changing audit guidelines and significant international audit standards emerging through bodies such as ISO. Yet, in the end, you can't manage what you can't measure, and ultimately, what you don't know can hurt you.

NOTES

17. The Price Waterhouse study, "Progress on the Environmental Challenge," was released in January 1995 and was the third in a biannual series by Price Waterhouse on how Corporate America manages environmental issues.

18. Ruddock paraphrase collected by the author in informal conversations.

19. "Elimination of Penalties Could Lead to More Environmental Auditing," Price Waterhouse press release, April 6, 1995.

20. "Elimination of Penalties Could Lead to More Environmental Auditing," Price Waterhouse LLP news release, April 6, 1995.

21. *Arkwright Mutual Ins. Co. v. Nat'l Union Fire Ins. Co.*, U.S. Dist. LEXIS 174 (S.D.N.Y. 1993).

22. Partham, Donald J. Jr., JD and John M. Brown, JD, "Environmental Audit Legislation: EPA vs. the States," *Environmental Protection*, March 1998.

23. "CIEA White Paper Supporting a Qualified Self-Evaluation Privilege for Internal Environmental Audits," Coalition for Improved Environmental Audits, July 27, 1994.

QUESTIONS FOR FURTHER THOUGHT

1. What are some of the potential advantages and disadvantages of performing an environmental audit?

2. Considering the type of work that is done, what types of skills—both professional and personal—are needed to be an effective auditor? What sorts

of interpersonal conflicts could arise from an environmental auditing job? How is upper management commitment crucial to the job?

3. What sorts of things should be considered when creating and implementing an environmental auditing system? How does the ever-changing public, scientific, and legal environment affect an auditing scheme?

4. Even though WMX incorporates a proactive environmental auditing system into their overall corporate environmental strategy, facilities may still manage to fall out of compliance. As a corporate strategist, how would you address this problem? Is it realistic to require companies to adhere to a "100 percent of compliance" doctrine? Are some industry sectors more at risk to fall out of compliance based on their business and the specific regulatory environment?

5. What are the potential complications and solutions for establishing a worldwide environmental auditing system? Are there cultural, sociopolitical, or market differences that could adversely affect a corporate auditing system? How could they be remedied?

The Question of Measurement

MEASURING FOR CORPORATE ENVIRONMENTAL PERFORMANCE

A strategic response to corporate environmental compliance needs and business opportunities requires knowledge of where we are now, where we are going, and where we want to get to. Strategy is always this mix of past mistakes, present predicaments, and future solutions. As with WMX's audit program, companies looking to take the first, often cautious steps toward compliance and beyond need to measure their entire corporate performance with reliable management systems. This "strategic needs" kind of assessment gets us closer to the heart of what makes a corporation tick, and while issues of regulatory compliance are often only perceived as necessary legal costs of doing business, they are a small part of corporate strategy.

Ultimately, measuring for corporate environmental performance boils down to the fundamental questions: What to measure? How to measure? and How to communicate those measurements both internally and externally? Underlying these questions are the concerns of aligning measurements with environmental needs and business goals, making measurements accountable, and allowing for continuous improvement. This is further complicated as voluntary initiatives such as the International Chamber of Commerce's Business Charter for Sustainable Development and ISO's environmental management standards create additional pressure for firms to adopt specific measurement protocols and standards.

As regulatory requirements have evolved over the last thirty years, firms have been required to develop measurement systems that record amounts of permitted air, land, and water emissions, as well as information such as number of accidents and spills, lost workdays, amount of hazardous waste generated, and nonpermitted emissions. As corporate responses to environmental requirements have evolved over the years, environmental, health, and safety

(EH&S) managers have incorporated additional metrics that more accurately link environmental responsibilities to business costs.

A 1995 National Association of Environmental Managers survey of 41 firms indicates that companies now include metrics such as number of notice of violations, type/volume of nonregulated materials recycled and disposed, total cost of fines, amount of fuel, material, and water used, and bottom-line annual costs of EH&S operations.[1]

More progressive firms are blending the fundamental environment metrics with more strategic indicators—acknowledging where they are, where they have been and where they want to be. These "leading" and "lagging" indicators, shown in Figure 4–1, present an example of these two types of metrics. This mix of required and business-related environmental measurements allows decision-makers to prioritize past problems, seek business opportunities, and address their most pressing concerns.

What follows by Ronald Van Epps and Susan Walters attempts to give us a rapid glimpse of the upward stairwell to corporate strategy. If you can accurately represent corporate functions in the performance terms of time, cost, and quality, then you can accurately take a big-picture snapshot of your environmental liabilities and opportunities. Strategy is about choice and about mobilizing a few good options. Van Epps and Walters explain how good environmental performance measures allow you to see more clearly your total opportunities and your key choices among all the costs, fines, staff mishaps and mechanical failures or public discharges.

The question of reliable corporate measurement always raises itself in strategy sessions. Do we really know our past mistakes? Can we accurately measure ways to improve our current performance? What telling performance indicators exist that can ensure our future and increase our market share?

A recent survey of leading environmental professionals conducted by the Global Environmental Management Initiative led to the following set of valuable recommendations for planning, implementing, and evaluating an environmental measurement system. These are presented in brief in Figure 4-2.[1]

	Lagging Indicators	**Leading Indicators**
Measure	end-of-process or output indicators	in-process or management indicators
Approach	quantitative	quanitative and qualitative
Example	pounds of toxic chemicals released to air	# of facilities conducting audits
Strength	easy to quantify and understand	reflects not only past performance
Weakness	root causes not identified	hard to build support for use

Figure 4–1 Leading and Lagging Indicators

Source: GEMI's *Primer on Environmental Measurement, 1997.*

- One size doesn't fit all—consider the company's operations, organization, and unique environmental impacts.
- Determine whether health and safety metric will be included in the program.
- Ensure that the program is sustainable, even as the business environment changes.
- Select metrics that drive performance.
- Select metrics that are understandable and compatible with the company's operations and information systems.
- Define performance expectations and identify who is accountable.
- Get upper management support and business unit support.
- Ensure that the right people are getting data quickly so necessary actions can be taken.
- Ensure the metrics are driving the right or intended behavior.
- Get stakeholder feedback on the system from employees, business units, the public, and stockholders.

Figure 4-2 GEMI's Advice for Environmental Measurement Systems

Source: GEMI's *Primer on Environmental Measurement, 1997.*

As you read through both Van Epps' and Walters' account of linking environmental responsibilities with business needs and Walter Liggett's discussion of the technical considerations for such a measurement system, keep the recommendations presented above in mind.

NOTE

1. Global Environmental Management Initiative's *Measuring Environmental Performance: A Primer and Survey of Metrics in Use*, GEMI, Washington, DC, 1997.

Why Are Environmental Performance Measures Necessary?

Ronald Van Epps and Susan Walters

Ronald E. Van Epps, based in Chicago, is a partner with Arthur Andersen's Environmental Services practice. Since joining Arthur Andersen in 1984, Van Epps has worked with clients of various industries on issues of environmental management systems, performance measurement, activity-based costing, cost/benefit analysis and process improvement. He has a BS in accounting from Indiana
Continued

University and is a CPA and a member of the American Institute of Certified Public Accountants.

Susan D. Walters is a manager with Arthur Andersen's Environmental Services practice and is also based in Chicago. With experience in a number of areas of environmental management services, Walters was a key player in the development of Arthur Andersen's EcoAccounting@ methodology and software development team and she is a lead instructor of Environmental Services EcoAccounting@ and Performance Measure training. She has a BS in accounting from Indiana University.

Corporations are coming under increasing pressure to improve environmental performance. Officers and boards of directors are asking pointed questions of EH&S managers: Exactly how much do we spend on EH&S? Are we staying out of trouble? Why do we have so many people in this department compared with five years ago? How and where can we reduce environmental costs and not sacrifice compliance? Are we receiving adequate return for our investment in environmental management?

These questions are being asked more often as companies are merging EH&S activities into the business. Too often, companies have few quantifiable or fact-based answers to these fiscal questions. They lack clear definitions of how to define environmental performance. Performance measures provide the common language that is essential to the integration of EH&S into business.

In business, we can effectively manage only what we can measure. As Tom Malone, president of the textile manufacturer Milliken & Company, puts it: "A team without a scoreboard is not playing the game; it's only practicing."[2] In business, the purpose of any performance measurement scoreboard is to change behavior. The same approach used to change and to improve traditional management procedures (that is, keep score by measuring how well processes perform) must also be used to evaluate environmental performance.

Facing a growing regulatory burden, companies that do not control their EH&S programs run the risk of stumbling financially. Yet, even companies that are committed to high environmental standards can run into difficulties when it comes to establishing comprehensive, cost-effective programs to address EH&S risks. Companies need measures that consider the key elements of time, cost and quality in the evaluation of processes throughout their organization.

For many successful companies, the goal is to embrace continuous improvement. It is critical to change from a reactive, problem-solving approach (identify the difficulty and solve it) to a "proactive" environmental stance (anticipate the problem and avoid it). This philosophical change is analogous to the Total Quality Management movement, which advocates the need to build-in quality. Many businesses and government regulators agree that this is the best approach, in terms of both improved quality and cost-effectiveness.

The proactive approach clearly pays off. Dow Chemical has stated that, based on its experience, the company receives a 55 percent return on investment for environmental projects done in order to anticipate and avoid environmental issues. Proactive projects include process changes to reduce certain waste streams, material substitution efforts to reduce or to eliminate certain chemicals, and making capital investments to reduce energy consumption. These projects represent a few examples of the types of environmental initiatives that can generate significant returns. Conversely, the business noted a 15 percent *negative* return on expenditures arising from reactive approaches to resolve environmental problems or to address government mandates. The fundamental problem that arises stems from an inability to evaluate and to pursue multiple options. Often, companies must respond to government regulations or environmental issues on an accelerated time frame, leaving very little time to explore less costly alternatives. While all of this is intuitively obvious, many companies continue to invest a very small portion of environmental spending in proactive initiatives. Why is this?

One reason is the lack of adequate performance measures (i.e., the inability of companies to evaluate properly the financial return on EH&S investments). In a March 1994 survey performed by the Global Environmental Management Institute (GEMI, the multinational professional association created to address corporate environmental management issues), 12 out of 18 Fortune 500 companies indicated that financial measures (such as return on investment or net present value) were not used in evaluating environmental compliance capital projects.[3] A survey performed by Arthur Andersen in July 1996, in conjunction with Organization Resource Counselors (an H&S trade organization), found that only 38 percent (of the 21 respondents from 14 Fortune 500 companies) consider H&S operational impacts qualitatively and quantitatively in their operational investment evaluations. The leading reasons for limited use of quantitative H&S data in investment evaluations include an inability to define activities, an inability to quantify money spent on key H&S activities, and an undefined relationship between H&S activities and their operational impacts.[4]

WHAT IS AN EFFECTIVE PERFORMANCE MEASURE?

Consider what a performance measure is. Many managers think they know, but if they do, they're not effectively implementing their knowledge. Many organizations say they have performance measures in place, but their environmental measures tend to be limited-focused on failure rates and end-of-pipe controls. Because these measures are limited to tracking costs, emissions, or other outputs, they fail to measure adequately the efficiency or effectiveness of the underlying processes. In truth, most company strategists focus on being in compliance, but many cannot tell if they are efficiently complying with environmental regulations or how to improve performance.

WMX Technologies, Inc. is a good example of a company that has gone beyond the traditional output-related environmental measures. While output measures (such as the number of notices of violations (NOVs) and total emissions) remain part of the company's monthly report, WMX now tracks and reports measures such as percent of energy usage per ton of waste managed and the number of self-identified audit issues over total issues. The company also tracks the percentage of operating personnel receiving environmental training and the percentage of identified issues resolved within an established timetable. Clearly, performance measures are more robust than measuring only for compliance.

The additional measures adopted by WMX supplement the traditional output-oriented measurements and help management evaluate its investment in its environmental programs relative to the impact on the company's environmental performance and, ultimately, the company's financial performance.

Government agencies have begun to go beyond measuring the traditional output-orientated failure measures. A good example is Minnesota Pollution Control Agency (MPCA). This agency, through its continuous improvement efforts, has established several innovative performance measures that monitor the cost, time and quality of its activities. It has recently established stretch goals for the time that it takes to issue a permit, the number of permits issued per full-time equivalent (converting this measure into dollars spent per permit), and the amount of permit backlog. These measures have directed MPCA's focus and attention on those areas where it has direct control and can impact and improve performance. Furthermore, these measures have provided the data and tools necessary to communicate performance improvement to the stakeholders.

A performance measure, as defined in the Arthur Andersen volume *Vital Signs*, quantifies "how well the activities within a process or the outputs of a process achieve a specified goal." Since a correctly designed and implemented measurement system looks at processes as well as outputs, it does more than identify problems. It can help anticipate and prevent problems.

A measurement system must consider three measurement attributes: time, cost, and quality (see sidebar). Each of these attributes represents a key component that directly impacts business performance. In addition, the measurement system must be understandable and controllable by employees, it must be objective and consistently reported.

To be effective, measures must be well understood and controllable by employees. If not, employees are likely to lose interest because they know that they can't change the outcome. One example of this involves a company's attempt to measure and control waste water treatment costs. In an effort to establish accountability, the company began to allocate the costs of waste water treatment based upon the square footage of each process in the plant. While assignment of costs to process owners can be an effective tool, the use of poor

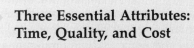

Three Essential Attributes: Time, Quality, and Cost

A performance measure can have many attributes. Based on Arthur Andersen's experience with hundreds of companies around the world, the three primary attributes are time, quality, and cost.

- Time measures focus on how quickly the underlying process functions. The less time it takes to complete a process or task, the sooner the new revenue-producing or compliance activity can occur. A few examples include the time it takes to obtain a permit and the percentage of internal assessment findings that are addressed within a period.

- Quality represents the delivery of results that meet the expectations of stakeholders. Quality measures focus on the perceived "goodness" of the product or service in the eyes of stakeholders or customers. Examples that use quality in the measure include the number of internal assessments performed, the number of waste-handler audits, the percentage of raw materials with recycled content, and the number of chemicals in use that are listed on the EPA Toxics Release Inventory.

- Cost represents the financial impact or output of a process, product, or decision. In other words, it reflects how much a process or product costs to meet the stakeholder requirements on time. Up until now, many companies have not scrutinized the economics of environmental compliance and performance. The cost per permit, training expenses per person, and the percentage of energy dollars saved as a result of environmental initiatives (such as capital expenditures, process changes, or material substitution) are examples of potential cost measures.

- Measures should be reported at the top levels and cascade down throughout the company. Business units, divisions, and plants should have goals and measures that are consistent and integrated, rather than being fragmented and isolated.

Source: Van Epps and Walters, *Corporate Environmental Strategy Journal, 1996.*

measures, such as the relationship between square footage in the plant and waste water treatment costs, can be counterproductive. The use of this measure has not resulted in a reduction in waste water treatment usage largely because that effort would not have resulted in a reduction of the costs to the process owners. As a result of an ineffective measure, management has not achieved the targeted reduction in waste water treatment usage that had been anticipated.

Measurements should also be objective and reported consistently. While the metric chosen may be a percentage or an element of time (days or months), it is important to design the proper measure and then figure out the proper metric. Examples of straightforward metrics include the percentage of audit findings that are addressed within 30 days or the elapsed time to obtain a permit. Other metrics might measure the percentage of employees trained for an environmental program and the training cost per employee. While this level of documentation sounds basic, few companies actually measure and track these items. An exception is Browning-Ferris Industries (BFI), which now requires all of its EH&S site managers to be certified under the company's environmental training program. The benefits to BFI are that it has established minimum criteria for training each of its site managers, it knows the number of employees and sites that are qualified, and it can begin to measure the training costs for this program. More importantly, BFI should be able to link improvements in environmental performance with its investment in the training program.

EARLIER PROGRAMS LACKED PROPER INCENTIVES

Until relatively recently, the government had not produced a measurement system that created an incentive for companies to go beyond compliance. The EPA began looking for measures of success as soon as it was formed a quarter-century ago. Ideally, the agency wanted to find measures that showed that the air, water, and land were getting cleaner, and that human exposure to pollutants was decreasing. The EPA, however, had trouble devising representative sampling protocols, and it was impossible to measure certain pollutants with existing field instruments.

In the late 1970s and early 1980s, government agencies became linked to laws that had a command-and-control framework, such as the Resource Conservation and Recovery Act. The environmental performance measure that the agencies used was based on a company's or individual's behavior and the fines and penalties incurred. It was determined that progress must be occurring as long as the number of fines and penalties continued to grow. Such negative reinforcements have failed as performance measurements primarily because they do not indicate whether facilities have improved their performance from the previous year. In addition, they do not provide any guidance on how to improve environmental performance.

3M is a good example of a company that has used effective performance measures, coupled with a commitment from management, to make significant improvements in its environmental performance. Beginning in the early 1970s with the adoption of the 3M environmental policy and the establishment of the Pollution Prevention Pays (3P) program, 3M began to recognize the importance of measuring environmental performance. Since its inception in 1975, the company's 3P program has produced the following documented, tangible results:

- Reduced air emissions by 134,000 tons
- Reduced water pollutants by 16,900 tons
- Reduced sludge and solid waste by 426,000 tons
- Saved the company $537 million

In an effort to build upon the success of the 3P program, 3M has continued to update its environmental goals and performance measures. In 1987, the company launched 3P+, a program to achieve Year 2000 goals of 90 percent reductions in all releases to the environment and a 50 percent reduction in waste generated by 2000. Then in 1990, 3M implemented the Challenge '95 program as another formal measurement tool. In Challenge '95, the company developed a waste ratio which is used to provide a simple measure to track major changes in the amount of waste generated by 3M divisions/plants. The ratio formula expresses waste generated as a percentage of total output per facility. By adopting this ratio, the company is able to benchmark performance across facilities and has established a five-year goal to reduce waste by 35 percent.

3M is one example of a company which recognizes the importance of linking environmental performance to financial performance. By utilizing a set of effective measures, 3M has dramatically reduced its impact on the environment while creating a competitive advantage in the marketplace. 3M's 3P program has changed the way business and government look at environmental strategies. It is now recognized that environmental improvement can be good for business and good for the environment.

EPA'S SHIFT FAVORS PERFORMANCE MEASURES

The EPA made a giant leap forward in performance measurement in 1986 under the Emergency Preparedness and Community Right to Know Act. The Act has required companies with significant quantities of hazardous materials to participate in the Toxics Release Inventory program. For the first time, pollutants were reported as an aggregate figure (pounds per year), and company executives were being held publicly accountable for an environmental performance measurement. These reports dramatically changed the way companies viewed themselves, as well as the way they were viewed by the general public.

Although the law did not require companies to reduce anything, it increased environmental awareness. Because such high numbers were being measured and reported to the public, companies were pushed into voluntary reduction. The media, investors, religious groups, and communities took notice. And companies began to take a closer look at the environmental performance of their suppliers. Suddenly, the regulators were not the only people interested in overseeing the specific performance of regulated entities. Intense public scrutiny not only caused many facilities to reduce emissions, it also caused regulated entities to begin to look for a new set of environmental performance measures. This initiative represented a move to demonstrate their commitment to the environment, a trend that continues to this day.

EXPLORING NEW PERFORMANCE MEASURES

By harnessing and using market forces, the government can achieve the same environmental goals of mandatory regulations at a significantly lower cost.

Voluntary incentives and government/business partnerships can go a long way toward pollution prevention and control. As Mary Gade, Director of the Illinois EPA (IEPA), pointed out in a roundtable discussion sponsored by the *Illinois Legal Times*, "Government has had far more successes when it has set goals for industry and has allowed it the flexibility to meet those goals, as opposed to [regulating] the exact technology to use, which often locks [companies] into technology that will be outdated or costly."[5]

The IEPA realizes the critical importance of the measures that it selects to evaluate the success of its programs. These measures not only keep track of state performance, they often become the same measures that corporations, and ultimately the public, use to focus their own priorities, and measure and communicate progress. Thus, it benefits both sides of the environmental regulatory coin to develop measures that accurately identify the true state of environmental performance.

LIBERATING TOOLS THAT RECOGNIZE OPPORTUNITY

If management is having difficulty seeing the link between its results and environmental efficiency and effectiveness, the proper performance measures can help make the connection. However, to be effective, the environmental measures should be integrated across the organization and should be consistent with the overall company goals. Furthermore, they should be consistent with the tools used in traditional business areas. For example, in order to recognize the importance of environmental performance, select environmental measures should be integrated with traditional monthly operating statistics such as sales, gross margin, and other operating metrics that are monitored and reported to senior management.

An H&S trade organization and fourteen of its leading industry members requested Arthur Andersen to facilitate the development of how to apply traditional financial evaluation tools to the H&S arena. Specifically, the group was attempting to tailor method(s), model(s), or process(es) to guide companies in the evaluation of the financial impact of H&S investment on overall business performance. Successful implementation of these measures depends on clear understanding and communication of the financial dimension.

An example of traditional cost measures applied in traditional business decisions includes cost ratios (e.g., return on investment, economic value added, etc.). However, the application of these tools to EH&S decisions is limited. In fact, it is considered groundbreaking innovation to apply these tools to EH&S business decisions. This is primarily due to the lack of guidance regarding how to apply these tools in these areas. Over the last several years, EH&S and operating professionals have found they are at a disadvantage in their ability to communicate their investment proposals in terms that are familiar to business managers. Recognizing the competition for funding, EH&S

COMMUNICATING WITH BUSINESS MEASUREMENTS

Goal: to identify cost and benefit inputs necessary to apply traditional financial performance measures.

Performance Measure	Costs	Benefits
ROI	Cost of prevention	Impact on H&S performance
EVA (Economic Value Added)	Cost of inspection/ implementation	Impact on H&S implementation costs
	Cost of failure	Impact on operational costs

Challenges:

- Defining the activity components that should be included in the cost calculations. For example: What should be included in the spiral cost of failure?
- Understanding and explaining the relationship between the costs and benefits and the H&S cost/activity.

Source: Van Epps and Walters, *Corporate Environmental Strategy Journal, 1996.*

and other professionals have concluded that they must find a way to communicate more effectively their project proposals' costs and benefits (see sidebar).

Success is further dependent on leadership from above, and achieving cooperation and communication across departmental boundaries. As a result, as Robert Shelton previously stated, EH&S managers should seek a "project champion" at a high level in the organization to spearhead a more proactive, integrated approach to environmental management. These steps are critical if EH&S performance measures are to be effective in mitigating risk and managing cost.

The importance of integrated measures is reflected in the following example. A major retailer, with approximately 1,200 stores nationally, recently began to integrate the company's environmental program with other initiatives within the company. In one specific case, merchandise was arriving in the stockroom on hangers that were thrown out and replaced with hangers suitable for display. Stockroom performance measures were based primarily on retail volume processed hourly per employee and waste disposal costs. However, the stockroom had very little opportunity to influence the packaging decisions that controlled their activities and the disposal costs to a large degree. Decisions on protective and merchandise packaging were made primarily by the merchandising department, who were evaluated on sales volume and retail margin. Because retail margin did not include stockroom labor or disposal costs, there was no incentive to spend any additional money to order hangers that could go directly from vendors to the sales floor.

By reevaluating the existing measures, the company realized it could decrease disposal costs, in addition to reducing handling costs and cycle time in the stockroom significantly. This type of opportunity also exists at many manufacturing facilities, and it highlights the importance of integrated EH&S measures. In manufacturing facilities, many of the product decisions are made by Research and Development during product design; however, accountability for disposal costs often resides with the plant manager, who has very little input into the bill of materials used in the process.[6]

The importance of management commitment and the need to properly align environmental measures can be demonstrated in the following example. At Tenneco Gas, one of the country's leading suppliers of natural gas, the company's goal was to self-identify and correct, on a timely basis, as many environmental deficiencies as possible. In the minds of many environmental site managers, however, pointing out a significant number of deficiencies was inconsistent with the company's goal of environmental excellence. One of the general managers clarified the company's vision when he presented an award to the facility that identified the *most* deficiencies during the year. He gave them an award—much to the shock of site managers who had self-identified far fewer items—because he felt this facility had done the most thorough job of self-examination and *correction*. While the general manager stressed the importance of seeing improvement in that number the following year, he encouraged all of his facility managers to identify and address environmental deficiencies actively before they became an issue.

While this specific scenario occurred several years ago at Tenneco Gas, many companies today are still suffering from a lack of properly aligned environmental measures. Employees sometimes confuse the goal of zero environmental violations with the objective of self-identifying and correcting problems or potential problems on a timely basis. A good set of performance measures can help to make that link. (See the accompanying article by Ditz and Ranganathan for lessons on this.)

Working in isolation can also present problems. For example, if the only metric on which EH&S professionals are being evaluated is how fast they can obtain a permit, the result may be onerous reporting and monitoring requirements, and higher-than-necessary costs. EH&S professionals should seek operations involvement in the drafting of the permit. This integrated approach arises from the knowledge that the ongoing monitoring and reporting should be considered as an integral component of the permit cost. An effective set of performance measures will consider the cost as well as the quality and timeliness of the process.

TACTFULLY IMPROVING THE BOTTOM LINE

How does a company establish overall environmental priorities, define activities, and design integrated performance measures for continuous improvement? An appropriate methodology identifies and quantifies critical activities and their drivers. This cost quantification and activity driver identification provides the basis for performance measure development. By categorizing environmental activities into five fundamental cost pools, which include (1) strategic/tactical positioning, (2) business risk management, (3) program administration, (4) impact minimization, handling, and disposal (operations), and (5) penalties and injury to human health or the environment, management can evaluate the cost effectiveness of its environmental programs by identifying the key activities and associated cost drivers of the company's environmental program. Properly classifying the costs and understanding their drivers allows management to begin to evaluate the nature of the environmental costs, whether proactive in nature to avoid potential issues, or reactive to address and resolve internal or external failures.

The first step in evaluating the cost effectiveness of a company's environmental program is to define what constitutes an environmental activity. While this can often be a long and difficult process, it doesn't need to be. The important factor is to develop a comprehensive list of environmentally related costs. In beginning of this process, it is important to assemble a multidisciplinary team which includes representation from operations, EH&S, and finance, at a minimum. The next step is to analyze all of a facility's payroll and non-payroll costs to identify those associated with the environmental activities. This step should lead to a cost matrix which often follows the 80/20 rule. In many cases, 80 percent of a facility's environmental costs are driven by 20 percent of the activities. This point is especially relevant to the next step. In designing a set of environmental performance measures, the facility should focus on the key environmental activities (e.g., those 20 percent that are driving the costs). It is not critical to track and report costs for all environmental activities. In addition, it is often too costly and time consuming to attempt to track all these costs at a detailed level. Instead, the facility should establish and track measures for the key activities on a monthly basis; then on an annual basis it should revisit the overall cost pool to determine if there were any significant changes in the key environmental costs. Analysis of these costs and their drivers often leads to opportunities for improvement. In addition, understanding the activity drivers leads to controlling the costs. Therefore, it is these activity drivers that are excellent candidates for performance monitoring.

The process of identifying and measuring costs is not an easy one, as many of these costs are buried in overhead cost pools. However, if done correctly at a facility level, with the proper resources, management should be able to complete the initial analysis in two or three months. After the initial review, measuring and tracking environmental costs should be part of the every-day routine, requiring little additional effort.

PERFORMANCE MEASURES DESIGNED TO CHANGE BEHAVIOR

Effective performance measures should be designed to change behavior and the environmental performance of the organization. They also should provide internal and external stakeholders with goals and measurements to track progress and continuous improvement. Finally, they need to be designed with a business purpose in mind: to improve bottom-line performance by increasing quality and reducing the time and cost it takes to do a process the right way.

One example of where this approach to environmental cost management and performance measure development was applied is a project in which Arthur Andersen worked with a petrochemical facility. The project team highlighted the EH&S activities where the most resources have been spent. Further, by developing an understanding of what drives these activity costs, they were able to highlight opportunities for performance and cost improvement. To monitor these activities on a continual basis, the team developed a set of performance measures. For example, one of the significant activity costs was the EH&S-related maintenance. An understanding of this activity demonstrated that the primary driver for this was in response an emergency expense and, thus, these costs included overtime and short-notice ordering and delivery fees. Through activity analysis, the team identified opportunities for improving the EH&S maintenance process and reducing the spending on the activities. For example, the team suggested that their preventive maintenance schedule be reviewed, that they establish a limited inventory of vital emergency maintenance materials, that a description of what constitutes an emergency work order be defined, and that they negotiate better rates with their outside contractor for labor and supplies. To monitor the performance of this activity, they developed performance measures for the key activity drivers— for example, the percentage of material that is bought on an emergency basis, the amount of dollars saved due to rate negotiations and elimination of overtime and emergency delivery charges, and the percentage of emergency maintenance calls. These performance measures allowed them to monitor and to communicate their process improvement.

CONCLUSION

When key measures are aligned with the company's vision and focused on those activities within a given process, management objectives can be reached in a cost-effective and environmentally responsible manner. Properly focused performance measures ultimately improve the overall quality and strength of a company, which is something that investors and analysts demand.

Ultimately, performance measures provide companies with tools that can help their integration of EH&S activities into the business (see Figure 4–3).

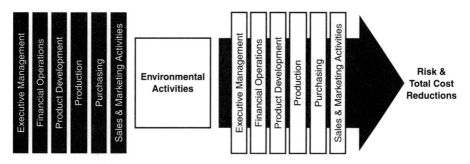

Figure 4–3   Measuring Environmental Activities Throughout the Business

Source: Van Epps and Walters, *Corporate Environmental Strategy Journal, 1996.*

Performance measures are one way to quantify and to communicate the EH&S impact factors and positively manage the effects of those factors on the bottom line.

NOTES

2.   Interview and communications between the authors and Milliken.
3.   Please see GEMI's "Measuring Environmental Performance: a Primer and Survey of Metrics in Use." For additional information go to www.gemi.org.
4.   Survey conducted by authors and not published.
5.   Mary Gade comments made at event sponsored by the *Illinois Legal Times* in 1994.
6.   Due to client confidentiality, the name of this retailer cannot be disclosed.

Lessons from the Field: Research Perspectives on Environmental Performance Indicators

Daryl Ditz, Environmental Law Institute,
and Janet Ranganathan, WRI

Daryl Ditz is Director of Environmental Management Programs at the Environmental Law Institute (ELI) in Washington, D.C. Before working at ELI, Ditz was at the World Resources Institute where he worked on corporate environmental accounting, new policy frameworks for the electronics industry, sustainability in the U.S. forest sector and international technology cooperation.

Janet Ranganathan is an associate in the program in the Management Institute for Environment and Business at the World Resources Institute (WRI) where she works on sustainable business strategies. Since 1993, she has led work on corporate environmental accounting and the role of emerging monitoring technologies for better management and accountability.

Except for such mandatory reporting requirements as pollution emissions, most firms are still in the dark about the environmental performance of their business activities. This makes the firm vulnerable to changing regulations, stakeholder expectations, and customer demand. Excellence in environmental performance will become an integral part of business economic viability. The following recommendations, from a 1997 World Resources Institute study, are aimed at helping firms better measure, manage, and improve environmental performance.

1. *Firms should establish environmental goals corresponding to these environmental performance indicators (EPIs).*

   Indicators provide critical links in the chain of vision, strategy and implementation. With a strategy of resource productivity, pollution prevention, and product stewardship, firms will realize both economic and environmental benefits. A growing array of companies are already using EPIs to quantitatively track progress toward corporate environmental performance goals. Judging by voluntary corporate environmental reports (discussed in Part III), companies are moving in this direction. What's more, Dow Chemical recently announced ten-year environmental goals that include reducing chemical emissions and waste generation per pound of production by 50 percent and energy use per pound of production by 20 percent.

2. *Firms should use these EPIs to benchmark their performance internally and against other companies.*

   Systematic comparison of environmental performance is valuable to provoke questions about performance and opportunities for improvement. Others outside of companies are already beginning to do such benchmarking. With the expansion of publicly available data sets, such as national pollutant release and transfer registers, firms will benefit from greater access to comparable international information. Internally, firms should use these EPIs to measure the effectiveness of their environmental management systems.

3. *Companies should revamp their information systems to integrate these EPIs into their internal management and reporting systems.*

   Embedding quantitative measures of materials and energy flows in the corporate information architecture will help ensure that environmental performance is factored into business decisions throughout the firm. In 1992, for example, GM's Europe Technical Development Center in Germany began developing an information system to support materials management as well as environmental reporting. The resulting system is now being piloted at other GM facilities in Europe and North America. Lessons learned in this experience will be incorporated into new plants in Thailand and Poland with the goal of creating a tool to support pollution prevention, lifecycle assessment, and regulatory reporting on a global basis. Companies in the process of overhauling their internal systems for management information, accounting systems and technical communications have a golden opportunity to fold these EPIs into the design.

4. *Firms should integrate these EPIs into managing their supply chain.*

Companies committed to improving environmental performance along the product chain should require standardized information on these EPIs from their tier-one suppliers. The resulting information can serve the downstream firm in two ways. First, it flags environmental issues that might otherwise pass unnoticed, issues that could interrupt supply or tarnish the reputation of their products. Second, it helps shift some of the responsibility for answering customer environmental performance. This shouldn't won't replace cost, quality and reliability as key criteria in choosing suppliers, but it should be a factor in responsible management.

5. *Firms should incorporate EPIs into internal incentive schemes.*

Since these EPIs are linked to resource productivity as well as environmental improvement, firms that factor them into internal incentives can drive the organization in the desired direction. A few firms are beginning to tie salary bonuses and other rewards to such EPIs as pollutant emissions and nonproduct output, but a WRI-Tellus survey suggests such opportunities for aligning employee incentives with corporate goals remain largely untapped.

This article is taken from Ditz and Ranganathan, *Measuring Up: Toward a Common Framework for Tracking Corporate Environmental Performance,* World Resources Institute, Washington, DC, 1997.

Editor's Note: Given the new mandate to make the environmental responsibilities of a firm yield sustainable business value, the corporate strategists of the next century must center their efforts not only on public relations and the many small symbolic victories of government relations. Instead, these new corporate planners must use performance measures to reposition the firm so its environmental improvements are based on more competitive machines and more appealing products, not just changes in their advertising budgets. In short, the new executives must train themselves first by learning the compliance language of lawyers and engineers, and second by giving that language more immediate business value.

Part II of this text explores how leaders come to recognize business opportunity. Part III then explains how these same high-reaching executives then broadcast their results to a suspicious public, or a set of price-sensitive consumers.

It would be a lie if we suggested that such corporate moves by environmental executives are easy. They are, in fact, riddled by serious risks and substantial uncertainties. Nevertheless, one smart way to understand business value is to measure it in terms of time, cost, and quality. Too often, refusing to do this, the environmental professional gets lost in the corporate mansion and fails to gain the attention of top management.

Environmental leadership requires a balanced skill base that includes management savvy and technical competence. In the following piece by Walter Liggett, you will read about the skills that environmental leaders need in order to understand environmental measurement and performance evaluation. These skills are used to take firms beyond the mere foothold of compliance and toward a more profitable view of corporate environmental performance.

Lessons from the Field: Environmental Measurement Feasibility

Walter Liggett

Walter Liggett is a statistician with the National Institute of Standards and Technology (NIST). Building on NIST expertise in physical sciences measurement, he has published in the field of environmental measurement. He currently serves on committees for the American Statistical Association. Before joining NIST, he worked for the Tennessee Valley Authority.

INTRODUCTION

Environmental managers often face the serious challenge of communicating with technical staff in the company on issues of environmental performance and measurement. Both management staff and technical personnel work toward common corporate goals, but they often speak entirely different languages. Moreover, these measurements are only useful to decision-makers when they lead to evidence helpful in achieving strategic business goals. In achieving these strategic goals environmental measures can help corporate strategists in four fundamental ways:

1. Demonstrating acceptable risk
2. Providing a record of current conditions
3. Showing improvement
4. Assuring stakeholders through credible measurements

Environmental managers realize that the decision to go ahead with certain types of environmental measurement depends on both usefulness and cost. This delicate judgment is often the focus of communications between senior management and technical staff. No one finds justifying environmental measurement in these terms easy. Moreover, both the cost and the utility of the resulting conclusions are hard to predict. The costs may be high and conclusions may be weak. On the other hand, small, timely investments can lead to strengthened conclusions. So how should these questions of environmental measurement be addressed by corporate leadership? In order to achieve effective decisions, senior-level strategists and middle management need to understand the broad measurement concepts underlying their final decisions.

Although definitive scientific evidence is everyone's first choice as a way to secure agreement, environmental managers cannot assume that they can somehow obtain *complete* evidence with these measurements to make logical decisions. The cost and feasibility of obtaining suitable scientific evidence depends on each of the specific corporate goals and the available alternatives for achieving those goals. For these reasons, managers cannot use technical complications as an excuse for assigning decisions about environmental measurement to the technical staff. Knowledge of the strategy, vision, and resultant goals is needed to judge whether the evidence will be useful and whether past measurement practices will serve in the current situation. Thus, middle managers and senior executive staff alike must accept responsibility for judging the outcomes of resultant environmental measurements—be it regulated air emissions, packaging materials use, or energy consumption.

Enabling the decision-makers to assess the significant lessons learned from these environmental measurements involves linking the environmental concerns and business strategy with the performance required of the measurement system. For example, when the risk to humans (i.e., floor personnel, surrounding neighborhoods) in a particular corporate project is shown to be acceptably small, then the tactics for achieving agreement among stakeholders on the project may become more clear. In this case, the relevant performance requirement may be, in a broad sense, accuracy. Likewise, if it is possible to show improvement in environmental conditions around a facility (i.e., reduced groundwater contamination), for instance, then decisions for further facility renovation may become feasible and stakeholder assurance becomes easier. In this case, the ability to discriminate between the changing impact of the facility and other external changes, and ultimately, to communicate those changes both internally and externally is the relevant performance requirement.

With elements of feasibility, purpose, cost, and outcome in mind, we can talk briefly on four implicit uses of environmental measurements for strategists.

DEMONSTRATING ACCEPTABLE RISK

An environmental manager can take one of two definitive positions with respect to measurement for risk assessment. One is to pursue an agreement among all parties on what to measure and how well.[7] The other is to recommend abandoning the use of risk assessment altogether. Measurement for risk assessment usually requires accuracy from both the physical sampling and the laboratory analysis.[8] Especially for the physical sampling, this may be a problem.[9] Since "sufficient" accuracy is hard to establish, managers should seek consensus among technical staff and senior management before obligating themselves to the costs of measurement.

Nevertheless, the measurement feasibility of risk may determine the course of regulatory negotiations. For example, an environmental risk that can be measured is more easily accepted by the public than risks where no credible measurement exists. (Negotiation based on measurement feasibility is illustrated in Part III of this text with the discussion of the voluntary agreement between EPA and the American Forest & Paper Association.)

PROVIDING A RECORD OF CURRENT CONDITIONS

From the point of view of compliance and business decision-making, knowing "where we are" is at least half as important as the strategic goal-setting process. For this reason, measuring to check the current state of the firm is a necessity for organizational environmental leadership.

Many corporate environmental issues involve the measurement of trends over periods of months and years (i.e., emission monitoring). The staff member who makes measurements at the beginning of such a period are often not available when there is finally enough data to draw conclusions due to personnel turnover. Thus, the information needed to interpret the original measurements must be stored in a database along with the measurements. Such information is often called "metadata."[10] In thinking about what information to store, environmental managers should try to anticipate what interpretations may be required in the future.[11]

The first item to consider is the measurement protocol. In many situations, comparisons are made in terms of indicators rather than accurate measurements of specific site properties. Comparison of indicators depends on faithful execution of protocols (i.e., sound collection techniques); thus the particular protocols must be spelled out in detail as part of the metadata as well. There may be reason to change the protocols, but even in this case, the old protocols must be known so that the new way can be compared with the old.

One approach to studying trends involves resampling the same sites over time. The advantage of such an approach is that background trends can be separated from local trends. Generally, trends due to elements such as changes in the weather and changes in far-removed pollution sources will be the same at all sites and thus will be part of the total background trend. Also, drift in the measurement system, which is a serious concern in long-term studies, will generally show up as part of the background trend.

Another approach to assessing trends is sampling over an entire region so that inferences can be made about the average over the region, or better yet, predictions can be made for any point in the region. The advantage of such an approach is that the same sampling sites do not have to be used; thus the possibility of sites becoming inappropriate for sampling is avoided. Finally, all metadata should include auxiliary information thought to be useful in interpreting trends, including weather data and information on anthropogenic activity.

Provisions for inclusion of metadata with measurement must be made in the management information system (MIS). Such provisions require more complicated data models, which must be anticipated when the MIS is configured. The use of metadata can complicate information systems. Data are usually input into an MIS with the understanding that they are a snapshot in time and space, yet the use of metadata includes an understanding that the data are interdependent—an opposite assumption of traditional data management.

What is actually involved is likely a reconfiguration of MIS. This, of course, is an expense and may meet some resistance. Nevertheless, it is necessary. Proponents of the use of MIS envision anyone in the organization using these environmental measurements. What is surprising is how complicated interpretation of measurements is, and thus, how much work has to be done in order to properly configure the MIS. Likewise, stakeholders outside of the organization may also gain access to information and, of course, one cannot guarantee that outsiders will use the available supporting metadata to interpret the measurements. Nonetheless, if the metadata are available but ignored, then discrediting an outside study becomes much easier.

SHOWING IMPROVEMENT DESPITE
PROBLEMS WITH SELECTIVITY

Selectivity is the biggest problem in the use of performance indicators. An indicator that works well at one facility or for one company might not be selective enough to work nationwide. There are ways to deal with lack of selectivity, however. Often in ecological studies, several indicators are used at each site and time with the intention of sorting out "what affects what" during the data analysis. This approach has been the basis for successful studies although considerable scientific expertise is needed to implement it. By attaching realistic cautions and qualifiers to measurement results, the effects of a lack of selectivity, as well as other inherent measurement weaknesses, can be addressed. Without a doubt, qualifying the conclusions of corporate environmental performance—in both site-specific and companywide measurements—helps in the business decision-making process.

The problem of selectivity also raises issues when planning for data analysis. Environmental managers should be skeptical of any plans to draw meaningful conclusions from existing measurements that were made to answer completely different questions. All too often, the commitment to answer particular questions can lead to technically gifted staff spending a large amount of time without usable results.

ASSURING STAKEHOLDERS THROUGH
CREDIBLE MEASURES

Assuring stakeholders of the minimum environmental impact associated with a facility (or an entire company) requires measurement systems that are credible. Organizations concerned with the technical and scientific quality of measurements, including the American Society for Testing Materials, the National

Institute of Standards and Technology, and the Environmental Protection Agency, offer accepted parameters for credible measurements. Yet, firms themselves should look to assume quality of measurement as well.

What is required in assessing the performance of an environmental measurement system? Obviously, one cannot judge the quality of a single measurement by itself at a facility. Moreover, complete information on a property of interest is rarely available. This distinguishes laboratory measurement from environmental measurement in the field. In assessing the performance of laboratory measurement systems, technical staff usually has reference materials with known values that can be used to accurately gauge performance. In the field, however, firms must often make replicate measurements and measure the same sites with two or more related protocols in order to evaluate measurement systems effectively.[12] Generally, to evaluate the performance of environmental measurement systems, one must measure the same thing more than once. This once again translates to additional cost, but it is the cost of credibility.

An organization can maintain a credible measurement capability only through in-house experiments aimed at improving the current measurement system. A technical staff that knows how to evaluate measurement systems is expert enough to make quality measurements. How, for example, can one determine if a protocol is sufficiently explicit and is being followed faithfully except through measurement system evaluation? Managing environmental issues in a way that answers the public's expectations and assures stakeholders includes a reasonable program of such in-house experiments and measurement validation.

CONCLUSIONS

Environmental managers typically look to EPA for guidance in choice of measurement method, and indeed, EPA continues to make advances in the development of effective measurement systems. Nevertheless, EPA's priorities are generally not the same as those of the regulated community. EPA is generally interested in methods that are applicable nationally, whereas facility monitoring only requires methods that perform well locally. Likewise, EPA is concerned with protecting public health—policy questions—while a firm's commitment to measurement must be tied to both compliance needs and business goals. Not every firm in every business requires the same level of measurement quality or quantity. Yet, an organization with particular manufacturing processes might find some measurements so central to their business interests that the development of nonregulated measurements are worthwhile even when the additional cost and resource requirements are considered.

Environmental management often involves decisions made in the face of uncertainty: uncertainty in the conclusions of environmental impact, uncertainty in how much to spend on measurement, or uncertainty in the evaluation of environmental measurement system performance. These uncertainties will continue to complicate the role of environmental staff in organizations and muddle the decision-making process in business. True leadership comes with handling these uncertainties effectively.

NOTES

7. *Guidance for the Data Quality Objectives Process,* EPA QA/G-4, U.S. Environmental Protection Agency, Quality Assurance Management Staff, Washington, DC 20460, September 1994.

8. Gilbert, Richard O., *Statistical Methods for Environmental Pollution Monitoring,* Van Nostrand Reinhold, New York, 1987.

9. Gy, Pierre M., *Sampling of Heterogeneous and Dynamic Material Systems,* Elsevier, Amsterdam, 1992. For a more accessible account, see Francis F. Pitard, *Pierre Gy's Sampling Theory and Sampling Practice,* 2nd ed., CRC Press, Boca Raton, 1993.

10. Sundgren, Bo, "Making Statistical Data More Available," *International Statistical Review,* 64, 1996:23–38.

11. Michener, William K., James W. Brunt, John J. Helly, Thomas B. Kirchner, and Susan G. Stafford, "Non-geostatistical Metadata for the Ecological Sciences," *Ecological Applications,* Vol. 7, 1997.

12. Liggett, Walter S., and Kenneth G. W. Inn, "Pilot Studies for Improving Sampling Protocols," Chapter 10 in Larry H. Keith, *Principles of Environmental Sampling,* 2nd ed., American Chemical Society, Washington, DC, 1996.

QUESTIONS FOR FURTHER THOUGHT

1. Why are measurements important to managers at the business enterprise level? What are some of the common measures that are used? What effective performance measures did WMX Technologies develop?

2. How can performance measures be used to integrate EH&S objectives into other departments?

3. Van Epps and Walters recommend that companies should embrace a "proactive environmental stance." What could be done to facilitate this? Could the organizational structure affect the proactivity of a company? Is proactiveness a function of corporate culture? Does one shape the other?

4. Van Epps and Walters highlight the benefits of a proactive management style over a reactive management style. Why might reactive approaches to environmental risks be more expensive than proactive approaches? Are there risks with being proactive?

5. Consider the Tenneco example. Can performance measures have unexpected results? Should the goal of performance measures be to make the company or EH&S department look good, or to improve the company by finding problem areas?

6. The 80/20 rule says that 80 percent of a facility's environmental costs are frequently driven by 20 percent of activities. What kinds of activities would constitute this 20 percent?

7. Ditz and Ranganathan list a series of recommendations for corporate strate-

gists to measure corporate environmental performance. Based on your reading of the piece by Van Epps and Walters, what other recommendations would you include?

ON THE NIMO INTEGRATIVE CASE

In the preceding chapters, we explored the ground floor of environmental management. Our floor plan brought you into the rooms where most corporate environmental personnel spend the majority of their professional lives. The dominant features of this floor include audit systems, self-assessment tools, and performance indicators. These are today's primary tools for achieving and maintaining compliance, the core of corporate environmental functions.

All of these management tools are embraced by Tom Fair in our integrative case. Mr. Fair, as the vice president of Environmental Affairs at Niagara Mohawk (see the Executive Spotlight for a full biographical sketch), needed to master each of these fundamental tools before he could carve out the described strategy to "go green." Yet, he had to do more as well.

You'll see the author become a "change agent," utilizing many skills to build buy-in throughout the firm. In order to scale Shelton's "Green Wall" at NiMo, Mr. Fair needed to select performance indicators that not only showed business value to his senior managers, but were usable and understandable by the business unit line operators.

This is no small accomplishment. As you read the case, please note the following items:

1. The EH&S vice president's comfort in utilizing the language of general management.
2. Fair's ability to roam with confidence into his firm's technical challenges regarding NO_x, SO_x, SPDES violations, and dielectric fluids.
3. Fair's readiness to appeal to his superiors and his colleagues for additional support and direction. (You cannot scale the Green Wall alone.)
4. Fair's endurance throughout the entire process. In order to discover the business value in environmental challenges, one must be able to construct performance indicators that make sense to multiple audiences—from the legal staff to the engineer and field operator.

In fact, if you reread the opening reflections in Chapter 1, you will see that Mr. Fair engages most, if not all, of the described environmental leadership traits.

It is so easy to get bogged down in compliance, spending 99 percent of your time and your best energy meeting legal demands. Yet the leader must prevail, cutting deals with environmentalists on the Adirondacks as he settles accounts for the senior management at the top of NiMo's headquarters.

Fair makes it all seem so easy. The close reader will ask, while observing each move, how Tom Fair stayed above the fray, measuring with exactness the changes that added value to his firm. But it is important to assume that many of these moves were difficult and risky, and some of them took guts. Read Donald Philips' excellent book, *Lincoln on Leadership* (Warner Books, New York, 1992), for another example of this; but as you read the following, please also remember that corporate success requires a strategic mix of panic and resolve.

INTEGRATIVE CASE I

Going Green: The Niagara Mohawk Story

Thomas Fair

Industry realizes that a regulatory game is still in place, but half the game now is to be part of the regulatory process.
—David Sokol, CEO and President of Ogden Products[1]

Why would a normally conservative utility company decide to "go green?" Growing public concern for the environment, the impact of environmental issues on the economics and technologies of the electric utility industry. Niagara Mohawk's particular regulatory context provides only half the answer. The other half lies in the Company's internal process of direction-setting; a process that involves assessing its environmental assets, liabilities, vulnerabilities, and opportunities and weaving them into a coherent agenda. That agenda is an important element of Niagara Mohawk's broader corporate strategy to meet the competitive demands of the future.

THE VITAL ENERGY-ENVIRONMENT CONNECTION

Why is the environment so important to Niagara Mohawk? Contemporary technologies that produce and distribute electricity and natural gas to end users are inherently intrusive on the environment—save those technologies yet tested. They utilize and affect our air, land, water, and ecosystems. Most of today's power plants burn fossil fuels to create steam that is used to turn turbines and generate an electrical current. Converting primary energy to electricity thus creates numerous byproducts from the combustion of coal, oil, and natural gas, such as sulfur dioxide, nitrogen oxides, carbon dioxide, and particulate matter. Hydroelectric energy is a clean, renewable, and indigenous source of low-cost energy; however, tradeoffs made in the early part of this century with respect to fisheries impacts are being revisited today. Nuclear power, although devoid of the pollutant emissions associated with fossil fuel combustion, has been plagued by public concern over an accidental-release scenario, and the disposal of nuclear waste. Construction of new electric transmission lines, distribution lines, and natural gas pipelines require corridors that transect ecosystems and communities. Oil used in electrical equipment for insulation can contain traces of PCBs, a chemical outlawed due to concern over its environmental fate and effects. And, various types of hazardous wastes are produced by utility operations in the course of operating and maintaining machinery. Thus, Niagara Mohawk contends with a very broad range of issues relating to its impact on the natural and human environments.

Although considerable progress has been made since the early 1970s toward making utility operations compatible with the environment, the energy-environment nexus

Who Is NiMo?

The Niagara Mohawk Power Corporation is an electric and gas utility company serving approximately 1.5 million electric customers and a half-million gas customers in the Upstate New York region between Buffalo and Albany. "NiMo," as it is commonly referred to by many of its customers, traces its corporate roots back to 1823 and the establishment of the Oswego Canal Company, an offspring of the Erie Canal system, which was, in turn, the wellspring of commercial and industrial development in Upstate New York in the early 1800s. Such origins led Niagara Mohawk's forebears to pioneer in hydroelectric development at Niagara Falls, on the Mohawk and Hudson Rivers, and elsewhere in the Upstate area. In 1950, some 500 companies were finally coalesced into a single corporate entity named Niagara Mohawk Power Corporation. Today the Company owns and operates a diverse array of coal, oil, natural gas, and nuclear electric generating stations in addition to 74 hydroelectric plants, and a system of electric transmission and distribution lines connecting all parts of its 24,000-square-mile service territory. The 1950 mergers also created a large gas distribution business, the successor of numerous local gaslight-era businesses formed in the mid- to late 1800s.

Source: Niagara Mohawk Annual Report, 1997.

characterized by those issues is likely to remain on the public policy agenda well into the next century. Global warming, urban smog, acid rain, and remediation of former industrial sites are inherently controversial and present daunting challenges to utility managers. Such issues have the potential to profoundly impact our economy and pattern of energy use. Laws and regulations designed to reduce such environmental risks drive costs and technology, and are thus a source of both business risk and, perhaps, opportunity for those who get "ahead of the curve."[2]

THE STRATEGIC DECISION TO "GO GREEN"

Managing through turbulent times is nothing new for Niagara Mohawk. Construction of its second nuclear generating unit at Nine Mile Point on Lake Ontario during the 1980s led to a severe financial crisis and a write-down of hundreds of millions of dollars in assets in the late 1980s. Financial recovery was achieved following a comprehensive Settlement Agreement with the Public Service Commission in 1990 that called for an assessment of the company's structure, management systems, and direction.

The company decided to expand the self-assessment using it as an opportunity to identify and address weaknesses, and to prepare itself for the challenges that lay ahead. Aided by McKinsey & Co., Niagara Mohawk's management identified a number of key areas where dramatic change was needed in order to prepare the company for its future; these key areas were designated as Change Initiatives. An executive sponsor was assigned for each Change Initiative to guide initiative teams comprised of middle management personnel, one of these being the Environmental Awareness Initiative Team. The teams benchmarked, identified best practices, and developed recommendations that contained implementation plans complete with budgets, schedules, and responsibilities for each area. While a need to lessen the company's impact on the environment was identified early on by Niagara Mohawk's senior management, the Initiative defined what direction to take, how far the change process should go, and how to get it done. The company's customers, regulators, and investors desired a more responsive organization—one that would proactively address the public's growing concern for environmental quality. Niagara Mohawk's management was keenly aware of the need to aggressively address regulatory vulnerabilities stemming from decrepit facilities and outdated practices. The company's management also recognized that a "green wave" was breaking in the early 1990s that would have significant repercussions for all of industry, but particularly for utilities.

After a great deal of discussion, five arguments emerged that supported taking a green path:

1. *It's the right thing to do,* based on an understanding of what it means to be a "responsible corporate citizen."

2. *Our stakeholders want it.* Customers, regulators, shareholders, and employees want it. Societal norms have dramatically shifted over the past 20 years to favor increased environmental protection. It follows that it is good business to align the Company with the environmental wave, just as it would be futile to resist it. A corollary consideration is that doing the minimum is not enough to satisfy the key stakeholders.

3. *Competition.* Due to the impending deregulation of utilities, it is important to establish a positive track record and reputation, and to move toward environmentally preferred technologies, processes, and services over the long run.

4. *Enlightened risk management.* Dealing proactively with increasing environmental liabilities, regulations, and risks is a matter of enlightened self-interest. Growth of *opportunities for failure* (increasing regulation) and *consequences of failure* (litigation, enforcement, civil and criminal penalties, and cleanup costs) have substantially escalated the business risks associated with environmental matters.

5. *Enhanced reputation.* A positive corporate identity on the environmental dimension has real value, especially one based on actual deeds, not smoke and mirrors. NiMo wants to be an organization held in high regard by customers, investors, regulators, and environmental groups for positive commitment and performance, and one that all employees from the CEO on down are proud to be a part of.

Like other dimensions of corporate strategy, the decision to become an environmental leader was a product of the world view, vision, and values of the top management team and a product of the concern for what is (1) right and responsible for all the Company's stakeholders, given the important connection between energy and the environment, and (2) responsive to society's desire for a greater level of environmental protection.[3]

THE CHANGE PROCESS: WHAT IT REQUIRES OF THE ENVIRONMENTAL MANAGER

The strategic decision to take a green path led Niagara Mohawk's top management to make three key changes in corporate governance and organization in 1990–91. First was recruitment of two additional outside directors with environmental expertise who would become members of the Board's Corporate Public Policy Committee, renamed the Corporate Public Policy and Environmental Affairs Committee, and would be given the expanded scope of setting policy and overseeing the company's environmental program. Second, the Corporate Environmental function was moved from an engineering group into the CEO's portfolio, where it would report at a higher level and provide direct input to corporate strategy and more effective advocacy (see Figure I–A). Third, a new officer position, Vice President of Environmental Affairs, was created. In addition, top management gave the Environmental Awareness Initiative team a high degree of freedom to promote change, and the clear goal of planning for a leading-edge, environmental management program (see Figure I–B). As work on the Initiative progressed, its key recommendations were presented in progress reports to the CEO, president, and other members of the top management team for approval. Decisions were made to immediately implement some of the recommendations. Thus, by April 1991, the Company's CEO and its Senior Vice President of Legal and Corporate Relations had completed the first stage of their strategy to move Niagara Mohawk to the forefront on the environment:

- Doug Costle, former administrator of the U.S. EPA, and Dr. Bonnie Guiton, a consumer affairs expert and former president of Earth Conservation Corps., had joined the Board of Directors.
- The Corporate Public Policy Committee's charter and membership had been expanded to include oversight of the Company's environmental policy and performance.

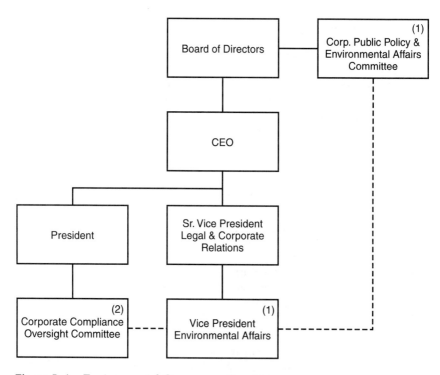

Figure I–A Environmental Governance Structure
(1) Established in 1991 as part of the corporatewide Environmental Awareness Initiative.
(2) Established in 1994. Chaired by the vice president of envoronmental Affairs and comprised of officers from each line organization and the General Counsel.

Organization	Environmental awareness is an important component of corporate governance
Environmental Policy Statement	Set "beyond compliance" direction
Issue Management	Early decisions, coordinated action, and adequate resources
Communications	Awareness of the company's policy, positions, and accomplishments
Training	Understanding of policy and compliance requirements
Environmental Procedures	Operationalize regulations and corporate policy
Information System	Tracking analysis, and reporting capabilities
Planning	Build policy into corporate strategic and operational planning
Risk Assessment	Identify, analyze, and manage risks
Environmental Auditing	Find, fix, and prevent recurrence of problems

Figure I–B Elements of 1991 Environmental Awareness Initiative

- The author had been recruited to fill the newly created position of Vice President of Environmental Affairs.
- The Environmental Awareness Initiative Recommendations and its 30-month implementation plan had been approved by top management.
- The cornerstone of the Initiative, establishment of a corporate environmental policy, had been discussed by the senior management team on a conceptual level and agreement reached that its overall theme would be going "beyond compliance."

THE SECOND STAGE: LEADERSHIP AGENDA

The appointment to Vice President of Environmental Affairs initiated the next stage of Niagara Mohawk's green strategy: carrying out the Environmental Awareness Initiative. The first few months were dominated by five priorities that flowed from the Initiative:

1. Working with the company's management team and the Corporate Public Policy and Environmental Affairs Committee of the Board to develop a written environmental policy statement.

2. Assessing the company's environmental assets and vulnerabilities, and setting environmental goals that would begin the process of translating the Policy Statement into specific actions and accomplishments.

3. Overhauling the company's environmental management system.

4. Realigning the internal structure and mission of the Environmental Affairs unit with the corporate policy, the Initiative elements, and the corporate environmental goals articulated to the Board Committee.

5. Visiting with key external constituencies (these early visits paid off when the company experienced an embarrassing environmental incident in July 1991, but was able to resolve the problem by working with these constituents—see below).

The most fundamental and far reaching of these tasks was adoption by the company's Board of Directors of the "beyond compliance" environmental policy statement. Through consultations with the CEO, the president, several board members and other members of the company's top management, it became clear that those charged with the Company's governance desired an action-oriented policy that would place it on the forefront of corporate environmentalism. Building on what the Environmental Awareness Initiative team had already accomplished, a statement was crafted that reflected the inputs of these consultations and drew upon other published corporate environmental policies, including the International Chamber of Commerce Business Charter for Sustainable Development, and the Valdez (now known as CERES) Principles. [4] The Policy Statement also addressed Niagara Mohawk's particular environmental setting and issues, such as the extensive landholdings in and around the Adirondack Park region, the company's inherited ownership of gas manufacturing waste sites, as well as interest in promoting consumer energy efficiency.

One of the most telling quotes on achieving environmental compliance is the following from the Roman lawyer, Paulus, circa 200 AD: "That which is permissible is not always honorable." Another way of saying this is, "The law often doesn't tell you what you *should* do, only what you *may* do." Doing only what is "permissible" is often unwise as well from a narrow financial perspective. Those knowledgeable in the field of

---

EXECUTIVE SPOTLIGHT   Mr. Thomas Fair, Vice President of Environmental Ethics Affairs and at Niagara Mohawk Power Corporation

I have had a twenty-five-year career in managing environmental issues in the power industry, starting in 1972 with a consulting firm, Gilbert-Commonwealth Associates, where I was responsible for impact assessment and siting of energy projects throughout the United States. I hold an MBA, an MS in Urban Planning, and a BS in Architecture.

I joined Florida Power & Light Company in 1975 where I served as Director of Environmental Affairs from 1989–91. While at FP&L, I began seeing the value of using Total Quality Management tools to improve environmental performance. I was also involved in directing the licensing of major power generation and transmission projects and environmental compliance activities.

In 1991 I moved to New York, where I was elected Vice President of Environmental Affairs at the Niagara Mohawk Power Corporation (NMPC). In addition to my environmental responsibilities, I have recently been appointed NMPC's Ethics Officer.

I have been an advisor to the North American Commission on Environmental Cooperation and participant in the Aspen Institute Series on the Environment in the Twenty-first Century. I have served as a liaison to the President's Council on Sustainable Development Energy Task Force, as an advisor to the Electric Power Research Institute, and as chairman of the environmental committee of the Florida Electric Power Coordinating Group.

corporate environmental management wryly note that companies whose policy is only to "comply with regulations" are typically those with the worst compliance performance and environmental problems. Why? Because in trying to do only the minimum to get by they create no "margin" to account for the inherent variability in the performance of individuals and physical systems, and the need to prevent problems. Moreover, they simply do not set their sights high enough considering the gap that seasoned managers know always exists between desired performance and that which is actually achieved in the field. The payoff for such uninspired policies is most often a "black hat" reputation together with higher environmental costs.

In May 1991, Niagara Mohawk's Board of Directors adopted the "Corporate Policy on Protection of the Environment" (see Figure I–C). The statement embodies the belief that doing the right thing is good business and that compliance, though essential, is an insufficient principle to guide corporate behavior in today's world.

With the strong support of top management and the Board of Directors for the Policy, the Vice President of Environmental Affairs was charged with developing a plan that would translate intentions into actions and tangible achievements. In June 1991, two goals were presented to the Corporate Public Policy and Environmental Affairs Committee of the Board:

1. Achieve Excellent Environmental Performance.
2. Be Recognized as a Corporate Environmental Leader for Performance and Accomplishments.

Achieving these goals would depend on three factors: (1) the effectiveness of the environmental management system being put in place; (2) how well the Corporate Policy on Protection of the Environment would be integrated into planning and operations companywide; and (3) the quality of relationships established with external stakeholders. These factors became the objectives around which all of Environmental Affairs' activities were organized.

BUILDING THE ENVIRONMENT INTO PLANNING AND OPERATIONS

During the latter half of 1991, the Company took a critical step in translating its Policy into specific actions. With encouragement from the Public Service Commission staff, the

▶ Meet or surpass the requirements of all environmental laws and regulations.

▶ Promote the wise use of energy.

▶ Assume a responsible stewardship role for the natural resources under our management.

▶ Reduce pollution and conserve raw materials.

▶ Fully account for law and environmental considerations in our planning and decision-making.

Figure I–C Key Elements of Corporate Policy on Protection of the Environment

Environmental Affairs Department developed a Corporate Environmental Performance Index (see Figure I–D) comprised of 18 parameters falling into three categories:

1. Waste and emissions
2. Compliance
3. Enhancements

The object was to give each of the company's Strategic Business Units, the company's top management, the PSC, and other external stakeholders a comprehensive, objective, and verifiable means of measuring the company's progress in implementing the Environmental Policy. The Performance Index was developed by an internal task force led by Environmental Affairs with representatives from each of the Strategic Business Units. The task force visited other companies to determine the state-of-the-art in environmental performance measurement. It then developed a number of options which were evaluated based on how well they would: (1) further the corporate environmental policy; (2) represent the interests of various stakeholder groups; (3) use high-quality, verifiable data, obtainable at reasonable cost; and (4) capture all aspects of the company's performance. Options for parameters and index rollup methodologies were critiqued by three outside consultants and the PSC staff before a final selection was made.[5]

NiMo's experience with the Performance Index has shown that the management truism "what gets measured gets done" holds in the environmental arena. Performance baselines for each of the index parameters provide an opportunity to set improvement targets in annual business plans, and enable future external benchmarking. The Performance Index quantifies about 80 percent of the Corporate Policy objectives and serves as a strong and auditable link between the Policy and operational planning.

In 1992, Niagara Mohawk's CEO issued a directive requiring that all business units incorporate actions implementing the Corporate Environmental Policy and Index improvement targets in their annual business plans. He also directed that the Policy be incorporated in all major corporate planning efforts, such as plans for investment in and utilization of the company's generating units. Such plans now give explicit consideration to environmental factors associated with options. They incorporate quantified environmental regulatory scenarios rather than being based solely upon today's regulatory standards.

In 1993, NiMo enlisted the aid of Research Triangle Institute in facilitating and organizing a pilot project to develop protocols for measuring environmental performance across the utility industry, based on the Environmental Performance Index. This project,

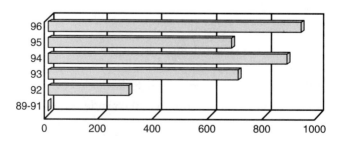

Figure I–D Environmental Performance Index

with the initial support of twelve utilities in the Northeast, has grown to include some thirty U.S. and Canadian utilities. In addition to environmental performance measurement benchmarking, NiMo has monitored environmental expenditures for major U.S. utilities based upon publicly available data. [6] As a result the company has found that the environmental performance profile is very good, and environmental costs have been quite low over the last five years, thus reinforcing the view that a proactive "beyond compliance" approach to managing corporate environmental responsibilities is a prudent business policy.

The view that policy not only can but should contribute to the corporate bottom line is illustrated by Figure I–E, the policy matrix of environmental performance and environmentally driven costs. Several important points can be made using this "which company would you like to be?" matrix.

First, all senior executives (and environmental managers!) want their company to be number four, the one with better-than-average environmental performance *and* lower-than-average environmentally driven costs. The policy goal for the environmental dimension of a company's business should be the same as that for any other important dimension, such as customer service, safety or product quality—*high performance at low cost*. This is the only position sustainable over the long run from both a financial and societal perspective.

Second, just as with other important dimensions of the business, environmental excellence can actually be an avenue to *lower* costs. This point has been written about by many and is discussed throughout this text.

On the other hand, companies in the second cell of the matrix that "buy" environmental excellence by throwing money at it are failing to effectively harvest the fruit of being environmentally responsible. Companies in the second cell are not sustainable over the long run, given competitive pressures.

Lastly, laggards are either in the worst position (cell number one) with poor performance

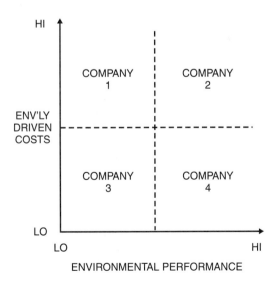

Figure I–E Which Company Would You Like to Be?

and high costs, or have poor performance and low costs (cell number three). The problem with the latter position is that such companies end up in disrepute, as environmental pariahs that fall farther behind as the bar of societal expectations is raised. Eventually they will be forced to spend catch-up money. The risks such laggards face is from adverse customer reaction. They risk forfeiting the measure of cost avoidance and control over expenditures that comes with being proactive. Laggards are constantly fighting battles with regulatory agencies, and environmental and community groups that could push them into the first or second cells of the matrix.

SCALING THE "GREEN WALL"

When designing the Environmental Awareness Initiative in 1991, Niagara Mohawk's strategy was to continuously improve all aspects of its program to "stay ahead of the curve." Over the last several years, improvement efforts have focused on three broad areas:

1. Improving environmental management system with innovations such as the Environmental Performance Index.
2. Continually improving measured environmental performance through incremental reductions in waste and emissions, pollution prevention, and measures to assure tighter compliance.
3. Maintaining a leadership posture on key environmental issues.

Thus, in 1993 NiMo began a series of new self-assessments and benchmarking efforts that have continued to the present. The firm engaged management consulting firms to perform a focused assessment of the company site investigation and remediation program and a comprehensive environmental management system review. NiMo employed the GEMI guidelines, the U.S. Sentencing Commission Draft Guidelines for Prosecuting Environmental Crimes, and agreed to participate in several environmental management system benchmarking analyses performed by consultants for other utilities that had identified Niagara Mohawk as a "best practices" company.[7] In addition, NiMo requested audits by the internal audit department to review the program, and assure integrity of all data inputs to the Environmental Performance Index. The project to engage other utilities in quantitative environmental performance benchmarking has been noted above. Finally, Niagara Mohawk has continued to focus a great deal of attention on analyzing mistakes (from environmental audits, incidents, agency inspection results, etc.), including those of other companies. Careful review of these hard and soft data has been a vitally important source of improvements to the program.

EMPLOYEE ENVIRONMENTAL AWARENESS: MAKING CHANGE MAKE SENSE

A substantial part of the Environmental Awareness Initiative focused on communicating with the line personnel ultimately responsible for making it happen. This is often referred to as "where the rubber meets the road" in corporate environmental management. During 1992, over 90 percent of Niagara Mohawk's entire work force (close to 11,000 employees) was given environmental awareness training that explained the Company's new environmental policy, and reinforced what top management expected of each employee to meet the company's overall environmental goals. Environmental procedure documents were prepared for each environmental program to aid line supervisors in interpreting regulatory requirements on the job. The general awareness training was followed by a series of formal "nuts and bolts" compliance training programs in 1992 for the hundreds of operations personnel with environmental compliance responsibilities for air and water quality, hazardous waste, PCBs, oil spill prevention, mitigation of wetland impacts, and storage tank management. Over one thousand employees participate in these training programs each year.

Employee environmental awareness was also enhanced, through creation of an environmental audit unit. This unit was established in 1992 as an instrument of continuous improvement. Also, the environmental audit unit helped disseminate "lessons learned" throughout the organization through (1) annual training, (2) a cross-functional auditing task force, and (3) issuance of written advisories that identify regulatory issues of concern.

The audit program was augmented by formal day-to-day compliance surveillance in business units with significant environmental responsibilities. The computerized environmental information management system procured and installed during 1992 began to support the environmental performance index, permitting, and waste management activities in the Environmental Affairs Department in 1993. The actions contained in the Strategic Business Unit business plans directive translated into significantly improved environmental results.

In 1997, the Environmental Affairs unit convinced the Company to pursue certification of all its generating facilities under the ISO 14001 Environmental Management Systems standard. NiMo became the first utility in North America to achieve certification of two of its generating plants, with the others scheduled for certification in late 1997 and early 1998.

LEADERSHIP REQUIRES ACCOMPLISHMENTS BEYOND THE NORM

Putting a state-of-the-art environmental management system and an aggressive corporate environmental policy in place is necessary but not sufficient to achieve environmental leadership. The real strength of any company's commitment to the environment is demonstrated by the actual results it achieves on issues that are important to its constituents. Results must match rhetoric, or your company will be discredited.

Real environmental leadership is focused on the substance of how machines work, not just on management systems. Therefore, concurrent with upgrading our management system, NiMo placed a heavy emphasis on the development of specific strategies and action plans for seven high-priority issues. These affect how the company runs the machines, not just the law.[8]

- *Clean Air.* Through a cost-effective combination of antipollution controls, cleaner fuels, and greater reliance on cleaner sources, Niagara Mohawk is reducing its SO_2 and NO_x emissions substantially (see Figure I–F).
- *Global Warming.* In 1992 the company became one of the first utilities in the United States to publish a Greenhouse Warming Action Plan describing its plans to reduce its CO_2 emissions through use of lower CO_2-emitting energy sources, improved nuclear performance, and energy efficiency programs (see Figure I–F).

In 1994, Niagara Mohawk scored a first, by completing an agreement with the Arizona Public Service company (APSCo), the U.S. Department of Energy and Environmental

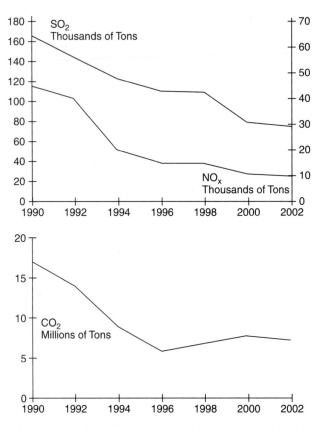

Figure I–F   Niagra Mohawk SO_2, NO_x and CO_2 Air Emissions (1992–2002)

Defense Fund under which Niagara Mohawk will trade 2.5 million tons of CO_2 credits from its reduction activities to APSCo for 20,000 Clean Air Act sulfur dioxide (SO_2) allowances held by APSCo (see Figure I–G). The allowances will, in turn, be "retired" through donation by Niagara Mohawk Power Corporation to an environmental organization. The donation will generate a tax benefit valued at over $500,000 that Niagara Mohawk Power Corporation will invest in projects that further reduce CO_2 and other pollutants.

In October, 1997, the Company was specifically cited for its proactive approach by President Clinton at a White House symposium on global warming.

- *Adirondacks Protection.* Niagara Mohawk was able to demonstrate responsible stewardship for the natural resources under its ownership through comprehensive planning of a ten-mile stretch of the Upper Hudson within the Adirondack Park. This included conveyance in 1992 of 1,200 river corridor acres to the Conservation Fund and additional acreage to the Adirondack Nature Conservancy and Adirondack Land Trust in 1993. A similar comprehensive planning program was adopted for the Salmon River in 1994, and another is underway along the Middle Hudson corridor.

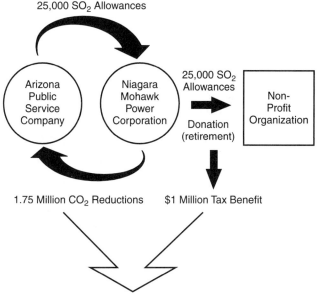

25,000 SO_2 Allowances

Arizona Public Service Company

Niagara Mohawk Power Corporation

25,000 SO_2 Allowances

Non-Profit Organization

Donation (retirement)

1.75 Million CO_2 Reductions

$1 Million Tax Benefit

Funding for Additional CO_2 Reductions

Figure I–G   Interpollutant Trade Agreement

- *Gas Manufacturing Waste Sites.* As an alternative to an enforcement-driven approach, NiMo took the initiative to investigate and remediate properties containing wastes left from the 100-year era when gas was manufactured from coal. The master plan for dealing with the MGP site—the first of its kind in New York State—has been enthusiastically embraced by the New York State Department of Environmental Conservation (DEC), the EPA and the communities in which the sites are located.

- *Recycling.* The company has expanded operations at its in-house, money-making recycling business, known as the Investment Recovery Center, by increasing paper and metal recycling by 50 percent and 30 percent respectively since 1991. In addition to recycling 15 million pounds of paper since 1987, the Center has added the capability to recycle glass, plastics, rubber, and wood.

- *Renewable Energy R&D.* Niagara Mohawk's R&D Program has pioneered the development and use of wind power, photovoltaics, biomass, and other environmentally friendly energy alternatives, clean transportation using electric- and natural gas–powered vehicles, and cost-effective solutions to existing pollution problems (advanced emission control systems and site remediation technologies).

COMMUNICATING WITH CONSTITUENCIES: MAKING STRATEGY AVAILABLE

Environmental professionals sometimes view communications as an activity belonging to the Public Relations Department, rather than as an integral part of their jobs. The Environmental Awareness Initiative addressed this critical element of environmental performance by focusing on all internal and external stakeholders and constituencies.

Integrating the Environmental Policy throughout the corporation requires a sustained campaign involving the CEO, the President, and the Environmental Vice President. This campaign includes frequent discussion of environmental goals and projects at employee meetings and through internal news and information channels. Over the past three years, Niagara Mohawk's internal newsletters have run over two-dozen features on the corporate Environmental Policy, its application, and some of the environmental challenges the company faces. These activities are regularly reported on at officers' meetings and to the Corporate Public Policy and Environmental Affairs Committee of the Board. The employee environmental awareness training mentioned above utilized a video featuring the CEO and the President, underscoring their commitment to the Corporate Policy on Protection of the Environment and their expectations for employees' behavior.

Through its best-practices analysis the Environmental Awareness Initiative team learned that it is equally important to communicate the company's environmental policy, positions, and accomplishments to external stakeholders, and to engage in dialogues with them. Organizations and key individuals that have a lot to say about the company's success or failure need to know what NiMo is doing to address its environmental responsibilities, and generally welcome the opportunity to exchange views provided the effort is a sincere one. It is also true that positive feedback from outside sources, particularly recognition by government officials and regulators, reinforces positive behaviors within the company.

The importance of effective external communication was evidenced by an incident that occurred only four months after my arrival at Niagara Mohawk. One afternoon in July 1991, the commissioner of the DEC called to inform the CEO that the Department was about to announce a major enforcement action against Niagara Mohawk for unpermitted discharge from the Company's headquarters complex. As soon as the initial shock wore off, a five-point action plan was developed which called for:

1. Rapid response—immediately determine the cause and possible countermeasures for the discharge.
2. Openness—tell it all and tell it early to regulators, key external constituents, and the community through the news media.
3. Taking responsibility vs. ducking it, minimizing it or being defensive. Put a program in place to find and correct similar problems.
4. Careful follow-up to ensure that all commitments are met and plans carried out.

The company's open communications enabled it to use the incident as an opportunity to build credibility and demonstrate to all its employees and its external constituencies how it would deal with the environment under its new corporate policy. The Company's response to the incident drew praise from the DEC and local opinion leaders, who helped convince people throughout the company that we were on the right track.

THE CHALLENGES AHEAD: WHY NO POSITION REMAINS FIRM FOR LONG

Practitioners of corporate environmental management are keenly aware that their field is highly dynamic. Indeed the status quo is the enemy. The onset of new issues, the rebirth of old issues, new scientific findings and technologies, and the ever-increasing accumulation of laws and regulations demand continual adaptation, at times complete overhaul, of the way companies address their environmental responsibilities. Although environmental departments must constantly acquire new knowledge and skills, and re-deploy their resources, most of the corporate changes required for effective adaptation must occur elsewhere in the organization and at times strike at fundamental business assumptions. Therefore, effective environmental managers are change agents, capable of persuading line and staff organizations outside their chain of command to signifi-cantly alter their work routines, spending priorities, and plans, often before evidence of the need for such changes is visible.

As change agents, environmental managers must address three issues that emerged in the late 1980s. These issues are challenging companies to rethink some of their basic assumptions about how the environment affects their business, and what their response should be.

SUSTAINABLE DEVELOPMENT AS A STRATEGIC CONCERN

The first issue, the most far-reaching theme for twenty-first-century environmental man-agement, is "sustainable development," a concept set forth in "Agenda 21" and the ac-companying "Rio Declaration," at the UN Earth Summit in Rio de Janeiro in 1992. When translated into corporate management principles such as "system optimization," this concept gives new and broader meaning to the phrase "environmentally responsible behavior" (see Figure I–H).

System optimization is really a family of closely related concepts such as "pollution prevention," "life-cycle design," and "industrial ecology," all of which look at the en-vironmental and economic ramifications of every step in the production process and then optimize the whole process.

Sustainable development and system optimization share three elements: (1) a focus on process, (2) a holistic approach versus piecemeal problem solving, and (3) the goal of harmonizing economic production and ecological processes. Moreover, the kinds of

---

- More Efficient Production Processes
- Cleaner Production Processes
- Consideration of the Entire Product Life Cycle, Hence Minimizing or Avoiding Wastes
- Environmental Management a High Corporate Priority
- Stewardship
- Dialogue with Employees and the Public, Environmental Awareness and Training
- Annual Environmental Conduct
- Codes of Environmental Conduct
- R&D of Environmentally Sound Technologies and Environmental Man-agement Systems

---

Figure I–H   The UNCED Charge to Business and Industry

Source: Chapter 30 of Agenda 21.

changes in thinking and the behavior they imply go far beyond tweaking existing products and production processes. They require rethinking processes from the ground up. Consistent with these insights, Niagara Mohawk is continually pushing its operations to become more environmentally "efficient" (i.e., reducing the environmental burden per unit of output) to develop renewable energy sources, to dramatically increase reuse and recycling of materials, and to take creative approaches to issues such as global climate change and acidic deposition.

COMPLIANCE IMPERATIVE IN A TIME OF CORPORATE DOWNSIZING

A second overarching environmental theme that is causing widespread consternation in corporate board rooms is the tightening enforcement vice, especially the increasing use of criminal sanctions. The business risks associated with compliance failures have escalated to the point where some of the "best practices" Niagara Mohawk instituted through its 1991 Environmental Awareness Initiative, such as environmental auditing and training, are becoming universal. To tighten the compliance program further, in 1993 NiMo initiated three management tools: (1) a compliance-monitoring category in the Environmental Performance Index referred to above, (2) internal surveillance and reporting to detect, review, and act on incipient compliance problems that can arise between audits, and (3) root cause analysis and corporatewide dissemination of "lessons learned." In 1994, NiMo established a Corporate Compliance Oversight Committee chaired by the Vice President of Environmental Affairs, and comprised of the General Counsel and officers from each of the company's line organizations. The Oversight Committee meets quarterly to review the company's compliance status across all operations using the results of environmental audits, agency inspections, emission/discharge data, and other types of information compiled by Environmental Affairs (see Figures I-A and I-I). It provides a very useful, action-oriented forum for addressing compliance issues and ensuring that improvement actions are taken. The results of its work are reported to the company's president.[9]

Finally, considering the need to deepen the organizational roots of compliance at work locations where the environmental risks are greatest, Niagara Mohawk proceeded with a plan to achieve ISO 14001 certification for all its generating facilities in 1997–98. Putting the environmental management system to this test (a) further institutionalized our compliance assurance system and beyond-compliance practices, (b) raised employee awareness and pride, and (c) led to a number of further EMS improvements as each facility prepared to undergo the ISO audit.

Ironically, the relentless management focus required to meet the compliance imperative can result in a manifestation of Gresham's Law, where efforts to avoid the negative crowd out efforts to achieve the positive. This can be an unintended consequence of government's harsh enforcement of absolute, unwavering conformance with the millions of words and numbers found on thousands of pages of regulations—but only if you let it.

"LEAN, GREEN, AND CLEAN": WHAT THE NEW MANTRA CAN MEAN

The third environmental management theme is a result of increased consumer demand for environmental quality. It is the recasting of the environment as a competitive issue. As the influence of the environment on products, processes, costs, and technologies has grown, so too has the pressure on environmental managers to suggest and carry out environmentally related business strategies that improve the company's ability to compete. Considering the variety of ways in which the environment can influence a company's competitive position points to three distinct types of environmental strategies:

1. Assuring that questions about the interpretation of environmental regulations, permit conditions, or compliance as well as inquiries, complaints, or allegations are referred in a timely manner to the Environmental Affairs Department as well as through the SBU chain of command;

2. Assuring that communications with the EPA, DEC or any other governmental entity relating to environmental compliance fully involve the Environmental Affairs Department as well as the SBU chain of command;

3. Assuring that SBU personnel who supervise compliance with permits and/or handling and disposal of materials or substances subject to environmental regulation receive continuing training concerning environmental compliance responsibilities;

4. Identifying ways to derive greater benefit from environmental auditing;

5. Incorporating environmental compliance as a component of business plan goals as well as performance goals for individuals with compliance responsibilities;

6. Identifying (on a systemwide basis) and implementing countermeasures for the root causes of noncompliance; and

7. Aiding in the communication of environmental compliance information throughout the company to those persons responsible for implementation of the September 8, 1994 directive.

Figure I–I Charter of the Corporate Environmental Compliance Oversight Committee

1. Management strategies—avoiding costs and reducing risks; smart compliance.
   Example: Environmental training and auditing to prevent costly and embarrassing incidents.

2. Regulatory strategies—figuring out how to stay ahead in the public policy arena (a survival skill for the next century).
   Example: Negotiation of a comprehensive, multisite plan for investigation and remediation of waste sites owned by Niagara Mohawk versus defaulting to a much more costly, reactive, site-by-site approach.

3. Product/service strategies—creating value for environmentally attuned customers; becoming part of the solution to the problem when possible.
   Example: Pushing NO_x control technology to create tradable overcompliance "credits" at low marginal cost, which can be used to aid the company's industrial customers who may lack cost-effective control options or who desire to expand and require a NO_x offset.

Most companies will probably struggle to comprehend and adapt to the environmental challenges ahead because they imply significant change. On the other hand, those companies whose leaders have engaged in serious internal discussions concerning the environmental dimension of their companies' business and have made environmental protection a part of their self-concept and "persona" should be in a position to make opportunities out of the same environmental challenges that their competitors treat only as threats.

Although one might like to assert that Niagara Mohawk is now in the latter group, the validity of such an assertion can only be demonstrated by the company's continuing performance against ever-changing constituent expectations, set against a backdrop of other dramatic changes in the electric utility "business environment." Will what Niagara Mohawk has done to weave an environmental consciousness into the fabric of the core business make the company stronger, more resilient, and better prepared for the future? Only time will tell.

NOTES

1. *Changing Course: A Global Perspective on Development and the Environment,* Stephan Schmidheiney with the Business Council of Sustainable Development, MIT Press, Cambridge, MA, 1992.

2. *Lean, Green, and Clean: The Profitable Company of the Year 2000,* the Tom Peters Group, Palo Alto, CA, 1990.

3. Please see "Business and the Environment," SRI International, Business Intelligence Program, Report No. 809, 1992; and "Our Common Future," report of the World Commission on Environment and Development, Oxford U. Press, 1987; and "Choosing a Sustainable Future," report of the National Commission on the Environment, Island Press, Washington, DC, 1993; and *Agenda 21: The Earth Summit Strategy to Save Our Planet,* edited by Daniel Sitarz, Earthpress, Boulder, CO, 1993.

4. *Business Charter for Sustainable Development: Principles for Environmental Management,* International Chamber of Commerce, 1990.

5. "Sustainable Development by Design: Review of Life Cycle Design and Related Approaches," G. A. Keoleian and D. Menerez, *Air and Waste Journal,* May 1994.

6. "Industrial Pollution Prevention: A Critical Review," H. Freeman, et al., *Journal of Air and Waste Management Association,* May 1992.

7. "Factors in Decisions on Criminal Prosecutions for Environmental Violations in the Context of Significant Voluntary Compliance on Disclosure Efforts by the Violator," U.S. Department of Justice, 1991.

8. "Measuring Environmental Performance at Niagara Mohawk," Joseph Miakisz, *Total Quality Environmental Management,* Autumn 1994.

9. "How Niagara Mohawk Incorporates Environmental Factors into Policies, Plans, and Procedures," Joseph Miakisz, *Total Quality Environmental Management,* Summer 1995.

QUESTIONS FOR FURTHER THOUGHT

1. Why is internal leadership and commitment needed within an organization for compliance challenges? How can this be accomplished?

2. How can compliance-based goals and incentives lead an organization to "ahead-of-the-curve" environmental performance?

3. Why does the author assert that environmental managers are "first and foremost change agents"? Would a manager focusing only on compliance agree with that statement? Why?

4. Embracing environmental issues can reap benefits for any company, but it also brings risks. What risks does NiMo face during their transition toward achieving environmental excellence?

5. How did NiMo evaluate its progress in implementing its Corporate Environmental Policy; specifically, how does the company Performance Index operate? (Focus on quantitative vs. qualitative measures and the importance between the distinction.)

6. How did the information captured in the Performance Index allow the Corporate Environmental Policy to be integrated into the core business operations and decisions?

7. Express opinions on how NiMo handled its first public environmental problem since getting on the "green path." Discuss the reactions and effects on both internal and external stakeholders.

SUGGESTIONS FOR FURTHER READING

- Friedman, Frank, *Practical Guide to Environmental Management,* Environmental Law Institute, Washington, DC, 1993.

Considered the environmental managers' "bible" by some, in this book Friedman presents a realistic view of the role that an environmental manager plays inside a corporation. With a strong grounding in the legal requirements of the field—Friedman is trained as an environmental lawyer—the book offers a comprehensive view of management programs, legal reporting requirements, mergers and acquisitions, auditing, and dealing with stakeholders, from the perspective of a regulated entity.

- Daugherty, Jack E., *Industrial Environmental Management: A Practical Handbook,* Government Institute's, Inc., Rockville, MD, 1996.

For anyone interested in the technical components of corporate environmental compliance, Daugherty offers a detailed account of "coping with compliance." Like Friedman, Daugherty presents information on the functional tasks of environmental managers, such as audits, inspections, permitting, and controlling pollution, but his focus is more on the technical aspects of compliance (i.e., ppms, pollution technology, absorption models). Still, it is a useful resource for professionals.

- Findley, Roger W., and Daniel A. Farber, *Environmental Law: In a Nutshell,* West Publishing Company, St. Paul, Minnesota, 1992.
- Sullivan, Thomas F. P. (ed.), *Environmental Law Handbook,* 13th ed., Government Institute's, Inc. Rockville, MD, 1995.

These two books on environmental law offer distinctly different, yet useful, presentations on the federal and state environmental laws that drive environmental compliance. Findley's book offers a readable summation of the major statutes, while Sullivan gives readers a slightly more encyclopedic and thorough recitation of our American legal framework.

- Masters, Gilbert M., *Introduction to Environmental Engineering and Science,* Prentice Hall, New Jersey, 1991.

For those interested in understanding the technical nuances of remediation, fate and transport, pollution air dispersion and risk, Masters' book on environmental science offers readers a good look at the field.

- Wehrmeyer, Walter (ed.), *Greening People: Human Resources and Environmental Management,* Greenleaf Publishing, England, 1996.

This collection of readings linking human resource management and environmental management is a timely discourse on the needs of including employees throughout the company in environmental initiatives. More than most management initiatives, the implementation of environmental strategies requires wholehearted staff attention. This text contains a number of valuable chapters on facets of human resources management such as employee incentives, change and corporate culture, training, and employee responsibility.

- Piasecki, Bruce, *Beyond Dumping,* McGraw-Hill, New York, 1984.
- Piasecki, Bruce, and Gary A. Davis, *America's Future in Toxic Waste Management,* Quorum Books, Connecticut, 1988.

Both of these books by Piasecki offer a glimpse at the technical complexities of achieving baseline, legal compliance. In *America's Future*, Piasecki looks to some of the ahead-of-the curve models of compliance and stakeholder involvement in siting, remediation technology selection and pollution controls. *Beyond Dumping* offers readers a look at the dominant technological options of pollution abatement and avoidance during the 1970s and 1980s.

- Keith, Larry H., *Principles of Environmental Sampling*, 2nd ed., American Chemical Society, Washington, D.C., 1996.

This multi-author compilation is not likely to be read cover-to-cover, but any student with some technical background could read selected chapters and obtain familiarity with the way environmental measurement problems are framed. The book also gives an introduction to some of the tools used in solving applied measurement problems.

PART

2

RECOGNIZING BUSINESS OPPORTUNITY

CHAPTER

Defining Strategy in the "Age of Environmentalism"

WHAT BUSINESS CAN EXPECT NEXT CENTURY

You can't win in business without being able to recognize opportunities that bring you profit, talented staff, and the chance to pursue other opportunities that matter. This takes strategic thinking. The discipline of strategic management—as an area of academic inquiry—is often described as "relatively young." As Richard Rumelt states in *Fundamental Issues in Strategy:*[1]

> The field has not, like political science, grown from ancient roots in philosophy, nor does it, like parts of economics, attract scholars because of the elegance of its theoretical underpinnings. Rather, like medicine or engineering, it exists because it is worthwhile to codify, teach, and expand what is known about skilled performance of roles and tasks that are a necessary part of our civilization. Its advancement as a field increasingly depends upon building theory that helps explain and predict organizational success and failure.

This passage explains why strategic thinking in business is more about practice than theory. It is a clinical art, like medicine or applied engineering, not a pure science. We believe that sound strategic thinking allows leaders to recognize reliable business opportunities and integrate superior environmental programs, and we believe this kind of thinking will gain in significance for corporate leaders across the next century.

But what exactly is corporate strategy, and how does it respond to environmental needs and pressures? Here are three recent, thoughtful attempts at defining "strategic thinking," which is as hard to capture as the word "jazz."

95

First Definition

Strategy is the determination of the long-run goals and objectives of an enterprise, and the adoption of courses of action and the allocation of resources necessary for carrying out these goals.—Alfred D. Chandler Jr., *Strategy and Structure: Chapters in the History of the Industrial Enterprise*

Second Definition

A strategy is the pattern or plan that integrates an organization's major goals, policies, and action sequences into a cohesive whole. A well-formulated strategy helps to marshal and allocate an organization's resources into a unique and viable posture based upon its relative internal competencies and shortcomings, anticipated changes in the environment, and contingent moves by intelligent opponents. —James Brian Quinn, *Strategies for Change: Logical Incrementalism*

Third Definition

What business strategy is all about is, in a word, competitive advantage. The sole purpose of strategic planning is to enable a company to gain, as efficiently as possible, a sustainable edge over its competitors. Corporate strategy thus implies an attempt to alter a company's strength relative to that of its competitors in the most efficient way.—Kenichi Ohmae, *The Mind of the Strategist*

Chandler, Quinn, and Ohmae are mostly focused on corporate strategy.[2] Let's not forget that strategic thinking also occurs in warfare, politics, and world diplomacy, and that it involves what we call "street smarts" as well. Perhaps Robert Grant offers the most simple, yet most effective, definition of all in his book on strategy. Simply stated, "strategy is about winning," and you can't win often without a steady stream of captured business opportunities.[3]

Born of military action, the creation and study of business strategy evolved from early research on business planning for organizational success. Grant continues by purposefully distinguishing these two.[4]

We should distinguish strategy from detailed planning; strategy is not a rule book, a blueprint, or a set of programmed instructions. Strategy is the unifying theme that gives coherence and direction to the individual decisions of an organization or person.

Sometimes, mission statements indicate strategic direction. Moreover, the subtle significant actionable elements of strategy are often communicated through a collection of policy statements, acquisitions, new staff hires, user's guides for internal staff direction, and even smart, somewhat deliberately revealing press clips. The public face of a strategy doesn't stay in bloom for very long.

Strategy is mostly secret. What goes public are the parts designed to win public approval, intimidate competitors, or convince regulators, as explored in Part III of this book.

THE BIRTH OF BUSINESS STRATEGY

Prior to the 1960s, the link between strategic management and academic research was essentially nonexistent—apart from a few researchers in the field. The prehistory of strategic study lies in the fields of economics, organizations, and bureaucracies. Adam Smith's "price theory" left little room for real strategic planning in organizations. All decisions on inputs, outputs, and market selection would be coordinated, according to this drastically simplified model, through market price, which would lead to the highest level of market efficiency. Yet the world of technical performance, public choice, and environmental demands make a price-based theory too simple to be an effective mapping of today's real and quite dynamic world.

Strategy, as a framework for understanding business decisions, evolved slowly. Frederick Taylor's "science of work," presented in *The Principles of Scientific Management* in 1911, developed the idea that functional practices (i.e., industrial operation) could be improved through careful observation and analysis. This perspective focused completely on "the right way to do a job" on a shop floor. In 1938, Barnard stressed the difference between managerial work that made the organization *efficient* versus managerial practice that led to organizational *effectiveness*—in many ways the root of strategic management research. What's sad about most of the last 25 years of environmental efforts is that firms focused exclusively on efficiency, at the neglect of effectiveness.

Further development toward a working paradigm of business strategy came from Simon, (1947) and Selzinick (1957) with their developments on the idea that organizations held "distinctive competencies" that differentiated them from their competitors. The strategic concerns and resultant advantages tied to "environmentalism," expressed in this text, are tied closely to this notion of distinctive competency. When companies like ARCO or Volvo create product advantages tied to environmental issues (as noted in this part), they are effectively leveraging this distinctive competency.

Three additional texts presented in the early and mid-1960s helped to crystallize the notion of a "strategic framework" for understanding and categorizing a firm's behavior. Each of these texts (shown in the accompanying sidebar) offered evidence which helped to break the understanding of corporate behavior free from the neoclassical, predetermined framework previously postulated by the followers of Adam Smith and other determinists.[5]

With all these texts now in the library, the field of strategy took shape during the 1960s, 1970s, and 1980s. Yet it would be another twenty or thirty years before folks began exploring the intersections of strategy and technology, and

Published Models on Corporate Strategy: Getting Closer to A Modern Reality

- Alfred Chandler's *Strategy and Structure* examined the way executives defined their long-term roles in organizations. Likewise, Chandler also presented an exciting, more dynamic model that recognized the role that differing organizational structures played in long-term organizational evolution and decision-making. Such variances are a common aspect of reliable corporate environmental strategy today.[6]

- Kenneth Andrews's *The Concept of Corporate Strategy* took Chandler's ideas and added Selzinick's notion of "distinctive competencies" and external environmental pressures on a firm. Andrews went on to state that "corporate strategy has two equally important aspects, interrelated in life, but separated to the extent practicable in one's study of strategy. The first of these is formulation, the second implementation." This text was developed through the Harvard Business School, already differentiating itself from other business schools in this new area of management. Formulation can be thought of as the shaping of the pitcher's spout; implementation is about using the handle to pour out the new direction.[7]

- Igor Ansoff's *Corporate Strategy* looked to develop an idea of strategy as a means to maximize economic returns in a smart, organized manner. Ansoff saw strategy as a "common thread" for choices on (1) product-market scope, (2) growth vectors (old versus new products and markets), (3) competitive advantage (unique opportunities for the firm based on products and markets), (4) synergy internally generated by a combination of capabilities and competencies, and (5) make-or-buy decisions. (Few, in the last twenty-nine years, have thought to adapt Ansoff to environmental concerns.)[8]

more appropriately, strategy and environmental needs. There were a few rare exceptions, but overall the literature avoided any discussion of the "environmental" and business strategy until the 1990s.

LINKING ENVIRONMENTAL MANAGEMENT WITH BUSINESS STRATEGY

Understanding the role of "environmentalism" in business decision-making requires an understanding of history. American environmental regulatory policy first came as a wave of change crashing on the political and corporate landscapes during the 1960s. Rachel Carson's book, *Silent Spring*, published in 1962, ignited the public and helped spark the environmental movement. Lake Erie was declared dead, the Cuyahoga River in Cleveland caught fire and burned

Some Dominant Lessons in Strategy: 1965–1985

Further shifts in the understanding of corporate strategy took place in the mid-1960s. Stemming from the Boston Consulting Group's work on their "experience curve," some fundamental patterns were noted (i.e., first-mover advantage leads to lower costs and higher margins, and ultimately to a strengthened competitive position). This enhanced view of strategy made both empirical and conceptual sense. In short, during the birth of legislated environmentalism, the 1970s brought about research that furthered the distinctions between strategic choice, content, and process. By the 1990s, distinctions concerning strategy and its environmental consequences, began to be noted by Bruce Smart, Stephen Schmidheiny, and others.[9]

At the same time, pragmatic researchers were beginning to note how the world of real strategy was far more complex than any theory or model. Examples of consequence include Lindbloom's "muddling through," Quinn's "logical incrementalism," and Mintzberg and Waters's "emergent strategies." These students of strategy noted the dynamic, ever-changing nature of actual strategic thinking. They got us all closer to how environmental matters play at the strategic level, and a more complex view of strategy in business resulted.

Additional work in the 1980s represented the attempt to test tangible connections between strategy and firm performance:

- Following Chandler's research, Harvard researchers empirically demonstrated a relation between growth strategies, organizational form, and the expected performance of the organization—thereby classifying diversification strategies of firms. They mostly ignored environmental matters.

- Purdue University researchers examined business strategies and noted the high amount of heterogeneity in strategies and performance in single industries. This led to a notion of strategic groups and competitive advantage and showed that strategy could be measured by real variables. While many real variables were studied, the environment was not.

- Harvard's Michael Porter used the field of industrial organization economics as an alternative lens through which to view strategy and performance. Porter moved strategy beyond the vague concept of external forces and recognized five distinct forces that made up a structured competitive industrial environment.

for five days, the nation's proud symbol, the bald eagle, was near extinction from DDT poisoning, and smog in some U.S. cities was often visible and noxious. As a result, public outcry for federal leadership in protecting the country's natural environment and public health took strong hold of Washington, as well as other national capitols.

The litigious response to environmental concerns erupted throughout the 1970s and into the 1980s. This is expressed vividly in Figure 5–1. The corporate response to the "environmental movement" was reactive at best—

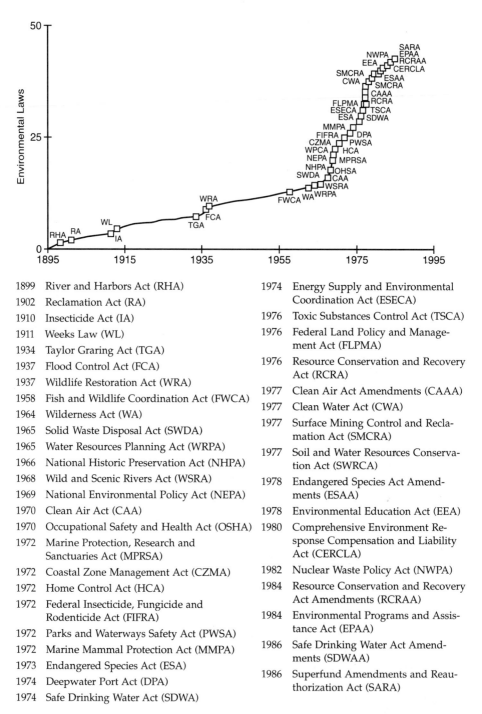

1899	River and Harbors Act (RHA)
1902	Reclamation Act (RA)
1910	Insecticide Act (IA)
1911	Weeks Law (WL)
1934	Taylor Graring Act (TGA)
1937	Flood Control Act (FCA)
1937	Wildlife Restoration Act (WRA)
1958	Fish and Wildlife Coordination Act (FWCA)
1964	Wilderness Act (WA)
1965	Solid Waste Disposal Act (SWDA)
1965	Water Resources Planning Act (WRPA)
1966	National Historic Preservation Act (NHPA)
1968	Wild and Scenic Rivers Act (WSRA)
1969	National Environmental Policy Act (NEPA)
1970	Clean Air Act (CAA)
1970	Occupational Safety and Health Act (OSHA)
1972	Marine Protection, Research and Sanctuaries Act (MPRSA)
1972	Coastal Zone Management Act (CZMA)
1972	Home Control Act (HCA)
1972	Federal Insecticide, Fungicide and Rodenticide Act (FIFRA)
1972	Parks and Waterways Safety Act (PWSA)
1972	Marine Mammal Protection Act (MMPA)
1973	Endangered Species Act (ESA)
1974	Deepwater Port Act (DPA)
1974	Safe Drinking Water Act (SDWA)
1974	Energy Supply and Environmental Coordination Act (ESECA)
1976	Toxic Substances Control Act (TSCA)
1976	Federal Land Policy and Management Act (FLPMA)
1976	Resource Conservation and Recovery Act (RCRA)
1977	Clean Air Act Amendments (CAAA)
1977	Clean Water Act (CWA)
1977	Surface Mining Control and Reclamation Act (SMCRA)
1977	Soil and Water Resources Conservation Act (SWRCA)
1978	Endangered Species Act Amendments (ESAA)
1978	Environmental Education Act (EEA)
1980	Comprehensive Environment Response Compensation and Liability Act (CERCLA)
1982	Nuclear Waste Policy Act (NWPA)
1984	Resource Conservation and Recovery Act Amendments (RCRAA)
1984	Environmental Programs and Assistance Act (EPAA)
1986	Safe Drinking Water Act Amendments (SDWAA)
1986	Superfund Amendments and Reauthorization Act (SARA)

Figure 5-1 Exponential Growth of U.S. Laws on Environmental Protection

Source: Bruce Harrison's "Going Green: How to Communicate Your Company's Environmental Commitment." *Business One,* Irwin, IL, 1993.

resulting in a grudgingly posed series of lobbying tactics, avoidance, and reluctant acceptance. Somewhere in the 1980s, the smarter companies began to take a different approach to their new environmental responsibilities, choosing to look at them from a strategic vantage point rather than as a legal burden alone. In the wake of the statutory barrage of the 1970s and 1980s, companies like Du Pont, Dow, and Xerox began to look for the right waves to surf in order to bypass their competition and avoid the avalanche. The result was the legitimate birth of corporate *environmental* strategy.

With this new view, corporate planners began to recognize environmental customers, suppliers, statutory opportunities, new product niches, process efficiency opportunities, and the real potential for enhanced public image and social responsiveness. An entirely new corporate response began. As such, the language of environmental professionals inside business organizations began to change as well, as a result of this new mindset (see Figure 5–2). Environmentalism was beginning to have an entirely new, potentially friendly face *inside* the corporation—requiring a cautious reexamination of current environmental management practices. Progressive firms, and, perhaps more accurately, progressive individuals directly concerned with environmental management inside the corporate mansion now began to lead the business down a new, greener path, marrying the green goals of the environmental community, the public, regulators, and most certainly the employees themselves with the equally green goals of business—profit.

Even with the accumulated success stories of this altered view of "corporate environmentalism," this new strategic view of environmentally related challenges strangely continues to elude some corporate planners and many researchers. The entrenched, compliance-laden history of the environmental movement still seems to taint their view. As Stuart Hart states in the January–February 1997 issue of the *Harvard Business Review*:[10]

Figure 5–2   The Changing Language of Environmental Management

TERMS FROM 1970 THRU 2000	TERMS FOR NEXT CENTURY
• permitting requirements	• consumer preference
• end-of-the-pipe	• pollution prevention
• liability and risk	• sustainability and profit
• hazardous waste management	• product stewardship and life-cycle assessment
• reporting to regulator and required reporting and disclosure	• environmental annual reports and voluntary environmental disclosure beyond the law
• minimizing costs	• enhancing competitive advantage
• environmental threats	• environmental opportunities

Source: Assembled by Kevin A. Fletcher from informal interviews with environmental professionals at RPI's EMP Program Corporate Affiliates Events 1993–1997.

Few executives realize that environmental opportunities might actually become a major source of revenue growth. Greening has been framed in terms of risk reduction, reengineering, or cost cutting. Rarely is greening linked to strategy or technology development, and as a result, most companies fail to recognize opportunities of potentially staggering proportions.

It is this new, enriched strategic response to the threats and opportunities of "environmentalism" that will serve as another significant form of competitive advantage next century for firms—just like quality, distribution, and cost are now primarily strategic items. The prior "mechanistic" views of corporate decision-making were dissolved away by researchers and practitioners alike, acknowledging the dynamic and organic nature of business. This is even more evident when one begins to look at the environmental choices being made by corporate strategists.

From the environmental advocacy perspective, the understanding of the marriage of corporate strategy and decision-making with environmental concerns is a fundamental and inevitable requirement. The importance of this new corporate role is summed up in the following passage from a 1996 *Harvard Business Review* article.[11]

> Like it or not, the responsibility for ensuring a sustainable world falls largely on the shoulders of the world's enterprises, the economic engines of the future. Clearly, public policy innovations (at both the national and international levels) and changes in individual consumption patterns will be needed to move toward sustainability. But corporations can and should lead the way, helping to shape public policy and driving change in consumers' behavior. In the final analysis, it makes good business sense to pursue strategies for a sustainable world.

By 1998, some twenty-eight years after the start of American environmental regulation, corporate environmental strategy is beginning to get past the primal state of adolescent excitement and childish uncertainty, and is instead becoming ingrained in the dominant institutions of law, science, and business. A telling quote on this issue of the new corporate environmentalism comes from Paul Gilding, former executive director of Greenpeace International, who stepped down from his post in 1994 to consult with firms directly on issues of environmental consequence.[12]

> In little more than 10 years, the environment has become a mainstream issue, from living rooms to corporate boardrooms. What the world needs now is a behavior change that is speedy enough to avoid catastrophes on ecological and economic levels. Business is the only vehicle for this type of change.

Leveraging the real economic engines of the world for positive environmental change takes time, patience, skill, and leadership. As you enter the mansion of possibilities we've constructed for you, please keep in mind that it was built because "strategy is all about winning." When you look through the cases and professional insights assembled in this text, you begin to realize that strategic responses to "environmentalism" can take many forms. Whether it be examples of terrain advantage, opportunity advantage, or moral advantage, as shown in Figure 5–3, identifying the business opportunities inherent in our "environmental" playing field is new for corporate strategists. This requires knowledge of both the functional and the visionary facets of strategy.

When an ARCO reinvents the traditional product rules of the petroleum industry, an entrenched industry usually dependent upon stability and slow change, then you're seeing an example of a strategy that recognizes environmental "opportunity advantage." This type of strategy is much more risky than traditional strategies related to cost, quality, and distribution, but the higher risk relates to a higher potential reward as well. AT&T's role in eliminating ozone-depleting chlorofluorocarbons (CFCs) directly related to the "terrain advantage" they created by developing technically sound and economic alternatives to CFCs.[13] The "moral advantages" that firms like the Body Shop, Patagonia, or Ben & Jerry's leverage with selected customers, and stakeholders serve as their strategic foothold in the marketplace.

In Part III of this text, on environmentally related business opportunities, please keep in mind that environmental leaders *only add cost*, and little value, to the big-dollar business functions *unless* they know how to fit and fix the strategic direction of their firms. Leaders keep those painful realities in mind throughout their careers.

FIVE MEASURES OF CORPORATE ENVIRONMENTAL STRATEGY

In Part I, we studied how "Achieving Compliance" serves as a basis for a strategic response to environmental threats and opportunity, driving executives, managers, and line staff alike to reach compliance objectives and move beyond. Once companies gain a handle on their legal requirements, there is the opportunity—with added time and resources—to jump the higher hurdles of new product development, process refinement, and environmental management

Figure 5–3 Three Kinds of Strategic Advantages in Environmental Management

Opportunity Advantage	Terrain Advantage	Moral Advantage
When you have an early lead in a technical skill base or approach, and when others are not yet ready to replicate.	When the convention of science and law support your direction of growth, as does your market position.	When the public and the press constantly want your "corporate" position. This is about image and prestige.
ARCO's reformulated gasoline strategy.	AT&T's strategic role in reducing the use of CFCs.	The Body Shop or Patagonia product strategy.

Source: Assembled from Piasecki's "Environmental Management Seminar" course at RPI. See Figure 5–4 for book reference.

systems integration. In Part III, those efforts to answer environmental needs and win public points for some firms are examined.

In order to hold tightly onto these potential opportunities, a strategy must address each of the "five fingers" required to steer in a new direction. Each of these "fingers," expressed in Figure 5–4, represents the core set of concerns that should be folded into any environmental strategy. Part II begins to examine how the functions of business opportunity recognition can be profitably focused on environmental concerns and related customer demands.

First, the role of the budgetary process is evaluated by Richard MacLean and Anne Rappaport. Understanding the importance of budgetary decisions in environmental strategy is the first step toward fully integrating business goals and environmental concerns.

In our final teaching case, Sandra Rothenberg's and Jeff Maxwell's look at Volvo's efforts to design and market an "environmental" car is striking at first. Unlike the limited efforts of boutique environmental shops, Volvo's core business—automobiles—is not easy to make "green." Yet, we see a similar effort to add business value through environmental innovation in ARCO's creation and positioning of reformulated gasoline. Such concrete cases show us how the spout of strategy and new product creation can redirect the budgeting process.

The third section of Part II gives you the experiences of AT&T's "Design for the Environment" efforts. Brad Allenby and Joseph Mon's reflections, along with the other glimpses into management systems by David Rainey, present the important argument for aligning business concerns with environmental threats and opportunities through effective management systems and models—thereby continuously improving the overall corporate response to environmental issues.

Finally, it takes solid information to tie environmental functions together tightly, weaving them in with the traditional business goals of revenue enhancement and market share development, while ensuring compliance and fortifying the strategic environmental response. Thus, we end this part with a

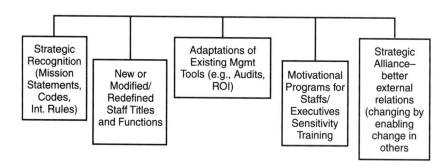

Figure 5–4   The Five Recurrent Elements of Success

Source: From Piasecki's *Corporate Environmental Strategy: The Avalanche of Change Since Bhopal,* New York, Wiley, 1995.

discussion of management information systems (MIS). Relatively new to even business strategists, information systems play an important role for environmental strategists as a tool that helps makes sense of environmental compliance and business information. At last, you can lead both with concepts and data. This allows business decision-makers to think more strategically. Charles Knapp and Richard Cervin help us understand this new, increasingly important facet of strategic management, while we see a corporate vignette in action through the eyes of Audrey Mason Bamberger at Anheuser-Busch.

From these concrete examples, the web of information, tools, and skills required for environmental leadership begins to take shape (see Figure 5–5).

If you wish to get a better handle on these issues, you may need to consider how corporate change regarding environmental choices involves a complex mix of disciplines and personnel. It is never just a legal, economic, or purely technical affair, but a matter of blended training, and when business strategists begin to link the skill of opportunity recognition with environmental concerns, we see this blended training in action.

Please read our integrated cases at the end of each part with this need for multiple competencies in mind. Chapter 1 outlines the needed skills to cross disciplines as well. As we end this century, environmental strategy is most reliably defined by those who can achieve compliance as they recognize business opportunity.

- Knowledge of the budgetary process, financial concerns, and how environmental initiatives fit into the corporate balance sheets.
- Communication in business language in order to effect change in the firm, as seen in Shelton's presentation in Part I.
- Leveraging the basic knowledge of staff potential, mergers, and the other aspects of the corporate strategist's "five fingers" of conventional management.
- Self-assessment programs facilitated through the use of information systems and performance metrics.
- Acknowledging the strategic limitations of merely achieving compliance.
- Environmental management systems designed to stimulate continuous opportunity recognition through new products and services.

Figure 5–5 EH&S Skills for Identifying Business Opportunities

NOTES

1. Rumelt, Richard, Dan Schendel, and David Teece, *Fundamental Issues in Strategy,* Harvard Business School Press, Boston, 1994.

2. Please see Rumel, Schendel and Teece for additional passages on the meaning of "business strategy."

3. Grant, Robert M., *Contemporary Strategy Analysis: Concepts, Techniques and Applications,* Blackwell Business, Cambridge, MA, 1996.

4. Grant's definition best integrates military action and business competition.

5. Please refer to Rumelt et al. for a detailed and effective historical depiction of the field of strategic management.

6. Chandler, Alfred, *Strategy and Structure: Chapters in the History of the Industrial Enterprise* MIT Press, Cambridge, MA, 1962.

7. Andrews, Kenneth, *The Concept of Corporate Strategy,* 1965, Dow Jones-Irwin, Hennewood, IL.

8. Ansoff, Igor, *The New Corporate Strategy,* John Wiley & Sons, NY, 1988, an updated version.

9. David, Fred, *Concepts of Strategic Management,* 2nd ed., Merrill Publishing Company, Columbus, OH, 1987.

10. Hart, Stuart, "Beyond Greening: Strategies for a Sustainable World," Harvard Business Review January-February, 1997.

11. Please see Hart (1997) and also refer to "Stewards of the Seventh Generation," *Harvard Business School Bulletin,* Vol. 72, No. 2, April 1996.

12. Please refer to Ewire at www.envirodisk.com for the 1994 press release.

13. Piasecki, Bruce, *Corporate Environmental Strategy: The Avalanche of Change Since Bhopal,* Wiley, New York, 1995.

Environmental Accounting for Competitive Advantage

ALIGNING FINANCIAL CONCERNS AND ENVIRONMENTAL RESPONSIBILITIES

The concerns of environmental managers spill over into both the financial accounting and managerial accounting concerns of the company. Although MacLean and Rappaport discuss the significance of these concerns in the following piece, it is important to reflect on the basic reasoning behind integrating environmental issues into accounting metrics and decisions.

According to a recent article in *Managerial Accounting*, the accounting functions are considered "one of the primary groups responsible for developing firm's strategies."[1] While this assertion may be overstated, it is true that when it comes to decision making, as well as the selection of firm strategies, Watergate investigators and *Washington Post* reporters Bob Woodward and Carl Bernstein's credo to "follow the money" rings especially true.

In a very basic sense, accounting functions have three roles to fill for companies: aiding in strategic decisions, controlling current costs, cash flows and current decisions, and finally, filing required information (i.e., SEC, federal tax law, etc.).[2] The spillover that occurs on issues of environmental consequence covers these three areas as well.

Surprisingly, the same *Management Accounting* study of five firms revealed that of those three basic roles that accountants play in firms, often accounting information is most useful in the last two roles: controlling costs and adhering to filing requirements. As one corporate executive in the article stated, "while the strategic plan may contain little accounting information, accounting information is useful for the process."[3] As discussed in the environmental measurement section in Part I, the right *financial* information serves to guide the decision making process at a minimum.

Company	Finding
Amoco Oil	Nearly 22 percent of operating costs (excluding feedstock) were considered environmental at the Yorktown Refinery.
Ciba-Geigy	The environmental component was estimated at over 19 percent of manufacturing costs (excluding raw materials) for one chemical additive.
Dow Chemical	Between 3.2 and 3.8 percent of the manufacturing cost for a polymer-based product was considered environmental.
Du Pont	Over 19 percent of manufacturing cost was identified as environmental for one agricultural pesticide.
S.C. Johnson Wax	Environmental costs identified for one consumer product were approximately 2.4 percent of the net sales.

Figure 6–1 Results of WRI's *Green Ledgers* Study

Source: Ditz, Daryl, Janet Ranganathan, and Darryl Banks, *Green Ledgers: Case Studies on Environmental Cost Accounting*, World Resources Institute, Washington, D.C., 1995.

Studies on environmental accounting over the last few years have shed light on the lack of information reaching top management. A 1995 study on the state of environmental accounting practices conducted by the World Resources Institute (WRI) offers one clear example. The results of WRI's case research on a number of multinationals, shown in Figure 6–1, reveals how information on environmental costs often goes unrealized by corporate decision makers.

Identifying environmental costs and related financial opportunities is a tangible way of gaining the attention of upper management by linking environmental responsibilities with costs. The following piece by MacLean and Rappaport will help you to understand the significance of translating these environmental concerns into bottom-line considerations.

NOTES

1. Akers, Michael D., and Grover L. Porter, "Strategic Planning at Five World-Class Companies," *Management Accounting*, July 1995.
2. Please see Ditz, Daryl, Janet Ranganathan, and Darryl Banks, *Green Ledgers: Case Studies in Corporate Environmental Accounting*, World Resources Institute, Washington, DC, 1995.
3. Akers, Michael D., and Grover L. Porter, "Strategic Planning at Five World-Class Companies," *Akers*, July 1995.

Greening the CFO: Implementing Environmental Accounting in Industry

Ann Rappaport and Richard MacLean

Ann Rappaport holds a joint appointment as assistant professor at the Department of Civil and Environmental Engineering and Department of Urban and Environmental Policy, Tufts University. She worked with a team from the United Nations Environment Programme, the Prince of Wales Business Leaders Forum and Tufts to prepare Partnerships for Sustainable Development: The Role of Business and Industry (1994). Her book, *Development and Transfer of Pollution Prevention Technology*, was published by Quorum (1993); she collaborated with Margaret Flaherty on *Corporate Responses to Environmental Challenges: Initiatives by Multinational Management* (Quorum Books, Westport CT, 1992).

Richard MacLean is president of Competitive Environment Inc., a consulting firm headquartered in Scottsdale, Arizona. He is also executive director of the Center for Environmental Innovation (CEI), a not-for-profit supporting university environmental research. Prior to this he held executive environmental positions in several Fortune 500 corporations. When he was Manager of Environmental Protection at General Electric's corporate headquarters in Fairfield, Connecticut he developed one of the first full-cost models, *Financial Analysis of Waste Management Alternatives*, published in 1987. Since that time he has led a number of innovative projects related to environmental accounting, including accrual and disclosure issues related to due diligence.

For decades governments have relied on cost-based decisions to set environmental policy. For example, in Europe the "Polluter Pays Principle" assigns costs for environmental degradation to the industries that generate waste. The international agreement to phase out ozone-depleting CFCs balanced the long-term costs to switch to safer substitutes against the health risks from increased ultraviolet exposure. Much of the debate over the Clean Air Act Amendments of 1990 was driven by cost/benefit considerations. Corporate financial officers (CFOs) are beginning to notice such large-budget items and developments.

The 1990 Clean Air Act Amendments also embraced a move away from command-and-control legislation and toward market-based incentives for environmental protection. The acid rain program is structured on a SO_2 allowance trading system designed to achieve pollutant reductions with maximum economic efficiency. Proponents of the scheme produced analyses showing that total costs for compliance are considerably lower under the trading scheme than under the conventional approach of requiring each regulated facility to achieve a percentage reduction in emissions. But what exactly is environmental accounting, and what might we expect from it in the next century?

At the same time that cost considerations are being given increasing weight in national environmental policy, there is recognition that tools available for policy makers need further development. For example, economists have observed that indicators used for assessing national economic viability, the gross national product or the gross domestic product, have the perverse effect of rising when the environment is damaged. When primary resources are extracted, the country derives income, but there is no offsetting factor for resource loss. The massive oil spill from the *Exxon Valdez* had a positive impact on the gross national product because millions of dollars were spent on cleanup.

In *Saving the Earth*, Lester Brown, Christopher Flavin and Sandra Postel examine current efforts to develop alternative national accounting systems that do not require exploitation in order to value natural resources. All of the emerging systems, the authors note, require the use of data that are currently unavailable for many countries.[4] Emerging efforts are under way in companies to take a comprehensive enterprise-level approach to examining environmental costs, but like countries, companies face some data challenges.

WHAT IS ENVIRONMENTAL ACCOUNTING?

The systematic analysis of environmental costs offers real advantages for sound business decision making. According to Paul Bailey, senior vice president of the environmental consulting firm, ICF, environmental accounting is a useful modification of life-cycle costing. Life-cycle costing was developed in the 1960s and 1970s to reflect rising ownership costs of systems, including labor and energy costs. In addition to life-cycle costs, environmental accounting includes pollution control and waste management costs. Bailey describes environmental accounting as having four levels of costs (shown in Figure 6–2) that accumulate to strategic proportions:[5]

If a conventional project that produces waste is compared to a project that incorporates pollution prevention technology, the project with pollution prevention will often be financially more attractive when environmental accounting is used. This attempt to factor all environmental costs into enterprise-level decision making is similar in principle to environmental-cost-driven decisions emerging at the national level.

In practice, however, the considerations that guide a decision for a business—at the enterprise level—are different. In the United States, national-level

---

Conventional costs—include the usual capital and operating costs such as equipment, labor, materials, etc.

Potentially hidden costs—include hidden regulatory costs such as monitoring, paperwork, testing, training, inspections, etc.

Contingent liability costs—include penalties, fines, and future liabilities.

Image and relationship costs—include corporate image, community relations, consumer response, etc.

Figure 6–2 The Four Levels of Corporate Environmental Costs

environmental analyses involve government agencies, elected officials, non-government organizations, academics, industries and the public openly debating issues and assumptions. On the other hand, environmental accounting decisions by business are made in private. The outcome may impact customers, employees, shareholders and/or neighbors with limited access to the data and/or voice in the outcome. The distinction is crucial.

Environmental accounting is relatively new at the enterprise level; this guidance for its implementation is still emerging. Practical considerations for companies will allow financial decision makers to become full participants in environmental decision making.

SUPPORTING THE EXISTING ENVIRONMENTAL HIERARCHY

Environmentalists generally agree that there is a hierarchy of product, process and waste disposal options. Products and processes that use the fewest resources and least toxic raw materials, and/or generate the least waste, are preferred. If waste is generated, waste management practices that recycle or reclaim the material are better than those that treat it. At the bottom of the hierarchy is landfilling. This hierarchy has been an explicit part of federal waste management policy since the Resource Conservation and Recovery Act was amended in 1984.

It was around this same time period that the first discussions were occurring within industry and government over accounting techniques to fully capture the true costs associated with the generation and management of waste. It was recognized that, in principle, environmental accounting drives the decision up this hierarchy toward better choices, at least from an environmental standpoint. The assumption by proponents of environmental accounting is that any decision that moves the current practice up this hierarchy is better for the environment and best for business. In fact, it may not be better for either. As the following examples indicate, decision tools are imperfect and should be used with care.

CONCERN OVER WHAT YOU REJECT, NOT WHAT YOU APPROVE

Ideally, an environmental accounting analysis will lead to the selection of a new process involving nontoxic raw materials and zero waste generation. In the real world, the selection is rarely this clear cut. For example, a company may be considering alternatives for an existing waste stream. An environmental accounting analysis may indicate that on-site incineration with energy recovery of a nonhazardous waste is more cost effective than continued off-site disposal at a municipal landfill. The alternative of a process modification that will result in zero waste generation, although technically feasible, may not be cost justifiable, even after considering indirect costs and long-term liabilities.

The decision to reject the technically feasible process modification in favor of the more cost-effective incineration option may some day come under the scrutiny of hindsight. If a thorough analysis was conducted, the merit of the decision will stand. If a superficial analysis was done, problems, possibly more serious than if landfilling had continued, may result. Consider the following scenario:

An attorney files a toxic tort lawsuit on behalf of neighbors claiming that the emissions from the incinerator damaged their health. If the health concerns were not thoroughly evaluated and subsequent analysis confirms their potential existence, the defense is weak. If health issues were identified in the original analysis and not given sufficient weight, no precautions were taken and alternatives were available but rejected on financial grounds, the company may be subject to substantial punitive damages. In this case, a faulty full-cost financial analysis may be worse than no analysis at all.

UNCHARTED TERRITORY: ENTERING THE RAPIDS OF THE NEXT CENTURY

If a faulty analysis can be damaging, then what constitutes a good one? Unfortunately, there is little definitive guidance at the practical, operational level. In principle, the mechanics of environmental accounting is identical to any financial analysis that considers readily identifiable costs (e.g., capital, operating expenses, revenues) and displays these in a standard format (e.g., financial spread sheet). There are, however, significant differences: first, the time period is considerably longer (e.g., 20 years); second, a more rigorous analysis is conducted of potential future costs; and finally, it includes costs that are often very difficult to quantify.

This analysis might include projected regulatory changes (e.g., land disposal restrictions), indirect compliance costs (e.g., record keeping requirements) and other overlooked or "hidden" regulatory costs associated with waste generation. Potential incentives (e.g., loan guarantees) and disincentives (e.g., waste end taxes) may also be factored in. Less tangible factors, such as potential long-term legal liabilities or the loss of sales revenues due to adverse publicity arising from environmental incidents, can only be estimated from available data or established through some internal company policy mechanism.

While the financial principles are conceptually straightforward, it is extremely difficult to estimate long-term liabilities. Case law and remediation cost data have been accumulated only over the past 20 years. Both the technology choices and the legal settlements are in a state of flux. Without a stable platform and historical database, there is no commonly accepted and widely used approach to predicting future costs. This instability is the primary reason why non-sudden, environmental liability insurance is extremely costly and all but impossible to buy.

The bottom line is that the practical application of environmental financial analysis is in its infancy; the first journal devoted to these issues, *The Journal of Environmental Financing, Accounting, Taxation & Reporting,* first appeared in 1991. Over the past five years, however, there has been a wealth of information published on the theory and mechanism of environmental accounting.[6]

IS PRECISION NECESSARY?

From a practical standpoint, the inability to *precisely* estimate long-term liabilities and other hard-to-quantify factors is not a reason to avoid environmental accounting. Companies can use general, published guidelines and modify these to suit their degree of "risk avoidance" (i.e., how much risk the company is willing to accept).

Environmental accounting's advantage is that it provides a persuasive vehicle to communicate to the people who control resource allocation. Environmental managers have traditionally not been skillful in addressing environmental issues in business terms that executives can readily understand. Executives informed of the full range of issues are more likely to seek prudent environmental practices than they would if less quantitative methods were employed. Access to quantitative data is at the core of any informed business decision.

For example, the release of the first SARA 313 (Community Right-to-Know) emission estimates produced a flurry of programs to voluntarily reduce emissions. There is no question that avoiding negative publicity was a major factor. But many executives learned for the first time of the large volume of wasted raw materials and the potential liabilities created by these emissions. The information, available at a plant level, had never before been consolidated and presented to upper management. In a similar fashion, implementing environmental accounting, even if it is approximate at first, will provide top decision makers with new and useful information.

WHAT CONSTITUTES GOOD
ENVIRONMENTAL ACCOUNTING?

A good analysis—one that will stand the test of time—is determined by the thoroughness by which the alternatives are evaluated by a multifunctional team of professionals. Finance, legal, engineering, environmental, health, safety, R&D and production should be involved, at a minimum.

A thorough check list of costs to evaluate, a financial model and a software program to process the information facilitates the process but should not control it.[7] These tools are no substitute for an informed analysis. A team effort is critical; the surefire way to disaster is to place even the best financial analysis model in the hands of an engineer or finance manager and rely on a single individual's limited perspective. As noted earlier, corporate environmental strategy requires a range of expertise to remain viable.

Advice to Practitioners of Full-Cost Accounting

Build Alliances

You are trying to change the way the Accounting/Finance Department has traditionally reported data. It is essential that top management understand and support the need to better identify environmental costs. Their collaboration will facilitate this important change. You should establish a contact within the Accounting/Finance Department that has sufficient stature and knowledge to facilitate this process.

First Understand Their World

Accounting and budgeting systems were originally structured to answer specific business questions and to satisfy external requirements (e.g., Securities and Exchange Commission). Even in a new company, this framework will dominate how the accounting systems are structured. You will need to work within this structure to identify existing information and mesh new needs conveniently with the existing system.

Some internally or externally dictated accounting systems may prove especially challenging. For example, in the utility industry, much of the accounting practice and culture is centered around reporting according to Federal Energy Regulatory Commission (FERC) accounting practices. In the regulated utility environment, additional cost breakdowns were deemed unnecessary because all costs could be recovered through rates. Currently, accounts are not broken down by specific processes. If they were, costs could be easily categorized for their environmental impact. You will need to understand preexisting constraints, since these requirements will have to be incorporated into any future system.

Do Your Homework and Network

Ten years ago there was relatively little information available on environmental accounting practices. This is no longer the case, so take advantage of others' wisdom; read the available literature. Equally important is networking among your peers. They can give you useful insights into the do's and don'ts of working with the Accounting/Finance Department and management.

One of the best ways to sell full-cost accounting in your company is to explain to your management the progressive steps taken and the benefits gained by other companies. You may want to set aside a modest budget for benchmarking in this area.

Be Strategic in Data Collection

Determine the questions you need to answer for decision making now and in the future. Differentiate between nice-to-know data and must-know information. There is nothing that turns off line organizations more than their valuable time being spent gathering information of little value. On the other hand, you will gain staff and line support if they perceive that the data have an influence on the outcome of decisions.

It Is More Than a Numerical Exercise

Your financial analysis is just one part of the overall analysis. Legal, regulatory, and ethical issues, along with company philosophy, must be taken into consideration. Use a team approach to develop a balanced financial analysis.

Timing Is Everything

Trying to get the Accounting/Finance Department's attention during year-end close is unwise. On the other hand, good opportunities may present themselves; for example, the Finance and Information Systems Departments may be undertaking major overhauls in the way data are gathered and analyzed. Find out if these windows of opportunity are on the immediate horizon, even if you are not very far along in your activities.

This Is an Emerging Field—Precision Is in the Future

You are trying to assist management in making key decisions. These decisions are made by examining the most significant factors. Don't be overly concerned if future disposal liability has a sensitivity of plus or minus 50 percent. At this point, it is more important to inform management that there is, in fact, a future liability and that liability may be relatively large compared with other process costs. You are probably better off developing a workable system influencing management today and striving for continuous improvement over time, than waiting five years for a perfect system.

MAKING ENVIRONMENTAL ACCOUNTING SYSTEMS WORK

Even if there were no organizational issues, environmental accounting faces institutional issues that, unless addressed, will impede its future use. The most obvious is management's concern over the future use of records by adversarial parties. The situation is not unlike the sensitivity over facility compliance audits. Management recognizes their need, yet worries over the creation of discoverable records.

There is growing pressure from environmental groups to require public disclosure of environmental audit results.[8] In the European Community this issue has been resolved for the moment by making the Eco-Audit program voluntary. Despite the concern over environmental compliance audits, they typically use yes/no checklists and rarely create a liability concern if prompt corrective action is taken when problems are identified. In contrast, public disclosure of financial analysis for environmental projects can be very complex and subject to misinterpretation if taken out of context.

Also missing are widely accepted risk management guidelines for environmental accounting. Societies, not companies, define acceptable risk. There is a considerable body of literature that defines acceptable risk for catastrophic accident analysis, nuclear plant operation, remediation cleanups, pesticide use and so on. For environmental accounting, the accounting mechanics exist, but not with a framework to perform the accompanying risk analysis. Large corporations with specialized talent and resources can use internal expertise and external assistance to perform custom evaluations and feel relatively secure in their decisions. A concern is that companies with limited resources will perform simplistic evaluations, thus compromising the value of the decision-making tool.

Much easier to address is institutional guidance on how the information should be used in a financial context. The Financial Accounting Standards Board (FASB) and the American Institute of Certified Public Accountants (AICPA) have provided guidance on some environmental finance issues (e.g., capitalization of costs to remediate environmental contamination). [9] The Securities and Exchange Commission (SEC) has also provided some information on contingent liability disclosure requirements. Specific guidance for performing environmental accounting is still emerging. It is needed for several reasons.

First, there is a gray area between theoretical estimates of liability for planning purposes and actual estimates that must be accrued and/or disclosed. In general, the dividing line is over the certainty of actual funds being expended within a specific time frame. For example, there are sufficient data for many products to estimate and reserve funds to cover product warranties. On the other hand, an environmental accounting model may predict that for each ton of waste generated, $200 in liabilities will be generated. Do you accrue this amount? A project may have an estimated liability (remote, but very large). If you proceed, do you report the information as a contingent liability to the SEC, since environmental liability insurance is virtually unavailable?

With so little data currently available it seems unreasonable to accrue for these contingent liabilities. But could accruals be required in the future? Environmentalists might press a case even now that this should be done. Generating full-cost evaluations presents a dilemma. The more generally acceptable liability cost factors become, the more useful they are to guide business decisions. At the same time they become a powerful basis to justify subjecting industry to additional financial burdens (e.g., waste or raw material taxes such as those that currently finance Superfund). If long-term liability costs became predictable to the extent that industrial accidents are today, environmental liability insurance could become available at "reasonable" rates. Insurance would make it easier to make informed business decisions, since liability uncertainties can be translated into specific business costs.

For example, several years ago the managers of a business were considering starting a new venture to renovate used equipment that contained a hazardous substance. Although the numbers looked promising, management could not reach a decision because of their concern over the waste disposal liability issues. Waste minimization was not an option, since the hazardous substance already existed and would have to be disposed as a first step in the renovation process. An environmental accounting analysis was used to place the environmental issues in perspective: The liabilities were not significant when compared with the total venture.

Second, buy-in from the financial community is essential. Accounting managers by their very nature tend to be very conservative—"by the book." In the absence of widely accepted institutional guidelines, they will be reluctant to change current practice and institute new methodologies. Their actions are not only subject to scrutiny by regulatory auditors, such as the SEC, but also by external, third-party auditors that review their practices and disclose significant issues in the company's financial reports to the SEC and shareholders. [10]

Defining financial procedures, because of their potential significant impact, also raises political issues. For example, the EPA developed an extremely detailed financial model for evaluating the indirect costs of environmental requirements. The model has never been officially approved and released. If it were, it would serve as the standard for the Office of Management and Budget to evaluate the costs for EPA regulations. [11]

MAKING TOTAL COST ACCOUNTING WORK ON BEHALF OF THE ENVIRONMENT

Environmental accounting presents a dilemma. On the one hand it can be a powerful tool to systematically analyze environmental issues and convincingly communicate this information to management. On the other hand, it is so powerful that it has the potential to significantly change the products, processes and organizational structure of its users.

For environmental accounting to become a more vital part of corporate decision making, corporate decision makers and the financial community must:

1. *Define the risk management process appropriate to environmental accounting.* Companies need a framework within which to operate that will provide institutional approval and foster consistency. With this framework, companies will not be concerned about creating discoverable records or being criticized for the methodology used in their analyses.

2. *Consolidate the model information to date into a user-friendly package.* There is a growing body of information that can be consolidated into a tool that industry can readily use.

3. *Provide financial guidance.* Accounting groups can take the lead in providing institutional guidance on procedures, and can help with difficult questions, such as those related to liability analysis.

4. *Educate business and finance managers about the environment.* Business schools are beginning to address environmental issues in their curriculum. The process needs to be accelerated and expanded to include current managers.

Bristol-Myers Squibb—Cost Accounting for Productivity

As their contribution to companywide productivity efforts, in 1995, the Environment, Health and Safety group at Bristol-Myers Squibb launched several operational initiatives, one of which was environmental full-cost accounting. Five elements were identified for implementation over a four-year period: [12]

1. Develop and implement enhanced methodology for capital project evaluation.

   By justifying EHS spending on quantifiable financial benefits and compliance, approval and implementation of projects with positive financial returns will be accelerated.

2. Develop EHS capital project tracking and reporting system.

   By coding all significant EHS projects, the company will facilitate analysis and expect economies of scale in executing similar projects across the company.

3. Track and report priority EHS operating costs.

   Activity-based costing will help link EHS costs to specific products and businesses, and is expected to hold down increases in EHS operating costs by helping decision makers identify the most cost-effective areas of focus.

4. Develop electronic systems for managing remediation projects.

   Development of software and establishment of cost centers will reduce administrative time for data gathering, analysis and reporting.

5. Investigate revised treatment of workers' compensation costs.

   Just as companies' decisions to push responsibility for waste management costs down to the facility level has created an incentive for pollution prevention, Bristol-Myers Squibb is considering allocation of workers' compensation costs down to the department or facility level as an incentive for improved safety performance.

   These environmental full-cost accounting efforts complemented the company's commitment to pollution prevention throughout the product life cycle, a strategic approach to environmental issues launched in 1992.

   According to Bristol-Myers Squibb's Vice President for Environmental Affairs, Occupational Health and Safety, Dr. Thomas Hellman, the company anticipates significant cost savings and cost avoidance associated with the total package of EHS productivity measures. Implementation of environmental full-cost accounting may well result in additional savings beyond those initially anticipated.

EFFECTIVE ENVIRONMENTAL DECISION MAKING

Companies have been making environmental decisions for decades, yet they have been slow to make environment a core business issue. Rather, environmental decisions have been handled on the periphery, falling under government-business relations, ethics, public relations, or social responsibility. Company stakeholders, both internal and external, now expect more.

There is an expectation that environmental considerations can and will be woven into companies' decision making fabric, and environmental accounting represents a powerful tool for achieving this objective. Financial analysis is at the heart of companies' "real" business and when the environment is taken into account at this level, companies can legitimately claim to be proactive with respect to the environment. Business executives, especially the CFO, play a critical role in the greening process by encouraging the use of decision making tools that convert environmental strategy into action.

NOTES

4. Brown, Lester R., Christopher Flavin, and Sandra Postel, *Saving the Planet,* Norton, New York, 1991, pp. 121–130.

5. Bailey, Paul, "Environmental Accounting—Making It Work for Your Company," *Total Quality Environmental Management,* Summer 1996.

6. The United Nations has prepared a guide to literature on corporate environmental accounting called "Environmental Accounting: Current Issues, Abstracts and Bibliographies," United Nations publication No. E.92.11.A.23. Call the United Nations Publications Sales Section (212) 963-8302.

7. There are a number of commercially available software systems and tools to support environmental accounting. The EPA's Office of Pollution Prevention and Toxics published two reviews: "Incorporating Environmental Costs and Considerations into Decision-Making," EPA742-R-95-006, February 1996, and "Valuing Potential Liabilities for Managerial Decision-Making: A Review of Available Techniques," EPA742-R-96-003, December 1996, both available through the PPIC or NTIS (National Technical Information Service), (800) 553-NTIS.

8. The Canada Institute of Chartered Accountants, Toronto, Canada, has published relevant research reports and study group reports, including "Environmental Costs and Liabilities: Accounting and Financial Reporting Issues," (1993), and "Environmental Auditing and the Role of the Accounting Profession" (1992). To order call (416) 3322; fax (416) 204-3416.

9. The American Institute of Certified Public Accountants (AICPA) and the Financial Accounting Standards Board (FASB) have published accounting standards related to environmental accounting. Much of this work is related to accrual and reporting of environmental liabilities such as AICPA's "Statement of Position on Environmental Remediation Liabilities." For a current listing call AICPA at (800) 862-4272 and FASB at (203) 847-0700.

10. The Society of Management Accountants of Canada, Hamilton, Ontario, Canada, has published management accounting practices handbooks, including "Tools and Techniques of Environmental Accounting for Business Decisions, #40" and "Accounting for the Environment." Call (905) 525-4100.

11. The U.S. Environmental Protection Agency makes available a wealth of information on environmental accounting through the Pollution Prevention Information Clearinghouse (PPIC). Contact PPIC at (202) 260-1023, Fax (202) 260-0178, or e-mail

PPIC@epamail.epa.gov and request their list of available documents. This should be your first stop in obtaining additional information on environmental accounting. The EPA also sponsors a number of projects through the Environmental Accounting Project managed by Holly Elwood or Susan McLaughlin at EPA (202) 260-4362 or 3844 respectively; e-mail: elwood.holly or mclaughlin.susan @epamail.epa.gov, respectively. They publish periodic updates on EPA's activities in this area and maintain a Network Directory of professionals interested in environmental accounting.

12. Bristol-Myers Squibb, "EH&S Strategic Plan Update: Productivity, Growth, and Customer Focus," prepared by ERM, Inc., 1995, and Bristol-Myers Squibb, "Environment 2000: Pollution Prevention Throughout the Product Lifecycle," 1992.

QUESTIONS FOR FURTHER THOUGHT

1. Why do pollution prevention projects become more attractive when full-cost accounting is applied to the decision making process? Will they always be more economically attractive?

2. What are some of the challenges in gathering the data necessary to perform a full-cost analysis?

3. Do the uncertainties surrounding a full-cost accounting analysis obscure the value of the methodology?

4. What are the potential downsides of environmental full-cost accounting?

5. In the early 1980s, Du Pont led producers and users in opposing CFC regulations. At the end of the decade, it completely reversed itself and actively supported the phase-out. What could have motivated a company to willingly agree to discontinue a profitable product line? Can companies economically benefit from the discontinuation of environmentally unsafe products? If so, how?

6. What might be some of the techniques that a company could employ to measure—in financial terms—the impact of environmental issues on corporate image?

7. The legal system is significantly different in the U.S. from those in most countries. Concepts such as class action suits, adversarial expert witnesses, jury trials and punitive damages are relatively uncommon in other countries. How might these differences encourage or discourage the development of future innovative tools and techniques to identify and quantify environmental risk?

Environmentally Driven New Product Development

DRIVING THE PRODUCT DEVELOPMENT PROCESS

A reliable sign that environmental strategy has taken hold of a company is when the firm's products or services begin to include environmental attributes. Often companies inject environmental considerations at the end of the product line. This may come about as a result of legal requirements or public pressure, such as when the world's defense, telecommunications, and other electronics makers suddenly had to phase out CFCs in the late 1990s.[1] But strategic environmental concerns are sometimes voiced earlier in the product design cycle.

In the next case, please watch how ARCO extended their normal definition of the value chain to include environmental aspects throughout product design and manufacture. This is an exciting global business development and a significant development for next-century firms. However, it pays to be careful to distinguish actual product improvement from glossy public relations. Please reflect on this serious and tricky concern in the accompanying sidebar on Cannon.

In the next case, on ARCO, as well as in the final teaching case on Volvo, please do the following:

- Contrast "awareness" PR with PR based on superior products and technology.
- Suggest that such "answer-seeking" is more dependent upon R&D efforts than simple PR.
- Explore the claim that the slogan "new and improved" is quite new to the realm of environmental management and strategy.

Clearly, the world needs more efficient manufacturing processes and more environmentally benign products. In the next essays, please note how leading firms are taking this challenge seriously by reforming the very nature of cars and gasoline.

121

A Reflection on 1997's Environmental Public Relations Winner

Facts on the Cannon Clean Earth Campaign with the Rowland Company

- Cannon USA represents one-third of the Tokyo-based multinational's $20 billion annual sales revenue, so the image of Cannon in the United States matters greatly to its Japanese strategists.
- These strategists in Tokyo like America's grandest national parks, and their operating philosophy known as Kaosei (which means harmony between and among people and nature) gave the Rowland Company an award-winning opportunity and PR budget.
- Since 1990 Cannon has been rightly donating money to the Nature Conservancy in exchange for customers returning used toner cartridges, which Cannon then recycles.
- Rowland's PR agents rethought this low-visibility precedent by targeting more visible examples in the twenty key habitats nationwide, including key park sites. For example, Cannon committed $1 million annually to a new campaign called "Expedition into the Parks." Each selected park offered a discrete photogenic opportunity to capture honest public efforts to save critically endangered species.
- Suddenly, the Kemp's Ridley turtle had new, well-heeled allies. Both the Nature Conservancy and the National Wildlife Federation joined in, sharing their scientific knowledge and trust with the public.
- By 1997, Cannon had won the big PR prize in the environmental area, known as the CIPRA prize.
- Cannon has since logged nearly 600 million positive impressions in the most well-read and prestigious national news outlets.

Source: Cannon Clean Earth Campaign internal document, 1997.

Questions

- What does this case tell us about the nature and power of public relations, as well as its clever abilities to turn threats into opportunities?
- What does the case tell us about the national environmental groups and their interests in reaching national press and magnifying their name recognition?
- Can such corporate PR ever actually fix a serious environmental problem, or can it shape a positive social outcome? Is it, by its very clout, mostly reactive and informational?

These three loaded questions are posed for a reason: A big part of the search for answers resides in problem identification. Effective public relations can do that, but it takes a more concentrated corporate effort to deliver reputable results. Going into the next century, we need superior products, not just better advertisements.

We live in an age of environmentalism, but the immense gap between what we portray as our ecological ideals and what is actually bought and consumed will not come into a more reliable realignment until more firms follow the product innovation pathways outlined by ARCO and Volvo. The reenchantment of the world in the next century requires no less than a bold set of product changes in our homes, cars, and fixed manufacturing sites throughout the globe. This reenchantment will not be earned through simple public relations. It demands environmentally driven new product development.

NOTE

1. Please see Piasecki, *Corporate Environmental Strategy: The Avalanche of Change Since Bhopal*, Wiley, New York, 1995 for a full-scale case on CFC reduction.

Leading Change in the Face of Product Elimination: ARCO's Strategic Choices in a Cleaner-Burning Gasoline

Kenneth R. Dickerson

Kenneth R. Dickerson is Senior Vice President, External Affairs, for Atlantic Richfield Company (ARCO). Please see the "Executive Spotlight" for a full biographical sketch.

Air pollution certainly is not new to Southern California. The area has struggled with smog from its earliest human habitation when Native Americans burned wood in the Los Angeles basin. In this century, steps have been taken to reduce Southern California's air pollution. One of the most important was the introduction of the catalytic converter on automobiles in the mid-1970s. But every step forward seemed stymied by population growth—every new resident seemed to arrive with at least two cars and a determination to explore every nook and cranny of the new country. And we're still struggling with this problem. Despite remarkable strides in reducing the pollution emitted per mile by each car, the number of cars and miles driven continues to grow[2] (See Figures 7-1 and 7-2.)

As environmental problems reduced the quality of life, and as economic security became an issue with political flare-ups in the Middle East, advocacy groups lobbied to replace gasoline with other fuels. In Southern California, frustration grew to a point where state legislators and regulators established more stringent standards than mandated by the federal Clean Air Act. In the mid-1980s, the South Coast Air Quality Management District floated a plan that would mandate replacement of gasoline with methanol and then electricity within a 10-year period.[3]

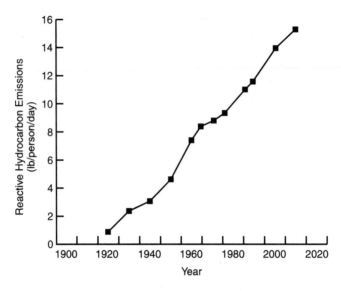

Figure 7-1 South Coast Air Basin Population Growth

The oil and automotive industries opposed these measures as impractical for economic and logistical reasons. We argued that the alternative fuels proposed as replacements for gasoline—such as electricity, natural gas, methanol, and ethanol—were untried on a large scale. Natural gas is clean but requires retooled cars and expensive central fueling stations. Ethanol is relatively clean but costly and energy-poor. Methanol is tricky to handle, hard on engines,

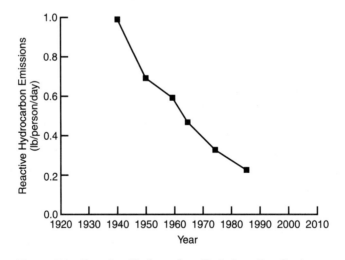

Figure 7-2 Reactive Hydrocarbon Emissions Per Capita

environmentally questionable, and only has about one-half of gasoline's energy. Battery-powered vehicles are expensive and limited in driving range, and large-scale battery disposal could dramatically increase toxic lead pollution.[4]

Storm clouds continued to gather over the oil industry in 1989. In the nation's capital, the federal Clean Air Act was coming up for renewal amid promises of more draconian air quality standards and the possible mandating of alternative fuels. Few in Washington had heard of "reformulated gasoline" and almost no one considered it an alternative fuel. In California, where summer and smog were like Siamese twins in the southern half of the state, regulators were beating the drums for a fuel known as M-85, a blend of 85 percent methanol, 15 percent gasoline. This "fuel of the future" would be the bridge fuel to electric cars—never mind the fact M-85 may have only a minor effect on reducing peak ozone concentrations. Methanol, said the chairman of the California Energy Commission, "holds the most promise for providing a secure, long-term energy supply, alleviating California's air quality problems, and winning acceptance from consumers, fuel retailers, and the auto industry." Meanwhile, the oil and auto industries were about to embark on an unprecedented study of the relative merits of alternative fuels, even as critics charged that the two industries were conspiring to rescue gasoline from the environmental executioner.[5]

The oil industry itself was split on how to weather the coming storm. Many companies favored a go-slow approach. The real solution, they said, lay with the auto industry. Cars from Ford, GM, Chrysler, and Japan were getting "cleaner" each year, and if auto makers would only install a few more antipollution devices, including an on-board canister to capture more emissions, air quality would keep improving and, in time, the problem would wither away. As for the oil industry's contribution to the mix, their answer was more fuels research. Above all, they said, avoid quick or costly action, hang tough, and the regulators would be proven wrong.

Other companies, including ARCO, believed very differently. The regulators, they argued, would not wait patiently for year-to-year improvements in Detroit's and Nagoya's offerings. Clean air was an issue of the greatest urgency, and the oil industry had a responsibility to deal with it, a responsibility it had largely been shirking.

AVOIDING PRODUCT ELIMINATION: MAKING A STRATEGIC CHOICE

By any measures, it seemed to ARCO that gasoline had the advantage over alternatives in cost, availability, convenience, and energy content. And when it came to air pollution, we believed we could convincingly demonstrate that gasoline emissions could be cut to the level of the likeliest competitors, such as M-85, a methanol-gasoline blend.

Even more to the point, as far as we were concerned ARCO's most important product, gasoline, was in danger of being eliminated by new regulations.

If that happened, we would be out of business, at least out of the Southern California refining segment of our business.

The proposed measures and fuels may have seemed draconian, but they clearly reflected the public's demand for cars that would not pollute the environment. Consumers wanted a fuel that would not make them feel guilty about their everyday energy needs. ARCO felt that it had to accept this challenge and develop cleaner fuels for the future in order to remain competitive.

At the outset, two important questions had to be answered: Which fuel would be the cleanest and most cost-effective for the producer and consumer? And what should ARCO's posture be? ARCO assigned two interdisciplinary teams—technical and policy—to find the answers. (See the companion article at the end of this chapter, "Convening Change at ARCO.")

The policy group was responsible for developing a strategy that would meet the needs of environmentalists, government regulators, and the public, and that would be the position the company would adopt to be economically viable for the foreseeable future. The technical team was assigned the task of developing a cleaner fuel without taking ARCO out of the oil business, its core for more than 125 years. The work of these two groups, and ARCO as a whole, not only changed the fundamentals of gasoline refining and marketing, it also changed clean-air management at the federal, state, and local levels. And it reinstated fossil fuels as a major player in the nation's efforts to improve its air quality.

OVERCOMING TECHNICAL HURDLES

In the beginning, our solution—cleaner-burning gasoline—faced serious hurdles. For example, without costly refinery retooling, we could not produce enough "clean" gasoline for our entire market. And we certainly couldn't invest in retooling until we knew we had a gasoline formulation that would work and also meet future state and federal requirements.

Therefore, ARCO targeted the dirtiest vehicles on the road—pre-1975 cars and pre-1980 trucks. We focused our efforts on reformulating a gasoline that would reduce emissions from these vehicles. Concentrating on these old polluters gave us the opportunity to develop a cleaner-burning gasoline within our refinery limitations. These older models were designed to run on leaded gasoline and lacked the catalytic converters that significantly reduced tailpipe emissions in subsequent models. Old clunkers were only 15 percent of the area's vehicle population but produced 30 percent of the vehicular emissions.[6]

Using Cal Tech's computer model of the Los Angeles basin's atmospheric composition—the same one used by the South Coast Air Quality Management District to measure air quality—ARCO's product chemists and refining specialists formulated a gasoline that significantly reduced emissions from our target vehicles. The gasoline was called EC-1 Regular. It was the world's first emission-control gasoline.[7]

EC-1 wasn't just another petroleum product. The formula to produce it was a significant change from past practice. It changed gasoline by—among other things—replacing aromatics with a new compound that added oxygen to the fuel. Unlike the other alternative fuels, EC-1 did not require new automotive engineering, new distributions systems, or retooling of cars and trucks. The formula was a change in gasoline blending that promised to make a substantial improvement in air quality.

DEVELOPING PUBLIC ACCEPTANCE WHILE SELLING PRODUCT

To convince government regulators of the product's advantages, ARCO brought them into the testing process right from the beginning. EC-1 was tested by two independent laboratories with the full knowledge and approval of the South Coast Air Quality Management District and the California Air Resources Board. Both agencies validated the results ARCO reported for EC-1.

The tests showed that if all of the pre-1975 cars and pre-1980 trucks in Southern California were to switch to EC-1, it would be equivalent to removing 20 percent of these vehicles from the road and would reduce air pollution by about 350 tons a day. EC-1 was clearly a breakthrough in clean fuels technology.[8]

Tests alone, of course, are not enough. One must also get the word out, which ARCO did in September 1989 when it introduced EC-1 at a press conference in Los Angeles. ARCO's chairman was joined on the dais by a number of elected officials and environmental and community leaders, including the executive directors of the South Coast Air Quality Management District and the California Air Resources Board. It was a story carried in newspapers and television news across the nation and even around the world—a remarkable achievement for a product sold only in Southern California.

EC-1's immediate success demonstrated the superiority of cleaner-burning gasoline over every other alternative fuel under consideration. It was much less expensive. It was immediately available. It worked in current vehicles. And it significantly reduced vehicular emissions. The implications for the nation were clear: Cleaner-burning gasoline should play a central role in cleaning up pollution from vehicles. To do so, it had to be included as an approved clean fuel in the 1990 Clean Air Act amendments then being written in Washington, D.C.

EXECUTIVE SPOTLIGHT   Kenneth Dickerson, Senior VP
External Affairs,
Atlantic Richfield Company

As a longtime ARCO employee and lifetime observer of both the good and not-so-good efforts of resource development companies, I learned at a young age that adjustment to change was the most critical factor in achieving success in any field. Hired by ARCO as a staff attorney, I was transferred to another job before I ever reported to work. Rather than a diet of litigation and title examinations in Dallas, Texas, I encountered revolution and social upheaval in Bolivia. As a manager of ARCO's interests in Bolivia, I accepted change as a daily occurrence to be faced with little prior experience that was transferable to this assignment. Survival and success in Bolivia, as well as in Venezuela where I was next assigned, required a willingness to be reeducated to understand centuries-old cultures with practices and customs unlike any encountered in the United States, decades before globalization became a popular word. Reeducation, above all, involved constant observation of others, the patience to listen and learn, and a willingness to adjust to the unexpected.

With the realization that the rest of the world was radically different from the United States, I returned home to undertake tasks that bore little relationship to prior work situations or assignments. For a time, there was a blur of mergers, acquisitions, antitrust trials, and work relocations, but each had a common element— change; change in the law, change in the businesses we owned, change in decision makers, and change in the attitudes of society toward ARCO and its future.

Perhaps the most radical change was the emergence of the environmental movement in the late 1960s and early 1970s. Nothing prepared business for the vigor of the environmental movement. A case in point: ARCO and its partners had obtained the right-of-way to build the Trans-Alaska oil pipeline and ordered the materials to begin construction. To everyone's surprise and shock, a federal judge ruled that no permit could be issued without an Environmental Impact Statement that many people felt would be impossible to obtain. With the wheels falling off plans to move Alaskan oil to market, I was dispatched to Washington to "get the permit." Eighteen months and one Yom Kippur later, the permit was in hand. To complete the pipeline, ARCO brought environmentalists inside the tent. Leading environmental groups from the Lower 48 went to Alaska to measure our progress in protecting the state. We funded their oversight of the pipeline's construction and accepted the fact that they would be a dominant force in our future. Without this compromise, we might still be litigating each mile of construction. Lessons learned: Listen to others, be patient, adapt to change, and embrace good ideas, whatever the source. These lessons became a permanent part of ARCO's culture.

ARCO has faced scores of similar challenges since the 1970s. Each one had its own special difficulties. As overseer of government affairs, public affairs, and environment, health, and safety matters, I have been privileged to be involved in many of these challenges.

CONVINCING LEGISLATORS AND THE COMPETITION

Until the introduction of EC-1, other fuels, particularly methanol, were favored by legislators, regulators, and environmentalists as the most appropriate clean-burning substitutes for gasoline. All, however, had substantial technical and economic disadvantages. Under current market conditions, electric vehicles, for instance, cost $10,000 to $40,000 more than comparable gasoline cars, require expensive battery replacement, and could create additional environmental problems due to the need to mine additional lead and to dispose of lead and cadmium batteries. Methanol requires extensive retooling or replacement of vehicles, and methanol itself is dangerous to handle. Natural gas as a vehicle fuel is expensive, if one considers the $300,000 cost of each refueling station and up to $4,000 in increased vehicle purchase price. Finally, natural gas vehicles can travel only about half the distance of comparable gasoline cars with the same amount of fuel space.[9]

We had to convince legislators that cleaner-burning gasoline was the better choice. At the heart of our strategy was a carefully targeted media campaign that included advertising in major newspapers—the *New York Times, Wall Street Journal, Washington Post, Detroit Free Press* and *Chicago Tribune*—as well as national magazines. We also sent a series of letters from our chairman to leaders throughout the nation, and we met directly with members of Congress and other government officials.

In a November 1989 article in *Oil and Gas Journal* (two months after the introduction of EC-1 Regular), then-ARCO chairman Lodwrick M. Cook wrote: "A need for cleaner-burning fuels has clearly emerged, and the health of the petroleum industry in the years to come will depend on its ability to respond to that mandate." Although there was no industry consensus on how to proceed, reformulated gasoline began working its way into the market as other refiners followed ARCO's lead. ARCO, meanwhile, moved ahead at its own fast pace, adding a cleaner-burning premium gasoline to its EC inventory in 1990, then developing an even more advanced formulation that would require a refinery retrofit running into the hundreds of millions of dollars. Unless the entire industry joined the effort, said ARCO's chairman, ARCO would be at a competitive disadvantage if it proceeded on its own. At this point, the California Air Resources Board stepped in (M-85 being a distant memory), built on ARCO's EC experience, and mandated an industrywide changeover that culminated with CARB Phase II reformulated gasoline in 1996.[10]

Our best argument for cleaner-burning gasoline was EC-1 itself. It gave tangible and verifiable evidence of improved air quality on a daily basis as emissions into California's air were being reduced. In 1990, ARCO introduced the second phase of the product line, EC-Premium, and our contributions to clean air grew. In the fall of that year, we achieved our goal of having cleaner-burning gasoline written into the Clean Air Act Amendments as an approved clean fuel.

ROLLING OUT THE PRODUCT LINE

Inclusion in the Clean Air Act was an important step for cleaner-burning gasoline. But greater challenges lay ahead in California where standards more stringent than the new federal requirements were being considered. All gasolines would have to be reformulated to meet these mandates. In response to the California Air Resources Board initiatives, ARCO proposed a formulation, EC-X, that reduced tailpipe emissions below EC-1 and federal requirements.

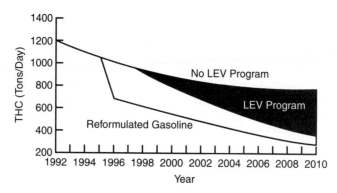

Figure 7-3 Total Hydrocarbon Emissions: California Light-Duty Gasoline Vehicles. LEV means low-emission vehicles under California law.

ARCO pointed out that if EC-X were used by all the cars and trucks in the state, vehicular pollution would drop by 3.8 million pounds a day, the equivalent of taking eight million vehicles off the road. That's nearly a third of all cars and trucks in the state. Ozone-producing tailpipe emissions would be 38 percent below that of conventional gasoline in late-model vehicles. (See Figure 7-3.) The good news for consumers was that EC-X would cost only about 15 cents a gallon more than current gasolines.[11]

We told the California Air Resources Board that we believed the EC-X formula should set the standard for California gasolines. In 1992, the state board agreed with us, adopting an EC-X type formula and mandating that it replace conventional gasoline in the state beginning June 1, 1996. With this decision by the California Air Resources Board, ARCO's EC strategy was being fully implemented.

MAINTAINING PUBLIC AWARENESS AND ACCEPTANCE

As the June 1, 1996 date neared, ARCO management wanted to remind the motoring public in California of the company's role in developing the state's new reformulated gasoline standard. ARCO's corporate advertising agency recommended full-page insertions in major dailies throughout the state.

A nagging question needed answering before the ads ran: With May gasoline prices sharply higher in California due to a combination of factors, would ads extolling the environmental benefits of reformulated gasoline (RFG) seem irrelevant, even provocative, to an enraged public? Focus groups assembled in San Francisco and Los Angeles were reassuring. Shown the ads, participants displayed a surprising grasp of the issue, with most recognizing the necessity for slightly increased pump prices to pay for cleaner gasoline.

The ads pointed to progress such as eliminating 98 percent of hydrocarbon emissions compared with vehicles of 25 years ago—and it includes a promise:

Through the use of cleaner-burning fuels like EC-X, we would continue to build a future of cleaner air and an environment "we can live with."[12]

Public awareness of the benefits of cleaner-burning gasolines has also been boosted by environmental writers like Gregg Easterbrook. In an April 9, 1995 article in the *Los Angeles Times,* Easterbrook noted that cleaner-burning gasoline "is a leading environmental success story. Invented by ARCO, it is a reason Los Angeles smog has declined by more than half since the first Earth Day in 1970 even as the car population of Los Angeles nearly doubled." Easterbrook repeated this message in *Newsweek* soon after that.[13]

Reformulated gasoline has led to a win-win scenario. For the oil industry, it has given gasoline a new lease on life and positioned it as a fuel that can compete environmentally with other alternatives. For U.S. auto makers, who were among the first to cheer the development of RFG, it enabled them to meet increasingly stringent emission standards. It also forestalled a possible rush to methanol-powered cars and an upheaval in fuels marketing that would have seriously impacted the auto industry.

The development of RFG also led to a multiyear, joint industry study known as "Auto/Oil" that has shed new light on gasoline technology and ways to optimize the interaction of fuel and engine to reduce hydrocarbon emissions. And finally, for the general public, it has meant enormous improvement in air quality, especially in the most smog-prone cities.

ONGOING CHALLENGES TO THE PETROLEUM INDUSTRY

The battle for clean air is far from over. As we look to the future and an ever-burgeoning vehicle population, we continue to seek new ways to lower pollution caused by the automobile.

Remarkably, much of the progress has come from research conducted jointly by those old antagonists, the oil and auto industries. Historically, the question of where the responsibility lay—on the fuel or the engine—was a hot potato tossed back and forth between the two industries. Then, in October 1989, the Auto/Oil Air Quality Improvement Research Program (AQIRP) came into being to attack the auto pollution issue on a joint basis. The six-year, $40 million research effort has conclusively shown that changes in both fuel and light-duty vehicles are leading to substantial reduction in ozone air pollution. The data is helping legislators and regulators meet the nation's clean air goals through the development of new and innovative testing techniques for measuring the effect of fuels and vehicles on emissions.[14]

One particularly promising area under study by the Oil/Auto group is On-Board Diagnostic (OBD) systems. OBD is a system that would be incorporated in every vehicle. Among other things, it would monitor the efficiency of the vehicle's catalytic converter. An indicator light on the dashboard would warn the motorist when the catalytic converter needed service, as well as alerting them to other emissions problems. We are hopeful that OBD systems will become standard equipment on new vehicles within the next few years. The oil and automobile industries are working together on this new technology.

Even as the oil and automotive industries continue to attack pollution through systems such as OBD and cleaner-burning gasolines, new challenges appear on the horizon. For instance, researchers believe the haze in national parks may drift from densely populated areas hundreds of miles away. Arizona's Grand Canyon, for example, traces its smog to areas as far away as Southern California and northern Mexico.

Another challenge is the ongoing pressure that the states are under to attain national ambient air quality (NAAQ) standards. We've made considerable progress in this area but many major cities still fall short of NAAQ requirements. And those requirements may become more stringent to address new health concerns.

There is also the troubling Energy Policy Act of 1992 mandate requiring alternative fuels to be used in fleet vehicles: 10 percent of gasoline would be replaced by 2001 and 30 percent by 2010. For obvious reasons, ARCO opposes mandates of this kind, and believes that market forces should determine the best transportation fuel.

Like the supply question, environmental issues seem to attract government-imposed decisions. Worldwide concern about global climate change, for example, has produced international agreements to reduce emissions of greenhouse gases such as carbon dioxide, a byproduct of fossil fuel combustion. Thus far, the agreements have been voluntary, but there is strong pressure to make them mandatory.

In dealing with these issues, there may be reason to turn to alternative fuels in certain niche market applications. Natural gas, for example, is an efficient substitute for gasoline in powering delivery vans or buses along local routes with access to central fueling. Electric vehicles will likely play a more important role at some future date, although EVs at present lack efficiency or cost-effectiveness for widespread use. To its credit, the California Air Resources Board recognized this technology lag when it waived its mandate that by 1998, two percent of new cars sold in California be electric. CARB still demands, however, that 10 percent of new cars sold in the state by 2003 be EVs.[15]

The best solution may be a hybrid—a car that runs on both electricity and some other fuel, such as clean-burning gasoline. The liquid fuel could be converted to electricity on board by an internal combustion engine or fuel cell. Demonstration models of automotive fuel cells are just now emerging from the laboratories. As we enter the twenty-first century, widespread commercial use is still years away.

LESSONS FOR BUSINESS AND ENVIRONMENTAL STRATEGISTS

Until successful replacements emerge, cleaner-burning gasolines are likely to carry us decades into the new century. Reformulated gasoline burns as emission-free as most of the alternative fuels, and with the recent expansion and diversification of major oil production sources in Latin America, Asia, and Russia, reliance on petroleum presents no immediate national security problem as first feared.

The emission reductions promised by a switch to cleaner-burning gasolines, predicted by air quality models, are now being verified through air quality monitoring—taking air samples and measuring the amount of pollutants. And as air pollution control agencies and refiners become more sophisticated and confident of the benefits of reformulated gasoline, more flexible gasoline formulas will be developed and authorized that will provide equivalent air quality benefits at a lower cost to the public.

Despite important progress, there are continuing problems with certain geographical areas of the country that are required to use reformulated gasoline to improve air quality. Refiners, oxygenate producers, and state governments anxiously seek guidance from EPA on how to comply with sweeping RFG rules, particularly the "opt-in" and "opt-out" rules for states that may or may not choose to be part of the RFG program. And the road map may change again if Congress reopens parts of the Clean Air Act, including RFG rules. Producing reformulated gasolines imposes heavy costs on refiners since expensive changes to refining facilities are required. Changes in the program now could result in the inability of these refiners to obtain any return at all on these massive investments. Also uncertain are the specifications for Clean Air Act Phase II gasoline that will be decided by the federal Environmental Protection Agency.

Yet, despite solid progress toward meeting the current standards, EPA has adopted new air pollution ambient standards for ozone and particulate matter that are more stringent because new medical studies associate even low levels of these pollutants with health problems. Combustion sources—including gasoline vehicles—may be principal targets of the new standards. One effect of these new standards probably will be to throw large parts of the eastern United States out of attainment for these pollutants. Vehicle emissions in the East have already come under heavy scrutiny under the current rules because of a growing concern that ozone created in cities is transported over long distances. This has led to pressure for adoption of cleaner, California-type vehicles and fuels across the rest of the United States—the so-called "49-state car" and "49-state fuel." The new, tighter standards will surely add momentum to arguments that once again California successes should be adopted by the rest of the nation.

It has become very clear that what this nation needs to solve its air quality problems is close coordination between refiners and auto makers with the objective of optimizing transportation systems to reduce emissions. Further, we need to develop air models that accurately measure the quality of air and what contributes to its deterioration.

In managing these and other environmental/transportation issues that will come up, ARCO's approach (may serve) as a model for future solutions: Our company's emission-control gasoline strategy has developed into a principal for effective environmental management. ARCO, to begin with, was eager to respond to the concerns of the public. We analyzed the problem from both a technical and public-policy point of view, looking at the big picture of how our product fits into the future of our economy and our society. We involved the regulators from the beginning, using their standards and computer models. We let the product speak for itself. And we never flagged in our commitment to getting the word out on our results.

Enthusiastic claims are often made for new products, and usually consumers ignore them because they are unverified or can be easily discredited by scientific evidence. But ARCO's contribution to clean fuels technology has been verified—by both science and government. What's more, it offers immediate benefits that are otherwise unattainable.

Just as the invention of gasoline helped make cars convenient a century ago, our decision to produce cleaner-burning gasoline has made autos conveniently cleaner. Reformulated gasoline significantly reduces emissions from conventional internal combustion vehicles that are on the road today.[16]

NOTES

2. Passell, Peter, "Economic Scene: Clean Air, At What Price?" *New York Times*, 11/27/91, p. D2.

3. California Energy Commission, "Critical Review of Reports by the Western Oil and Gas Association and the California Council for Environmental and Economic Balance on Alternative Fuels as an Air Quality Management Strategy," April 1989.

4. "ARCO Platform Goes Easy on the Environment," *Oil and Gas Journal*, February 10, 1992, pp. 42–43.

5. Lee, Patrick, "ARCO Introduces Low Emission Gas to Replace Leaded Regular on September 1," *Los Angeles Times*, August 16, 1989.

6. "Bumpy Road Ahead for Gas Guzzlers," *U.S. News and World Report*, August 28, 1989.

7. Maugh, Thomas, "ARCO Hype May Be Right—Gasoline Can Be Cleaner," *Los Angeles Times*, September 28, 1989.

8. California Air Resources Board, press release: "Air Resources Board Chairwoman's Response to Auto/Oil Study on Cars/Gas," Notes 4-A, February 14, 1992.

9. White, Robert M., "Technological Challenge at the Earth Summit," *National Academy of Engineering*, October 2, 1991.

10. Please see *Oil and Gas Journal*, November 13, 1989, "New Transportation Fuels: The Challenge Ahead," pp. 72–79.

11. California Air Resources Board, Staff Report, "Proposed Regulations for California Phase 2 Reformulated Gasoline," October 4, 1991.

12. Wald, Matthew, "ARCO's Surprising Stance on Air Debate," *New York Times*, November 21, 1991.

13. Please see Gregg Easterbrook's *A Moment on Earth: The Coming Age of Environmental Optimism*, Penguin Books, 1996. As well as David Kiley, "ARCO's New EC-1 Gasoline: A PR Coup in the Face of Mounting Pressures," *Adweek*, August 21, 1989 and Kristine Stiven, "ARCO Steps on the Gas for EC-1," *Adweek*, August 21, 1989.

14. California Energy Commission, press release: "Energy Commission Rejects Auto/Oil Industry-Sponsored Study on Alternative Fuel," February 14, 1992.

15. Wald, Matthew, "Vote Sought on Gasoline in California," *New York Times,* March 18, 1992.

16. Please see the following for additional information on ARCO: Council on Economic Priorities, "ARCO: A Report on the Company's Environmental Policies and Practices," November 1991; Peter Coombes, "Responsible Care: ARCO; DOW; Union Carbide; BASF; Cabot," *Chemical Week,* 148 (26): 42–52; David Faber, "The Best Annual Reports," *Institutional Investor,* 24 (11): 153–159; Investor Responsibility Research Center, Inc., "The Valdez Principles and Corporate Environmental Practices: ARCO Chemical Company," April 15, 1991.

QUESTIONS FOR FURTHER THOUGHT

1. Who did ARCO include in the development process and why? (CARB, etc.)

2. Besides new technology, what did ARCO include in the overall strategy to gain product acceptance?

3. With all the challenges ahead for ARCO, what should be their strategic direction for the future? Is there anything ARCO could have done to prevent the negative backlash and what should they do now?

4. Consider the succession of factors that have caused gasoline manufacturers difficulty over the past several decades. Include OPEC and shortages of the 1970s, Gulf War, California smog, CAA, and so on. How have these difficulties helped shape ARCO's strategy? Will this strategy work in the long run?

5. Why did ARCO develop a reformulated gasoline for the "regular leaded" market before pursuing larger opportunities for unleaded and premium unleaded? Include environmental reasons and economic reasons (retooling costs, etc.)

6. Discuss whether ARCO is strategically an energy company or a gasoline company. Why is the difference so critical for R&D decisions, investments, lobbying, and so on?

7. What strategic motives did ARCO have for sharing the formula of their reformulated gasoline? Did it work? (Focus on regulatory and market, and PR issues.)

8. What difficulties does ARCO face in trying to make its reformulated gasoline a national instead of a regional product? How has it attempted to overcome these challenges?

9. How should America choose which energy inputs to use into the next millennium? Explain the positives and negatives of using science, markets, or government to determine these choices. Is a combination of all three the best alternative?

Postscript
Convening Change at ARCO

Kenneth R. Dickerson

A dramatic change in corporate strategy can be the result of extensive analysis and deliberation or of swift reaction to a crisis. Both are part of the daily life of a corporate executive or middle manager. But meaningful change is increasingly driven by external forces and shaped by personal experiences and training of those who regularly analyze and recommend courses of action. This is particularly true when strategic decisions involve issues of social and political policy.

This case describes what was done at ARCO in 1989 and why the company charted a course different from its peers. What is not described are the deliberations of a group of middle managers, which shaped the final decisions made by ARCO executives. Several dedicated ARCO employees, receptive to change and emboldened by a corporate culture that rewards creativity, were brought together to recommend how the corporation could maintain environmental and market leadership in the face of growing demands to discontinue the use of fossil fuels. What would they do if they were in charge of ARCO's future? After several extended discussions, a 10-point list was developed, beginning with the manufacture of a product that would reduce emissions without disrupting the lives of consumers, be low-cost, and enable ARCO to maintain its sales and environmental leadership. Every item on the group's list of recommendations was eventually adopted by the corporation and is now part of ARCO's fabric. Most important of all, cleaner-burning gasolines became a reality.

My role was to convene the right people, encourage them to disregard conventional wisdom, steer them away from "quick fix" solutions, and assure them that their careers would not suffer if they advanced radical ideas. The "change team" needed little encouragement, having lived through other ARCO experiences where the unconventional was required and appreciated. They were well-prepared to chart a new course for the company.

A single person seldom makes a pivotal decision within a corporation. Almost always a team or task force, sometimes loosely stitched together, shapes recommendations for executive decision. ARCO's clean fuel decision in 1989 was a product of this environment. I had the good judgment to listen to the right voices and champion their causes. Individual and corporate success, in large measure, depends upon receptivity to change, the desire to cause change, and the willingness to see it through to successful completion.

Editors's Note: Since retiring from ARCO in 1998, Ken Dickerson has become one of 16 senior advisors to the AHC Group Inc. and its journal of Corporate Environmental Strategy.

CHAPTER

Environmental Management Systems

FROM PLAN TO ACTION: IMPLEMENTING CORPORATE ENVIRONMENTAL STRATEGY

In the complex effort to realize environmentally driven business opportunities, companies often fall short—not from a lack of effort, but rather as a result of failed implementation. Like any significant initiative in company practice, environmental strategies can cause a great deal of dreaded change in an organization. When corporate strategists create a proactive response to environmentally driven threats and opportunities, they often ignore the gap that lies between plan and action. In some companies, this gap gradually erodes at the core and presents itself as an insurmountable fissure that denies any positive results.

Looking at traditional models for change in an organization can help decision makers think about not only the content of this strategic response, but also the process of realizing that vision. The following catch-phrases describing organizational change may help you sense the difficulties inherent in such efforts:

- *Corporate culture.* Recognizing the peculiar nature of each organization is more of an art than a process. Sure it's easy to differentiate among small and large, dynamic and static, or one-dimensional and multidimensional organizations, but beyond this superficial knowledge of the firm lies a complex understanding of corporate culture and its nuance. Grabbing hold of this knowledge often means the difference between realizing the corporate strategic vision and falling short of that vision.[1]
- *Change management.* Changing organizational systems and behavior takes time and patient planning. Too often, management will dive headfirst into changing the way things operate. The management literature is rich with cases of well-intentioned organizational change backfiring as a result of poor planning, employee resistance, and a lack of understanding

among staff. John Kotter talks about this common disconnect in his book, *Leading Change*. Some of the common errors on change that he has uncovered are presented in Figure 8-1. Understanding these missteps can help management better implement its environmental strategy and vision.[2]

- *Communicating change.* Part of the failure in Corporate America in fully realizing the opportunities inherent in addressing environmental issues has come from failed communication. Whether it be failed communication between executive staff and line staff, or with external stakeholders (i.e., regulators, customers, stockholders), effectively communicating the strategic vision often fails to be a part of the overall realization of a corporate environmental strategy.

With a basic understanding of these likely impediments to implementing environmental strategies, the next century's leaders will not only idealize the appropriate business response to the corporate environmental terrain, but they will also effectively move the entire organization in that direction.

Often, it is merely understanding the many facets for planned changes in your company that makes the difference. Changing the direction that the corporate ship is taking can be laced with potential complications. It requires a full view of the horizon and an understanding of the roles each staff member plays in charting the new direction. Some tools for change are expressed in Figure 8-2.[3]

Tomorrow's environmental leader must supply the corporate captains with the right tools, maps, and personnel to help guide the appropriate and profitable decisions of course, speed, and direction. By speaking the "captain's" language and gaining respect, she can help determine when to hoist the "product sails," turn the budgetary rudder, and structure the work of the crew so that the course chosen leads to environmentally responsible and profitable shores.

---

1. Allowing too much complacency
2. Failing to create a sufficiently powerful guiding coalition
3. Underestimating the power
4. Undercommunicating the vision by a factor of 10 (or 100 or even 1000)
5. Permitting obstacles to block the new vision
6. Failing to create short-term wins
7. Declaring victory too soon
8. Neglecting to anchor changes firmly in the corporate culture

---

Figure 8-1 Common Errors of Organizational Change

Source: John Kotter, *Leading Change*, Harvard Business Press, 1997.

Vision + Skills + Incentive + Resources + Action Plan = Effective Change
Change without Vision = Confusion
Change without Skills = Anxiety
Change without Action Plan = False Starts
Change without Incentive = Gradual Change
Change without Resources = Frustration

Figure 8-2   Kolb/Forhman's "Five Factors for Effective Change"

Source: Kolb and Forhman, *Sloan Management Review,* 1970.

As the century closes, firms are preoccupied with refining their environmental management systems in order to more effectively track corporate environmental performance (as evident in the growth of standards such as ISO 14001). Yet, some also see this as an opportunity to better integrate environmental issues into strategic decision making. The gap between plan and action is often large, but the pieces in this chapter show how effective environmental management systems can make strategic vision a reality.

This chapter begins with a piece by David Rainey, faculty member at RPI's Lally School of Management & Technology. With new product development and team-based product creation expanding, Rainey takes a look at the logical convergence of integrated product design and Design-for-the-Environment (DfE) initiatives. DfE has become a popular catch-phrase in the 1990s, and it offers a way of incorporating environmental impacts into product design, sale, and use. In many ways, Rainey's piece echoes the earlier discussion of ARCO's gasoline reformulation and foreshadows the final case in this part on Volvo by providing concepts that explain the executive actions in both firms.

This seemingly far-fetched practice of DfE is given substantial weight in the piece by AT&T's Braden Allenby and Joseph Mon. AT&T, one of the world's largest communications providers, has taken the concepts of DfE to heart throughout their company. By embracing this new and exciting design process, AT&T is beginning to address environmental issues with more ease.

As one steps from plan to action, there will always be some slippage. It is a basic fact of organizational dynamics. The trick in the future is to prevent small slips from becoming a costly stumble. Next century, environmental management will need the tools of design and product development as key allies in implementing environmental initiatives.

NOTES

1. Please see Edgar Schein's *Organizational Culture and Leadership,* Jossey-Bass, New York, 1992.
2. Kotter, John, *Leading Change,* Harvard Business Press, MA, 1997.
3. Kolb, David A., and Alan L. Forhman, "An Organization Development Approach to Consulting," *Sloan Management Review,* Vol. 12, 1970, pp. 51–65.

Converging Integrated New Product Development with Design for Environment

David Rainey

Dr. David Rainey is professor and Curriculum Chair of Environmental Management at Rensselaer at Hartford, in Hartford, Connecticut. He teaches Environmental Management and Technology Innovation, and he is also a faculty member of Rensselaer's Lally School of Management & Technology. Trained as a mechanical engineer, Rainey has held several management positions for major corporations and currently serves as a consultant with the AHC Group.

After some thirty years of environmental regulation, multinationals are ending this century with two new powerful drivers behind the product creation process, namely: integrated product development and design for the environment. The rapid development of new products in telecommunications, electronics, defense, and elsewhere has become an important precursor for sustaining a competitive position in the dynamics of managing customer satisfaction. Creating customer value and satisfaction are essential for achieving superior performance in the next century and for providing the necessary focus to link corporate environmental initiatives with product change and manufacturing reform.

The product creation process is key to all modern businesses and includes market and technology assessments, product innovation, technology development, product development, process selection, and life cycle management. Integrated product development is difficult to define in a concise way. It is based on understanding what customers need, analyzing the options, and marshaling the available resources to quickly achieve the desired new product outcomes. The basic aspects of integrated product development are identifying the critical requirements, devising a holistic game plan, mobilizing the company's resources and talents, then executing the program and measuring the results. The critical features are product/market assessment, process management, and speed to the market. Today's firms, like Lucent Technologies, Lockheed-Martin, and Intel, don't neglect environmental attributes, but instead, insert them throughout the product creation process. What follows explores the meaning of these developments to businesses at large.

Design for the environment is a relatively new concept pertaining to the cradle-to-grave evaluation of the environmental impacts associated with products and technologies. It focuses on life cycle assessment of products and processes and the design of products based on environmental considerations to improve their potential and impacts. (Please see the fuller examination of DfE in this chapter written by the international corporate leader in the field, AT&T's Brad Allenby.) As noted in the Allenby essay, the concept of DfE is evolving in scope and may soon include significant technological and economic drivers as well. The fundamental approach is to design products that are environmentally and economically sound *before their release* to the marketplace.

The primary objective of the product creation process is to obtain sustainable competitive advantage through new product introduction. The purpose of design for the environment is the achievement of sustainability of products and processes in environmental and economic terms. The fundamental objectives are in concert with each other. What follows is a conceptual evaluation to determine key similarities and important differences for next-century applications.

LINKING PRODUCTS WITH SPEED OF DELIVERY

Rapid product development has become a reality because customer expectations require continuous improvements in product performance. Shortening life cycles mean that fast product design and introduction are an ongoing requirement to maintain viable and effective products. The proliferation of all of the products that are available for customers to choose forces a multifaceted approach for satisfying customer demand. Products have to be tailored to meet the needs of each market segment or reinvigorated to sustain their appeal and keep in line with expectations. You can see these forces at work in most electronic, telecommunications, and defense shops these days.

Speed is essential because the product creation process is a continuum. Customers force their suppliers to improve product development cycles, which forces individual competitors to reduce lead times of the product creation process. Speed of delivery and rapid deployment of new design features have become key factors.

Rapid product development requires a flexible approach for managing new products and processes. The concept necessitates a management framework that allows management to make a rapid assessment of the feasibility of a new product opportunity and to quickly decide upon an appropriate course of action. The concept is based on an architecture that enables senior management and product managers to make quick determinations about the feasibility and acceptability of a new product situation, to review the expected requirements and results, and to forge an effective game plan of the development project that focuses on market acceptance of the expected outcomes. This requires a management system that focuses the integration of all of the elements and resources into an effective framework. At this point, most readers may ask where there is room and time to consider environmental needs in such a realm.

In the traditional post-World War II model of product development there wasn't much room at the design floor for environmental drivers. This was because the traditional product creation process was relatively slow. Each element was developed in *series*, rather than in *parallel*. This sequential approach allowed each functional organization to develop its contribution to the overall process essentially independent of the other participants. The upstream activities were executed based on the input available at the time without much regard for the downstream (or environmental) considerations. A typical new product development program flowed from research and development to design and engineering, production, marketing, and commercialization in that order. The approach was viewed as efficient since it tended to minimize the resources devoted to the project at any point of time. There was very little collaboration and the design from the upstream activity team was handed off to the downstream participants without much direct involvement.

Whereas the sequential approach may have been seen to be efficient, it was not very effective. There tended to be many mistakes due to the lack of downstream input. The product design phase tended to incorporate specifications that proved difficult to include from a production perspective. The design engineers were doing their best but failed to achieve good designs because they lacked the necessary input. Downstream players were similarly disadvantaged because they did not know the reasons why certain selections were made. The lack of coordination slowed the process and caused additional activities to correct the inconsistencies and mistakes. The failure to truly integrate the process cost both money and time.[4]

Ironically, as a result of these other nonenvironmental reasons, firms began to reopen the questions of parallel product development strategies. Nonetheless, such fundamental reconsiderations of energy consumption, materials usage, and waste generation allowed a significant revolution in approach in the 1990s. We saw this most clearly in the search for alternatives to ozone-depleting electronic solvents like CFC-113.

THE EVOLUTION OF INTEGRATED PRODUCT DEVELOPMENT

The traditional approach did contribute to new product successes, but the pathways were too long and difficult. There were missing links: (1) a comprehensive framework of a management system for new product development; (2) a clear view of the interrelationships between the key participants, and (3) a systematic process for achieving and measuring results on a timely basis.

These missing links were discovered and reconnected in the 1990s. The more robust approach is articulated in Steven Wheelwright and Kim Clark's book, *Revolutionizing Product Development:*[5]

> Our research on and experience with firms that have superior development capabilities suggest that a much more comprehensive framework for a development strategy provides a far more secure foundation for an individual project. This framework addresses the four main purposes of development strategy:
>
> - Creating, defining, and selecting a set of development projects that will provide superior products and processes.
> - Integrating and coordinating functional tasks, technical tasks, and organizational units involved in development activities over time.

- Managing development efforts so they converge to achieve business purposes as effectively and efficiently as possible.
- Creating and improving the capabilities needed to make development a competitive advantage over the long term.

The Wheelwright and Clark model deals with the strategic aspects of technology assessment and forecasting, along with market assessment and forecasting. At last, there is reason to incorporate environmental costs and features into the product creation process. Their framework links these strategies with the aggregate product plan and the individual new product projects. They suggest that the integration of marketing, manufacturing, and design functions leads to speed, quality, efficiency, and effective problem solving. They argue that the capability to conceive and design quality prototypes and bring a variety of superior products to market quicker than competitors is increasingly the focus of competition. Along with this, many in practice began to note improvements in environmental performance as well.

The new product development framework focuses on the assessment, selection, design, development, and implementation of new product opportunities. It includes identifying and characterizing the dimensions of the new product design and development process, positioning new product opportunities in light of market realities, building flexibility into the process, managing accelerated new product programs, determining the mechanisms that management uses to guide the product development through the organization, and defining the metrics for monitoring performance. It is sequenced to produce a logical flow of the key elements of a program and provide a systematic process for managing the complexities involved in any situation.

For ease of comprehension, Figure 8-3 offers a generic breakdown of the new product development approaches. Please note management's intense involvement in each phase of product creation. While an engineer may carry out the design orders, it is quite clear from this chart that the parameters that might address environmental attributes are set early in the management process.

Figure 8-3 suggests concurrent development. The main functional areas execute their responsibilities simultaneously as the project develops. This approach minimizes the downstream mistakes caused by a lack of upstream involvement. It is based on a philosophy that success is achieved through a systematic process of time-dependent elements that must be formulated and implemented concurrently. The main aspects of proper integration are:

- Establishing the management processes for project execution.
- Creating a project team that understands the interactions required to achieve success and manage complexity.
- Infusing information and knowledge into the process.

Figure 8-3 Key Elements of the New Product Framework

Innovation Stage	Policy	Product	Process	Marketing	Market
Strategic Logic	Vision Strategy Objectives	Key Success Factor (Principles)	Core Capabilities	Driving Forces Competition	Situation Analysis (Opportunities)
Generating Ideas	Opportunities & Threats	Technology Assessment & Forecast	Production Resource Analysis	Market Assessment & Forecast	Market Research (Needs/Wants)
Developing New Product Concepts	Market & Product Strategies	Product Positioning (Generations)	Resource Linkage	Marketing Knowledge	Market Attractiveness
Selecting Candidates	Aggregate Planning	Concept Design & Specification	Process Leverage	Competition Testing of Concept	Market Selection & Segmentation
Business Analysis					
Planning & Analysis	Financial Analysis & Business Plan	Technology & Product Plans	Production/Operations Plan	Marketing Plan	Market Analysis
Feasibility Assessment	Financial & Managerial Capability	Technically Viability	Process Capability	Marketing Skills & Position	Market Profile Analysis

Figure 8-3 Key Elements of the New Product Framework *(continued)*

	Policy	Product	Process	Marketing	Market
Screening	Strategic Fit Leverage Financial	Quality; Cost; Reliability Performance	Resources Productive/ Ability	Marketability Growth Life Cycle	Value/ Price-to- Performance
Commitment	Sustainability	Platform & Generations	Strategic Capacity	Product Management	Stability Long Term
Design & Development					
Specification	Potential	Features	Inputs	Outputs	Attributes
Design	Risk to Reward	Detail Design & Engineering	Materials Plant & Equipment	Market Testing	Environmental Usability Functionality
Prototype	Validation	Features Performance Quality	Cost; Efficiency; Reliability	Product Life Testing	Acceptance; Strengths & Weaknesses
Preproduction	Confirmation	Product Testing	Process Setup Planning	Packaging; Distribution	Life Cycle Analysis Channels
Launch					

- Developing a network of relationships with stakeholders, customers, and suppliers that are part of the system and integrating them into the process.
- Testing concepts and designs and evaluating performance on an ongoing basis.

Such goals are noble, and if effectively earned, allow considerable success in the marketplace. Yet the key is teamwork. Cross-functional team integration is an organizational structure established to achieve collaborative behavior in a highly interactive new product development environment. It is a paradigm that enhances the skills and capabilities of the project participants by forming interdisciplinary teams for project execution. The emphasis is on the achievement of the overall results and excellence. Creating a spirit of high performance and collaboration is pivotal for success. Team members establish the basis for performing the work, set the priorities, specify the design and development activities, assess the alternatives, and evaluate the results. Here many firms now mix product champions with environmental champions.

Rapid product development requires close coordination and cooperation among all of the participants. Cross-functional teams link downstream activities with upstream decision making. The knowledge of the downstream capabilities and limitations allows the team to select solutions that are appropriate for each aspect of the project.

DESIGN FOR THE ENVIRONMENT: MAKING IT REALLY HAPPEN

Design for the Environment (DfE) is the systematic approach for evaluating the environmental consequences of products and processes and their impact on human health and the environment. As shown by the Brad Allenby case, DfE is a compelling environmental management concept that is based on a cradle-to-grave assessment of products and production processes. It examines all of the inputs and outputs in qualitative and quantitative terms and links products and processes to all of their precursors and resultant outcomes. The ultimate objective is to design or redesign products and processes that incorporate environmental considerations and analysis in the selection process and to make choices based on achieving a sustainable environment and reliable corporate profile.

The primary focus is the identification of the ingredients and their environmental implications, the determination of the effects that the products and processes have on the environment over their life cycles, and the development of environmentally compatible products and processes. A detailed understanding of the positive and negative aspects of products and processes with respect to economic, market, regulatory, social, and political factors contributes to more environmentally acceptable practices and outcomes.[6]

DfE initiatives entail a broad scope, requiring an assessment of the life cycle implications of products and processes from the extraction of the raw materials at the mine to the final disposal of the products and their resultant emissions, effluents, and waste. This often requires comprehensive and time-consuming analyses in order to minimize and improve the effects of a product and its related processes on the environment.

Despite these exploring complexities, DfE is increasingly becoming an important environmental management tool. It is now a generally accepted method for studying product-related issues and problems and their environmental implications and impacts. By the next century, it may prove a key tool in linking business strategy with environmental management.[7]

If you return to Figure 8-3, you'll see a significant role for life cycle assessment (LCA). Life cycle assessment is a systematic tool used to analyze and evaluate the resource requirements and environmental burdens associated with a product, its related processes, distribution requirements, and applications. The analysis is undertaken to identify, quantify, and evaluate the materials and energy used to produce and use a single corporate product over its entire life cycle. It is a multistage input/output model that examines all of the inputs and their impacts, and all of the outputs including products, derivatives, byproducts, and wastes and their impacts. The model evaluates the current picture and explores the possibilities for systematic improvement through product design considerations.

Product life cycle assessment is the principal method used today to evaluate products and processes from the design-for-the-environment perspective. It is an evolving dynamic method that currently consists of inventory, impact, and improvement analyses.[8] While entire books are now being written on these phases of LCA, Figure 8-4 sums up the key elements and goals.

ADVANTAGES AND DISADVANTAGES OF LIFE CYCLE ASSESSMENT

Life cycle assessment is a powerful tool that provides a comprehensive understanding of the underlying issues related to product design and production. It offers an increasingly reliable view of the product realities from an environmental perspective, allowing the decision maker to find solutions to potential problems or issues whenever possible. This broad view stimulates interest in producing environmentally compatible products that meet the expectations of customers and stakeholders (see Figure 8-5).[9]

The most significant benefit from a sustainability perspective is the in-depth analysis of the precursors to the product, the production processes, and the applications and retirement aspects. This comprehensive review of the complete value chain provides a tool for making decisions based on a life cycle view that weathers the driving forces of change. The information and knowledge gained from the process allows decision makers to minimize environmental defects that may be built into a product that could cause its premature death.

The main negative is the time and money required to perform the assessments and to incorporate the results into products. Another significant hurdle

Figure 8-4 Life Cycle Assessment Steps

	Inventory Assessment	Impact Assessment	Improvement Assessment
Elements	An objective quantification of environmental burdens	A subjective evaluation of the effects of the burdens	A systematic evaluation of the opportunities to improve the burdens
Key Aspects	Identify the elements and quantify in terms of inputs and outputs	Resource depletion, human health risks, safety, environmental degradation	Changes needed to bring about the desired improvements
Goals	Identification of inputs and outputs and evaluation classification of levels and loading	Understanding their potential implications on sustainability of products and processes	Opportunities to reduce the environmental burdens leading to sustainability

is whether the analysis serves the customer in any way that enhances sales of the product in question.

CONVERGING DfE, LCA, AND PRODUCT DEVELOPMENT

Both DfE and LCA techniques can be applied to the new product creation process described earlier. It is easier to develop the analysis concurrently with the design and development of a new product. The required work would parallel the elements of the product development plan and provide decision makers with real time information on the environmental implications of their designs. Some designers could even solicit comments from customers and stakeholders during the process, thereby obtaining information that could prevent a major problem. We know this already happens in cosmetic and eye-care product strategies.

A full life cycle assessment could uncover potential issues pertaining to compliance with environmental laws and regulations or undergo the scrutiny of environmentalists who may offer suggestions that could improve the viability of the product. Figure 8-6 presents some suggestions.

The outcomes can exceed the expectations. A reduction in solid and hazardous waste tends to improve products and processes from an economic and technical point of view. Waste minimization reduces process flow requirements and provides a better, more efficient process. Managing inputs and outputs that do not have economic value adds to process complexity without contributing

Figure 8-5 Benefits and Concerns about Life Cycle Assessment

Benefits (Positive Aspects)	Concerns (Negative Aspects)
Identification of potential problem areas early in the product creation process, providing the opportunity to make low-cost and impact changes.	The process takes time, effort, and money to achieve appropriate results, possibly delaying the commercialization of a new product.
Preventive actions and effects are easier to include in a product design than corrective actions.	An assessment of existing products may indicate the need for costly changes that are difficult to accomplish.
Decision analysis is framed in an objective view of the life cycle aspects of the product's environment, including impact on stakeholders.	There are uncertainties associated with the discovery of hidden defects that are not addressed in the product design or redesign activities.
Priorities are identified by the analysis, offering a systematic means to judge the most important design parameters and their relationship to environmental considerations.	Yet such priorities can conflict with existing staff or market needs and indicators.
A valuable input into the design aspects, helping to avoid serious mistakes due to a lack of knowledge.	The knowledge gained in the assessment process may cause the designers to incorporate changes that are not time tested, resulting in unforeseen or potential risks.
A systematic framework for assessing the environment consequences and impacts.	The consequences and impacts are complex and it is difficult to know the implications.
A reliable evaluation of product parameters leading to better understanding of the differences between product offerings.	Again, there is some concern over whether DfE and LCA findings are in advance of real customer interests.

to customer value creation. Environmental outcomes can flow in parallel to economic and technical goals.

Life cycle assessment can be used in the redesign of existing products. The existing design parameters tend to constrain some of the options that may be employed in the new product design situation. The redesign situation offers opportunities to improve the product by reducing or eliminating defects that stall the viability or success of the product. Life cycle assessment has been carried out on a limited scale based on the needs of the product redesign program, or on its full scope depending on the time available and the objectives of the program.

Please consider how all of these LCA and DfE tools are made more viable and useful with the software capabilities described by Charles Knapp in Chapter 9, which focuses on management information systems.

Figure 8-6 Uncovering Potential Product Alternatives

Raw Materials	Production	Distribution	Use & Reuse	Retirement
No Hazardous Materials	Increase Process Yields	More Efficient Sources	More Product Knowledge	Recovery Methods
Use Recovered Materials	Improve Production Practices	Improved Emissions	Alternative Applications	Infrastructure Development
Renewable	Less Energy			Recycling

DESIGN FOR THE ENVIRONMENT AS AN INTEGRAL ASPECT OF PRODUCT CREATION

The convergence of DfE principles with integrated product development concepts now offers senior management a comprehensive framework for developing sustainable new products or improving existing products by minimizing their negative aspects. As we enter the next century, such an approach has been used by defense, telecommunications, and electronics leaders. The framework integrates DfE principles with the economic and marketing perspectives of existing product management and product creation models. It sets the stage for a descriptive, analytical, and structural understanding of the needs, opportunities, threats, requirements, specifications, and flow of product creation and product management. With such a wide scope in focus, you can see how this involves strategic product choices.[10]

The purpose of the described methodology is to analyze and describe all of the key elements required to characterize a new product opportunity in sufficient detail so that management can be assured that nothing has been overlooked and that the best choices for inputs and outputs have been made. Herein lie its existing prospects for superior environmental performance. With the integration of DfE concepts into the new product development process, new products can be designed and built using the most effective corporate resources while maximizing the beneficial product features and minimizing environmental impacts.[11] Someday, you can expect more environmentally friendly computers, phones, and other devices derived from these two approaches.

NOTES

4. Ulrich, Karl and Steven Eppinger, *Product Design and Development*, McGraw-Hill, New York, 1995.

5. Wheelwright, Steven and Kim Clark, *Revolutionizing Product Development: Quantum Leaps in Speed, Efficiency and Quality*, Free Press, New York, 1992.

6. Keoleian, Gregory and Dan Menerey, *Life Cycle Design Guidance Manual,* "Environmental Requirements and the Product System," EPA/600/R-92/226, Environmental Protection Agency, January 1993.

7. Lennox, Michael and John Ehrenfeld, "Design for Environment: A Framework for Strategic Decisions," *Total Quality Environmental Management,* Vol. 4, No. 4, Summer 1995.

8. Veroutis, Agis, et al., "Achieving Competitive Advantage Through Product Stewardship and LCA," *Environmental Quality Management,* Vol. 6, No. 2, Winter 1996.

9. Keoleian, Gregory, Dan Menerey, and Ann Curren, "A Life Cycle Approach to Product System Design," *Pollution Prevention Review,* Summer 1993.

10. Fiksel, Joseph, *Design for Environment: Creating Eco-Efficient Products and Processes,* McGraw-Hill, New York, 1996.

11. Conway-Schempf, Noelette and Lester Lane, "Pollution Prevention through Green Design," *Pollution Prevention Review,* Vol. 6, No. 1, Winter 1995-6.

Leveraging Innovative Potential: Design for Environment at AT&T

Joseph Mon and Brad Allenby

Joseph M. Mon, PE, CHMM is Environment, Health and Safety (EH&S) Operations Director for AT&T. He received a BS in Chemical Engineering and Materials Engineering at the University of Connecticut. Mon is EH&S Process Leader, leads the Process Management Team (PMT) addressing worldwide compliance and EH&S program development, and is an integral member of the EH&S strategic planning team, sharing accountability with the EH&S Vice President for strategic direction.

Dr. Braden R. Allenby is currently the Environment, Health and Safety Vice President for AT&T. From 1995 to 1997, he was Director for Energy and Environmental Systems at Lawrence Livermore Laboratory, on temporary assignment from his position as Research Vice President, Technology and Environment, for AT&T. He graduated cum laude from Yale University in 1972, and received his Juris Doctor from the University of Virginia Law School in 1978 and his Masters in Economics from the University of Virginia in 1979. He received his Masters in Environmental Sciences from Rutgers University in 1989 and his Ph.D. in Environmental Sciences from Rutgers in 1992.

The quality revolution has swept its way globally through most companies. Focusing on improving the quality of products and services delivered to the customers and on companies' internal processes, the success of these programs has supported the application of these principles to the area of environmental, occupational health, and safety management.

In some ways this approach is nothing new. The Bell System, as a vertically integrated monopoly, not only manufactured telephones and telecommunications equipment, but leased these products to consumers. Periodically, these products were returned to the company, then refurbished and reintroduced into commerce. At the end of their life, they were taken back and disassembled into their component parts for reuse, recycling, and disposal. This wasn't done because recycling was on everyone's minds, but because it made good business sense.

When divestiture created the new AT&T in 1984, the economics supporting internal recycling systems changed, and the company had to develop a new approach to environmental concerns. Traditional compliance activities had to be augmented in order to meet increasingly stringent and detailed legal requirements such as those in 1984 amendments to the Resource Conservation and Recovery Act (RCRA) and the Superfund Amendments and Reauthorization Act of 1986 (SARA). The company had to sort out its role in connection with developing international requirements such as the Montreal Protocol (which banned the use of ozone-depleting CFCs), and had to become even more responsive to the growing environmental concerns of employees, stockholders, and customers around the world.

During 1995, AT&T was restructured into three independent firms: AT&T retained its core business of service provisioning, Lucent Technologies retained the manufacturing function, and NCR remained the network computing component. AT&T chairman and CEO, Bob Allen, reaffirmed the firm's commitment to EH&S leadership during the change in the introductory letter to the company's 1996 EH&S annual report:[12]

> AT&T has long enjoyed a reputation as a leader when it comes to corporate commitment to environment, health and safety issues. Our strong environmental efforts have even helped build the AT&T brand, one of our most valuable corporate assets. So it should come as no surprise that we intended to maintain our role as a top corporate champion in the areas of environment, health and safety despite our strategic restructuring which has led us to focus almost exclusively on services, with minimal manufacturing activity.

A strong commitment to environmental, occupational health, and safety performance did not alleviate the competitive pressures faced by the company due primarily to the Telecommunications Reform Act of 1996.

In order to meet these pressures, and go beyond them to integrate environment and technology throughout its operations, the company had developed, and is continuing the implementation of, a process-based management system that incorporates the concept of design for environment (DFE). DfE is based on the principles of industrial ecology.

AT&T also has a long history of quality initiatives as witnessed by the many products and services that have received the International Organization for Standardization (ISO) 9000 certification. The company has utilized quality methodologies for the past few years to turn the environmental focus from end-of-pipe waste management to proactive and preventive strategies. The application of quality principles to the EH&S discipline, also known as Total Quality Environmental Management (TQEM), is fundamental to the management system. Through TQEM, AT&T now approaches the reduction of wastes and emissions generated today through a multimedia approach in the initial product/process design. TQEM is also now driving DfE programs and procedures, recognizing that addressing environmental, health, and safety issues in the initial design process is the most cost-effective means for minimizing impact on the environment as well as employees' workspace.[13]

For AT&T, having a consistent, quality-based management system is essential to ensure improved compliance across its facilities, which number in excess of five thousand. DfE as a proactive, anticipatory, and preventive operating and engineering design approach is a key component of the management system. The goal of DfE is to avoid potential environmental problems for a technology, process, service, or product over its total life cycle by addressing them during the product concept and design stages.

Like most companies, AT&T began by looking at the wastes and emissions that were being generated; in fact, waste reduction and prevention has always been a part of any successful enterprise. Historically, as within AT&T, it was part of cost-reduction programs to increase efficiencies and maintain competitiveness for manufacturing products. With the onset of more restrictive waste management regulation, and skyrocketing waste management, treatment, and disposal costs, waste reduction and prevention were, and still are, seen as playing a greater role in remaining competitive worldwide.

Beyond simply achieving compliance, however, customers began to demand that products and services be built with a minimum of impact on the environment. They were trying to influence manufacturers through the direct purchase of products they perceive to be better for the environment and through their political backing of "green" representatives and programs. Legislation at all political levels was being written that mandated: the reduction of use of toxics; process emission and waste minimization; product waste minimization through recycling; and product life extension. The answers to these pressures seemed to lie in the implementation of TQEM and DfE practices.

DfE provides the company with a comprehensive and integrated corporate approach to operating as an environmentally responsible company. AT&T's system for environmental change has both internal and external dimensions. Internally, it includes the corporate environmental vision, how the company is organized to focus on strategic environmental concerns, the current corporate environmental goals, the developing information systems and tools that support DfE, and the lessons learned from introducing DfE into the organization. Externally, the company is supported in the efforts to build a global environmental infrastructure through alliances and partnerships with industry, government, and educational groups.

AT&T at a Glance

AT&T is the world's premier communications and information services company, serving more than 90 million customers, including consumers, business, and government. The company has annual revenues of more than $52 billion and 130,000 employees.

AT&T runs the world's largest, most sophisticated communications network and is the leading provider of long-distance and wireless services. AT&T operates over 5,000 locations in more than 200 countries and territories around the world. The company also offers on-line services and access to home entertainment, and has begun to deliver local telephone service. In addition, AT&T offers outsourcing, consulting, systems-integration, and customer-care services to large businesses and manages one of the world's largest credit card programs.

Source: Annual Report, 1996.

In 1973, AT&T's manufacturing subsidiary, Western Electric, first issued a corporate environmental policy that laid the foundation for a waste minimization program. With divestiture and a restructuring of the company in 1984, an AT&T Policy for Environmental Protection was issued recommitting us to the concepts of the original policy. Policy deployment was the process used to implement this environmental policy throughout the company.

AT&T'S EH&S Vision

- The policy for environmental protection went beyond just meeting regulatory compliance. It committed decision makers to develop and use nonpolluting technologies, minimize wastes, increase recycling, design products and processes with the environmental impact as a critical factor, and instill in all employees an awareness of environmental responsibilities and practices. Most fundamentally, it committed the company to the life-cycle approach and the use of DfE practices throughout the organization. AT&T deployed this policy as part of the overall quality policy, and it became an integrated part of the business plans.

- As a result of the transition into three distinct companies during 1995, AT&T decided to reevaluate its environmental policy. The new policy, signed by the Chairman in March 1997, supersedes the former environmental and the former occupational health and safety policy through a holistic approach, including DfE components, derived from AT&T's EH&S vision.

- AT&T's new EH&S vision is to be recognized by customers, employees, suppliers, shareowners, and communities worldwide as a world-class company that protects human health and the environment by fully integrating life-cycle environmental, health, and safety considerations into our business decisions and activities.

- This vision statement provides a framework for DfE and makes clear the corporate commitment supporting the company's developing DfE activities and environmental partnerships. The new vision is also consistent with and supportive of AT&T's longstanding safety creed: "No job is so important and no service so urgent that we cannot take time to perform our work safely." It is a cornerstone that makes it possible to continue building the rest of the infrastructure needed to define and meet AT&T's environmental goals.

Source: EH&S Annual Report, 1996.

HOW POLICY DRIVES EH&S INNOVATIONS

In the realigned AT&T, many of the manufacturing-related EH&S goals no longer apply. Rather, the challenge is to understand EH&S activities in the context of a services company, so that metrics appropriate to its activities can be developed. As a part of this process, the AT&T EH&S leadership team's goal is to integrate environmental, occupational health, and safety processes throughout the corporation, to increase environmental and economic efficiencies, and to enhance quality of life.

As a result of the services-oriented nature of the company, the environment, health, and safety policy had to be fine-tuned. The new policy builds on the vision and links environmental, occupational health, and safety stewardship to the AT&T Code of Conduct and core values of the company.

The New EH&S Policy

AT&T is committed to engaging its employees and leveraging its technology to protect human health and the environment in all operations, services, and products, and to contribute to the achievement of an environmentally efficient national and global economy. Implementation of this policy is a primary management objective and the responsibility of every AT&T employee.

Goals and Guidelines

- Comply with all applicable laws, regulations, and AT&T standards and practices governing environment, health, and safety.
- Support the development of responsible, technically and scientifically valid, cost-effective environment, health, and safety laws, regulations, and standards.

- Engage and educate employees to implement this policy and encourage them to further contribute to the achievement of an environmentally efficient national and global economy through volunteerism.
- Support environmental, health, and safety efficiency by purchasing environmentally preferable products and services.
- Promote the conservation of raw materials and other natural resources, including energy, by eliminating or reducing waste and emissions, and by recycling and reusing materials, components, and products.
- Continuously improve environmental and safety management systems to support the integration of applicable environmental, health, and safety considerations into our business decisions and planning activities.
- Promote achievement of environmental, health, and safety excellence by designing new generations of processes, products, and services to be environmentally preferable to the ones they replace, and by enabling our customers to increase their environmental and economic efficiency.

Source: EH&S Annual Report, 1996.

These qualitative goals and guidelines help all employees incorporate the policy into all facets of the business, from design through implementation and maintenance activities. They also provide the "golden thread" from EH&S activities to the business direction for AT&T. From these goals and guidelines, functional organizations within AT&T can develop quantitative goals to drive the business toward a more sustainable future. The EH&S organization has accordingly implemented a process approach that makes good business sense. At AT&T, process has been shown to be the best way to ensure consistent, across-the-board results.

The EH&S process has four subprocesses, (see Figure 8-7).[14]

The *Stakeholder Contact and Needs Analysis* subprocess team identifies and contacts key stakeholders, listens to their perspectives, and analyzes their needs. This team also builds relationships and manages them on behalf of the company.

Once stakeholder requirements are analyzed, the *Program Development* subprocess team works with the operating units to fund new programs and develop the goals and objectives to meet those requirements. The *Technical Management and Implementation* subprocess team consults on EH&S technical management issues and supports the implementation of new programs for compliance with legislative and regulatory requirements, including those of the Occupational Safety and Health Administration and the U.S. Environmental Protection Agency. The *Assessment* subprocess team measures, tests, and analyzes company performance and provides feedback to ensure continual improvement. The process benefits the corporate bottom line and leads to positive long-term results in the compliance area and to consistent improve-

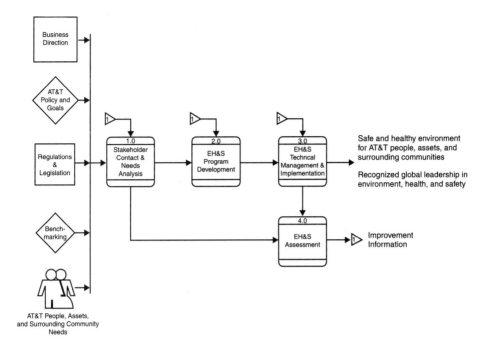

Figure 8-7   Macro Process Flow Diagram: AT&T EH&S Subprocesses

ment within AT&T. The output of the process is a safe, healthy workplace for AT&T employees and a protected environment.

The new AT&T process framework also includes the opportunity to create an environmental management system based on the principles of the AT&T quality management system and other best-in-class approaches, such as the ISO 14001 Environmental Management System standard. The new management system is also consistent with elements of the Environmental Charter of European Telecom Networks and other critically important international or national standards, such as OSHA's Voluntary Protection Program. A management system is only a means to an end. But it sets the stage for success and encourages the discipline necessary to achieve the EH&S goals. A management system is also only as good as the organization that is staffed to support it. We have also spent a considerable amount of effort developing an organization that is flexible and customer focused.

The environment, health, and safety organization now has a new structure, a sharpened strategy, and ambitious objectives. The new plan of action includes redefining industrial ecology priorities as a services company; continuing to integrate environment and safety practices into everyday operations; engaging AT&T people by communicating about these issues and encouraging them to consider community activities that support the environment; and assisting our stakeholders by offering telecommuting and other services that allow them to use energy more efficiently.

In an increasingly service-based economy, the intent is to provide a framework for services companies to use in establishing visible, measurable commitments to environment, health, and safety issues.

LEADERS MAKING THE TEAM WORK

The Vice President of Network Operations, whose function is the efficient operation of the network, also supports the process as the EH&S chief compliance officer for AT&T. The Executive Vice President of Network and Computing Services links the process to the AT&T Senior Management Team in his role as AT&T Chief Quality Officer. In addition, the Vice President of Law and Solicitor General for the firm provides legal support for EH&S. These three officers of the firm support the EH&S vice president who, in turn, supports a new EH&S leadership team. The team is a quality council that serves as a board of directors for the organization and creates EH&S strategies for AT&T. The team consists of AT&T representatives from key groups, including the EH&S Stakeholder Contact and Needs Analysis team and the Design for the Environment team, as well as representatives with EH&S responsibilities from several business units and business partners: AT&T Wireless, Supplier Management, Global Real Estate, Law and Government Affairs, Health Affairs, International and Universal Card Services.

Since the new AT&T operates in more than 200 countries and territories around the world, the EH&S organization must also have a global perspective. The international telecommunications business is undergoing rapid, almost daily changes. The company is involved in joint ventures with telephone companies throughout the world, including but not limited to Unisource in Europe and Alestra in Mexico. For example, Alestra is a joint venture between AT&T, Grupo Alfa, an industrial conglomerate, and Bancomer Visa, an investment bank. Alestra is planning to offer long-distance services in 60 of Mexico's major cities and is installing a fiber optic network.

The challenge is to integrate EH&S considerations into business decisions as the entire company works with joint venture partners. The goal of EH&S international operations is to promote a consistent standard of EH&S care for AT&T operations worldwide. New international EH&S managers are being strategically located in Mexico, to support Central and Latin America; in Spain, to support Europe, the Middle East, and Africa; in the United Kingdom, to support extensive intracountry operations; and in Hong Kong, to support the growing Asia-Pacific regional activities. These regional EH&S managers support facilities and business divisions within their regions, help develop global EH&S policies, standards, and goals, and develop environmental, occupational health, and safety infrastructure, resources, and expertise at locations within their regions. They team with the Real Estate and International Health Affairs organizations to provide integrated services worldwide.[15]

The new EH&S organizational structure provides more flexibility and a closer alignment to company operations. This alignment helps foster a sense of ownership by operating officers of the company not only of compliance-related issues, but also of revenue and brand-enhancing possibilities that are generated as a result of DfE initiatives.

Much of the company's success in reaching its environmental goals results from advances in technology. For example, these advances have supplied the alternative needed to help eliminate the use of CFCs and reduce toxic air emissions in manufacturing. AT&T still utilizes DfE principles to design, develop, manufacture, and market products, processes, and services worldwide with environmentally preferable life-cycle properties, and to promote achievement of environmental excellence by designing every new generation of product, process, and services to be environmentally preferable to the one it replaces.

No matter how compelling a corporate vision, no matter how effective a quality blueprint, and no matter how clear a policy to integrate technology and the environment, they are of no value unless teams of individuals are personally committed to making a difference in performance. The extent of AT&T's success is due to employees around the world who take their environment and safety responsibilities personally. It is the enthusiasm of the engineers, clerks, office staffs, installers, researchers, and managers on the front lines of the business that is making the real difference in performance. They are the ones who devise process and product improvements that have helped AT&T exceed its environmental goals while satisfying its customers and shareowners.

SOME KEY ADVICE

Rapid change offers enormous opportunities to those who seek them. In 1996, AT&T chose to accept the challenge to renew the companywide commitment to EH&S and to take the opportunity to construct a new EH&S infrastructure to reflect the changing needs of the business. The company has tried to look hard at itself and is building a long-term strategy, as embodied in the new policy. The past successes are the foundation for future excellence.

The review and modification of internal EH&S programs, including DfE, for application to the company is clearly a long-term challenge. This will be an ongoing process as corporate strategists reevaluate and redesign the training and technical programs to better address our needs as well as our performance measures and metrics and to better reflect our services orientation. We are now poised to set solid, measurable goals to implement our new policy. Now that our manufacturing presence is very much reduced, we can accept this opportunity to redefine industrial ecology for a services company and to expand our sense of social responsibility as a services company with more than 130,000 employees.

Implementation of DfE within the firm is again becoming a necessity, as it is for all companies looking to compete globally. Customer demands, government regulations, international standards, constrained natural resources, and other forces are combining to make the environment strategic instead of just overhead. The application of TQM provides many of the basic tools, methodologies, and principles needed to implement the necessary changes within a company in a systematic, cost-effective, and customer-focused manner. In the wave of successful quality implementation programs throughout companies, it is critical if change is to be implemented to show the linkages between DfE and the other quality improvement programs. Here are some other key thoughts and lessons learned for getting started:[16]

- Dedicate people to the effort and don't just add it to the responsibilities of already overloaded individuals.
- Keep it simple in the beginning so you can get started now, and learn as you go.
- DfE will be a little different for everybody, and, as it is still in its earliest stages of development, there are very few definitive answers out there.
- As with all quality improvement processes, focus on continuous improvement, and begin now instead of waiting to start when you think you have the ultimate solution.
- Solutions are not going to come easily, because we continue to see the definition of "environmentally preferable" as a moving target as the technology in this area advances.

When are you successful? When DfE is imbedded in the product or service realization process and routinely considered by designers, and the verifiable result is that each new generation of product, service, or offering you provide is more environmentally preferable than the one it replaces.

NOTES

12. *AT&T Annual Environmental Report,* 1996. Published by AT&T.
13. Allenby, B. R., in press. *Industrial Ecology: Policy Implications and Implementation,* Prentice Hall, Upper Saddle River, NJ.
14. *AT&T Annual Environmental Report,* 1997. Published by AT&T.
15. Graedel, T. E., and B. R. Allenby, *Industrial Ecology,* Prentice Hall, Upper Saddle River, NJ, 1995.
16. Graedel, T. E,. and B. R. Allenby, *Industrial Ecology and the Automobile,* Prentice Hall, Upper Saddle River, NJ, 1997.

TQEM: Total Quality Management Systems and the Environment

David Rainey

Dr. David Rainey is Curriculum Chair of Environmental Management at Hartford, in Hartford, Connecticut. See page 140 for the author's full biography.

INTRODUCTION

Total Quality Management is a widely accepted management system used to increase product and service quality and promote an ideology of continuous improvement throughout an organization. TQM provides a companywide integration of the processes necessary to meet customer expectations in terms of quality, reliability, and responsiveness. The essence of quality is customer satisfaction.

W. Edwards Deming, Joseph Juran, Armand Feigenbaum, Kaoru Ishikawa, Philip Cosby, and Genichi Taguchi, principal architects of the quality movement, laid the foundation for TQM and its derivative management systems. The total quality philosophy is based on a systematic, integrated, consistent methodology involving the entire organization. It emphasizes customer satisfaction (in the broadest sense of defining customers) and continuous improvement in every aspect of the system. The TQM philosophy emphasizes not only identifying and correcting defects, but most importantly, preventing them from occurring. Defects and variations to customer specifications are seen as losses under the TQM philosophy while consistency is viewed as the goal.

Total Quality Environmental Management is a derivative of TQM that uses many of the TQM methods and applies them to the environmental component of product and service delivery. TQEM was coined in April 1990 by the Global Environmental Management Initiative (GEMI) to foster environmental excellence corporatewide. GEMI's goal, developed at this 1990 conference, was "to promote a worldwide business ethic for environmental management and sustainable development, to improve environmental performance of business through example and leadership, and to enhance the dialogue between business and its interests."[17] GEMI identifies the basic elements of TQEM as follows:

- Identify your customer.
- Focus on continuous improvement.
- Do the job right the first time.
- Take a systems approach.

Like TQM, TQEM is a philosophy of focusing on customer needs and expectations, management commitment, a management system, and continuous improvement. It can serve as a blueprint for an environmental quality plan that provides the tools and methods for planning, control, and improvement. TQEM has helped to shift the environmental management emphasis from a regulatory-driven, compliance-based approach to market-driven, customer-based methodologies. It involves creating environmental policies and objectives that are implemented through a well-formed, trained, and empowered work-force.[18]

ENVIRONMENTAL MANAGEMENT STRATEGIES

Developing an environmental management system (EMS) is usually the initial step in the process of instituting a formal TQEM approach. An EMS includes the overall strategies, policies, objectives, and organizational structure established to manage and sustain the business and its operations.

Commitment by senior management is vital to the process. Senior management must send a clear signal to all employees to encourage their involvement. According to Phillip Green of Cambridge Management, one of the most important tactics in mobilizing the commitment of the entire organization to environmental protection is to create a focus on the benefits of TQEM, which are backed by a clearly defined environmental management policy. He views improved productivity as one of the most significant benefits of TQEM. Likewise, the pursuit of quality can lead to the elimination of defects and wastes. Defects and wastes are non-value-added elements that lead to economic loss and environmental problems.

The most important strategic element of TQEM is the identification of cus-

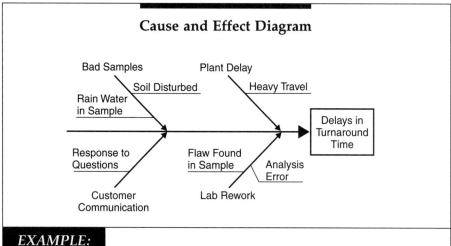

Cause and Effect Diagram

Bad Samples

Plant Delay

Soil Disturbed

Heavy Travel

Rain Water in Sample

Delays in Turnaround Time

Response to Questions

Flaw Found in Sample

Analysis Error

Customer Communication

Lab Rework

EXAMPLE:

A facility whose environmental managers complained that soil contamination analyses were taking too long to complete assembled a team to (1) arrive at a specification for turnaround time and (2) analyze the reasons for the existing turnaround time. The team first agreed on the major causes of the delayed turnaround time; then they constructed a diagram that listed the detailed causes contributing to each major factor.

Figure 8-8 Sample Tools in TQEM Decision Making: Cause and Effect Diagram

Source: GEMI's *Total Quality Environmental Management: The Primer,* 1993.

tomer and stakeholder requirements. As Richard Wells states, "the vision for both TQM and TQEM programs… is to add value to customers and thereby contribute to shareholder value. In TQEM, this means satisfying not only product customers, but also our internal customers and external stakeholders."[19]

The process of TQEM requires an ongoing management commitment to review operations, processes, and policies to ensure that they are in concert with overall business goals. Problems are identified and solved through a systematic approach that focuses on the long term. GEMI, and others, have developed new tools and modified traditional TQEM tools to enable such management review to occur. These tools (see Figure 8-8) allow environmental managers and senior management alike to identify current or potential problems with their environmental management systems and take corrective action. These types of tools and mindset have allowed companies like AT&T to go beyond their regulatory requirements and identify business opportunities through cost avoidance (efficiency) and revenue enhancement (effectiveness).

NOTES

17. Global Environmental Management Initiative, *Total Quality Environmental Management: the Primer,* 1993.
18. Green, Phillip E. J., "Environmental TQM," *Quality Process,* Vol. 26, 1993.
19. Wells, Richard, "Why We Need Value-Added Environmental Management," *Total Quality Environmental Management,* Summer 1995.

CHAPTER

Management Information Systems and Environmental Management

THE WHEEL OF CORPORATE DECISION MAKING: INFORMING THE EXECUTIVE

Regulatory pressure and financial constraints can fetter corporate environmental management to compliance requirements, limiting the integration of environmental concerns and business opportunities. Achieving these compliance requirements is hard and can consume the majority of a department's time. However, focusing on mere compliance prevents the discovery of strategic value in managing environmental issues—which may affect the bottom line. The result is similar when management tools such as information management systems are used solely to achieve compliance.

Used properly, information management systems enable environmental leaders to set goals and prioritize environmental expenditures for the greatest return, ultimately linking performance to shareholder value and customer loyalty. In the following pages, Knapp and Cervin's "Innovations in Environmental Information Management" discusses the use of information management tools to facilitate ongoing functions such as the accurate and timely processing of voluminous environmental monitoring data. Information management systems manage data on critical regulatory issues, allowing employees to make more informed decisions. The use of information management systems to achieve compliance requirements is crucial, but it is the extension of information technology to external communications and business development that will allow the systems to be beneficial.

Figure 9-1 presents an image of a firm's EH&S capabilities as a wheel, guided by the "hub" of strategy and supported by the functional "spokes" of an effective EH&S program (i.e., audits, environmental accounting).

164

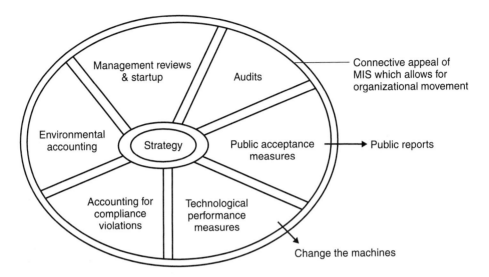

Figure 9-1 Management Information Systems

Source: Adapted by Piasecki and Chris Renaud for this text.

Management information systems are able to inflate this wheel with a flow of continuous information and connect these often-disparate functions.

According to the work of Deming and Juran, information management systems can be used to promote business advances through the improvement or innovation of processes or products. Knapp and Cervin's piece conveys the Health and Safety department practice of manually translating and disseminating information. In this example, an information management system assists in achieving compliance by allowing data to be entered and shared electronically. However, the lasting business value of the system lies in its other, more strategic uses.

Anthony Buonicore, CEO of Environmental Data Resources, states that data management systems can impact the five elements of a successful pollution prevention program: planning and organization; data collection; assessment; feasibility analysis; implementation. The value of the collected data lies in its application in establishing goals and prioritizing targets for pollution prevention alternatives and feasibility assessments. Feasibility studies are used to analyze the costs and benefits of alternatives by synthesizing data from purchasing, manufacturing, marketing, and research and development. Without an enterprisewide system, a proper feasibility statement would be too cumbersome. An information management system allows for an assessment of the pollution prevention alternatives, based on technical and economic criteria: emissions produced, current and anticipated regulatory requirements and the cost to meet them, cost per unit of product produced, and the financial implications of alternatives.[1]

Upon implementation, an information management system allows the firm to track the progress of the chosen alternative against a baseline, to measure performance against goals, and to implement corrective action. An information management system also allows upper management to align employees with corporate directives. Employees can view environmental policies, corporate objectives, and their responsibilities. According to Audrey Bamberger's essay in this chapter, engaging employees to create new business opportunities reaps important benefits: Ensuring regulatory compliance, identifying new opportunities for cost savings and cost reductions, and enhancing the corporate image.

Information management systems add value to a firm by improving the effectiveness of information flows. Data on prioritized pollution prevention targets, cost-benefit analyses, and progress toward goals are valuable kinds of information to use in a dialogue with investors and consumers. Investors gain insight into the financial and legal benefits of integrating environmental considerations into business, affirming the purpose behind change. Consumers witness an openness and social responsibility, usually allowing enhanced revenues through an appeal to new and more loyal customers.[2]

When properly utilized, an information management system enables leaders to become more effective change agents. Time formerly spent on compliance issues can be spent on analysis, research, benchmarking, and forecasting. At this level, information management systems allow leaders to discover opportunities that are not yet manifest, and to forestall error, to attain competitive advantage. To attain this advantage, an information management system must be used to add value to the firm, connecting the many functions of EH&S departments and enlightening decision making.

NOTES

1. Buonicore, Anthony, "The Role of Data Management in Developing Pollution Prevention Strategies," *Corporate Environmental Strategy,* Vol. 1, No. 1, 1993, p. 65.
2. Beyster, Mary Ann, "The Need for Integrated Information Technology," *Corporate Environmental Strategy,* Vol. 1, No. 3, p. 65.

Innovations in Environmental Information Management

Charles Knapp and Richard Cervin

Charles Knapp is currently Project Manager of Editorial Tools for Micromedex, Inc. Before this, Knapp was President of Environmental Health & Safety Management Systems, an ISO 14000 management, measurement, and Internet communication services firm. He has worked for a variety of businesses and government agencies in regulatory compliance and business management during the previous two decades, and has been a key architect of several successful business management software packages.

Richard Cervin is Consulting Manager for the EHS Venture Group of Andersen Consulting. During the previous two decades, he has worked with a wide variety of firms in selecting and building environmental, health, and safety business management software packages, as well as numerous business process reengineering and management consulting engagements.

At any meeting of environmental, health, or safety professionals, consultants and clients alike talk of the difficulties of dealing with information. The volumes of data and tasks of collection, accumulation, and record maintenance present formidable challenges. Fortunately, strategies and technologies can be applied by the individual and the organization, facilitating effective, proactive, performance-enhancing design and operations-management decisions that then lead to reductions in overhead and fines, improved planning and performance, and other benefits.

Corporate America has applied advanced techniques and technologies for managing many kinds of corporate and plant information. However, automation frontiers remain. Without a doubt, one of the least mature areas of business information automation is environmental, health, and safety performance management. One reason is that the business requirements have been very dynamic, particularly for the environmental portion of EH&S activities. Given the recent appearance and exponential growth of requirements, many professionals have found themselves in a continual catch-up mode, focusing much of their daily effort on project backlogs. Figure 9-2 recaps the major U.S. federal mandates and data requirements.[3]

INFORMATION MANAGEMENT ACTIVITIES AND THEIR BURDENS

EH&S performance management typically relies on five interrelated information management activities: knowledge acquisition; data warehousing; data mining; knowledge communication; and performance and compliance reporting.

Knowledge acquisition means the collecting of information. This includes including manual efforts, such as plan document preparation. It also includes automated electronic measurement, such as continuous emission monitoring.

Data warehousing is the activity of recording and maintaining knowledge in readily accessible repositories. Management activities include the coordination of information storage schemes across multiple environmental media, regulations, corporate departments, and facilities.

Data mining is the activity of selecting or sorting through the data warehouse knowledge repositories. For much of the twentieth century, this was either a manual task or, if computer-assisted, was in the domain of computer

Figure 9-2 Major U.S. Federal Mandates and Data Requirements

Time Frame	Focus	Compliance Requirements	Data Implications: Unstructured Data	Structured Data
1970s	Air, Rivers Workers	Planning permitting monitoring reporting	Planning documents, regulation text, chemical information (MSDS), maps and drawings	Monitoring and reporting: high transaction volume, low degree of manipulation and summation
1980s	Right to Know	Accounting, disclosure	"	Accounting and disclosure: high degree of summation
Early 1990s	Pollution Prevention Consolidated Enforcement	Multimedia pollution reduction	"	Accounting: more comprehensive tracking of transactions Disclosure: high degree of summation
Late 1990s on	Greenhouse-Gas Reduction, International Standards	Continuous emission monitoring, plans, audits	"	Monitoring: high transaction volume Permit compliance reporting: high degree of summation

programmers. Modern data mining tools enable a moderately skilled knowledge worker, such as an environmental engineer, to perform these activities without being dependent on computer programmer assistance.

Knowledge communication is the communication of information, such as material safety data sheets MSDS or emergency plan distribution, via paper or electronic means (such as corporate intranets or the Internet).

Performance and compliance reporting delivers quantitative information to management, shareholders, and regulators. You might regard this activity as a subset of knowledge communication. This activity is given special attention at this point in our discussion because it is such a prominent part of business management activities. In many cases the measurement parameters, printed forms, or electronic data interchange (EDI) formats are dictated by government regulations.

HYPOTHETICAL CASE STUDY: WHAT WILL WE FIND BEHIND YOUR DOORS?

Take a plant tour with us. On the eastern side of the plant is the Health & Safety office, with its collection of MSDS. It is an amazing collection—many sheets for several thousand commercially produced chemicals. The intention is to distribute MSD sheets to all workers for materials brought in from off site.

Clerks type MSDS information into one dedicated personal computer, generating printouts that list the important details in a standardized corporatewide MSDS format. Photocopies are sent throughout the plant. The information could be shared electronically. Why not? Neither the Health & Safety director nor the other department directors are willing or able to pay the cost of connecting Health & Safety to the plant computer network. So, this department remains an "island of automation."

Some companies distribute MSDSs solely via photocopies. Some companies such as this client prefer to minimize the worker training requirements on how to interpret the vastly varying formats and labels on third-party MSDSs, so they interpret the manufacturer's sheet and distribute their own standardized-format sheets. Other companies rely on electronic scanning, taking a digital snapshot of each page of a material manufacturer's MSDS. They may choose to use optical character recognition (OCR) software to convert the digital snapshot into text files, fully searchable by any worker's text search software.

Next to the MSDS computer is a stack of manufacturer's MSDSs, waiting to be entered or updated into the central MSDS repository. It takes fifteen to twenty minutes to type all the text, with about a third of this time spent translating from the MSDS text labels to the corresponding data entry fields which are specified on-screen in the PC MSDS software. For example, a published MSDS might specify "relative density," and the PC operator must intelligently pick out the corresponding PC field of "specific gravity." Once MSDSs are entered into the repository, it is time for distribution. Standardized MSDSs are printed from the PC, then photocopied and mailed to production (shop floor) departments. Given the task time requirements and available staffing, it took this firm more than a year to catch up with the backlog.

Then we walk over to the packaging plant. We see a binder of MSDSs, in the standardized company format. The binder only has sheets for about one-third of the products in actual use. (Fortunately, no OSHA inspectors have looked into the timeliness or completeness of the binder.)

We ask, "How are the SARA inventory and TRI release reports prepared?" The answer in this department is that estimates are prepared at year-end, and cross-referenced with regulated chemicals on the Title III List of Lists and corresponding MSDSs. The figures are sent to the front office, where the environmental director's staff summarizes most of the departmental figures and prepares compliance reports. Needless to say, this redundant work could be greatly minimized if this company had a shared, corporatewide repository containing the relevant "structured" information off of the manufacturer's MSDS, particularly the names and percentages of constituent chemicals. Without such sharing, it takes two environmental engineers four months, using paper and a home-grown PC spreadsheet. It is an expensive compliance reporting effort, but the engineers remain very proud of their spreadsheet.

Now we walk across the street to one of the several manufacturing buildings. U.S. SARA reporting on inventories and releases to the environment is a repeat of the previous scene. One difference here is that they ask the purchasing department for an annual printout of storeroom stocked-inventory levels, and a printout of purchases. They use paper and a PC, in this case with a stand-alone PC database software package (purchased for more than $10,000) that prints a Tier II and Form R report, which they send directly to the authorities. No information is shared with other departments, making this an "island of information."

Then we walk over to the construction department on the western edge of the plant. They use large quantities of regulated but not obviously hazardous materials—paints, lubricants, welding rod, and so forth. To assist in preparing inventory and emission reports, the construction department might ask the purchasing department for a printout of material usage, but most of their purchases never go through an electronic PO or inventory-receiving process. That is because they need orders fulfilled faster than the purchasing department can deliver, and most products that construction orders are not pre-listed on the purchasing department database. The construction and maintenance departments buy about 4,500 of the plant's 5,000 chemicals. And purchasing lacks the staffing to enter and maintain database information, unless the product is an office supply or one of the principal plant chemicals, purchased in bulk.

In addition, the receiving department cannot electronically log a product receipt if it is not in the purchasing database. The receiving department manager does not want to fix the problem, or process additional paperwork. The result is that most departments must do their own chemical ordering and receiving. So, when construction materials are received, invoices go to the accounts payable department. A check is cut, with no electronic record of what was received. Since little information is accumulated, this is what we call a "desert of information."

Another problem with the decentralized chemical receiving is that widely varying quality of materials management yields widely varying materials storage conditions, ranging from those that are in full regulatory compliance to those that not only are a compliance liability, but also are an accident waiting to happen. And few workers can tell you what kinds of storage conditions are safe or compliant with regulations. A storage-area fire is a real possibility.

Seeking a safer vantage point, we head up front to the Corporate Environmental Director's office in the executive building. We ask what the Director thinks of how business is being done. The answer is full of concern:

> We're doing the best we can, and we have a very dedicated crew in the field. But we spend so much time preparing regulatory reports and engineering plans. When I want to do some forward planning, it takes forever to collect any usable information from the field. We need more resources, but with our perpetual downsizing, it's not going to happen. Outside contractors can only help us so much in complying with changing regulations, and they are very expensive. I know we'll be fined more than we need.

This manager's concerns are common. The information-handling processes at many firms need a major overhaul.

In the late 1980s, many corporate officers and environmental specialists openly discussed their fear of personal (as well as corporate) penalties for compliance failures. In the middle 1990s a new air of fatalism became widespread. For example, the *National Law Journal* surveyed 233 corporate attorneys with firms having annual revenues in the $50 million to $10 billion range. Sixty-seven percent said their companies violated environmental laws in the previous year. Moreover, 67 percent also said that they believe that full compliance is impossible.[4]

Today we rarely have less concern over governmental enforcement. Part of the reason is, of course, due to increasing levels of corporate compliance, and decreasing backlogs dictated by recent regulations. Nevertheless, the major objective expressed by many local environmental specialists is to keep up with the regulatory paperwork enough to keep their jobs. Stated another way, keeping one's job often outweighs personal desires for improved corporate environmental performance.

At the same time, the major objective of many corporate officers is to improve the competitive edge. Increasingly, the questions asked of senior environmental management are "How can we improve our bottom line? And how can we use environmental information management to improve our bottom line?"

FOUR FUNDAMENTAL INFORMATION MANAGEMENT STRATEGIES

Companies are now experimenting with four fundamental environmental information management strategies. What follows explores each approach at length; usually the mix that fits your culture works best:

1. Strategizing for proactive management
2. Reengineering business processes
3. Upgrading and deploying information technology across the enterprise
4. Planning for the full life cycle of information technology utilization

The assumption is that strategic use of MIS tools in environmental management can help to improve the corporate bottom line. Figure 9-3 illustrates what one large chemical manufacturer forecasts as the U.S. return on investments in these strategies.[5]

These changes are far more comprehensive than traditional, incremental quality improvement programs. One author calls this "reengineering the corporation," while another refers to it as "process innovation," and yet another calls it a "paradigm shift."[6] The objective is an improvement not just in efficiency, but also in effectiveness. The key question is "What is the desired end?"

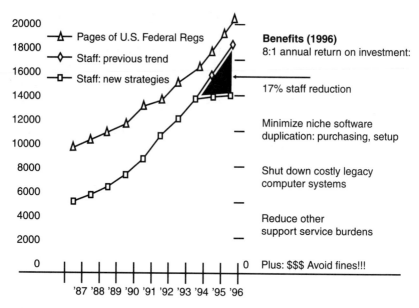

Figure 9-3 Manufacturer's Return on Investment

Source: A large U.S. chemical manufacturer.

As Steven Covey phrases it in *First Things First*, it is not a matter of doing things better, but rather a matter of doing better things.[7]

Strategizing for Proactive Management

The objective here is to facilitate proactive tasks, while continuing to perform traditional tasks. It involves careful planning of technology deployment, utilization, and support. It typically necessitates upgrading technology from the common standalone solutions to newer technology.

The primary step in creating a strategic MIS involves assessing existing business processes. Whether the manufacturing activity is process oriented or discrete (finished products can be disassembled into components), whether continuous or batch, a modeling of MIS issues helps create a broader vision of how these information systems will enhance the company. Figure 9-4 illustrates the variety of business activities and issues.

In sum, environmental information systems must support business management. They must be able to deal with a wide variety of manufacturing activities, and they also must support proactive management that goes beyond the goal of achieving compliance and toward the goal of integrating environmental concerns with the core business (see Figure 9-5).

The management transformation leverages advanced information technologies to integrate across the enterprise, encompassing geography, organizations, and information systems. The products employed yield enterprisewide

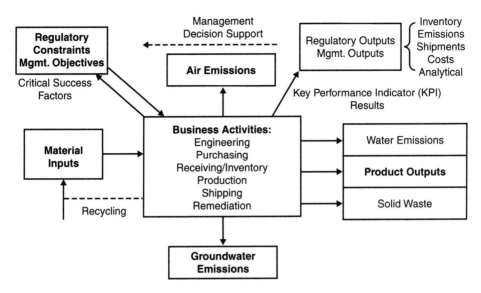

Figure 9-4 Typical Process Model

information warehouses, viewable by dynamic decision-support tools. As a result, information from disparate locations, departments, and information repositories is leveraged for proactive management.

A key step is to define the desired ends. For example, the managers of the companies mentioned in the hypothetical case study decided that they wanted a corporatewide environmental information system, one that could meet both

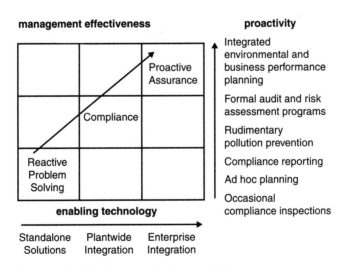

Figure 9-5 Enabling Technology and Effectiveness

the needs in the field for generating compliance reports and the needs of management for a corporatewide overview of environmental performance. They concluded from feasibility surveys that there are suitable commercial products, so custom software development was unjustifiable. They also decided that this new information system should share information with existing plant systems; links would be built during package deployment.

Reengineer Business Information Processes

Companies are reexamining how environmental information is handled and looking for opportunities to make major changes and improvements in workflow processes. This task goes hand in hand with the related task of planning for proactive management. It involves identifying relevant corporate objectives and processes, then redesigning workflows to better fulfill the objectives, a process that can only enhance management's ability to meet its mandated tasks and devote time to forward-thinking proactive projects. As a result, there is an effective match between business processes and corresponding information (see Figure 9-6).

Reengineering is dramatically different from quality management. It is ambitious, aiming for order-of-magnitude improvements in key performance measures, such as compliance report accuracy and days to prepare and submit reports. It focuses on processes from an individual's viewpoint, unconstrained by functional and organizational boundaries. It engages in creative rule-breaking, finding and challenging fundamental assumptions about normal business practice. Its objectives are to identify and address genuine needs. It utilizes information technology to enable new ways of working, rather than acting as a driver of

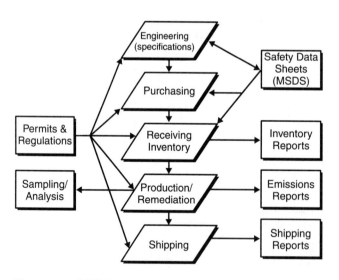

Figure 9-6 MIS Reengineering of Business Processes

incremental change through substitution and automation. In sum, reengineering facilitates effective change by examining people, processes, and technology.

There are three key caveats in this effort. First, almost no one truly wants reengineering. Resistance to change is inevitable. Second, some corporate managers have given reengineering a bad name by focusing on staff and cost reductions, rather than process reengineering. Third, failure to anticipate and deal with these issues will doom a reengineering effort.

The reengineering effort extends beyond analysis. A successful effort will educate and communicate, turning the "changees" into positive, supportive change agents. The effort will encourage innovation, through means such as brainstorming and other "what-if" activities. The effort will seek integration with nonenvironmental business processes, such as simulation and forecasting or operations control.

In the hypothetical case study referenced earlier, the company wished to adopt a multiplant environmental tracking and reporting system. Examining workflows revealed that there was a desert of information, whereby no records existed for most of the materials purchased. It turned out that three-fourths of the plant chemical purchases were not trackable in current workflows, even though supporting information systems were operational. To alleviate this problem, chemical receiving (except for labs) was centralized at a single Chemical Receiving building, and lab chemical suppliers agreed to provide monthly electronic summaries of telephone orders shipped. As a result, all chemical receiving transactions were recorded into the plant materials management inventory system. In addition, the Health & Safety department agreed to better maintain the MSDS database. Together these steps lead to a major improvement in the completeness and accuracy of the company's MSDSs, inventory tracking, and usage reporting.

Upgrade Professional Skills

For most EH&S professionals, there was little demand for information management skills in the 1970s through the early 1990s, despite the proliferation of the corporate personal computer. In this period, many traditional environmental compliance managers and engineers did not appreciate the value of acquiring personal information technology skills or tools in assuring regulatory compliance and optimizing business management. In the late 1990s, this picture is changing.

One key driver is the proliferation of inexpensive, easier-to-use personal computers. A second key driver has been the continual reorganizing and downsizing of the 1990s. Many displaced EH&S professionals found that their engineering or scientific or regulatory expertise alone is insufficient to deal with changing business needs given an oversupply of applicants, and as a result spend a surprising amount of time before landing new work.

Some have called this an illustration of the need to continually retool your professional skills. Author Daniel Burrus calls this retooling "reengineering yourself."[8]

For example, one EH&S engineer with a major railroad became so adept at information management that he was promoted to director of EH&S. How? Not by becoming a "programmer." Rather, he learned to mine corporate data repositories (including cost information not owned by the EH&S department) to quickly find answers to management questions. His manager looked good as a result. When the manager was promoted for superior business management, my friend filled the newly vacant slot. His new skill created new professional opportunities.

One information management tactic to consider involves interconnecting the data of environmental systems with plant and corporate information systems. Devising electronic connections with nonenvironmental systems storing related kinds of information, such as purchasing, can also boost bottom-line efficiency. Interconnecting systems in this way can transform environmental information into a strategic corporate asset. Another interconnection that is commonly desired is to connect environmental decision support tools with corporate electronic mail and fax facilities, usually triggered by monitoring the data warehouse for specified conditions (such as a sample measurement close to or exceeding a permit limitation). This speeds the responses to business problems, such as a processing-equipment failure.

This tactic creates data interfaces, where information in one functional repository, such as production, is cross-referenced with related information residing elsewhere, such as in an environmental system. One benefit is that information can usually be entered and maintained in one place, minimizing redundant labor. Another benefit is that information can be collected and viewed from across a number of disparate functional repositories, and perhaps distributed geographically across a number databases in a number of locations.

For EH&S professionals, one specific advantage of open (nonproprietary) databases over previous technologies is that the open architecture and standard query languages facilitate using add-on software packages for a variety of input and output functions, such as continuous emission monitoring, pollutant dispersion modeling, and electronic data interchange.

There are a number of issues, however, that must first be addressed in order to effectively integrate data:

Levels of Interchange

To *interface* or to *integrate*, that is the question. Truly integrating data can imply extensive redesigning and rebuilding of multiple information systems. In many cases, the more cost-effective approach is to build data interfaces, such as copying transactions (selected, common fields only) between systems.

Interchange Triggers

When should data be exchanged, based on specified *events*, or specified *chronological intervals*? For example, some databases allow the creation of event-driven "trigger" programs, such as notifying a specified user when a sample measure exceeds environmental permit limits. For example, an event-trigger-enabled database could read and record air stack emission parameters every fifteen minutes.

Timeliness

Should interchange tasks be carried out immediately, one at a time (*real-time*), or grouped together for periodic (*batch*) processing? Answering the question involves the following three issues:

1. *Value over time:* How soon does a change in one system need to appear in another? immediately? within an hour? the next day?

2. *System performance:* How will either approach affect the user's workstation, and associated data warehouse servers? How long will the workstation or server be unavailable during the interchange operation (can be a critical issue with some mainframes)?

3. *Costs:* What are the costs for development and operation of each approach? For example, will one approach require an expensive server hardware upgrade in order to maintain satisfactory performance?

Openness

Are file structures readily understood? For example, do any of the package manufacturers provide a listing and diagrams of file structures? Some environmental software package manufacturers provide both hardcopies and electronic. Having open, readily understood and accessible file structures can dramatically speed the interchange development effort.

Are there any time constraints on when interchange can take place? Some mainframe databases, in particular, require all users to exit before performing data import or export activities.

Tools

This gets to the basic question of whether the software is user-friendly. Is there a great deal of programming and computer language required? Some database tools provide menu-driven trigger and procedure-building capabilities, helping knowledgeable super-users to quickly devise or update the trigger logic.

Integrate Across the Enterprise

This strategy is different from the approach taken in many environmental departments. Older commercial environmental software packages are difficult and expensive to connect with other company data repositories because the underlying database technology was meant for standalone or departmental use and often uses proprietary (closed) architectures. Today, packages using more advanced, open database technologies designed for multidepartmental, enterprisewide automation are becoming available.

In our case study, open systems were deployed across all plants. These systems were interconnected with purchasing and receiving systems. Redundant data entry was minimized, information entered in one field location could be readily shared with other locations, and management was assured of common field approaches and similar environmental performance.

One end product from the reengineering effort was the set of systems linking information warehouses, organizations, and facilities, as depicted in Figure 9-7.

Deploy Across the Enterprise

Companies can leverage their investment by addressing the needs both of the field and of corporate management. Utilizing the approaches detailed above, field personnel are able to accumulate, retrieve, and manipulate information as needed. This helps in a variety of ways, such as fulfilling worker right-to-know requirements, generating plant-specific regulatory compliance reports, and empowering field workers to readily respond to emergencies. Corporate needs often entail the summation of field data, enabling comparisons by location to plans and objectives. Our case study is a good illustration of planning for deployment from the bottom to top. A detailed implementation plan was put in place, focusing first on populating the data warehouse with referential

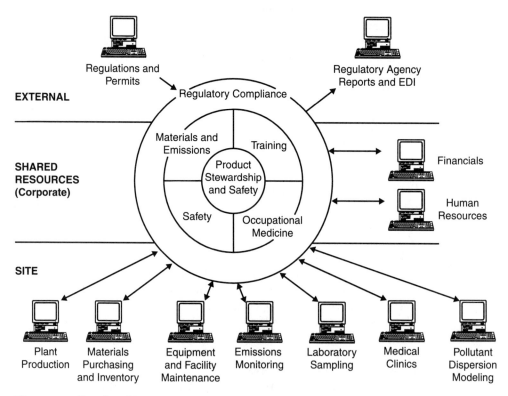

Figure 9-7 Results of Reengineering

setup information, then on capturing appropriate transaction information from daily operations. The final phase focused on training field personnel and corporate managers respectively on how to use the compliance reporting, decision support, and ad hoc data mining tools for their varying needs.

Plan for the Full Life Cycle of Information Technology Utilization

Many companies select environmental software in a manner more resembling the purchase of a word processor than a financial or tax-compliance package. As a result, many crucial issues, such as staffing and infrastructure, are inadequately resolved. For example, the company in our preceding case study had a one-year backlog on distributing MSDSs.

Using the deployment of a software package as an example, the first item of business is to identify what should be implemented initially and what should come later, and at which locations. This is commonly assessed by identifying key outputs (such as highest priority regulatory reports), and then identifying key inputs and any software-mandated order of set-up and testing.

Successful implementation of a package requires considerable analysis of the issues raised in defining data sources. These issues are important. They guide decisions as to what data will be captured, whether existing systems capture such data, where data will reside, how data will be accessed, and whether any existing processes need to be redesigned. These issues may validate existing processes (many of which are followed for regulatory compliance) or invalidate them, indicating a need for modification or elimination. Understanding these issues leads to a faster and more satisfactory deployment of the package.

Proven, advanced information management strategies are increasingly being used in a variety of business processes, including environmental, health, and safety operations. Approaches that reengineer and integrate systems can maximize effectiveness and efficiency to ultimately improve company performance. In support of this effort, a wide variety of software products are commercially available today. As a result, companies have leveraged their environmental information to better manage the core business, while simultaneously minimizing the commonly excessive burdens of information and systems maintenance. Restated, the net result of innovative information management approaches and skills is that environmental professionals have ready access to the information they need in order to make effective, proactive, performance-enhancing design and operations-management decisions. This will become more common in the next century.

NOTES

3. Regulatory portion of table suggested by Chris Fitzgerald in the *Environmental Software Report,* Donley Technology, April 1992.
4. *Rocky Mountain News,* August 23, 1993, quoting a *National Law Journal* and Arthur Andersen Environmental Services study dated June 1993.

5. This information is based on confidential client interactions with the authors.

6. Hammer, Michael, *Reengineering the Corporation,,* Harper Business, 1993; and Thomas H. Davenport, *Process Innovation: Reengineering Work Through Information Technology,* Harvard Business School Press, 1993.

7. Covey, Stephen R., *First Things First: To Live, To Love, To Learn, To Leave a Legacy,* Simon and Schuster, New York, 1994.

8. Burrus, Daniel, *Reengineering Yourself: Using Tomorrow's Success Tools to Excel Today,* Simon & Schuster, New York, 1996. Also see Charles Knapp, "Reengineer Yourself," Environmental Software Report, Donley Technology, March/April 1997.

Information Challenges at Anheuser-Busch Corporation

Audrey E. Bamberger

Audrey E. Bamberger is a Senior MIS Business Analyst for Anheuser-Busch Companies in St. Louis, MO. She is working with Anheuser-Busch to develop and implement environmental information management strategy. Bamberger holds a Bachelor's degree in Computer Science from Wayne State University as well as a Master of Science degree from the Environmental Management & Policy program at Rensselaer Polytechnic Institute.

In 1997, Anheuser-Busch had worldwide beer sales of 96.6 million barrels. The company accounts for more than 8 percent of the world market and 45.5 percent of the U.S. market in brewery sales. In 1995, the company divested several businesses to focus on the brewing-related businesses. In alignment with this focus, the company owns packaging and theme park subsidiaries. The primary business of the packaging subsidiary is producing aluminum beverage cans and lids. In 1993, Anheuser-Busch began to respond to a set of complex information challenges indicated by Knapp in the previous essay.

The size and diversity of the Anheuser-Busch subsidiaries presents a special challenge for environmental information managers. Though focused on beer and entertainment, the information management requirements seem to end there. The variety of each of the subsidiaries requires that managers contend with diverse types of environmental management issues, including farming, anaerobic wastewater treatment, cogeneration of electricity, brewing, aluminum beverage container production, and wildlife and theme park management. Each facility has varying information needs and resources to apply to those needs, and varying degrees of environmental expertise.

At a brewery in New York State, a bioenergy recovery system converts wastewater byproducts to energy and at the same time provides environmental benefits to the entire community. On a farm in Florida, process water applied to acreage converts land into thick, rich grass and hay. At a can manufacturing plant in the Midwest, energy efficiency measures provide a competitive advantage by lowering overall production costs. At the brewing subsidiary, energy and water use are monitored and balanced with quality production needs. Nearly four million people annually visit a display of more than 12,000 fish, mammals, birds, reptiles, and invertebrates at Sea World in San Diego. Water splashed from the whale shows is cleaned and recycled back into multi-million-gallon life-support systems while visitors munch on snacks served on reusable trays.[9] What is the best way to capture such diverse environmental indicators in one reliable format?

STARTING WITH A COMMITMENT

In 1994, senior-level management formally added *Respect for the Environment* to the Anheuser-Busch Companies' Mission Statement[10] (see Figure 9-8). This priority on environmental responsibility is transforming environmental management from a reactive to a proactive mode, where issues are anticipated and holistically managed. The ultimate goal is to make every employee responsible for environmental compliance and to engage management participation in the process. The benefits for attaining this new, strategic goal are great: ensuring regulatory compliance, identifying new opportunity for cost savings and cost reductions, and enhancing the corporate image.

At Anheuser-Busch, achievement of a proactive position is occurring through the Commitment to Environmental Excellence (CTEE) program. Management participation is necessary as facilities can become proactive only through management commitment and a collaborative effort from all ranks of employees. Based on principles of total quality management, the CTEE program defines the pathway to environmental excellence as an effective,

---

At Anheuser-Busch, through all of our products, services, and relationships, our mission is to add enjoyment to life. Our behavior while working toward this goal will be guided by five fundamental beliefs:

- Exceeding customer expectations is our first priority.
- Quality has always been and will always remain our key competitive advantage—for products, people and services.
- Well-trained and motivated employees acting with the highest integrity are critical to our success.
- Responsible consumption of our beer products is in the best interest of society and Anheuser-Busch.
- Respect for the environment is a guiding principle in the conduct of our business.

Source: A-B Corporate Environmental Report, 1997.

Figure 9-8 Anheuser-Busch Mission Statement

integrated environmental management system. The success of the management system is dependent upon completion of three major actions:

1. Integrating environmental business needs into company core business activities

2. Incorporating environmental management objectives into the strategic goals of all subsidiaries

3. Finding the right information solutions to support these integrated business needs

THE INTEGRATION OF INFORMATION SUPPORT WITH BUSINESS NEEDS

Finding the right information solution requires an understanding of the overall corporate environmental objectives. In 1994, the company's senior-level Environmental Policy Committee approved an updated corporate environmental policy. This policy addresses expectations in employee and management accountability, integration of environmental considerations into business planning, requirements toward vendors and suppliers, and employing cost-effective methods to reduce the environmental impact of operations. The full EH&S Policy is shown in Figure 9-9.

To implement the policy, a specific set of Corporate Environmental Requirements was developed. These requirements transform the policy of environmental excellence into management guidelines that can be implemented. These are defined by three categories: environmental management, environmental performance, and environmental protection. Each requirement is based on regulatory and/or internal responsibilities. Internal requirements are responsibilities above and beyond mandatory regulations. In 1997, work began to enhance these requirements to include health and safety. Twenty EH&S requirements were approved in 1998 for implementation at all facilities; these are shown in Figure 9-10.

A LONG-TERM SOLUTION OPPORTUNITY

Information systems are vital support tools. Environmental processes, such as ensuring compliance, measuring performance, and monitoring regulations, require systems to collect and manage large amounts of data. Much of this required data exists in other business areas and systems outside of environmental. For example, managing emissions and hazardous waste reduction goals requires information from operations, purchasing, production planning, and environmental. Providing a system to manage environmental information forces the sophisticated analysis of other information systems, such as cost accounting, material management, production planning and control, quality management, plant maintenance, and human resources management. Anheuser-Busch's approach is to integrate environmental data and processes into the right business system.

Anheuser-Busch will uphold its position as a global leader by promoting environmental, health, and safety excellence. Through management leadership and employee involvement, Anheuser-Busch pledges to do the following:

Employees

- Create a safe and healthy workplace
- Build a respect for the environment
- Conform to the spirit as well as the letter of applicable laws and regulations and to the Company's EHS requirements
- Set EHS targets and measure progress toward them
- Integrate EHS considerations into business planning, decision making, and daily activities
- Provide the resources and training to carry out this policy

Community

- Prevent accidents and minimize environmental impacts
- Communicate our EHS performance
- Respond to our neighbors' concerns
- Support EHS public policy development
- Support wildlife and habitat conservation efforts
- Conserve resources and minimize waste by reducing, reusing, and recycling

Contractors, Suppliers, and Customers

- Encourage, support, and recognize EHS innovations
- Assist in the integration of EHS excellence into products and services
- Exchange EHS knowledge and technology

Shareholders

- Increase shareholder value through EHS excellence

Figure 9-9 Anheuser-Busch Companies, Inc. Environmental, Health, and Safety Policy

As environmental management systems are implemented at Anheuser-Busch, the corporate information system (IS) strategy must change to meet the demand. Historically, data processing departments met customer business information needs by providing standalone or partially integrated solutions—both being isolated approaches. The new information systems strategy focuses on total business systems integration. Projects are in development integrating the key functional areas of the company: financial, operational, and managerial. Major areas of the corporation have undergone business process analysis and redesign.

1. Management Systems
2. Employee Responsibilities
3. Property Management
4. Suppliers
5. On-Site Contractors
6. Product Stewardship
7. External Communications
8. Regulatory Relationships
9. Variance from Internal Requirements
10. Incident Response and Preparedness
11. Awareness and Training
12. Measurement and Improvement
13. Process Risk Reduction
14. Pollution Prevention and Resource Conservation
15. Capital Project and Process Change Review
16. Regulated Material Management
17. Transportation
18. Environmental Programs (air, water, wastewater, groundwater, waste management, stormwater)
19. Safety and Occupational Health Programs
20. Employee Medical Care and Wellness

Figure 9-10   Corporate EH&S Requirements

Source: A-B Corporate Environmental Report, 1997.

This information management strategy change provides a unique opportunity to help support the environmental management system by integrating environmental information needs into the corporate business systems of the future. The entire integration project is a multiyear challenge and presents a strategic opportunity for Anheuser-Busch. Without this level of integration, true environmental excellence would be elusive. Claudette Hennessey, regulatory project manager at Ciba-Geigy, echoes this imperative:[11]

> The rate of change of the [EH&S] regulations has been estimated at 40 percent a year if you count all sources; to put this into perspective, conventional computer science wisdom says to rebuild from scratch if more than 30 percent of the requirements change. Because we cannot trash our systems every year, we must develop requirement-absorbing processes that will allow us to identify and integrate changes, keep our business focus, and maintain our day-to-day output of tracking and reporting.

As seen in Charles Knapp's article, achieving flexible integration means designing environmental information systems around business processes. At Anheuser-Busch, this approach requires understanding environmental and other business process areas that control environmental data, such as cost accounting, material management, manufacturing, and operations. Achieving the vision of environmental excellence seems insurmountable without the enabling mechanism that information technology and business process understanding provide. For Anheuser-Busch to develop an environmental information systems plan, the first step was to define the environmental business processes.

DEVELOPING THE BUSINESS MODEL

In 1994, Anheuser-Busch began development of an environmental business process and data model. The model identifies and defines required data, ideal environmental business processes, and relationships between environmental and other business processes. Through a series of meetings, participants helped to define processes providing added value to the organization, such as removing redundant tasks and improving business process flows. The modeling sessions provided an opportunity for teams comprised of facility, subsidiary corporate, and corporate staff to reengineer business processes and document a standard blueprint for corporatewide environmental management.[12]

Once the teams defined enough of the model to anticipate some benefit, a technical team installed a "proof of concept" pilot at a selected facility. The pilot's main purpose was to prove that the idea of business process mapping could provide improvement and add value to the organization. A wastewater reporting process, previously an intensely manual one, was chosen as the pilot. The technical team developed and implemented a computer-based solution based on the defined business processes. Results included resource reductions, time savings, and improved data quality and accuracy. A survey conducted six months after pilot installation revealed an estimated monthly labor savings of over 100 hours.

The processes set the standards for best environmental, health, and safety practices. The business process model will be updated in the future to reflect the integration of health and safety with environmental business practices. The model links customer business needs and system requirements. Although the model identifies best business processes, it does not define everything to be automated. Technical analysts, together with development teams, evaluate automation as a potential enabler to implement the business processes. In some cases, benefits are achieved through business process improvement alone.

MOVING TOWARD THE VISION

The business process model provides information specific to environmental management. The next step was to apply information to move closer to achieve the vision of environmental excellence.

Figure 9-11 demonstrates the integration of corporate business and plant floor systems as an environmental management tool. Environmental information systems are integrated, whenever and wherever possible, with plant floor and business systems. On paper, complete integration of environmental requirements into business systems provides the ideal setting for environmental management. In a practical sense, however, resource constraints limit which environmental requirements are included into the business systems. Where a fully integrated solution cannot provide data needs, other environmental systems will be used. Building this network of information solutions requires a blueprint, the business process model. Where environmental requirements are not fully integrated into operational, managerial, manufacturing, or plant floor systems, interfaces are needed to complete these requirements transparent to the user.

At the center of the triangle is the environmental customer. This is the responsible person, trained in understanding business needs and corporate policy and their role in the system. This individual draws from all angles of the well-designed triangle such that he/she is specific to environmental management, not data management. Once achieved, all requirements that have been mapped in the environmental processes have their respective positions in the triangle.

The major lessons Anheuser-Busch has learned over the past three years encompass organizational needs, management issues, and human relations in the development of an integrated environmental management system. The most complicated issues and problems in a project this size are not as much technical hurdles as they are "people-related" issues. The following ten areas reflect that point:

1. Communication of the Vision

Management must set and commit to the communication of the environmental vision throughout the company. Employees have to believe that change is going to happen. At Anheuser-Busch, corporate distribution of the new

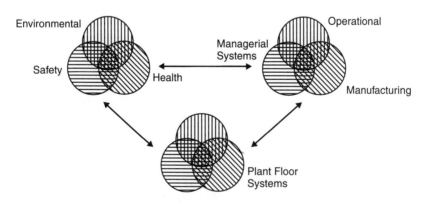

Figure 9-11 Managing Environmental Information

environmental policy and the updated Corporate Mission provide the highest level of support and commitment for the environmental management and information system changes taking place. These documents provide the foundation for helping all employees understand the importance of environmental responsibility.

Equally important is ongoing communication between corporate, facility, and information systems staff. Becoming familiar with the intent of the vision is the first step toward understanding and supporting implementation of the vision. Customers at all levels, from corporate to the facility, need to provide input to the requirements and the implementation of the processes. Project leaders need to ensure that this input is reflected genuinely in the direction of the management system and the implementation of the requirements. *Communicate, communicate, communicate;* this is ultimately the final bottom line.

2. The Journey to Integration

The journey to systems integration will be long. It's going to take awhile to bulldoze silos and replace them with the mechanisms to exchange and share information. Theory is easy to expound on, but results are harder to come by. We are anticipating those bumps in the road. And, if we're all aimed at the same target, we can succeed. But we cannot accomplish this at a corporate level alone. We need to be integrated with business strategy. Information systems support is vital to that end.

Here are some measures designed to make the journey a little less bumpy:

- Take the time to do it right.
- Define and understand the goals and objectives of the environmental management system.
- Define and understand the environmental business processes.
- Keep all relevant parties involved. Communication is vital.
- Provide interim, flexible information solutions that support the long-term goals of the organization.
- Set and keep moving toward the long-term target.

3. Commitment to Quality

Anheuser-Busch maintains a historical record on its commitment to quality and the environment. The goal of integrating environmental performance into the other business activities of the company is based on building quality into manufactured products. This ongoing corporate commitment to quality and continuous improvement provides a key component necessary to meeting the environmental information system challenge.

Quality systems development depends on having the right people committed to defining the business processes. Teams need to be comprised of individuals from all levels of the organization and from relevant departments, such as finance, legal, and operations. Team involvement shortens development time, contributes to system accuracy and efficiency, and helps secure customer buy-in. In addition, team development puts everyone on the same plane pointing toward the same target.

4. Satisfying Short-Term Needs

A vision and strategic plan are necessary to achieve environmental excellence. But defining the work in smaller pieces can provide quick, measurable results, thereby promoting success in high-priority areas and encouraging efforts to continue.

As Anheuser-Busch progresses toward the long-term solution of corporate business integration, project leaders still must address short-term information needs. Technology exists today enabling quick computer solutions to meet some of the pressing needs. The Environmental Quality Manual (EQM) mentioned in Figure 9-12 is a tool satisfying short-term needs. However, the company's short-term solutions must be aligned with long-term corporate business goals and the information strategies of the company.

The challenge to information managers is to implement a long-term information solution to help facilities maintain compliance with all environmental requirements. Corporate staff took the first step to meet this challenge and developed a PC-based EQM. The EQM is a one-stop toolbox performing four major functions. The EQM:

- Shows each facility how to comply with the corporate requirements through development and use of a customized EQM
- Tracks activities using a calendar feature
- Measures performance through a self-assessment tool
- Provides consistency and backup for facility environmental management in cases where regular staff is unavailable or replaced

In addition, the EQM provides a useful support tool for part-time staff who may be involved in other responsibilities besides environmental concerns. Anheuser-Busch is in the process of developing and implementing an EQM at each facility.

The EQM derives additional value from the platform where it resides—Lotus Notes groupware. In addition to the benefits the EQM provides, Lotus Notes solidifies the application by providing rapid application development and establishing communication links. With a minimal amount of training, developers can create simple, comprehensive systems designed for information exchange among users. Facilities may now connect to a central information storage device, eliminating the need for complex networks. In this way, the EQM platform becomes an electronic communication link between facility and corporate locations.

Source: A-B Corporate Environmental Report, 1997.

Figure 9-12 Meeting the Information Challenge via the EQM

5. Quantifying Costs and Benefits

Selling information solutions internally to the organization requires an understanding of both tangible and intangible benefits. Solutions must be cost effective and provide value. At Anheuser-Busch, internal customer needs are high priorities. Implementation of information solutions must provide benefits contributing either to pressing compliance needs and/or to the financial health of the company.

Projects must have established tangible and intangible measures, and be followed through with analysis and results. Implementation teams need to understand the benefits of process improvement with and without technology support. As projects proceed, some of the intangible benefits become more quantifiable through gains in understanding. Do not discount the costs or benefits of intangibles just because they are more difficult to identify; sometimes they become the biggest selling points.[13]

Speaking the language of business by communicating costs and benefits helps sell solutions internally. Customers need to understand that systems are not being implemented for the sake of technology or change but to provide benefit for the entire organization. Providing specific cost and labor savings brings more support to the project.

6. Side-Stepping Communications Barriers

Providing the best solution to environmental information management requires the efforts of environmental and information systems professionals. Achieving the solution means the two disciplines must learn how to communicate in common terms. Technical engineering and environmental terms can bring this gap in a variety of ways:

- Defining the business processes documents the environmental world in business and information technology language.
- Developing pilots and projects brings both disciplines together to discuss work on issues in understandable terms.

Crossing this communications barrier requires that each must take the initiative to learn about the other's discipline. Because solutions integrate business processes with technology support, this additional education contributes to a better understanding of relevant issues and applicable options.

7. Understanding Organizational Readiness

Accomplishing an environmental system integration strategy requires commitment by environmental and information systems management. This is a unique opportunity that does not take place often in large organizations. As organizations downsize, the challenge for remaining staff is to accomplish at least the same amount of work with less resources. The new requirements of the environmental management system place even more responsibility on staff. Information systems can help relieve some of the pressure. The entire organization needs to be ready to successfully meet the challenge of integration. One well-intentioned individual or department alone cannot achieve the massive and far-reaching business and thought-process change that is required to effectively succeed.

8. Supporting Changing Roles

The approach to environmental management at Anheuser-Busch creates new roles and opportunities for everyone in the organization. The new management system challenges corporate, subsidiary corporate, and facility staff to shift to proactive management activities. While corporate personnel need to provide expertise and more useful support tools, facility environmental staff are challenged to maintain compliance and build continuous improvement into their work. This means providing value-added solutions supporting environmental tasks and enabling staff to shift from reactive to proactive activities.

Information professionals need to develop a keen business knowledge of the organization, a clear understanding of environmental customers' business needs, and an understanding of technical solutions. Providing value-added information solutions that support corporate business objectives and departmental needs requires this cross-education.

9. Breaking Down Old Information Silos

This may well be the most difficult obstacle to overcome. To provide value, information needs to be shared. Building departmentally-oriented systems encourages data isolation. Understanding environmental business processes and the relationships among core business processes is fundamental to avoiding this trap. In addition, it takes information management one step closer to supporting the entire organization. The individuals of an organization have to want to break down those silos. This is difficult, especially if the silo happens to report to you.

10. Converting the Fear of Change to the Excitement of a Challenge

> Change has considerable psychological impact on the human mind. To the fearful it is threatening because it means that things may get worse. To the hopeful it is encouraging because things may get better. To the confident it is inspiring because the challenge exists to make things better.[14]

These poignant words are over thirty years old, but they still reflect the attitudes of today. Automation, to some individuals, provokes pictures of unwieldy, data-hungry monsters. These systems are more apt to add work to the day than provide help and support. Overcoming this resistance requires communication, interaction, and proper planning.

Management sets the direction for change. Employees' understanding of the need for change has to overcome their comfort level with the status quo.

In addition, a planned, positive approach to change inspires the confidence to help employees deal with change.

CONCLUSION

At Anheuser-Busch, the new approach is corporatewide business process integration to manage environmental information. The company can meet these challenges by focusing on quality, business process reqiurements, and the right application of technology. J. William Sugar, Senior Director of Environmental Affairs, is cautiously optimistic about these solutions:

> Long-term integration is a great opportunity, but we can't put everything on hold while we wait for a system. At the same time, we can't make this too grandiose that people won't get it or bring on overwhelming challenges too fast and risk failure. We need a balanced solution that builds on our ultimate goal of total integration.[15, 16]

NOTES

9. Anheuser-Busch Companies, Inc. *Corporate Annual Report,* St. Louis, Missouri, 1997.

10. Busch III, August A., Chairman of the Board and President, Anheuser-Busch Companies, Inc. From an excerpt in an employee-awareness video released in conjunction with Earth Day, April 1995.

11. Hennessy, Claudette, "The Clean, Green Information Machine," *Chemtech,* November 1993, pp. 16–22. Ms. Hennessy is Regulatory Project Manager at Ciba-Geigy.

12. Interview by the author of John L. Stein, Director of Strategic Environmental Initiatives at Anheuser-Busch.

13. Savings are based on post-implementation reviews conducted six months after initial system implementation at the facility.

14. Quoted in *Wall Street Journal,* June 7, 1967. King Whitney, Jr. President, Personnel Laboratory, Inc. Remarks at a sales meeting.

15. Interview by the author of J. William Sugar, Senior Director of Environmental Affairs at Anheuser-Busch.

16. The author wishes to thank the following individuals for their contributions toward this piece: Bill Sugar, Jack Stein, Lynn Murdoch, and Leslie Migliozzi.

QUESTIONS FOR FURTHER THOUGHT

1. Think about the various business functions of a manufacturing firm. What kinds of environmental information could be useful internally to the staff of chemical manufacturers? of other manufacturers (as chemical consumers)?

2. What kinds of business environmental information could be useful internally to the staff of government regulatory compliance agencies?

3. What are some computerized information repositories you might expect to find within a manufacturing firm, particularly among various business functions?

4. What kinds of environmental information could be calculated from performance metrics about daily manufacturing business operations?

5. What kinds of environmental information about a particular business might be useful to distribute to the public (including stockholders and plant neighbors)?

6. What are some means a business might employ to distribute information to the public?

7. What kinds of computer skills are needed for managing a business's environmental information?

8. Given the continual introduction of new information technologies and products, what are some useful criteria for deciding whether a new technology is worth the investment?

INTEGRATIVE CASE II

Extending the Umbrella of Social Concern: Volvo's Strategic Approach to Environmental Management

Sandra Rothenberg and John Maxwell

Sandra Rothenberg is a doctoral candidate in the Organization Studies program at the Sloan School of Management, MIT. As a research associate with the International Motor Vehicle Program and MIT's Technology, Business and Environment Program, she has studied corporate management of environmental issues for the past five years, with a focus on the automobile industry.

James Maxwell, Ph.D., is the director of the Center for Environment and Health at John Snow Inc. and a visiting scholar at MIT's Center for International Studies. He previously served as co-director of MIT's Technology, Business and Environment Program, and has written and consulted extensively on environmental policy and management issues.

In the late 1980s, Volvo CEO Pehr Gyllenhammar and other top managers believed that heightened environmental pressures directly threatened the survival of Volvo's products. Gyllenhammar had recognized the conflict between environmental protection and Volvo's products as far back as 1972, when he declared: "Volvo does not wish to protect the auto at any price and under all conditions. It is in Volvo's best interest that the auto is used in such a way that it does not cause environmental damage."[1] It was not until a decade later, however, that Volvo expanded its commitment to environmental protection.

This policy is unique in both its breadth and its early emergence in the field of environmental management. Cornelius Smith, Vice President for Environmental Affairs at Union Carbide, would later describe Volvo's policy as being among the most progressive corporate environmental policies that he had ever come across.[2] It preceded similar moves by many other leading companies, and also preceded the formulation of such industry initiatives as the Coalition for Environmentally Responsible Economies, the Chemical Manufacturers Association's Responsible Care Program, and the International Chamber of Commerce's Business Charter for Sustainable Development.

By establishing this new policy, Gyllenhammar sought to make environmentally conscious operations, like safety, a cornerstone of Volvo's corporate strategy and image. This meant developing a comprehensive approach to address the total life-cycle impacts of Volvo's products. The policy called for Volvo to strive continuously to reduce the environmental impacts of its products and manufacturing processes and mandated that the company go beyond applicable regulations to improve environmental performance. To implement this progressive policy, Volvo created a variety of new organizational structures and management systems.

Positioning Volvo for Change

Volvo was incorporated in 1915 as a subsidiary of AB SKF, a Swedish ball-bearing manufacturer, and in 1935 it became an independent company. Today, the Volvo Group consists of four product companies: Volvo Car Corporation, Volvo Trucks and Busses, Volvo Penta (marine and industrial engines), and Volvo Flygmotor (aircraft and space engines), with cars, trucks, and buses as its largest operating sector. Under the leadership of Pehr Gyllenhammar, Volvo's business strategy has been to focus on niche markets. With a reputation for safety, quality, and durability, Volvo has targeted a number of high-end niche markets, and has traditionally held a strong and relatively stable position. Intense competition in the early 1990s threatened Volvo's position in these markets, and several changes have been undertaken to address these problems. Organizational changes, such as the consolidation of the truck and bus divisions, have been instituted to make more efficient use of Group resources. Joint ventures and alliances have reduced the cost of research and development.

Volvo's activities have always been strongly influenced by the social commitments of its leaders. Gyllenhammar expanded the scope of the group's social commitments beyond product safety, a focus as far back as 1927, to include workplace issues. Explains one employee, "If one were to go back to the 1970s, a young Pehr Gyllenhammar came into Volvo. He was very interested in the 'quality of life' and made several dramatic moves to increase the quality of Volvo work life . . . . His fundamental concern was with the compatibility of industry with humanity." Gyllenhammar introduced new manufacturing systems at two of Volvo's automobile plants to address these concerns. Although some questions remain as to whether these new systems offer either the human fulfillment or productivity that can be found when using alternative production techniques such as lean production, Gyllenhammar's actions have inspired the people at Volvo to be concerned about worker safety and job satisfaction.[3] With the announcement of the new environmental policy, Gyllenhammar further extended Volvo's umbrella of social concern.

Volvo has a long history of environmental activity, and was one of the first industrial manufacturing corporations in the world to adopt a formal environmental policy.[4] Until the mid-1980s, the primary emphasis of Volvo's environmental strategy was compliance with applicable regulations. It had some notable achievements in this regard, such as the development of the three-way catalytic converter with Lambda Sond. During the course of the 1980s, a general growth in environmental awareness in Sweden and throughout the world alerted Volvo managers to the elevated importance that environmental issues would exert on business decisions.

Even more important, Volvo managers were strongly influenced by local changes in environmental activism. In the mid-1980s, Volvo applied to the Swedish Licensing Board for Environmental Protection for a permit to expand the Torslanda paint shop, its largest paint shop in Sweden. Volvo's environmental activity was subject to unprecedented scrutiny. Environmentalists also protested Gyllenhammar's active support of the "Scan Link," a road and railroad running from Oslo down the West Coast of Sweden to Denmark. Thousands of seals were dying in the North Sea off the coasts of Sweden; environmental concerns were rated the number-one political issue; and for the first time members of the Green party were elected to the Swedish Parliament. Angry environmentalists directly confronted Volvo, Sweden's largest corporation, about its environmental record.

As Volvo's top managers faced this change in the salience of environmental issues to the public, they became aware of the need for environmental action within Volvo that went beyond compliance. Gyllenhammar decided Volvo should expand its commitment to environmental protection. Remembers Inge Horkeby, Manager of Environmental Protection in Volvo's Technical Development Department, "Gyllenhammar heard [the changing interests from the public] and realized that we have to have our own goals in the future. It was a way for him to manifest a true conviction that industry had to show the way and to find a . . . better image for the company. We were not the ones trying to back off from our responsibilities. We wanted to fix them." "Fixing" these problems early and communicating these actions to stakeholders could also give Volvo competitive advantage.

A New Environmental Strategy that Reshapes Volvo

In October 1988, Gyllenhammar formed an Environmental Task Force, whose members included the top managers of each Volvo Company. The Task Force was charged with creating an environmental policy for the Volvo Group and programs to implement this policy.

One goal of Volvo's environmental strategy was to increase its legitimacy and credibility in the environmental arena. This first required gaining control of and improving Volvo's environmental performance. Gyllenhammar had already begun to "sell" Volvo in Sweden on its environmental performance; he had observed that although Volvo was working hard on environmental issues, it could not effectively communicate what it was doing. Gyllenhammar felt that he had to have stronger evidence to back the claims that he and Volvo were making.

At the same time, managers realized the competitive opportunities presented by environmental issues, and, as they already had with safety, wanted to build environment into a "cornerstone" of the company. Explains Olle Boethius, Manager of Environmental Affairs at Volvo Car Corporation, "At the time of the policy, we had to define our own strategy. We had to decide whether or not our environmental activities should be used to profile the company." In other words, it was a matter of whether environmental issues should be used commercially, and, if so, how the company should present itself with regard to these issues. Volvo decided to develop a unique company environmental profile, as had previously been done with safety. If, however, Volvo managers were going to claim that they "cared" about the environment, it was necessary to be able to back up these claims.

The Task Force designed the environmental policy to implement these ambitious strategic goals. Volvo pledged to take a "total view" with respect to the environment, which meant considering environmental impacts over the product life cycle. This required that the company look beyond its own walls to suppliers, distributors, and even customers, and required that they actively communicate with these stakeholders about Volvo's environmental activities. A credible image also requires consistency in environmental performance across geographic areas. Therefore, Volvo pledged to strive for a uniform, worldwide environmental standard for process and products.

Given the ambition of this strategy, the Task Force placed these goals in the financial and product constraints of the organization. To accommodate financial constraints, the Task Force decided that while the company had sufficient resources, it should "opt for manufacturing processes that have the least possible impact on the environment," and invest in environmentally oriented activities to the greatest extent possible. If the financial situation were reversed, however, the statement allows for an appropriate modification of environmental activities.

Matching the Ambition with a New Management System

Once this strategy had been developed, programs needed to be designed to implement it. In 1989, the Task Force produced a report that described Volvo's new environmental policy and programs for implementing this policy. The report outlined guidelines based on a list of management initiatives created by Gyllenhammar and given to the Environmental Task Force.

The management choices made by Volvo can fit into six generic areas:

1. Procedures and structures for environmental policy
2. Mechanisms to monitor and review environmental performance
3. Incentives and controls to encourage environmental achievements
4. Methodologies and tools to assist environmental decision making
5. Guidelines for environmental investments
6. Guidelines for communication with stakeholders

These categories are outlined in Figure II-A.[5] Within each of these categories, companies can choose from a variety of options. Volvo's managers realized that the company could not completely live up to their new commitments within existing systems for environmental management; therefore the Task Force outlined several programs to implement its environmental strategy.

Procedures and Structures for Setting Internal Environmental Goals

The Task Force Report detailed new mechanisms for the Volvo companies to set dynamic internal goals. Long-term environmental goals are set in three- to five-year plans (the length depends on the company's own planning cycle), reviewed and updated yearly. Using these long-term plans as guidelines, one-year goals are then set and revised annually. These plans and goals can cover such areas as production and product performance, information gathering and dissemination, environmental training, overall management structure and programs, internal and external communication, and public relations. The goals, explains Ulf Jansson, Environmental Manager in Product Engineering at Volvo Car Corporation, are explicitly meant to push Volvo ahead of regulations. "We could just say 'meet all the legal requirements and nothing more.' Then we wouldn't need the minimum standards. We have decided to go further."

Each section of the Volvo Group, including divisions like the Data Group, is required to participate in the planning process. Goals are set at each level of the organization. While top managers in each subsidiary set broad long-term goals for their company,

Figure II-A   Choices in Environmental Management

PROGRAMMATIC CATEGORIES	
Procedures and structures for environmental policy	A structure for environmental management helps firms to internalize and meet their regulatory and more proactive environmental goals. In addition, this helps to allocate environmental responsibility, specify the flow of internal and external information, and offer guidelines on how to carry out environmental activities.
Mechanisms to monitor and review environmental performance	The potentially severe consequences of poor environmental performance necessitates accurate monitoring of environmental achievement. Two main mechanisms accomplish this: direct reporting of environmental activity and environmental auditing.
Incentives and controls to encourage environmental achievement	Incentives and controls are important to emphasize commitment to environmental performance, and to encourage employees to perform in a manner consistent with this commitment. Incentives recognize and reward environmental achievements, innovations, and programs in order to motivate employees. Control mechanisms assess environmental performance in performance evaluations.
Guidelines and tools for environmental investments	Environmental investments frequently do not offer short-term financial pay-backs when evaluated by traditional accounting procedures. Financial guidelines suggest how managers can consider such benefits as long-term financial savings and avoid costs when making environmental investments. Tools to help evaluate environmental performance in financial terms can be created.
Methodologies and tools to assist environmental decision making	One of the most difficult tasks of environmental management is to assist employees making decisions about complex environmental issues. To reduce uncertainty in environmental decision making, companies can employ tools to help evaluate the environmental impacts of product and process decisions, systems to record company activities and their associated risks, or standard operating procedures to guide employees when performing environment-related tasks.
Guidelines for communication with stakeholders	To ensure external support of the environmental strategy, managers have to communicate with company stakeholders. These programs could include participation in environmental debates and financial support of environmental activities.

Source: Rothenberg S., J. Maxwell, and A. Marcus for *Business Strategy and the Environment* (see Note 5 for full citation)

managers at the project level set both three- and five-year goals and very specific one-year minimum standards.

The Task Force Report also outlined a new decentralized organizational structure in which Group companies could set their internal goals. The new structure included a small corporate-level environmental group and environmental offices in each of the product companies,. This structure served several purposes for Volvo. First, it offered a forum in which environmental goals and decisions could be made and discussed. Second, along with the established reporting procedures, the structure facilitated the review of environmental activity, and would ensure that this activity was consistent with company and Group goals and policies. Third, the structure specified who in the company is responsible for environmental activities.

The president of each company, for example, holds responsibility for implementing the environmental policy. This is important because it clarified the legal and corporate responsibilities for Volvo's environmental performance, giving Volvo a greater amount of control over its environmental activities.

Review of Company Achievement and Group Consistency

The new environmental structure served as a mechanism to ensure that companies and divisions are meeting their internal goals and living up to the spirit of the Volvo policy. Yearly achievements at each level of the company are compared to the minimum standards set the year before and are then reported to a higher level in the company for assessment. In addition, The Task Force developed an environmental auditing program as another mechanism to follow up minimum standards and three- to five-year plans.[6] There is one permanent auditor who selects an audit team from a pool of about 20 employees throughout Volvo, depending on their area of expertise. This auditing structure was selected for three main reasons: (1) it would be small and flexible; (2) it would use experts within the organization, leading to a more effective audit; and (3) it would allow auditors to disseminate information about observed environmental performance throughout the organization.

Like the usual concept of an environmental audit, Volvo's internal audits serve to ensure that regulatory requirements are being met. For the most part, however, the audit team concentrates its activities on upcoming legislation and the plant and companies' own internal minimum standards. Environmental management and routines are also scrutinized to ensure that environmental responsibilities are delegated in a competent manner. To date, 38 of the 41 Volvo plants have been audited.

In 1994, the Board decided to start preparing for the introduction of an environmental management system common to the whole Volvo Group. The Volvo Environmental Management System (VEMS) is designed to encompass the current major standards. The first step for Volvo in the VEMS process was to prepare three of their plants to meet the European Eco-Management and Audit Scheme (EMAS) standards. There is significant overlap with Volvo's established auditing program for those plants targeted for EMAS verification and registration. However, EMAS audits are more detailed and comprehensive than Volvo's internal audits. Required elements of the EMAS review process are shown in Figure II-B.

Other Tools to Enhance Environmental Decisions

The Task Force Report outlined a plan for environmental training with three goals: (1) to show that Volvo was serious, (2) to teach Volvo employees about environmental problems and the corporation's contribution to them, and (3) to inform employees about environmental activities at Volvo and about what they personally could do to improve Volvo's environmental performance. The report outlines who should be trained, the nature of the training, and how often training programs should be repeated.

The first environmental training class, for 450 of Volvo's top managers, was given in January 1989. An employee remembers that at that first seminar, "Mr. Gyllenhammar stated that anyone that does not care about environmental issues [and] does not comply with environmental goals hasn't got a place in Volvo . . . . *It was very clear.*" He then

- Assessment, control, and reduction of environmental impact
- Energy management, savings, and choice
- Raw materials management, savings, choice, and transportation
- Waste avoidance, recycling, reuse, transportation, and disposal
- Noise management
- Selection of new production processes and changes to existing production processes
- Product planning (design, packaging, transportation, use, and disposal)
- Environmental performance and practices of contractors, subcontractors, and suppliers
- Prevention and limitation of environmental accidents
- Contingency procedures in case of environmental accidents
- Staff information and training on environmental issues
- External information

Figure II-B   Required Elements of the EMAS Review Process

made each company president get up and state how their company would commit to the environmental goals of the Volvo Group.

Many training classes follow a format similar to the original program. Environmental specialists from government, industry, and environmental organizations speak about the consequences of environmental phenomena, such as global warming, ozone depletion, urban air pollution, and the depletion of natural resources. Volvo uses the training programs to stress its commitment to solving environmental problems, repeating Gyllenhammar's strong declarations. This also enhances internal communication about environmental issues and creates a common base of understanding within the company. Training informs employees who in the company is knowledgeable about environmental issues, increasing internal communication with these experts. The Volvo Car Company has recently committed to train all its employees, as well as suppliers, market organizations, and dealers—in total, about 70,000 people.

Another tool developed to enhance environmentally sound decision making was a smart set of investment criteria. One choice facing managers designing environmental management structures is how to consider environmental impacts of decisions relative to other investment criteria. As with other companies, projects at Volvo must normally use certain return-on-investment criteria. To address this issue, the Task Force specified a guideline for managers to make investment decisions:

> Prior to making decisions concerning major process or production changes which result in pollutant emission or other adverse environmental effects, measures shall be taken to enable such decisions to be based on the utilization of the best technology from an environmental viewpoint. Decisions concerning deviations from this policy shall be made by top company management.

This type of criteria is important for a number of reasons. First, it ensures responsible delegation of environmental decisions, because it forces any decisions to adopt more adverse solutions up to top management. Boethius recalls, "We did not want any president standing there saying 'I didn't know.'" Second, the statement encourages managers to look at environmental investments differently than other investments. As a result, Volvo has started to put money into activities without the payback that was required before. This type of guideline is especially important for middle managers, whose main concerns are traditionally quality and cost. Without this clause, managers could easily block environmental initiatives before they would have the chance to get to the company Environmental Working Groups and Executive Committees. Third, the clause has an important "psychological" impact because it places the burden of proof on those supporting options that are not as environmentally compatible, regardless of the cost. Committed to taking a "total view" of environmental issues, Volvo needed to find mechanisms to enable employees to assess the environmental impacts of its products and processes at the initial design stages. To achieve this objective, Volvo helped to develop and introduce two decision tools, MOTIV and EPS, to help employees make more environmentally compatible material and chemical choices.

These tools communicate complex environmental impacts of material and chemical selection decisions in a way that can be understood by product and process engineers. The introduction of these technologies represents an important change for Volvo because it allows the organization to lower the level at which environmental decisions are made, bringing in life-cycle environmental considerations at the beginning of product and process development.

EPS was created to help designers compare the life-cycle impacts of their material choices. Developed in cooperation with the Federation of Swedish Industries and the Swedish Environmental Institute, the principal tool of the EPS system is the definition of "environmental indices" in the form of numbers. Taking into account natural resource depletion, raw material extraction, land use, and emissions into air, water, and soil, these indices measure the environmental impacts of various material choices at each stage of product production and use. The designer compares a single environmental load unit (ELU) for each material choice.

The simple choice that EPS presents to designers is unique in the arena of life-cycle analysis because it is the only system currently being used in industry that offers so simple a presentation. As such, it has had many critics. EPS was chosen, however, explicitly because of its simplicity. Explains Jansson, "Other [life-cycle systems] available are too complex—you need something like this to make it work." To avoid misuse of the numbers, the system is completely open for people to alter the assumptions underlying the final numbers, and each number is presented with its range of uncertainty, to help users understand the significance of the ELU.

Volvo also decided to adopt a computer database, MOTIV, which holds information on approximately 90 percent of the chemicals used in the company. The system gives users access to detailed information on environmental, health, and safety risks; in-company chemical use; and available chemical replacements for the chemicals in the database. MOTIV takes relevant information from several sources such as toxicologists, environmental regulations, and local in-house instructions, and converts it into a form that is understandable and clear to the users. The system, used by most of the major companies and divisions at Volvo, contains information from throughout the Volvo Group and is accessible to all Group members. Since its introduction in January 1991, more than 100 people have been trained on MOTIV.

The most important aspect of MOTIV, asserts Urban Wass, is *how* it is used in the organization. Usually, all new chemicals to be used in Volvo are reviewed by the Industrial Hygiene Department in Technological Development. MOTIV has changed this process by giving the information that is needed for these types of decisions to people in R&D, product development, and production. This information is used not only to resolve short-term chemical emergencies, but also to assist product and process chemical choices. The system helps environmental questions to be answered directly in production, the best place to make process decisions.

MOTIV cost approximately $380,000 to develop and $170,00 to maintain per year. From this investment, however, Volvo has actually saved approximately $170,000 annually after expenses. Savings come from identification of wasteful chemical practices and simplified access to chemical information reducing by 50 percent the number of chemicals that Volvo uses since MOTIV's introduction.

As part of the profiling effort, Volvo takes the job of communicating their environmental activities seriously. At the Group level, Volvo actively communicates their activities to stakeholders. One way this is done is through extensive involvement in local and global environmental debates. Another way Volvo communicates with regulators and environmental interest groups is by inviting them to participate as speakers in the environmental training classes. In addition, the Volvo Group has become more involved with the environmental community, through an annual 1.5 MSEK (approximately $225,000) environmental prize and other awards and scholarships to support environmental research and activities. Similar communication activity occurs at each product company, varying in intensity depending on the product and its market.

Making the Ambition Real over Time

As described earlier, the management system created for environmental activities was decentralized. Similar to other Group-level initiatives, it was designed so that most decision-making activities would occur at the company rather than the Group level. This would more actively involve individual companies in environmental initiatives and allow each company to adjust its management systems to meet its own unique needs and capabilities.

The danger of decentralization, however, is the chance of inconsistent environmental performance. A few years into implementation of the program, undesired performance inconsistencies were observed across the Volvo companies. Minimum standards across companies and divisions varied in breadth, specificity, and level of performance; and, possibly of greater concern, the effectiveness of the chosen management structures varied among product companies. A failed merger attempt with Renault in combination with a severe market downturn had also drawn attention from environmental issues in some of the companies.

In addition, as discussed earlier, Volvo's environmental policy allowed for a modification of environmental activities, depending on available financial resources. For a time, a financial downturn affected the types of environmental investments that were undertaken at Volvo's production facilities. In the late 1980s, the company had the resources to invest in large environmental projects. Remembers Horkeby: "There was a mutual understanding in Volvo as an entire company that processes were going to change . . . . [It was] so obvious what we had to do—at the same time there was a certain budget with which we could work . . . . Luckily, we had the money then!" This availability of finances allowed the program to get off to a strong start.

This positive financial trend, however, reversed in the late 1980s and early 1990s. While Volvo continued to invest its profits from earlier periods, financial constraints started to become a serious obstacle to program implementation. The flexibility of the management programs at Volvo allowed each company to accommodate its environmental activities to these new financial constraints. For example, some program planners shifted environmental activity from capital investments to less-costly monitoring, planning, and preparatory activities for future environmental improvements.

In light of these implementation issues, environmental leaders in the company knew that they needed to push harder if they were going to be a world leader in environmental performance, as the company planned. After the breakup with Renault in December 1993, Volvo Group executive members revisited the environmental strategy and started to push harder for environmental changes. As explained by the current Director of Environmental Affairs, Anders S. Rison Karrberg, "Volvo as a group has an objective to be considered as one of the world's top three automotive companies in environmental care by the year 2000. This vision is now communicated internally and externally. Improved financial performance of Volvo will allow a more aggressive response to this challenge."

Corporatewide "working groups" were established in six major areas: recycling, EMAS, environmental information, production, products, and city transport. The Group also developed the Volvo Environmental Management System (VEMS) to further direct member companies.

Where needed, company-level environmental structures were also changed to increase coordination and empowerment. The car divisions' structure was changed, for example, when the AB Volvo Board suggested that it had to have a clearer and stronger priority on environmental performance. The car company formed an Environmental Competence Centre, which brings together twenty-five environmental personnel in the Volvo Car Company; and approved Ulla-Britt Fraejdin-Hellqvist as head of the center. One benefit of this organizational form is that it acts as a strong pressure group to integrate environmental issues into company decision making. It also clearly identifies where responsibility lies within the company. Since these changes, environmental employees report more commitment to, and support and resources for, environmental initiatives within the company.

Evaluating Success in Terms of Volvo Culture and Key Stakeholders

Overall, Volvo has made significant progress in changing internal attitudes and decision-making procedures regarding environmental performance. One sign of the organization's change is in employee attitudes. Before, explains Inge Horkeby, it was difficult to communicate about environmental issues. "Now you can feel that there has been a big change in the attitudes and communication about environment in the company. It has been a hot subject in the past years and within Volvo there has been a tremendous amount of interest. You feel like you are really achieving something."

Volvo has also had some success in pushing environmental decision making down in the organization. Decision-making tools, such as MOTIV and EPS, distribute information to people lower in the organization and enable them to participate more actively in the decision-making processes. In addition, the new programs have fostered an atmosphere in which environmental innovations are more easily discussed and encouraged. Before the policy, there was no structure in which environmental decisions and goals could be systematically reviewed.

This structure, along with the guideline for environmental investments, has reduced resistance often encountered at middle management. Kerstin Sterner, Environmental Manager at the Truck Corporation, explains that the policy prevents middle management from blocking environmental initiatives that spring from lower levels of the organization. The Truck Corporation, for example, was considering using new types of plastics that had better environmental attributes but cost more. An employee formulated a proposal to introduce one of these plastics in the truck cab. The Working Group heard of this idea and invited him to an Environmental Council meeting, where they evaluated how the new product satisfied the relevant policies and technical requirements. Since it met these requirements, took less energy to make, gave off lower emissions, and was only slightly more expensive, the proposal was accepted. Sterner notes that "a few years ago, this was not possible—there was no one to go to before. As long as cost and quality requirements were met, it was okay."

The structure also helps Volvo influence current and future regulatory pressures. At Volvo's Technical Development Center, they have learned that if Volvo is in front of legislation, it can have more input into the development of new regulations. They feel that if a company waits, it will be forced to use technology that may not be the best choice for its plants and possibly for the environment.

While changing internal attitudes and approaches to environmental performance were important for legal reasons, Volvo also wished to enhance external perceptions of the company. Within Sweden, it is clear that Volvo has improved its image and reputation considerably. This increase in pride allows the organization to have a more satisfied work force and enables Volvo to attract more competent people to the company.

Swedish regulators reported that they saw a change in Volvo's attitudes during the late 1980s and felt that Volvo was serious about its commitments. Local regulator Kersten Aswald has observed large changes in the attitudes of Volvo employees. Before the policy, she thought many Volvo employees "just found environmental demands ridiculous. They only saw one problem at a time. Now they very much accept [that] their contribution to [environmental degradation] is a problem."

Environmental changes at Skovde engine plant provide an example of the kind of innovative environmental technologies Volvo has implemented. During the permitting of the Skovde plant, Volvo proposed to the Licensing Board for Environmental Protection that they add reverse osmosis to the ultrafiltration techniques already being used in order to concentrate and better separate the wastes from the cutting fluids. The Licensing Board did not mandate this proposal, as the proposal addressed the treatment of fluids that most plants in Sweden release directly into the environment. Instead, Volvo instituted this proposal because they felt it was unethical to release the waste untreated. According to Peter Adler, a regulator with the Swedish Environmental Protection Agency, at a meeting with the environmental manager from the Skovde plant, the "Licensing Board for Environmental Protection had to ask of Volvo twice: 'Can you really manage this?' Usually, it is the other way around!"

The Skovde case further illustrates how the new environmental policy and programs have encouraged more incremental environmental improvements in manufacturing processes. Many of the minimum standards at Skovde focus on smaller sources of waste, such as chemical durability, monitoring and reduction of small solvent losses, and mapping and subsequent reduction of energy usage. Environmental Manager Magnus Tholander explained, "The main objective is that we should not waste our natural resources. It may be that in the process the costs are reduced because we buy and destroy less, but these are secondary reasons. It is unethical to waste resources—here and in the rest of industry."

Local environmentalists, although more skeptical of Volvo's activities, have re-assessed their view of Volvo over the past several years. Chris Agren, the Swedish NGO Secretariat on Acid Rain, thinks that:

> [Volvo has definitely] been more thorough than other Swedish companies in try-ing to be green . . . . They do not just have a green CEO, but they are also per-forming education within their own company, which is very important for results. [For an effective environmental policy, you] have it at all levels, and Volvo has been conscious of educating at these levels . . . . They are one of the few compa-nies that did this fairly early.

He also appreciates the honesty in Volvo's approach. Comparing the company to one of its main competitors, he comments: "I don't like Saab's advertisements. They lead to a false understanding [of the environmental impacts of their cars]. They imply that you can improve the environment by using the car. Volvo has been more careful by not us-ing such vulgar arguments."

Agren can, however, still perceive a discrepancy between Volvo's actions and per-formance. This is most evident in fuel economy, and he points to the new 850's high-power engine as an example of this problem. When he questions Volvo executives about this, they reply that it is what the Volvo consumer wants. Ulla-Britt Fraejdin-Hellqvist, head of environment at Volvo Car Corporation, admits that legislators and industry do have a large responsibility in this area. At the same time, she explains, the customer must also do his or her bit. "The dream is to get everybody to use the gas pedal lightly. When it comes to driving, we are good at making demands on others, but most people reckon that 'if I press the accelerator a bit more, it doesn't matter so much.'"[7] Mr. Agren responds to this line of reasoning: "What they don't say, however, is that they [Volvo] have a large influence on the consumers!"

It may be too soon to determine how Volvo's environmental activities have influ-enced consumer perceptions of the company. If these issues become more salient fac-tors in the automobile marketplace, Volvo may benefit directly. Although most con-sumers currently seem unwilling to pay a premium price for environmental improvement, Volvo's target market may be more likely to break this mold. As with safety, these customers may be willing to pay a premium price for Volvo's environ-mentally superior products earlier than other consumers. Even if this does not occur, Volvo's environmental efforts may serve to strengthen their profile as a "caring" com-pany. "Now," explains one employee, "with Volvo, people are not only safe in the car but also safe from the car. It is the next logical step."

Can Others Ride with Volvo's Directions?

Like many other companies in the late 1980s, Volvo was under increasing criticism for its environmental record. Pehr Gyllenhammar recognized that the global environmental crisis would profoundly influence Volvo's core businesses, threatening the very existence of its products. He guided top managers to devise a new environmental policy and management system to build environment as a "cornerstone" for the future survival the company.

The approach taken by Volvo is unique in its early recognition of the strategic im-portance of the environment, and in its effort to integrate environment into its business strategy and operations. Part of this strategy was to take a long-term view of environ-mental issues and to operate under the assumption that environmental issues will even-tually exert an influence on consumer decisions. The decision to build a company and product profile that extends safety to include environmental responsibility drives many of Volvo's efforts.

To implement the new policy, Volvo initiated comprehensive change in their management system. A new structure for environmental decision making has opened paths for discussing environmental improvements and for setting and reviewing environmental goals. This structure, while creating new abilities within the organization, was designed to fit with the existing decentralized structure so as to reduce resistance to the change. Top management commitment led to increased employee concern for and participation in environmental decision making. With environmental auditing, these were the primary incentives and controls relied upon. This choice again fit with an existing company culture, which had a strong history of social concern and did not require the use of stringent control mechanisms to encourage environmental action.

A central piece of Volvo's program, the management system offered a method for Volvo to take a "total view" of its environmental performance, as well as the potential to improve continually its environmental performance throughout the product life cycle. Goal-setting activity directly enhances each division's capability for continual improvement. New technology systems have increased Volvo's ability to monitor and use environmental information over the total life cycle, making it easier to integrate environmental concerns into the design stages of products and processes. Environmental guidelines for suppliers and distributors, as well as research on vehicle scrapping and recycling, are additional components of this life-cycle approach. Volvo intends to continue this life-cycle focus and has publicly announced that by 2000, the first Volvo with a complete life-cycle declaration may see the light of day (the declaration will include about 80 percent of the life cycle).[8]

Larger questions still loom. With its competitors in the automobile industry, Volvo may have to ask what role the automobile can play in a sustainable society. Environmental, transportation, and mobility issues are all interacting to create a hostile environment for the automobile. This hostility can be seen in Europe, where cities are already implementing bans or restrictions on vehicle use.

As of 1997, Volvo had started to address these concerns in their new 850 line, designed with engines that are lighter and more compact than Volvo's old family of engines. In addition, in preparation for other future environmental trends, this engine is designed to work, and give peak performance, on methanol mixtures with only minor modifications. Volvo has also developed an experimental hybrid vehicle and created a "City Traffic" program to participate in the development of more proactive policies in the area of transportation. Related strategies such as "city cars" and IVHS show promise in addressing these concerns, but they may not be enough to satisfy societal demands. Automobile companies may eventually need to consider diversification into alternative transportation markets and public education on environmentally responsible use of the automobile. Since Volvo AB produces products related to a wide range of transportation vehicles, they feel that they are well prepared to adjust to society's changing transportation needs. When this time arrives, Volvo will be well positioned for leadership in its industry.

NOTES

1. J. Whelan, "We Can Save the Earth: A Special Advertising Section," *Time Europe Edition*, November 27, 1989.

2. Smith, C. C., "Proactive Corporate Environmental Management," *Environment: Another Challenge for Industry,* Rome, Italy, 1990.

3. Womack, J. P,. D. T. Jones, and D. Roos, *The Machine That Changed the World,* Rawson Associates, New York, 1990.

4. Langenius, Sten, Welcoming Address in *Managing and Developing Environmental Auditing Programs in European Industries: Seminar at Volvo,* Gothenburg, Sweden, November 27, 1991.

5. Rothenberg, S., J. Maxwell, and A. Marcus, "Issues in the Implementation of Proactive Environmental Strategies," *Business Strategy and the Environment,* 1(4): 1–12, 1993.

6. This program was developed along with the Federation of Swedish Industries. Members of the Federation, including Volvo, thought that auditing was something that industry should implement on their own before they lost control of the process to an undoubtedly less effective government auditing process.

7. As quoted in Maria Edstroem, "Ulla-Britt saetter alla pa Volvo I miljoeskolan" ("Ulla-Britt Puts Everybody at Volvo into Environment-School"), *Ny Teknik,* Issue 14, 1995.

8. "Volvo Miljoemaerks foere ar 2000" ("A Volvo Will be Environmentally Labeled Before the Year 2000"), *Ny Teknik,* Issue 6, 1994.

QUESTIONS FOR FURTHER THOUGHT

1. Volvo pledged to strive to attain a uniform, worldwide environmental standard for process and products. However, Volvo instituted a decentralized organizational structure in which group companies set their own internal goals. What are the ramifications of these changes in staff, title, and function on the attainment of environmental excellence? Does it make sense to use a decentralized structure to achieve uniform performance?

2. Volvo's environmental investment program is dependent on the financial health of the organization; when resources are available, environmentally oriented activities are invested in to the greatest extent possible, and are curtailed when resources are insufficient. This is a philosophy of the environment as a cost-center, and that Volvo has to make money elsewhere to support environmental care, instead of environmental care making the money. Is this reflective of the operating field in the industry, or is this reflective of Volvo? If a financial downturn stalls an environmental policy, has the firm moved beyond the Green Wall?

3. Volvo's environmental auditing program charges one permanent auditor with the task of selecting a temporary audit team from approximately twenty employees. What are the pro's and con's of this format, functionally and strategically? How does this strategy relate to the lessons detailed by Beaton in his piece on environmental auditing at WMX?

4. Pehr Gyllenhammer stated that it is not in Volvo's best interest to protect the auto at any price. How is it not in Volvo's financial interest to protect its core competency, from the perspective of new product development, cost, and employee satisfaction?

5. Volvo extends its environmental training to suppliers, dealers, and market organizations. What is the strategy behind this effort, and what are the obstacles to achieving it?

6. Deviations from Volvo's investment criteria shall be made by top management, to prevent the initiatives of personnel below them from being stalled on the basis of cost and quality issues only. What constitutes a reason to deviate from the investment criteria? Is there anything other than cost? Does this policy constitute greenwash?

7. Volvo's EPS is open for people to alter the assumptions underlying the final numbers. What did Van Epps and Walters write about such malleability in "Measure for Measure?"

8. Based on Charles Knapp's piece on information management systems, what would be the pro's and con's of Volvo's MOTIV database, in regard to new product development?

9. Volvo management displayed carrot-and-stick efforts to align employees with the new environmental agenda. Which strategy is more effective, and at which stages?

10. Volvo's Environmental Manager Magnus Tholander reveals that the main objective at Volvo is to function under an environmental ethic, with cost considerations secondary. Is this a smart strategy?

    Volvo's 850 series high-power engine is an example of a disconnect between policy and reality. Are there any other examples of this? What are the consequences of this disconnect?

11. What is a firm's responsibility in the influence of consumer actions? What is the benefit of influencing behavior toward a more environmentally responsible ethic?

12. Volvo's target market has paid higher prices, to receive greater assurance of safety and quality. Is it likely that the same target group will pay more for the environment? Do manufacturers of products that are targeted at affluent consumers have an advantage in selling environmental attributes that other producers do not have?

13. Imagine yourself as the CEO of Volvo, planning the role for Volvo in a sustainable society. How can Volvo position itself for the future, through new product development or by emphasizing other companies within the Volvo Group?

14. Consider the choice categories outlined in Figure II-A. How do Volvo's choices fit into these categories? What do you think are the organizational and environmental (i.e., external to the firm) factors that lead Volvo to make the choices it did? What alternative programmatic options are there in each of the categories?

15. Chris Agren mentions what he perceives as the inherent discrepancy between Volvo's products and protecting the natural environment. How is

Volvo addressing this discrepancy and why? What other options do they have, and in what ways are they restricted in following these options? Is it realistic to expect that Volvo will change their product strategy in response to environmental concerns?

16. A unique aspect of Volvo is its Swedish culture, which is known for its higher level of environmental concern. What can companies do to reduce resistance to proactive environmental programs when they are not working in such a supportive culture? What are the underlying assumptions held by most corporate managers regarding environmental issues and how must these assumptions change?

17. Part of the EMAS program is full disclosure. Consider the risks and benefits of full environmental disclosure. (At the time that the case was written, there was information available on Volvo's Web page.) Look up the Web page and compare it to that of Volvo's European competitors. What are the strategic implications of these differences?

SUGGESTIONS FOR FURTHER READING

- Fiksel, Joseph (editor), *Design for Environment: Creating Eco-Efficient Products and Processes*, McGraw-Hill, New York, 1996.

  Fiksel collected a fine group of practitioners operating under DFE principles. If you're interested in the nuts and bolts of using Design for the Environment principles in an organization, this thick book will help you better understand this evolving area.

- Piasecki, Bruce, *Corporate Environmental Strategy: The Avalanche of Change Since Bhopal*, John Wiley & Sons, New York, 1995.

  This text offers a glimpse at the strategies of four firms struggling to create competitive advantages through the alignment of environmental demands and core business. Looking at Union Carbide, AT&T, ARCO, and Warner-Lambert, the book presents the leadership needed in these organizations to spur new product creation and turn environmental costs into profits.

- Tibor, Tom, Ira Feldman (editors), implementing *ISO 14000: A Practical Comprehnsive Guide to ISO 14000*, Irwin, New York, 1996.

  This text will give the reader a rich knowledge of the ISO 14000 standards. Yet, look beyond the mere presentation of ISO standards and one can read a solid discussion of environmental management systems in a much more essential form.

- GEMI Primer on TQEM, Global Environmental Management Institute Publishing, Washington, D.C., 1992.

  The Global Environmental Management Initiative (GEMI) publishes executive primers that cover the various tools used in environmental management systems. This primer on TQEM offers a quick and useful summary of the dominant tools used to increase quality and responsiveness in a TQEM system.

• Welford, Richard, *Corporate Environmental Management: Systems and Strategies*, Earthscan Publications, London, 1996.

Welford discusses the importance of management systems to integrating corporate environmental strategies by looking at specific systems such as Life Cycle Assessment and Auditing schemes. He has collected a group of contributors that further the discussion of the role these systems play in effective strategies.

PART

3

ANSWERING PUBLIC EXPECTATIONS

The Public Face of Corporate Environmental Strategy

Frank Mendelson and Bruce Piasecki

An established element of strategic planning is identifying future trends. One reliable method involves comparing your firm against other leaders to benchmark performance and best practice. It is also wise to be aware of changes in the customer's thinking—purchasing habits, cultural and normative shifts, changing demographics, and evolving societal expectations; and most importantly, to develop the organizational capabilities to answer these new expectations. This section of our text focuses on those difficult needs.

Since Bhopal, a broadened field of stakeholders has emerged for environmental managers and corporate strategists. Internal customers have always included employees, but now add the board of directors and newly created special committees on the environment, holding management responsible to answer questions on corporate environmental performance. Personal liability for performance is a concern, too. Board members and the CEO are culpable for environmental degradation and accidents, as is the employee in the field. At the best firms, senior management is looking with greater interest at internal business unit reports, developing environmental cost accounting tools, and demanding performance measures that go beyond traditional compliance metrics.[1]

Sophisticated leaders are viewing environmental performance through three prisms simultaneously: reducing liability, reducing EH&S risk, and at the same time, finding competitive advantage though environmental opportunity. Goal-setting priorities are stretching to include zeros: zero exceedances, zero emissions, zero waste, zero accidents. All of these measures are not restricted to behind-closed-doors deliberations. Expectations voiced by stakeholders come from community members, regulators, creditors, insurers, public interest groups, municipal leaders, the Securities and Exchange Commission, academic researchers, trade associations, former employees, new customers, and new employees following mergers and acquisitions.

Investors, too, are demanding information that draws a connection between environmental performance and shareholder value. Financial reports and the growing trend to issue voluntary environmental reports still address material concerns, while also surfacing strategic ones. What is the company's environmental policy? How is it carried out and how is it measured? Internal customers and clients in the supply chain are responding to scrutiny over the entire life cycle of process, product, and eventual disposal. And just what is the corporation doing about sustainable development? How does the company answer questions like these from stakeholders, even before the terms of definition are fully understood? And who is responsible to provide the answer?

Although EH&S management has become an integral part of daily operations, it has traditionally been viewed as a cost center; for many companies, investment beyond compliance is still a tough sell. The response from executive EH&S leaders has been to integrate their staff and function within the core business process. But can a well-crafted and -executed environmental strategy and a formal environmental management system provide tangible benefit to a company's bottom line? Peter A. Soyka and Stanley J. Feldman of the ICF Kaiser Consulting Group state that "even though corporations may have developed superior environmental management systems, it is critical that these efforts lead to improvements in environmental performance . . . . Widely accepted financial theory holds that reduced investment risk is rewarded by a lower cost of capital, and all else being equal, a higher stock price."[2]

Their research reveals that the relationship between improved environmental performance and reduced stock volatility suggests that investors do seek out, evaluate, and value high-quality information regarding EH&S results.

Linda Descano, Vice President of Environmental Affairs for Saloman, Smith Barney, explains the necessity for corporate executives to communicate the financial benefit this way:[3]

> Since the perceptions of the capital markets are shaped primarily by information provided by companies, the challenge for the corporate community is to communicate the immediate and long-term financial implications of their progressive environmental practices. Until these linkages are clear, "beyond-compliance" environmental performance will continue to be undervalued by the markets . . . . Toward this end, companies should focus on the top two or three business-critical environmental drivers and discuss them in terms of the market, product, and cost impacts—both from an immediate and long-term perspective.

ANSWERING THE NEW EXPECTATIONS

The questions raised above are legitimate and are reaching into the very ingredients and packaging that become consumer goods. The growing needs of stakeholders and the strength of their expectations for a coordinated response to environmental issues are creating new job descriptions for environmental managers and new positions within the firm. Today, the senior vice president of external affairs often plays a key role in orchestrating a firm's environmental mission. (Simply look at some of the titles represented in this book to see this as evident.)

The growth of the global economy has stimulated initiatives to standardize environmental management systems, such as ISO 14000, becoming a minimum entry-level hurdle to doing business abroad. Even developing countries are enforcing practices that are regulated in the United States but have been historically ignored elsewhere. The customers are global, and so is the magnifying glass aimed at corporate practice.

At one time, customer satisfaction on environmental issues could be limited to a choice of one company over another, or by product preference. This is no longer true. Industry sectors are now responding to higher expectations of performance and accountability by the public and their watchdogs. A new way of doing business has emerged. Industry's voluntary management systems and attention to supply chain management have extended the meaning of corporate responsibility on environmental management. The formation of strategic alliances and the strength of business partnerships with government and public interest groups have become a necessary way to do business, remain competitive, and answer public expectations. These trends will continue to develop and become more normative over time.

The response to the public concern that created the U.S. Environmental Protection Agency and similar statewide departments in the 1970s—through an adversarial approach to legislation and micromanagement of regulation—is coming of age. The rise in the number of environmental disputes resolved outside the traditional means of the court system requires that leaders in industry, government, and NGOs understand technology, public policy, politics, science, and business, as well as a consensual approach to problem solving. Similarly, information management is no longer embedded within one department. Just as quickly as corporations are complying with the laws and regulations that increase the amount of data required to be disclosed, the public is receiving and interpreting those figures and trying to make sense of them. Keeping a corporate reputation intact requires environmental communication integrated within the strategic business plan. Anticipatory issues management, one tool of proactive management described by Deborah Anderson of Procter & Gamble, implies a constant awareness of stakeholder expectations, and the responsibility to educate as well as to inform. (It pays to revisit Part II for reflections on opportunity recognition with these next external concerns in mind.)

The chapters that follow trace the growth and influence of stakeholders on corporate environmental performance, and what this means for business and environmental strategists. As you think through these developments, please remember that every corporate mansion must now display a sophisticated information-rich public face.

THE LINK TO LEADERSHIP

In Part III, we reflect on environmental leadership through the analysis of responses to pressures from government and the concerned public. Dennis Macauley examines approaches that his industry, via their trade associations, has voluntarily taken to make environmental management systems transparent through programs like Responsible Care®, and we study the challenges of harmonizing domestic environmental policy abroad. A case example is provided to show how the demands of business and public welfare converged to productively address cleanup questions while avoiding the more costly and contentious legal battles.

We conclude by exploring voluntary environmental disclosure through environmental reporting. We see this as a key vehicle to answer public expectations. When done properly, environmental reporting provides a dual function: meeting the informational demands of a targeted audience, and initiating a feedback loop inside the business to develop new measures of environmental performance. As companies plan to adopt these metrics, they articulate more ambitious goal-setting, and ultimately the business becomes more responsive and competitive.

MAKING ALL THESE TRENDS MATTER

Of course, none of these new concerns for public expectations matter unless senior managers translate them into actual business practice. Stakeholders, however vocal or informed, are never exactly the same as purchasing customers, and a government claiming an openness to flexibility, new approaches, and alternative dispute-resolution techniques is not the same, in dollars and cents, as the current or near-future EPA regulations. Part III is designed so you can keep a perspective on these new developments.

So what can a strategic corporate planner do to ready his or her firm for these important developments? Often, the answer is "positioning"—the managers know how to situate their people, resources, and products for what's next, and they also know what one should do to forestall competitors. In the conventions of business training, these rare skills are deemed "the knowledge of strategy." Successful strategy captures business opportunities while it answers public expectations. But what exactly is *corporate environmental strategy*, and how can Part III of our text assist you in developing that special skill base?

In the end, all corporate strategy is about making your future more promising. Yet, in the age of environmentalism, where so many malfunctions make your people lose balance, the dangers of mismanagement, the surprises of delay, and the hardships of simple incompetence come in many serious forms. The everyday becomes our entangled agenda and what's next or what's promising gets short shrift. In order to keep your head clear, you must master the art of balancing the customer demands of today with answering public expectations of tomorrow.

Thus, it pays to invest time to position yourself despite the complex maze of present compliance and money-making responsibilities. This point is best captured by Miyamoto Musashi in his famous reflection on strategy, *The Book of Five Rings*. Musashi reminds us that strategy is about "the rat's head and the oxen's neck." Victor Harris, the translator, explores the phrase:[4]

> The rat's head and the oxen's neck means that, when we are fighting with the enemy and both he and we have become occupied with small points in an entangled spirit, we must always think of the way of strategy as being both a rat's

head and an oxen's neck. Whenever we have become preoccupied with small details, we must suddenly change into a large spirit, interchanging large with small. This is one of the essences of strategy. It is necessary that the warrior think in this spirit in everyday life. You must not depart from this spirit in large-scale strategy nor in single combat.

These words are selected with a serious end in mind. The modern corporation must answer its customers' expectations regarding the environment, and that's a serious battlefront. Clearly, the use of military metaphors for the softer realm of environmental management is itself a bit disconcerting. Yet, business, even environmental business, doesn't matter if it's not about winning.

Nonetheless, strategic thinkers can find many ways to advance their cause, with humor or destruction, with new hires, or with downsizing. What matters in the end is the positive overall thrust called "positioning." By positioning for the future, one best answers public expectations.

Practically speaking, it may be impossible to teach about strategy without profound "retreats" into the meddlesome, the combative, or even the egotistical. But, finally, the successful strategists have positioned their terms for the future, carrying ten thousand day-to-day details on their oxen's neck, while having a certain rat-like swiftness when they must.

Clearly, a dozen years after Bhopal, much of environmental strategy is driven by external expectations. Public-rating protocols are more common and more consequential than ever before. Part III is devoted to the study of these external, or public, drivers of corporate environmental change. Here you'll read about issues management, stakeholder relations, even about specific public-reporting techniques designed to shape public expectation. As you read these state-of-the-art renditions, please ask yourself how you might best equip yourself to answer public expectations at your firm. In focusing your skills in this ever-changing arena, you are developing a special set of leadership skills that remain rare but are increasing in corporate values.

NOTES

1. Piasecki, Bruce, *Corporate Environmental Strategy: The Avalanche of Change Since Bhopal*, Wiley, New York, 1995.

2. Soyka, Peter A. and Stanley J. Friedman, "Capturing the Business Value of EH&S Excellence," *Corporate Environmental Strategy: The Journal of Environmental Leadership*, Vol. 5, No. 2, pp. 61–68, Elsevier Science, Winter 1998.

3. Descano, Linda and Bradford S. Gentry, "Communicating Environmental Performance to the Capital Markets," *Corporate Environmental Strategy: The Journal of Environmental Leadership*, Vol. 5, No. 3, Elsevier Science, Spring 1998.

4. Victor Harris's translation of Miyamoto Musashi's *The Book of Five Rings*, Bantam Books, New York, 1983.

5. All references to *Corporate Environmental Strategy* are available on LEXIS-NEXIS at www./exis-nexis.com. Press .gu for a guide to our work once you sign on Lexis.

CHAPTER

Responding to Stakeholders

Responding to a New Social Charter: The Responsible Care Initiative

Dennis Macauley

Dennis Macauley is Director of Environment for Union Carbide. Please see the "Executive Spotlight" for a detailed biographical sketch.

One of senior management's key roles is to ensure the long-term prosperity of an enterprise by identifying and dealing with strategic issues. Today, one such strategic issue looms large: the lack of public trust and acceptance of corporate environmental responsibility. Voluntary environmental, health, and safety management initiatives are an effective way to earn trust and to achieve competitive advantage.

By focusing on the most comprehensive voluntary initiative in practice today, the chemical industry's Responsible Care® initiative, this essay explores the role senior management can play in restoring public trust. It explains what Responsible Care is, why it is important to individual companies as well as to the industry as a whole, and how it can be implemented. Although these pages focus on a chemical industry initiative, the principles are applicable in other industries such as paper, auto-making, steel, oil products, and metals, among others. Each of these industries is under increasing pressure to improve environmental performance and communication of that performance.

RESPONSIBLE CARE

Because corporations are social as well as economic institutions, they exist not only according to a formal written charter, but also according to an unwritten charter of societal expectations which include environmental concerns.[1] There is strong evidence, however, that the public does not believe the chemical industry is fulfilling the expectation of this unwritten social charter. Despite the industry's position as the fourth-largest manufacturing industry in the United

216

States and the highest contributor to the U.S. trade balance, public opinion surveys between 1980 and 1990 showed that:

- Unfavorable opinions increased from 40 percent to 58 percent.
- Favorable opinions fell from 30 percent to 14 percent.
- Those who felt the industry was underregulated increased from 57 percent to 74 percent.
- Those who saw the industry as essential decreased from 49 percent to 38 percent.[2]

Polls also regularly showed that the chemical industry ranked ninth out of ten industries in public confidence, ahead only of the tobacco industry. The industry's largest trade association, the Chemical Manufacturers Association (CMA), concluded that such an image would have a strong negative impact on the industry's long-term prospects, and that the root cause of the negative public image was not "bad press" but the industry's poor environmental, health, and safety performance.[3] In this spirit, the chemical industry, through the CMA, created a voluntary initiative called Responsible Care to address the negative impact of adverse public opinion.

Responsible Care was created by the Canadian chemical industry in 1985, and adopted in the United States by the CMA as a condition of its membership in 1988. It is the most ambitious and comprehensive EHS improvement effort ever attempted by any industry, but in essence it is very simple. In the words of Jean Belanger, the former president of the Canadian Chemical Producers Association (CCPA), whom some consider to be the father of Responsible Care, it is simply "doing the right thing,"[4] the Golden Rule applied to EHS management. The elements of the Responsible Care program in the United States are shown in Figure 11-1.

1. Guiding Principles
2. Codes of Management Practices
3. Public Advisory Panel
4. Member Self-Evaluations
5. Management Systems Verification
6. Measures of Performance
7. Executive Leadership Groups
8. Mutual Assistance
9. Partnership Program
10. Obligation of Membership

Figure 11-1 Elements of Responsible Care

EXECUTIVE
SPOTLIGHT Dennis Macauley

It's not surprising that attempting to experience "the great outdoors" within the confines of New York City can lead to unexpected results. In my case, that result was an interest in the environment way before the first Earth Day. During the 1950s as a child, my friends and I often took the subway to New York City's Jamaica Bay for a usually unsuccessful day of fishing. My father often told me how much better it was in the "good old days," before the bay had become polluted. A decade later, after my interest in science led me to chemical engineering at Manhattan College, I learned that environmental engineers solved such pollution problems. So, after completing my undergraduate degree, I became the first chemical engineer at Manhattan to attain a Master's degree in the civil engineering specialty of environmental engineering.

Upon graduation in 1970 (the year Earth Day finally occurred), I learned what the real outdoors was like when I moved to West Virginia to join Union Carbide for what would be a ten-year stint in the Research and Development Department. My work included designing and upgrading wastewater treatment plants, mathematical modeling, and fundamental research in reaction kinetics. After several years, I took charge of the firm's air quality and combustion research group. By 1979, I managed Union Carbide's air, water, and hazardous waste technology program.

I made a move from environmental technology to EH&S management in 1980, when I became environmental manager for a major division of the company. Well before ISO 14001 environmental management systems were conceived, I implemented an environmental management system, consisting of a strategic plan, environmental standards and training, and a comprehensive auditing program. In 1985, I extended that management system to cover health and safety within the division as well as environment.

The third phase of my career began in 1989 when I became corporate director of Safety and Health. My major contributions were the establishment of new safety standards and introducing a new process risk management program. In 1993, I assumed my current position as Director, Environment. Under this title, I am responsible for the company's system of worldwide EH&S standards and its environmental and site remediation program. I am also President of a Union Carbide subsidiary, the Umetco Minerals Corporation, as well as the company's Responsible Care Coordinator.

I have seen the industry go from the early days of command-and-control, to a more proactive approach through the implementation of Responsible Care. This has convinced me that top-notch EH&S performance and corporate profitability are mutually supportive in the companies that will be global leaders in the next decade. EH&S staff must help to achieve this by focusing on people, business alignment, stakeholder dialogue, technology, management systems, and by controlling costs.

Happily, the waters of Jamaica Bay have improved as dramatically as the industry. Finally, I can catch a trophy striped bass or weakfish in my old stomping grounds. It appears that the "good old days" may have returned.

Fundamentally, Responsible Care is nothing more than a strategic commitment to two principles: to continuously improve EHS performance, and to do a better job understanding and responding to public concerns about products and operations. The initiative, especially the aspect of interactive public dialogue, represents a major change in both strategy and culture of the industry.

THE ELEMENTS OF RESPONSIBLE CARE

Guiding Principles

If Responsible Care is essentially the Golden Rule applied to EHS management, then the Guiding Principles are the Ten Commandments. The executive contact of each member company (usually the CEO) must pledge to conduct business according to 10 principles:

1. To recognize and respond to community concerns about chemicals and operations.
2. To develop and produce chemicals that can be manufactured, transported, used, and disposed of safely.
3. To make health, safety, and environmental considerations a priority in planning for all existing and new products and processes.
4. To report information promptly to officials, employees, customers, and the public on chemicals-related health of environmental hazards and to recommend protective measures.
5. To counsel customers on the safe use, transportation, and disposal of chemical products.
6. To operate plants and facilities in a manner that protects the environment and the health and safety or employees and the public.
7. To extend knowledge by conducting or supporting research on the health, safety, and environmental effects of our products, processes, and waste materials.
8. To work with others to resolve problems created by past handling and disposal of hazardous substances.
9. To participate with government and others in creating responsible laws, regulations, and standards to safeguard the community, workplace, and environment.
10. To promote the principles and practices of Responsible Care by sharing experiences and offering assistance to others who produce, handle, use, transport or dispose of chemicals.

The Guiding Principles are the foundation of the Responsible Care ethic. They outline each member and partner commitment to environmental, health, and safety responsibility in managing chemicals.

Codes of Management Practice

The six Codes of Management Practice are the real heart of Responsible Care. They contain a total of 106 management practices derived from the Guiding Principles (as shown above), in the areas of community awareness and emergency response, pollution prevention, process safety, distribution, employee health and safety, and product stewardship. Collectively, these management practices, coupled with interactive dialogue with the public, describe a comprehensive process for performance improvement.

Member Self-Evaluations

Companies submit an annual self-evaluation to an independent contractor on their progress toward implementing the codes. This is done for one code every two months, so that by the end of the year progress has been reported on all six codes and the 106 management practices they contain. These reports are used by the CMA to track progress industrywide, to identify lagging performers, and to provide implementation assistance.

Public Advisory Panel

James Whiston, chair of the Responsible Care Committee of the International Council of Chemical Associations, describes Responsible Care as essentially a "listening program," in which companies listen to those with concerns about products and processes, and respond to those concerns.[5] Just as this applies to individual companies, it is critical for the industry as a whole. The Public Advisory Panel is a listening program for the entire industry. This fifteen-person panel, which is comprised of a cross-section of environmental, health, and safety thought leaders from outside the industry, including persons who have been longtime critics, has advised the CMA on all aspects of Responsible Care since 1988. As is appropriate, their annual recommendations pull no punches. Their early recommendations resulted in the establishment of the management system verification process, and objective measures of performance; their continuing input is essential if the initiative is to evolve and to succeed.

Measures of Performance

Several years ago, Robert Kennedy, then the Chairman of the CMA, said of Responsible Care, "Don't trust us. *Track us.*" The basic point is that when all is said and done, acceptance of the chemical industry will be achieved by recognized performance improvement as demonstrated by objective measures of performance. The CMA established performance indicators (Figure 11-2) to enable the public to judge for themselves whether the industry, or a particular company or plant, is meeting its Responsible Care commitment.

Management Systems Verification

Two thousand years ago, the Roman satirist Juvenal said, *Quis custodiet ipsos custodes?*, or, "Who will watch the watchers themselves?" Feedback from the Public Advisory Panel shows that Juvenal's formulation applies today to Responsible Care. They, and other stakeholders, hold the Responsible Care management practices in high esteem. However, they want independent verification that management practices are in place.

In response to this feedback from the Public Advisory Panel, the CMA adopted a voluntary management systems verification process in 1996, to help companies continuously improve their management and implementation of Responsible Care. The process involves a detailed review by external verifiers from other companies and the community to demonstrate progress toward goals to key stakeholders.

Executive Leadership Groups

Senior-level support continues to be an essential ingredient for success. Regional Executive Leadership Groups provide a forum for executive contacts to regularly address their progress and identify areas where mutual assistance is needed.

Partnership Program

Although CMA members represent 90 percent of the production capacity of the chemical industry, the remaining 10 percent, plus other chemical handlers and users, comprise a very large number of companies. It is important that as many of these as possible adopt the Responsible Care ethic. As Joseph Rees observed for the nuclear industry, companies in the chemical industry are all "hostages of each other" because poor performance by one company often has negative ramifications for the entire chemical industry.[6] Therefore, a

Figure 11-2   Measure of Performance

Code	Measure of Performance
CAER	Survey of employees, community, and emergency responders
Pollution Prevention	Toxic Release Inventory reportable releases and transfers
Process Safety	Number of fires, explosions, and toxic chemical releases
Distribution	Number of DOT reportable hazardous materials incidents
Employee Health and Safety	OSHA injury/illness rates
Product Stewardship	Customer perception survey

Partnership Program allows eligible non-CMA companies and state or national trade associations to participate directly in Responsible Care. At the end of 1996, there were forty-nine members in this Partnership Program.

Mutual Assistance

Member-to-member mutual assistance is one of the most effective methods for advancing Responsible Care. Through a mutual assistance network, companies come together at the executive contact, Responsible Care coordinator, and code steward levels to share information vital to success.

Obligation of Membership

In 1988 the bylaws of the association were changed to require every CMA member company to participate in Responsible Care. Members must subscribe to the Guiding Principles, participate in the development of the codes and programs, and make good-faith efforts to implement the program elements of the initiative.

THE BUSINESS CASE FOR RESPONSIBLE CARE

Perhaps the most obvious and meaningful question that arises when one considers whether to embrace a voluntary initiative such as Responsible Care is a knee-jerk reaction: "Why in the world would any senior manager in his or her right mind voluntarily undertake additional work when they can hardly keep up with all the work that is already mandated?" Although a strong social and ethical argument can be made to adopt a voluntary initiative such as Responsible Care, economic reasons alone can justify such a decision. As with any business decision, a commitment to such an initiative should not be made until the advantages are objectively weighed against the disadvantages.

ADVANTAGES

Potential advantages are shown in Figure 11-3 and fall into four general categories:

1. The right to operate
2. Cost reduction
3. Business opportunities
4. Social attractiveness of the business

These are called "potential" advantages because they will not be realized in all cases. Companies should carefully use the Checklist on the following page to identify which of these potential advantages are real for their situation, and then do their best to quantify these advantages.

CHECKLIST

Preserve the Right to Operate

- Enhance relationships with plant communities and regulators, resulting in more favorable response to expansion plans, permit renewals, incidents, or other issues.
- Convince the public that ill-conceived legal requirements, which would jeopardize the right to operate or render the industry noncompetitive, are unnecessary.

Reduce Costs

- Improve the efficiency and effectiveness of your management system through insights gained via the Management Systems Verification process.
- Reduce the likelihood of incidents, accidents, and litigation through improved, industry-consensus programs.
- Reduce waste disposal cost through improved pollution prevention programs.
- Reduce tendency toward overregulation and the associated costs.
- By sharing the work with other companies, reduce the cost of environmental, health, and safety tools, and improve their quality.
- Deal proactively with evolving trends and requirements using consensus approaches.
- Obtain more favorable financing and insurance rates.

Provide Business Opportunities

- Become more customer-focused through the increased involvement in customers' activities required by Responsible Care.
- Enhance corporate reputation as a reputable supplier by complying with an industry-consensus program.
- Involve sales, marketing, and R/D in environmental, health, and safety issues to identify "green marketing" opportunities.
- "Level the playing field" by establishing more uniform requirements throughout the industry.

Enhance the Social Attractiveness of the Business

- Help attract the "best and brightest" to join the company.
- Help employees feel good about their company and industry.
- Help senior managers feel good about themselves and their business by realizing they follow industry-consensus, socially responsible practices.
- Make the company more attractive to socially conscious investors.

Figure 11-3 Potential Advantages of Implementing Responsible Care

WARNINGS ABOUT RESPONSIBLE CARE

Any business decision must weigh the advantages against the disadvantages. The major disadvantage of Responsible Care is the direct cost to implement it. This cost will be strongly affected by two factors: the scope and quality of a company's existing EHS programs and performance and where the company would like to be relative to the competition when it has reached full implementation. For leading companies, many of the 106 management practices are already in place. The major cost, then, is that associated with enhancement of their EHS program. Other companies with less-developed programs will find the costs to be higher.

Another potential disadvantage is that, initially at least, dialogue with the community may be difficult. It is entirely possible that issues will arise as a result of this dialogue that would not have arisen (or at least not as soon) if Responsible Care had not been adopted. But managers should realize that it is just a matter of time until the public has access to the EHS issues associated with an operation. For example, the Clean Air Act accidental release provisions require that worst-case scenarios be made available to the public by the middle of 1999. Managers who have built community trust through Responsible Care will have much better success when such disclosures are made.

Finally, the last potential disadvantage is one of employee backlash to yet another program. The initiative may be regarded as just more work that management has dumped on an already overloaded work force. In the worst case, there actually could be hostility, but a more likely result is merely a state of apathy to the initiative. However, if employees are made aware of the real benefits of Responsible Care, such as improvements to workplace safety and health, the environment of their communities, and the long-term prospects for their company, they will be more enthusiastic supporters.

As with the potential advantages, a company should carefully identify and, to the extent practical, quantify the potential disadvantages. But the bottom line for most companies is that costs and other potential disadvantages usually can be managed, since Responsible Care is generally implemented over a period of about five years, and should not be an unreasonable investment considering the long-term advantages. But an even simpler solution to the cost/benefit equation is that Responsible Care and other similar initiatives are rapidly becoming a part of the business landscape that no leading company can afford to ignore.

ADVICE FOR LEADERS IN THE TWENTY-FIRST CENTURY

Responsible Care is now about a decade old. It has proven itself to be more than just a fad, and has already exceeded the life span of many industry programs. But in reality it is still in its formative years, at the beginning of a long journey. Key components of the initiative, such as objective performance indicators and an independent verification process, were not fully in place until

1997. It will take another ten to twenty years of sustained improvement for Responsible Care to bear its full share of fruit. Indeed, Responsible Care is not a sprint, but a marathon. As Responsible Care matures, its role in establishing an important link between business reputation and environmental strategy will grow in strength and consequence.

Nonetheless, the results so far have been impressive for Responsible Care companies:[7]

- Emissions to the environment decreased 60 percent from 1988 to 1994 while production increased by 24 percent.
- Occupational injury and illness rates decreased 30 percent from 1990 to 1995, although the industry had already been one of the safest in which to work. The 1995 injury and illness rate is almost a factor of four lower than the average of all U.S. manufacturing industries.
- The number of community advisory panels (a prime approach for understanding community concerns) increased from 56 in 1990 to 316 in 1995.

So, great progress is being made, but the jury of public opinion is still out. Success or failure will be determined by the industry's performance over the long term. During the mid-1990s, the chemical industry leadership that had the vision and courage to create Responsible Care has largely been replaced by a new generation of leaders. Responsible Care will succeed only if these new leaders have the perseverance to achieve that same vision.

Francis Fukuyama argues in *Trust: The Social Virtues and the Creation of Prosperity* that only those societies with a high degree of social trust will create the flexible, large-scale businesses required for successful global competition.[8] Voluntary initiatives such as Responsible Care provide the best solution to regain this trust if applied effectively and over the long term. The implementation costs for any such initiative are not insignificant and the culture change required is perhaps even more difficult, but the strategic manager will recognize its value to the long-term prosperity of the enterprise.

NOTES

1. Wilson, I., *Rewriting the Corporate Social Charter,* SRI International, Palo Alto, California, 1992.
2. Hirl, R., Opening Address to *Senior Executives' Responsible Care Seminar,* Lisbon, October 6, 1992.
3. "Environmental Health and Safety Performance Report 1995–1996," Chemical Manufacturers Association, October 1996.
4. Chynoweth, E., "Doing the Right Thing," *1996 Responsible Care Handbook,* Asian Chemical News/CAREline, September 1996, Singapore.
5. Whiston, J., " One Standard for the Whole World," *1996 Responsible Care Handbook,* Asian Chemical News/CAREline, September 1996, Singapore.

6. Rees, J. H., *Hostages of Each Other: The Transformation of the Nuclear Industry Since Three Mile Island,* University of Chicago Press, Chicago 1994.
7. "The Year in Review, 1995–1996: Responsible Care Progress Report," Chemical Manufacturers Association, October 1996.
8. Fukuyama, F., *Trust: The Social Virtues and the Creation of Prosperity,* Free Press, New York, 1995.

PREEMPTING THE CRISIS

Can crisis be avoided though a strategy that tries to identify issues before they become problems, and proactively responds to public opinion before a crisis emerges? The editors of this text, and the author of the next essay, believe the answer is yes. The focus of the next essay, by Procter and Gamble's Vice President of Environmental Quality-Worldwide, Deborah Anderson, discusses the concepts and principles that can assist business in getting ahead of an issue before it becomes a problem. The expectation is that the following discussion may help some corporations and future leaders improve their overall understanding of what is involved in anticipatory issues management—and what can be done to improve prospects for better outcomes in handling products and processes that are viewed by a suspicious and perhaps cynical public.

Key Concepts in Anticipatory Issues Management

Deborah D. Anderson, Ph.D.

Dr. Anderson is Vice President of Environmental Quality-Worldwide and Emerging Issues Support-Worldwide at Procter & Gamble. She reports directly to the Chairman of the Board and Chief Executive and has responsibility for environmental policy and strategic planning, and coordinates P&G's worldwide efforts on environmental government affairs, product stewardship, manufacturing H&S and product environmental safety. She serves as an international spokesperson for the company's environmental efforts. As Vice President of Emerging Issues Support, Dr. Anderson applies her extensive expertise in global issues management to assist business managers with new product introductions to the marketplace.

Over the past thirty years, the world has seen many examples of business impacting issues. There have been Exxon Valdez, the Brent Spar incident, Tylenol, the Dalkon Shield, oil-drilling rights, logging and the spotted owl, chlorine and dioxin, the Firestone 500 tire, the Sandoz fire in Basel, Alar, Nutrasweet, and Hamburger Clam Shells, to name a few. To the satisfaction of some corporations—and the dismay of others—the expertise with which these have been managed has been available to analysis by anyone with an interest in issues management. There is a gold mine of practitioner-based experience, which, if put to effective use, can enable any corporation to gain competitive advantage and strategic insight through smoother market introduction of their products and public acceptance of their actions.[9] This is especially true if issues are managed during the period in which they are emerging, maximizing the chance that a crisis will not occur, thus saving the business the substantial costs of crisis management.

Anticipatory issues management can be employed to manage an issue before it becomes a crisis. While written from the perspective of corporate environmental strategy, the following concepts and principles are broadly applicable to issues faced by many organizations and institutions. Indeed, if such work is done in a diligent manner, conditions that might lead to a crisis for any organization can be entirely changed so that they no longer exist. Once a crisis has occurred, you and your organization are dealing in *crisis management* and all opportunities to avoid a crisis outcome are forgone.[10]

ANTICIPATORY ISSUES MANAGEMENT PROCESS AND KEY CONCEPTS

The Issue Life Cycle

A "generalized" life cycle of an issue is shown in Figure 11-4. The word *general* should be emphasized because there are many variations on the course that any particular issue might take.[11] Many others have described the issue life cycle in various ways. The general life cycle consists of four phases:

Emergence

Emergence is the period when the issue is smoldering on the "fringes" of society, in a small part of academe, or on the agenda of a small interest group.

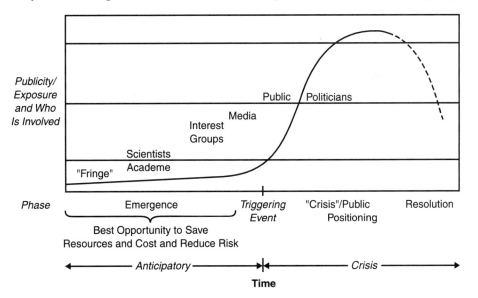

Figure 11-4 The General Life Cycle of an Issue

The fringe (not meant in a derogatory fashion) can be characterized as consisting of those less-conventional members of our society who tend to think five or ten years ahead of the mainstream. Some of these people might be in "think tanks" or the "underground." Many tend to be in campus groups since new thinking tends to surface first in universities. The length of time of this phase is highly variable and can be anywhere from a few hours to several years. The best opportunity to resolve an issue in a cost-effective way is during this phase.[12]

Triggering Event

The second phase usually, but not always, consists of some kind of triggering event thrusting the issue into the press and the public domain. This can be a spill or an accident—like Exxon Valdez or Bhopal. It can be Coca-Cola introducing New Coke or a news report of a death from the consumption of a product. It can be the publication of a book such as Rachel Carson's *Silent Spring*, or even something as simple as a barge filled with garbage that can't find a home. In this phase the issue becomes a crisis.[13]

Crisis

During the crisis phase, the issue is a matter of public debate—and the controversy is usually represented by the press. During this third phase, the public struggles to come to a position on the issue. The length of this period can again be very short or last several years depending on the issue

Resolution

The final phase is resolution. While some issues never get resolved (or so it seems), others resolve rather quickly. This may be dependent on how the corporation acts. If the response is quick and credible, the issue is more likely to resolve. Johnson & Johnson provided a model example of how to extinguish a crisis by their responsive actions during the Tylenol crisis. Resolution is less likely if the corporation responds with (what is perceived as) "stonewalling" or more corporate propaganda, as has been seen over many years with the response of tobacco companies to the tobacco issue.[14]

OPPORTUNITY FOR COMPETITIVE EDGE

Anticipatory issues management or managing an issue during the emergence phase is an opportunity for competitive advantage because costs can be greatly reduced by avoiding a crisis. (see Figure 11-5.)

It is clear from the history of many business examples that when management values anticipatory issues management during the emergence stage less cost and less disruption is incurred, and less risk is carried to the corporate reputation and image. One only need ask Exxon whether the Valdez incident

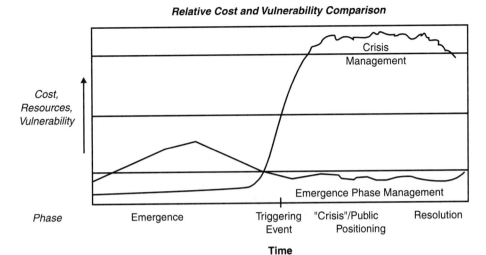

Figure 11-5   Emergence Phase Management versus Crisis Phase Management

impacted negatively on their business, or Dow about dioxin, or Intel about the Pentium chip to get an unequivocal answer. These are some of the most extreme and visible examples, but they serve to illustrate the point. The opportunity for continual improvement is ever present with new findings immediately available from watching the real world of one's peers managing their own issues and seeing the outcomes. The opportunity, then, is to achieve what is represented in Figure 11-6—resolution of the issue without a crisis.

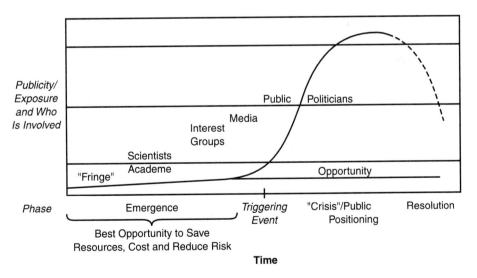

Figure 11-6   Resolving the Issue

WHAT THE PUBLIC DOESN'T KNOW COULD HURT YOU

An issue usually develops because a business wants to undertake an action or introduce a new product, ingredient, or technology that may (either in actuality or in perception) be contrary to or different from a prevailing or emerging public policy or social norm.

An issue can also arise because of an unforeseen event that has the potential to be interpreted by the public or others in a way that would be damaging to the business. This very important public policy/public values perspective needs to be appreciated in the development of an action plan to manage the issue. Often, businesses think that if they can just get the "science" or the facts out, the issue will go away. What is not realized is that stakeholders in a particular policy or social norm have not bought into the businesses' action.

Shell's Brent Spar incident provides a vivid example. Shell had done an excellent job of making a scientific determination that disposing of oil platforms by sinking them was an acceptable environmental risk. What was not anticipated was that this method of disposal would be unacceptable in terms of societal values that seek a clean earth free of such "rotting" structures.

Another example, closer to issues management strategy at Procter and Gamble, is the popular conception of the "landfill crisis," which impacted industry broadly in the late 1980s and early 1990s. Even though it could be shown—with scientific support—that any inert product or package was a safe environmental risk in a landfill, burying the world's garbage was contrary to the prevailing set of social norms that frowned on wasted resources, disposability, and "filling the earth with garbage."

THE PROCESS OF ANTICIPATORY ISSUES MANAGEMENT

While each issue is unique and requires its own unique solution, each can be analyzed and an action plan developed through the same general process or sequence of steps as shown in Figure 11-7.

Issues Identification and Prioritization (see Figure 11-7)

As discussed, early identification of issues that may impact the business is key to avoiding business-disrupting crises. There are several means of accomplishing early identification of issues and prioritizing them in terms of their potential to impact a particular business. One of these is *forecasting*.

Forecasting is not predicting. Forecasting is looking as far into the future as feasible, generally two-to-five and sometimes ten years, and making informed "guesstimates" about what the main trends will be in areas that can impact a particular business. Add to that the projected demographics, business

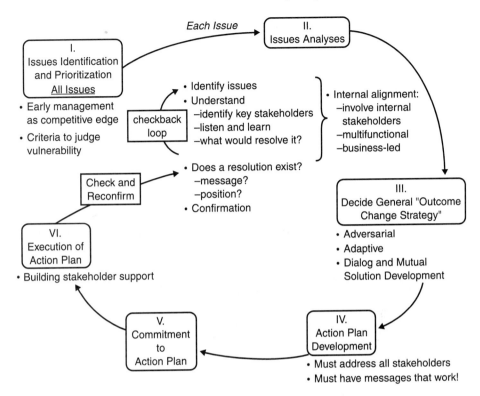

Figure 11-7 Process and Key Concepts for Anticipatory Issues Management

climate, political environment, and social trends and one can identify usually five-to-ten potential issues that might be expected to occur. Essential to successful forecasting is putting a comprehensive scanning system into place to keep abreast of issues circulating among various stakeholder groups ("fringe" thinkers, futurists, professional organizations, interest groups, public policy groups, think tanks, etc.).

In addition, you can identify so-called "wild card" events, which are events that have a very low probability of occurring but should they occur would have a dramatic impact on the business. For example, a forecasting research project conducted for Procter & Gamble (Institute for the Future, 1994) identified the millennial change as a "wild card" event. Knowing from previous research that the public tends to be more concerned about survival issues in proportion to the number of zeros on the time event (i.e., decade, centennial, millennial), it was a possibility that the millennial change could trigger exaggerated concern for the environment and "sustainability" of the earth. While the probability of this occurring was not high, should it occur, this would be a major issue for the business.[15]

The process of scenario building can also be used. This is similar to forecasting but tries to build a vision of a future time and considers the world political, social, economic, and technical backdrops against which an issue might play out. Consultants are often used to identify and forecast issues, or do scenario building. Prioritization can be done with the help of such tools as shown in Figure 11-8.

The table in Figure 11-8 lists the sorts of criteria that can indicate business vulnerability. A majority of responses in the "high" column most likely indicates that the business is highly vulnerable to attack by impacted stakeholders if the business proceeds with the anticipated ingredient or product introduction or company action. A majority of responses in the "low" column would most likely indicate that the business has a low vulnerability to the issue. Going through this type of quick analysis can give a good indication of vulnerability and, depending on the businesses' plans, how high a priority should be assigned to the issue.

Several years ago, P&G introduced the first baby diaper containing absorbent gelling material (AGM). This was a gel-like substance that absorbed water and held it away from the skin, thus protecting the skin from the wetness that made it susceptible to diaper rash. Even though extensive testing proving the safety of the ingredient and clinical studies demonstrating the efficacy of the diapers in reducing incidence of diaper rash had been conducted, there was concern for how parents would feel about such a novel diaper ingredient.[16]

Applying the criteria in the table in Figure 11-8 to introduction of the product produced the results seen in Figure 11-9.

It is clear from this analysis that the new product was probably very vulnerable to attack in the market place and could be a major issue for the company. As a result, special assignments were made several months in advance of product introduction to design a comprehensive program of anticipatory issues management to ensure successful introduction to the market place.

Issues Analysis

Once the key issues have been identified, each issue of high priority needs to be characterized to assess its potential to impact the organization (Figure 11-10). An internal group or task force of stakeholders is usually assembled to do this. If a key stakeholder is excluded from the issues analysis process, it can be difficult to ensure that the findings from analysis are incorporated into all resulting action plan. For example, if an advertising representative is not involved, advertising messages may not reflect an accurate understanding of the issue and, thus, may not be effective in addressing the concerns of external stakeholders. Also, it can be difficult to get internal alignment on a "change strategy" and an action plan if key internal stakeholders are excluded.

As a check on understanding, input on these questions is synthesized into concise statements and then reflected back to stakeholder representatives to

Figure 11-8 Prioritization Tool

Criteria	Slight	Medium	High
1. Degree to which skateholders perceive action, product, or ingredient to be dangerous: a. Perceived to be a "chemical"? b. Perceived to be associated with health? c. Perceived to be available to children? d. Perceived to be associated with uncontrollable, catastrophic, or dreaded risks?			
2. Degree of visibility/proximity to body: a. Used in household? b. Used on the body? c. Taken orally?			
3. Degree to which stakeholders perceive scientific or technological position to be uncertain			
4. Degree to which stakeholders perceive action, ingredient, or product to be trivial or superfluous, as opposed to important.			
5. Degree to which stakeholders perceive action, ingredient, or product to be threatening to the environment or "sustainability:" a. Short life span? b. Nonbiodegradable? c. Difficult to dispose of or socially unacceptable disposal method (i.e., landfill, incineration)? d. Intensive natural resource use?			
6. Degree of "foreignness" of manufacturer (local vs. domestic vs. multinational vs. foreign).			
7. Degree to which advertising/communication may be perceived as too much, adversarial, or not credible.			
8. Degree to which an alternative is available:			
9. Degree of social change required for action, ingredient, or public acceptance: a. Is it a new way to do something? b. Is it a new way to think about something? c. Will it impact a current social value?			
10. Degree to which the business is new to this product category, or this kind of action, or expects hostile competitive response: a. First product entry? b. Other players already firmly established? c. Business already a part of the "policy" network in this category? d. Hostile competitive response expected?			

Figure 11-9 Using the Prioritization Tool for Product Introduction: The AGM Example

Criteria	Slight	Medium	High
1. Degree to which skateholders perceive action, product, or ingredient to be dangerous: a. Perceived to be a "chemical"? b. Perceived to be associated with health? c. Perceived to be available to children? d. Perceived to be associated with uncontrollable, catastrophic, or dreaded risks?			*We knew that AGM would be perceived to be "chemical." It was also associated with health, and was a baby product.*
2. Degree of visibility/proximity to body: a. Used in household? b. Used on the body? c. Taken orally?			*The product was to be used on the skin.*
3. Degree to which stakeholders perceive scientific or technological position to be uncertain			*The science supporting diaper rash was complicated and AGM was a new material.*
4. Degree to which stakeholders perceive action, ingredient, or product to be trivial or superfluous, as opposed to important.			*Innovations to diapers would be perceived as essential innovations.*
5. Degree to which stakeholders perceive action, ingredient, or product to be threatening to the environment or "sustainability": a. Short life span? b. Nonbiodegradable? c. Difficult to dispose of or socially unacceptable disposal method (i.e., landfill, incineration)? d. Intensive natural resource use?			*There was concern about landfilling of diapers and that they were biodegradable.*
6. Degree of "foreignness" of manufacturer (local vs. domestic vs. multinational vs. foreign).		*Domestic*	
7. Degree to which advertising/ communication may be perceived as too much, adversarial, or not credible.			*A high degree of advertising was expected, and the advantage of AGM was difficult to explain.*
8. Degree to which an alternative is available.			*Many brands available.*

9. Degree of social change required for action, ingredient, or public acceptance:
   a. Is it a new way to do something?
   b. Is it a new way to think about something?
   c. Will it impact a current social value?

   Parents were not used to thinking of diapers as containing "chemicals" or as being something new.

10. Degree to which the business is new to this product category, or this kind of action, or expects hostile competitive response:
    a. First product entry?
    b. Other players already firmly established?
    c. Business already a part of the "policy" network in this category?
    d. Hostile competitive response expected?

    The company was well known in the diaper category, but . . .   *. . . This was a new way to think.*

Issue characterization involves answering the following questions in as much depth as possible, usually through a "listening and exploring" dialogue with representatives of external stakeholder groups. If the issue is considered to be too sensitive for company representatives to do such interviews, intermediaries can be used as long as it can be assured that an accurate understanding of the issue will be fed back to the company:

- *What is the issue?* All aspects of the issue (social, political, psychological as well as technical) need to be understood in as much depth as possible *from the perspective of those who have the issue.*
- *Who has the issue?* What are the groups that have the issue? Who are the issue stakeholders? (Physicians?, teachers? parents? activists? etc.)
- *Who are the "authority figures" for these groups?* To whom do these groups turn for advice? Whom do they believe?
- *What would they like to see happen? What do they think would resolve the dilemma?* What needs to change or remain the same? What do they want the corporation to do?
- *Has a workable resolution been suggested based on the analysis?* After understanding the issue and understanding what stakeholders want to see happen, often a possible resolution that would satisfy both stakeholders and the business becomes evident. This is usually one of two things: (a) a message that addresses stakeholder concerns and, thus, neutralizes the issue for them, and (b) an action or a position the company can take that neutralizes the issue for stakeholders.

Figure 11-10   Listening and Exploring to Accurately Characterize Issues

confirm understanding. If possible message ideas or positions that might neutralize the issue have evolved, these are also "tested" with stakeholders. It is important to determine whether such a message exists or can be developed because this will help determine which general change strategy might be chosen for managing the issue.

THE THREE APPROACHES

Once issues analysis has been completed, the general issue change strategy can be chosen. This is the general approach by which the business chooses to manage the issue and it is based on the ideal outcome the business wants to achieve.

There are three main strategy alternatives: adversarial, adaptive or dialogue with mutual solution development (see Figure 11-7). The business can take an adversarial stance and fight the issue; the business can change and adopt the action desired by the issue stakeholders; or the business can enter a dialogue with the issue stakeholders and develop a mutually satisfying solution to the "dilemma" presented by the issue. No one strategy is "right" for all issues.

Sometimes, even though the strategic choice is generally one type, the various pieces of the action plan might be a mix of strategic approaches. The "right" strategy can be chosen after a thorough analysis of the issue, including knowing what the issue stakeholders see as a desirable resolution and knowing whether a resolution is evident.

The Adversarial Strategy

An adversarial approach to issues management was the approach typically used by industry until about the mid-1970s. This was an era when industry found the idea of transparency especially threatening and not much in-depth communication occurred with stakeholders on issues of importance to them. This approach was typically employed for crisis management as well. In other words, there was not much attention to issues management during the emergence stage. Issues management and corporate actions to manage issues typically occurred after the issue had become a crisis and took the form of "damage control" activities often labeled as "stonewalling," "denial," or "corporate propaganda." This approach is used less frequently as more members of industry see the value of dialogue, but this does not mean that the adversarial approach is never the right strategy to use.[17]

For example, one can envision a situation in which an activist group wants a business to make a change that would be contrary to a longstanding corporate principle. The current principle is strongly supported by the majority of the businesses' other stakeholders. Analysis of the issue shows that even the activist groups' peers do not support the change and that, if the business adopted the change, it would lose credibility with its key stakeholders including many of the activist group's peers. Furthermore, analysis shows that the issue will be very short-lived in that an expected government action will make the issue moot. In such a case, the adversarial approach, characterized by the business simply stating that it doesn't intend to change, is a strategy that will most likely be successful.

The Adaptive Strategy

The adaptive strategy usually consists of doing what the stakeholders are asking or adapting to meet their needs in some way such as providing information on a particular issue. This strategy can be very effective and save time and effort when analysis of the issue shows that the change desired by stakeholders is consistent with the business' values, is neutral or adds value to the overall enterprise, and carries no risk to corporate credibility or reputation. It can also work to build a positive image for the business as "open to change" and "willing to listen to stakeholders." It can be a win-win for all involved.

For example, in connection with a detergent that Procter & Gamble markets in Europe, an activist group was concerned that the label did not convey information on ingredients as fully as they would like. In analyzing and understanding their concerns, Procter & Gamble determined that the suggested change would improve the quality of information on the label and that the requested change was consistent with all company policies. The company made the change and, besides improving the quality of information for stakeholders, helped to further build a reputation for listening and fairness.

Dialogue and Mutual Solution Development

This strategy is useful when analysis shows that a resolution is not immediately evident and that one that meets the needs of all stakeholders needs to be developed. In addition to issues analysis dialogue—to understand the issue in depth—this strategy involves further dialogue to "dilemma sharing." This means empowering stakeholders to help to develop a mutually satisfying solution and carefully building acceptance for the solution among all groups of stakeholders until the issue is resolved.

This process requires an attitude of mutual respect, superior listening and communication skills, and give-and-take dialogue. The business must be willing to acknowledge that some of its current ideas may change based on the new perspectives gained from the dialogue. It also needs to share ownership for the solution developed by the dialogue process. This can be a threatening situation for many businesses that consider such an approach *too risky* because the business gives up a certain amount of control in entering a mutual dialogue. But the mutual understanding and trust gained, the chance for innovative problem solving, and the building of relationships that will help manage future issues can make the process worth the risk.

Several tactics can be employed to successfully use this strategic approach. One in particular is a process for building stakeholder support. This process can also be used in situations where creating or catalyzing change in public policy or how the public thinks about a particular value is needed.

BUILDING STAKEHOLDER SUPPORT

No matter which strategic approach to manage this issue is selected, there may be a need to build support and acceptance for the solution among stakeholders. Sometimes this will only involve exposing key stakeholders to the right message or position and letting them share resolution to the issue. Other times, ownership of the issue solution needs to be generated by involving key stakeholders in development of the solution and then catalyzing a process by which their peers are enrolled in accepting the solution.

To successfully build stakeholder support, an appreciation of how external stakeholder groups (and we, ourselves) change their thinking is needed.[18] Thinking is changed only since stakeholders network continuously with their peers, changing their peers, thinking can be used to catalyze changes in their own social policy or even social values. This process can be effective even when stakeholder groups have been identified that hold extremely opposed views. Success of this model assumes that a "winning" message, company position, or issue solution has been identified during issue analysis or dialogue with stakeholders.

The process to build stakeholder support can be likened to "peeling an onion" (see Figure 11-11). The key stakeholder groups (as identified in issues

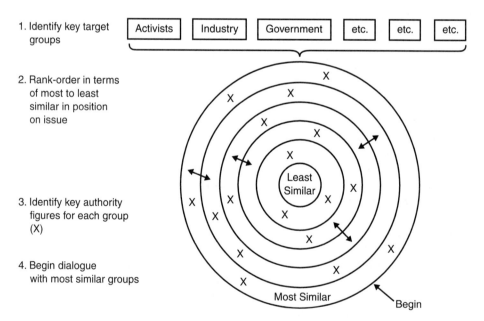

Figure 11-11 Building Stakeholder Support: Peeling the Onion

analysis) are ranked from those that hold views closest to the desired new way
of thinking to those that hold views most different or opposed to the desired
new way of thinking. These groups can be visually arranged as the various layers of an onion, with those most similar to the desired change on the outside
and becoming more and more different as one progresses to the inner layers.
The most different or those extremely opposed are in the center.

Authority figures for each group, again identified during issues analysis,
are targeted, and dialogue begins with those authority figures in those groups
in the outermost layer. Developing effective messages proven to help change
opinions on an issue is critical to success. As dialogue begins, authority figures
begin talking to one another within their own group and within the groups
closest to their own. As opinion changes and these groups begin to think differently about the issue, communication penetrates further and further toward
the center until authority figures in the most different groups are debating the
new ideas with each other. The process can be compared to the beating of jungle drums in the bush. One drummer starts a message and it spreads to nearby
villages. From there, it spreads to villages more distant until the whole jungle
is drumming the same message.

An interesting phenomenon occurs that enables management of even the
most opposed opinions. Those most opposed will, at this point, have the choice
of joining their peers as the new consensus develops or remaining opposed,
causing their position to appear extreme or somewhat unreasonable. Ultimately
their credibility suffers, and isolating them in terms of their ability to influence
their colleagues. These individuals can still make a lot of noise but their influence on their peers will be reduced. Often, a dialogue group or consensus conference may be held involving a representative number of authority figures. As
they achieve consensus, it further isolates any existing extreme opinions if they
have not yet joined the dialogue.

A certain momentum is associated with this process with varying amounts
of time needed to penetrate through to the inner layers depending on the scale
on which the process is being initiated (local, regional, national, or global). The
time needed to build momentum, and allow it to run its course, must be appreciated to maximize success. Also, it is obvious that the process needs to be
started early enough in the emergence phase of the issue to allow completion
if crisis is to be avoided.

The solid waste issue provides a good example of how building stakeholder
support through the use of this model was effective. During the early days,
when no one knew what was the right thing to do with garbage, it became a
popular answer to recycle everything. Unless the public understood that such
a solution was both technically and economically impossible and came to grips
with the best available solutions, Procter & Gamble would continue to see controversy around the disposal of our many products and packages. In order to
start to resolve the vast controversy and divergence of opinion, broad "dilemma
sharing" and dialogue needed to occur among key stakeholders to come to
consensus on a "right" way to manage solid waste. Then broad stakeholder

support (legislators, solid waste management people, the public, schools, press, activists, etc.) needed to be built for the solution so that policy in this area would embrace it.

The issues management strategy chosen for this was social dialogue and mutual solution development followed by the process to build stakeholder support. Authority figures, representing key stakeholder groups, were invited to dialogue around the technically "right" way to manage solid waste. A new consensus emerged. These policy makers realized that recycling was not the "magic solution"—and that a mix of solutions executed as an integrated system to most efficiently and effectively manage waste (i.e., Integrated Waste Management) was needed. These key leaders then dialogued with peers, catalyzing a broad change in thinking that became the basis of solid waste policy in America.

Action Plan Development

Once an overall issue change strategy has been chosen, the details of an action plan are developed. This will consist of the kinds of work that needs to be done to resolve the issue, and how the overall project will be coordinated among the various internal stakeholders. In the action plan, the needs of each external stakeholder group identified in issues analysis needs to be addressed. Depending on the change strategy selected and the complexity of the issue, the action plan may have many components. Most of these will be directed at developing and delivering communications tailored for each stakeholder group.[19]

Several years ago, Procter & Gamble found that publicity around the solid waste issue caused many parents to choose cloth diapers instead of disposables. Issues analysis showed that parents were very concerned about the environment and felt guilty using a product that they perceived to be bad for the environment. Furthermore, the reason they were choosing cloth diapers over disposables was: (1) because they thought cloth diapers carried no cost to the environment, and (2) they did not like the idea that diapers went to landfill. This analysis suggested that an adaptive strategy, helping parents understand the issue and making sure that other choices besides landfill were available, might be effective in neutralizing their environmental concerns.

Appropriate messages were developed and tested. Teaching parents that everything—even cloth—has an environmental cost and that, on a life-cycle basis, both cloth and disposables showed the environmental costs to be approximately equal, effectively neutralized part of the environmental issue for them. In addition, research showed that parents viewed composting as an acceptable alternative because of the resources recovered from the waste. To help neutralize the second aspect of the issue, Procter & Gamble began a technical program to ensure that communities understood and valued composting as part of their integrated waste solutions by providing technical expertise in building composting plants. This allowed parents to focus, more appropriately, on choice of a diapering product on the basis of benefits to the baby.

Commitment to Action Plan

Once the plan is developed and has the agreement of key internal stakeholders, it requires the commitment of senior management. Since much of the issues analysis process tends to occur at middle and lower levels of management, senior management needs to commit to undertake the actions outlined in the plan and to commit the resources to achieve the desired goal. They need to understand the risks of implementing the plan—and the risks of choosing not to. In some companies obtaining commitment to a program to avoid a crisis when there is no "fire at the door" is the final insurmountable challenge. This is the ageless quandary that all risk managers face—how to prove a particular action prevented a problem from happening. Using some examples may help. But obtaining senior management commitment and support at this point is key, making it nearly impossible to execute a complex action plan without the agreement of the senior stakeholders who are ultimately responsible.

Action Plan Execution

Finally, the plan is executed with frequent checkbacks to ensure that the desired results are actually being obtained. If not, issues analysis needs to be revisited to determine where a misunderstanding of the issue occurred or where some facet of the issue was missed.

LESSONS FOR CORPORATE STRATEGISTS

More than 30 years of experience has shown that anticipatory issues management or management of an issue during the emergence phase of the issue life cycle offers the opportunity to save cost, resources, and risk to reputation by issue resolution before a crisis can occur. A process is outlined by which this can be done and key concepts are discussed. Emphasis is put on understanding the issue life cycle, issue identification and prioritization, and issues analysis, which includes identifying and understanding subissues, identifying key stakeholders and their "authority figures," understanding stakeholder perspectives and desired solutions, and developing potential positions/messages aimed at these. Choosing a general issue change strategy, developing an action plan, and building stakeholder support for the solution are also discussed. This last concept is not only important in managing opposition but also can be used to help shape public policy and the public's perception of various social values.[20]

Even though the article is written from the perspective of business, the concepts and principles discussed are broadly applicable to issues faced by many organizations and institutions. It is hoped that this article might help some corporations improve their overall understanding of what is involved in anticipatory issues management and what can be done to improve prospects for better outcomes in issues management.

NOTES

9. Ashley, William C., and James L. Morrison, *Anticipatory Management*, Issue Action Publications, Leesburg, VA, 1995; J. K. Brown, *The Business of Issues: Coping with the Company's Environments*, The Conference Board, New York, 1979; W. H. Chase and Jones, B. L. *Guide to the Chase/Jones Issue Management Process Model*, Geyer-McAllister Publications, New York, 1979; Joseph T. Nolan, "Political Surfing When Issues Break," *Harvard Business Review*, 63, 1985, pp. 72–81; S. L. Wartick, and R. E. Rude, "Issues Management: Corporate Fad or Corporate Function?" *California Management Review*, 24(1), 1986, pp. 124–140.

10. Mitroff, I. I. "Programming for Crisis Control," *Security Management*, October 1989, pp. 75–79; Thierry C. Pauchant and I. I. Mitroff, "Crisis Management: Managing Paradox in a Chaotic World," *Technological Forecasting and Social Change*, 38, 1990, pp. 117–134; G. Siomkos, "Managing Product-harm Crises," *Industrial Crisis Quarterly*, 3, 1989, pp. 41–60; D. Smith, "Beyond Contingency Planning: Toward a Model of Crisis Management," *Industrial Crisis Quarterly*, 4, 1990, pp. 263–275.

11. Arrington, C. B., and R. N. Sawaya, "Managing Public Affairs: Issues Management in an Uncertain Environment," *California Management Review*, 26(4), 1984, pp. 148–160; J. Johnson, "Issues Management—What Are the Issues? An Introduction to Issues Management," *Business Quarterly*, 48(3), 1983, pp. 22–31; J. F. Mahon, and Waddock, S. A. "Strategic Issues Management: An Integration of Issues Life Cycle Perspectives," *Business & Society*, 31, 1992, pp. 19–32; Wouter Van Dieren and Steenwijk, R. Institute for Environmental & Systems Analysis, Amsterdam, The Netherlands, personal communication, 1996–1997; D. B. Yaffie, "Corporate Strategies for Political Action: A Rational Model," in A.M. Marcus (ed.), *Business Strategy and Public Policy*, Quorum, New York, 1987.

12. Hilgartner, S., and C. L. Bosk, "The Rise and Fall of Social Problems: A Public Arenas Model," *American Journal of Sociology*, 94(1), 1988, pp. 53–78.

13. Tombari, H. A. *Business and Society*, Dryden Press, New York, 1984.

14. Bigelow, B., L. Fahey, and J. F. Mahon, "Political Strategy and Issues Evolution: A Framework for Analysis and Action," in K. Paul (ed.), *Contemporary Issues in Business and Politics*, Edwin Mellen Press, Lewiston, NY, 1991, pp. 1–26.

15. Gitell, M. Procter & Gamble Research Study, *Consumer Attitudes Toward the Environment: The Next Ten Years*, Institute for the Future, Menlo Park, CA, 1994.

16. Procter & Gamble Research Studies, *Citizen Interest Groups and Corporate Interaction*, 1984, 1986.

17. Post, J. E. *Corporate Behavior and Social Change*, Reston Publishing, Reston, VA, 1978; L. E. Preston and J. E. Post, *Private Management and Public Policy: The Principle of Public Responsibility*, Prentice-Hall, Englewood Cliffs, NJ, 1975.

18. Helco, H. "Issues Networks and the Network Establishment," in A. Kings (eds.), *The New American Political System*, American Enterprise Institute, Washington, DC, 1978.

19. Dutton Jane E., Liam Fahey, and V. K. Narayanan, "Toward Understanding Strategic Issue Diagnosis," *Strategic Management Journal*, 4, 1983, pp. 307–323.

20. Buchholz, R. A. *Essentials of Public Policy for Management*, 2nd ed., Prentice-Hall, Englewood Cliffs, NJ, 1990; J. W. Kingdon, *Agendas, Alternatives and Public Policies*, Little, Brown, Boston, 1984.

Editor's Note: The essays by Anderson and Macauley are about responding to public expectations. The techniques of responsible care and issues management allow the resolution or containment of public pressure before it gets too big, or out of control. These executives know how to utilize the full resources of the mansion—from lobbying to advertisement and group meetings—to keep members of the neighborhood content and informed.

But what do you do when past mistakes have built up, and it is painfully clear that the public expects you to clean up? The following essay by Aliza Stern shows how leaders in Wichita, Kansas could clean up a real mess before it got too complex and too hot. Please note that this set of dispute-resolution techniques allows you to avoid the costly traffic jam of excessive court fees and negative press.

Fixing Past Mistakes by Managing Expectations

Aliza Stern

Aliza Stern is an attorney practicing law in New Jersey and Illinois. She has worked with environmental issues in both the public and private sectors.

In order to avoid the economic pitfalls of Superfund listing and to restore a contaminated site, the City of Wichita, Kansas united local businesses, lending institutions, and a state regulatory agency toward implementing an environmental cleanup plan. Wichita's approval for cleaning the Gilbert-Mosley site demonstrates the power of public-private cooperation. Property values were maintained, and an innovative program was implemented to enable property owners to buy, sell, and develop property without the fear of environmental litigation.

ENVIRONMENTAL PROBLEMS THREATEN RESIDENTS AND ECONOMY

In August 1990 the City of Wichita learned of groundwater contamination in a shallow aquifer underlying more than 1,800 acres of industrial, commercial, and residential property in and near downtown Wichita. The contamination was produced by area manufacturing, and consisted of chlorinated solvents, chlorinated hydrocarbons, and petroleum constituents. While the contamination had not yet affected drinking water, concern was expressed over the suburban drinking-water wells located six miles down-gradient of the contaminated area. Furthermore, the area of the contaminated groundwater, known as the Gilbert-Mosley site, was growing at the rate of 5,000 lineal feet per year.[21]

To protect the local economy from the impacts of being listed on the U.S.

Environmental Protection Agency's National Priority List (NPL), the city of Wichita decided to intervene and accept liability.[22] The Gilbert-Mosley site includes over 550 active businesses, more than 10 percent of the City's tax base, classified by the EPA as Potentially Responsible Parties (PRPs). Without local government intervention, each of the PRPs would be potentially liable for cleanup costs estimated at $15–$20 million. If the Gilbert-Mosley site were listed on the NPL, property values within the site would decline by 40 percent, translating into a loss of $5.06 million per year for the City and a $2.9 million decline in revenue for the local schools.[23]

When factoring in the estimated five-year period in which it takes the federal government to complete a Remedial Investigation/Feasibility Study (RI/FS) and Remedial Design for a Superfund site, Wichita would have incurred $25.3 million in tax revenue losses. After five years, the contamination plume would have grown an additional 25,000 feet, depressing the value of many adjoining properties.

Furthermore, the site could be listed for twenty years or more, preventing an economic recovery while the federal bureaucracy slowly progressed with the cleanup. Wichita was also aware of the stigma attached to listed property. City officials were attempting to circumvent public relations problems, including public perceptions of health problems, whether real or imagined, and adverse business effects, as wells as dramatic changes in life style if a water supply were affected.

Furthermore, NPL listing of the site would stop lending activities and property transactions within the city. Prior to the discovery of groundwater contamination, a $375 million revitalization plan for the downtown area was on the drawing board. However, these plans were withdrawn when the notice of contamination halted the availability of funding. City officials wanted to encourage local banks to continue lending to businesses and developers. Lending institutions had been extremely conservative in their lending practices and generally considered downtown redevelopment to be a risky venture. When these factors were combined with the presence of groundwater contamination, lenders were not willing to risk delinquent loans. Also, institutions were concerned about becoming a PRP for environmental cleanup costs through their lending activity.

In order to mitigate these various economic factors, to maintain public safety, and to move forward with the revitalization plan, the City of Wichita decided to intervene and accept liability for the cleanup. However, Wichita needed assurance that its plan was financially viable before it would enter into settlement agreement negotiations with regulatory agencies, lending institutions, and businesses. Part of the process included enlightening these groups of the benefits to all parties of forging an alliance.

First, Coleman Company, Inc. (Coleman), a PRP identified in the preliminary studies by the Kansas Department of Health and Environment (KDHE) as a major industrial contributor to the contamination, would have to agree to compensate the City for their portion of the contamination. Coleman had several forces drawing it to the negotiating table. Coleman would choose to enter into an agreement because if it did not negotiate with the City and Superfund were implemented, Coleman could potentially be liable for all of the expensive cleanup. Coleman also wanted to avoid any civil suits that could be brought by property owners for damages for the decline in property values due to the contamination. Coleman believed in the City's assumption that property values would rebound as a result of effective handling of the situation. Furthermore, Coleman had an interest in participating in the City's plan to solve the larger economic problems, as the company would also suffer from the economic decline of the City.

Second, the City needed to convince local banks that if it assumed responsibility for the cleanup, the banks would resume lending to local businesses regardless of the contamination. Thus, the banks were drawn to the negotiating table. Lenders agreed to negotiate because many of them already had investments in businesses located within the Gilbert-Mosley site and were at risk of becoming the "deep pockets" in the cost recovery should Superfund be implemented. Moreover, loan default rates in the area would be substantial without intervention to revitalize the economy. While agreeing to make further risky loans may seem like bad judgment on the part of banks, such loans were of secondary concern to cleanup liability.

SHAPING AN AGREEMENT THAT MEETS PUBLIC EXPECTATIONS

The Kansas Department of Health and the Environment (KDHE) was the lead agency determining the extent of the contamination at the Gilbert-Mosley site, and what action should be taken to remedy the problem. KDHE entered into a Cooperative Agreement with the EPA to determine the potential contamination in the area of the site. This early investigation was to determine the possible threat to human health and the environment, as well as whether the site should be listed on the NPL.

The City of Wichita avoided the NPL listing of the Gilbert-Mosley site by acting quickly and signing a Settlement Agreement with KDHE, accepting liability for the cleanup. In accepting liability, the City was concerned with financing a project that requires a substantial capital outlay. The City was concerned about the equity of the distribution of the burden. In this respect, those who contributed to the problem or those who would benefit from the remedy were the preferred bearers of the burden. Another consideration was determining who could afford the financial burden of the project; Responsible Parties are of little value if they do not have the means to contribute. Finally, there is the issue of the ease of collection. Often Responsible Parties (RPs) are identified who have the financial capacity to participate, but the difficulty of collecting makes the RP an unacceptable target. The agreement entered into with KDHE was framed to deal with each of these issues.[24]

The agreement gives the City the authority to implement measures to clean up the contamination and to revitalize the economy. However, the agreement will be void if the City fails to create a Tax Increment Financing District, negotiate an agreement with at least four lending institutions, and negotiate an agreement with Coleman Company, Inc. to share the activities and costs required by the Settlement Agreement.

TAX INCREMENT FINANCING: PUBLIC LEVERS THAT WORK FOR BUSINESS AND THE PUBLIC

In Wichita, property values began declining rapidly once contamination was discovered, and dropped further when banks stopped lending on property in the area. It is estimated that these values declined approximately 40 percent. To stop this hemorrhaging, the City of Wichita invoked Tax Increment Financing (TIF). TIF is a mechanism used by local governments in over thirty states to finance public improvements associated with development or redevelopment projects. The mechanism is based on the assumption that an area will produce greater tax revenues through improvements than would have been produced without such development. The "increment" is the difference between the property taxes paid before and after the development district was established. A certain portion of the larger revenues is then allocated to pay for the costs of development. Under state law, however, the tax revenue reserved for TIF district development may not exceed 20 percent of the total revenue received from the TIF district in any given year.

The TIF district was formally established on July 12, 1991, and tax collection from the TIF began in the 1992 budget year. In each year since its implementation (1992–1994), the City has collected $504,000, $414,000, and $423,000 respectively. These figures represent less than 0.3 percent of the property tax revenues available to the City, and the City has chosen to absorb these costs in its General Fund Budget instead of adding to the tax levies.[25] To date, no city services have suffered from the TIF. Furthermore, the TIF approach, in combination with the presence of a major, cooperative PRP, was designed to be a much less costly approach than the potential loss due to the contamination if a remediation plan were not implemented.

CERTIFICATE AND RELEASE PROGRAM: SHAPING PUBLIC GOALS

Under the authority of the Settlement Agreement between the City and KDHE, Wichita instituted a Certificate and Release Program. Through this program, landowners apply for release from cleanup liability. If the release is granted, the Certificate of Release document is filed with the Register of Deeds, and the holder of the Certificate can engage in property transactions without fear of incurring environmental liability due to the contamination. The release from liability applies to actions brought by KDHE, as well as the City. However, if the City fails to fulfill its obligations under the Settlement Agreement, due to lack of funding or other events, the Certificates will have no effect in relation to any environmental response actions not yet completed.

An agreement between the lending institutions and the City was established in April 1991, to assure the City that banks would resume lending to entities who obtained a Certificate of Release in the area of the contaminated site. This agreement was contingent upon a number of events: A TIF district had to be established for the site, a work plan had to be completed for the Agreement between KDHE and the City, and the Agreement had to be signed by at least four banks. All of these contingencies were satisfied, and banks have resumed lending in the Gilbert-Mosley area, with loans totaling approximately $96 million.[26]

SECURING A PUBLIC-PRIVATE PARTNERSHIP: LESSONS FOR LEADERS

Even though Wichita accepted responsibility for cleanup of the Gilbert-Mosley site, the City needed a private-sector partner to bear some of the financial burden. Under Superfund, local government has the authority to make any business that contributed to the contamination an economic partner through cost recovery. However, many businesses are unwilling or unable to meet their financial responsibilities for the cleanup. Wichita contained this problem by finding a willing private partner in Coleman.

Coleman, a manufacturer of camping equipment, is thought to be the largest contributor to the contamination. After approximately sixty days of negotiations between Coleman and the city of Wichita, an agreement was reached. Normally, RPs may not negotiate an agreement with EPA until after the RI/FS is completed. In this case, however, two factors enabled the City and Coleman to enter an agreement before the RI/FS. First, the City had already committed to accepting liability. Second, it was necessary to act quickly and to reach an agreement on the Remedial Investigation/Feasibility Study and the Remedial Design/Remedial Action (RD/RA) in order to revitalize the economy in the area.

The agreement between Coleman and Wichita establishes the conditions under which Coleman would contribute its share of the costs to the City's investigation and remediation of the Gilbert and Mosley site. Thus, Coleman agreed to reimburse the City with one million dollars for "direct costs" of the RI/FS. Such costs include payment for testing procedures, laboratory analysis, consultants, environmental contractors and subcontractors, interim response measures, and salaries of City employees assigned to project management. If the cost of the RI/FS exceeds this sum, Coleman will split the additional costs with the City.

The costs of the RD/RA will be shared by both parties according to a formula in the agreement. According to this formula, Coleman will contribute 100 percent of cleanup costs for areas in which they are primarily responsible for the contamination and 50 percent in areas where they share responsibility with other parties. The City will contribute the remaining 50 percent, but will seek contributions from other responsible parties as well. If any disputes arise between Coleman and Wichita, they will be referred to an arbitrator.

Furthermore, the agreement extends contribution protection and a covenant not to sue to Coleman for activities at the Gilbert-Mosley site addressed in the agreement. The covenant not to sue is the City's promise not to sue or bring administrative action against Coleman in order to force Coleman to perform actions or make payments beyond that required by the agreement.

Coleman has benefited financially from the plan and its success. Landowners in the area of the site who have tried to sue Coleman for causing a decline in property values and subjecting them to liability have had a very difficult time showing an actual decline in property values or potential future liability. For example, only six suits have been filed against Coleman, and only one of those went to trial. The jury in that case awarded the plaintiffs less than one-fourth of what they requested.

Another benefit Coleman received is that the negotiated agreement with the City has allocated a "fair share" of the cleanup costs to Coleman, avoiding the "deep pocket" allocation. However, Coleman's attorney expressed concern that Coleman's consulting firm and the City's consulting firm were not in agreement over what portion of the contamination is attributable to Coleman and where that contamination is located. Therefore, the percentages that Coleman must contribute to the cleanup under the formula in the agreement were undetermined. The cleanup, however, will not be delayed by an interruption in Coleman's participation should this issue require additional time to resolve, because adequate funding is available from the Tax Incremental Financing.

THE STRATEGIC BENEFITS OF MANAGING PUBLIC EXPECTATIONS

Even with the delay due to the state's review, the RI/FS was completed in record time. The full-scale remediation was underway by the summer of 1994, only four years after Wichita learned of the groundwater contamination.

The city addressed each of its concerns in its cleanup plan:

- The distribution of the burden of the cleanup is equitable: Coleman and other contributors to the contamination will pay the bulk of the costs, while the local population will pay a small percentage of the costs through taxes.

- Those bearing the burden can afford to pay the cost of remediation.
- The City's plan ensures ease of collection of contributions, as Coleman has voluntarily signed an agreement with the City and taxpayers must fulfill their payment obligations as usual.

The preferred course of action in any situation involving environmental contamination must always be determined by the particular circumstances. However, once the EPA has established the necessary elements of CERCLA liability and a statutory defense is lacking, a PRP's best strategy will generally be early settlement with the government.

The Gilbert-Mosley site settlement reveals a number of advantages over a litigious alternative. Massive legal expenses can be avoided and the savings used for the investigation and site cleanup. Also, settling parties will be able to exercise more control over the cleanup process, and circumvent the higher costs of an EPA-implemented investigation or cleanup. Therefore, potential damage to the local economy and property values may be avoided or remedied more quickly. For Wichita, the use of strategic alliances was successful in maintaining the economic stability of the city and avoiding the expensive and time-consuming process of assigning blame.

NOTES

21. Please see Lee Ann Groene's "Kansas Facing Weighty Environmental Tasks," *Wichita Business Journal*, January 1, 1990.

22. EPA's National Priorities List is a registry of serious Superfund sites—areas contaminated by past industrial practices and in dire need of cleanup.

23. Based on information collected by the author with the help of City of Wichita staff. The writer would like to thank Chris Cherches, the City Manager, City of Wichita, Kansas, for providing important information for this article.

24. Agreement between City of Wichita, Kansas and Coleman Company, Inc., April 23, 1991.

25. Please see Roger Olsen and Jack Brown, "Site-ing a Good Example," *American City & County*, August 1993.

26. Please see Robert Hauser, "Cleanup in Kansas: A Model of Innovation," *World Waste*, September 1996.

Editors' Note: Many companies are lost in the riddles and expenses of cleaning up past mistakes, or dominated by the new puzzles of present predicaments. Where the Stern minicase provides an example of how companies can rise above the fray and solve the riddles, the essay by Schilling is designed to give the next generation of environmental leaders some terms by which to understand these significant developments.

A Primer in Alternative Dispute Resolution Approaches and Terminology

Joseph Schilling

Joseph Schilling is currently the Director of Economic Development for ICMA in Washington, D.C., where he facilitates research on brownfields development. He has an L.L.M. in environmental law from George Washington University. Prior to working for ICMA, Schilling served for twelve years as a Senior Deputy City Attorney in San Diego.

Environmental issues are more complex and involve more interested parties than in the recent past—often with competing interests. Against this backdrop of multiple participants and differing attitudes, the legal landscape of ever-changing environmental laws, complex regulations, and inconsistent court decisions creates an atmosphere ripe for disagreement.

Given these complexities, environmental professionals can avail themselves of a continuum of conflict-management and dispute-resolution approaches.

Because conflict management is not a linear process, often various approaches or a combination of strategies may be appropriate. The dynamics of the dispute and the incentives to negotiate will dictate the relative success of the particular dispute-resolution approach.

For each conflict-management approach, focus on the relationship between the type of decision, the decision maker, and the parties' involvement. Approaches are divided according to the locus of decision-making authority (see Figure 11-12). In the alternative dispute resolution (ADR) strategies (collaborative problem solving, facilitation, and mediation), the disputants exercise

Continuum of Conflict Management and Dispute Resolution Approaches		
Informal Discussion Negotiations Collaborative Problem Solving and Facilitation Mediation	Arbitration Admin. Hgs.	Legislative Decisions and Rulemaking Judicial Decisions (Minitrials)
Decision Made by Parties	3rd-Party Decision Making	Legal (public) Authoritative Third Party Decision Making
COLLABORATIVE APPROACHES		ADVERSARIAL APPROACHES
Increased coercion and likelihood of win-lose outcome ➤➤➤		

Figure 11-12 The ADR Continuum

greater control and influence in making decisions. This contrasts with formal legal methods that are used to resolve disputes, where decision making is in the hands of a third party (judge, arbitrator, administrative hearing officer, or legislator). As the continuum moves from ADR to formal methods, the likelihood increases that a decision will create one party a winner and another a loser.[28]

THE CONTINUUM OF NEGOTIATION STRATEGIES

- *Informal discussions* are started by one or more parties to gather preliminary information about the situation. Informal discussions can help build trust and willingness to try creative ADR approaches. Even when the entities have a prior history, changes in personnel or management or the impact of external forces (media or citizens groups) may require informal discussions to reestablish levels of trust. An astute manager can use regular informal discussions as an effective approach to maintain important strategic relationships.

- *Negotiations* generally involve specific issues with the goals of persuasion, problem solving, and reaching decisions. In *Getting to YES*, Robert Fisher and William Ury of the Harvard Negotiations Project classify negotiations into two major types: positional vs. principled. The less-effective positional negotiations involve a give-and-take sequence of positions, arguing over what they do or do not want. Arguing over positions often tends to lock the negotiators into their respective positions.[29]

- *Principled negotiations* determine each party's underlying interest. The distinction between positions and interests is important in successfully using any of the ADR processes outlined on the continuum. The task is to separate or identify the interests from the positions. Fisher and Ury stress that positions tend to be concrete and explicit, while interests, once articulated, can be a divining force toward resolution.

- *Collaborative problem solving/facilitation/mediation.* The distinctions between collaborative problem solving and facilitation lie in the scope of the issues and the flexibility in the decision-making standard. Collaborative problem solving generally involve specific problems and concrete issues (e.g. regulatory negotiations), while public policy facilitations involve broader discussions where participants jointly identify and narrow the issues and then brainstorm about possible solutions. A true collaborative problem-solving process always uses consensus as the decision-making standard, while under some circumstances successful facilitations can happen without complete consensus.

  Mediation generally happens after the parties may have reached an impasse in their own negotiations. Mediation is usually a voluntary process, but it can also be mandated or encouraged by the courts, particularly in civil matters as a means to relieve the court's crowded dockets.

A mediator helps the parties communicate, negotiate, and reach agreements and settlements, but does not render a decision.[30]

- In *arbitration*, disputing parties present the facts of their case and argue the merits of their legal positions before an independent third party. The arbitrator then renders a decision and makes an award.

- *Administrative hearings* serve as the primary adjudicative process for many government agencies. Administrative hearings follow certain prescribed rules of procedure and many employ administrative law judges (ALJs) or hearing officers to decide individual regulatory claims.

- *Legislative decisions and agency rulemaking.* The legislative process, along with the courts, is adversarial by nature. Ultimately, the legislators' votes make winners out of one side and losers of another. While legislators and judges operate within these formal processes, the parties to the dispute do not directly participate in the decision making.

- *Judicial decisions* use judges or juries to make the final decision, not the attorneys or the parties. The scope of the decision, however, is limited by judicial precedent, statutory law, and the concept of legal rights.

NOTES

28. Bacow, Lawrence and Michael Wheeler, *Environmental Disputes Resolution*, MIT, Plenum Press, New York, 1987.

29. Fisher, Roger, William Ury, and Bruce Patton, *Getting to YES: Negotiating an Agreement Without Giving In*, 2nd ed., Arrow Business Books, London, 1991.

30. Susskind, Lawrence, *Breaking the Impasse: Consensual Approaches to Resolving Public Disputes*, Basic Books, New York, 1987.

Editors' Note: It would be naive and dangerous to give future managers the false feeling that all environmental disputes can be fixed and "made whole" as in the Wichita, Kansas cleanup. Such successful management of conflicting positions is rare, although indicative of the routes the future still holds as promising.

This chapter closes with two minicases designed to reveal real-world complexities in the effort to answer public expectations. The first of these cases is about failure, about a noble effort on the part of some paint manufacturers to fix an impending Clean Air crisis on volatile organic compounds (VOCs)—compounds that are both commonplace and costly to public health and industrial practice. Tim Herbst, an environmental counselor with the public relations firm Ruder Finn, does a superb job analyzing the elements of the failed agreement still looming large into the next century.

The second case, about a negotiated agreement between the EPA and forest and paper products manufacturers, echoes our opening on Responsible Care. The weight of public expectations after the tragic incident at Bhopal allowed firms like Macauley's Union Carbide to regroup and rethink. As a result, the twentieth century ends with chemical manufacturers assuming a real leadership role.

But what about industry types that have not yet felt the full weight of the Bhopal accident? Do they have the same reasons to mobilize change, and can they carry out strategic redirection with the same urgency and intensity of focus? This question is posed at the end of 1998, some fifteen years after Bhopal. It is still too early to tell if what worked for chemical manufacturers will work in the same logic and tactics, for other industries.

As these words are written, the Clinton Administration has proposed to extend some of the principles of Responsible Care and voluntary public disclosure to five other key industry types: oil products, steel, other metals, autos, and paper. That might inspire a decade of further change. According to John Cushman of the New York Times, *"if the Environmental Protection Agency has its way, people who live near hundreds of factories in five major industries will soon gain on-line access to mountains of data about the pollution given off by these plants."[31]*

Cushman continues, "the profiles will include each factory's pollution permit violations, inspections, toxic releases and the demographics of surrounding communities, which might help track whether any group is being disproportionately affected." Now that demands a serious new look at business and environmental strategy.

This is a part of ongoing efforts to expand what is known as "right to know" initiatives, first established in 1988 under SARA Title III and now commonly known as TRI—the Toxics Release Inventory. Yet, the suggested challenges go further than forced change by law. It inspires change by going public.[32] Since disclosure itself is a great corporate motivator.

Clearly, in order to operate in such a world of public disclosure, tomorrow's corporate leaders need to know how best to manage public expectations. Once again, the best learning here resides in the classics of political science and public management.

This chapter on stakeholder management ends with a case on how the EPA worked with the forest and paper products industry to resolve some significant environmental disputes. As you sift through the complete workings of this agreement, please note why simple public disclosure is no longer enough. Leaders of the next century will need to now how to apply improved government relations and public relations at the right intensity, at precisely the right time. This takes both strategic thinking and Deborah Anderson's advice on "anticipatory issues management."

In the beginning, practitioners solved environmental problems by throwing their best engineers and lawyers at the problems, instructing them to offer regulators and their publics a few doable options. That will always work to some limited degree.

In the next century, the public will expect a higher level of corporate citizenry. The CMA learned to let their high-rise executives meet with the host community. Other industries now voluntarily disclose some information on how they plan to reduce spills, emissions, or TRI numbers. The best suggestion for future leaders: Read some of the classics while in business school. They will prepare you for articulate and demanding stakeholders.

NOTES

31. Cushman, John, *New York Times,* Vol. CXLVI, No. 50,882, August 12, 1997.
32. For an insightful early study of TRI and SARA Title III, please see Michael Baram's *Managing Chemical Risks,* published by Tufts in 1990.

When an Agreement Is Not Profitable: The Paint Industry and Its Search for a National VOC Standard

Timothy D. Herbst

Timothy Herbst is currently an Environmental Councilor with the public affairs firm E. Bruce Harrison, a division of Ruder Finn. Mr. Herbst earned his M.S. in Environmental Management & Policy at Rensselaer Polytechnic Institute's Lally School of Management & Technology.

Calls for reinventing the EPA and demands for regulatory reform have escalated since the seating of the Republican majority in the 104th Congress in 1994. Trumping the evils of unfunded mandates and overburdensome environmental regulation has proved to be a powerful campaign weapon. But since early 1990, the EPA, and state regulatory agencies, have been practicing just such regulatory reform. Through regulatory negotiations, or reg-neg (see Figure 11-13), regulatory agencies have teamed with industry and other affected interests to build consensus over proposed rulemaking. Is this the start of an important next-century development?

The paint industry and other interested parties have recognized the potential for negotiated rulemaking to account for both an industry's economic well being and the goals of the regulatory agency. That recognition has resulted in working with the EPA in a reg-neg to develop uniform national guidelines for architectural and industrial maintenance (AIM) coatings to control volatile organic compound (VOC) emissions. By involving affected parties in regulation crafting, reg-neg was perceived by both the paint industry and the EPA as a means to reach sustainable and cost-effective VOC restrictions. As a consequence, a consensus regulation would achieve environmental goals while avoiding the delays, litigation, and resistance that traditional environmental rulemaking usually encounters from industry, thereby saving expense for industry, government, and the public.

Robert J. Nelson, the director of environmental affairs for the National Paint and Coating Association (NPCA), says that reg-neg offered:[33]

> . . . a unique opportunity for industry to help fashion a reasonable and rational regulatory scheme that [would] impact the formulation and sale of architectural and industrial coatings for the next decade, but it also [was] a chance to earn the

Just a few weeks after the Clean Air Act Amendments of 1990 were signed into law, the EPA and other agencies were handed an alternative to traditional adversarial rulemaking in the form of the Negotiated Rulemaking Act of 1990. By establishing statutory authority, the Act was created to encourage a wider use of regulation negotiation, a participatory rulemaking technique successfully used by some federal agencies.

Reg-neg is a process of consensus building with the goal of an agreed-upon text for a proposed rule. But reg-neg is not appropriate for all rulemaking. According to the Act, three criteria must be met to proceed with a reg-neg.

- All affected interests must be identified.
- Participants will negotiate in good faith.
- There should be a reasonable likelihood that a committee will reach a consensus. An agency can then opt to assemble a committee that represents affected interests—in a face-to-face forum usually with the help of a facilitator—to reach a consensus agreement. Reg-neg is designed to reverse time-consuming, expensive, and at times ineffective traditional rulemaking by allowing affected interests participation in the rulemaking process.

Reg-neg's interactive and open dialogue promotes effective rulemaking.

- It forces parties to understand and refine their own position to effectively educate others.
- The process forces participants to hear and consider alternative viewpoints.
- Open communication with diverse interests allows new, creative ideas to be voiced and considered.
- The exchange, in the interest of reaching consensus, allows parties to trade away less valuable priorities in exchange for critical priorities.
- An agreement that considers and accounts for all vital interests (in other words reaches consensus) is the desirable outcome.

A reg-neg consensus (if adopted by the agency) will still undergo the traditional public notice and comment and, perhaps, judicial review. If the consensus agreement, however, incorporates all vital interests, litigation is less likely. Any late-coming disgruntled parties will have less credibility since they failed to participate in the process and voice their concerns. While the process has been criticized by some participants for its time and monetary commitments, the end result avoids the traditional litigation, delays, and expense noted above. Even without an agreement, the open communication and exchange of ideas increase the chances of having at least some of the affected parties' interests considered in the proposed rulemaking before it is crafted. It is also an opportunity for regulators to test the creative ideas that might come out of a reg-neg.

Figure 11-13 Overview of Negotiated Rulemaking

respect and trust of the public by showing that ours is a progressive industry that, through the building of consensus, can solve its problems in a manner that balances the environmental needs of the nation and its own economic concerns.

Under the leadership of the NPCA the paint industry committed over two years to the AIM reg-neg. The negotiators, however, failed to reach a consensus. While it is uncertain the degree to which the EPA, armed with two years of knowledge, will incorporate the paint industry's interests into its rulemaking, a consensus agreement surely would have been more satisfactory.

The AIM reg-neg's failure stemmed from the complexity of establishing uniform national guidelines that will impact over 450 companies with a wide array of products. According to Nelson, over 65 percent of the total gallons of paints and coatings produced by those companies will be affected. For example, if VOC emission limits per gallon were set too low, uniform national guidelines would have unequal effects on the diverse paint industry. While larger manufacturers can take advantage of standardization to avoid the patchwork of existing state regulations, many small companies are disadvantaged by uniform regulations because of their relatively high market share of high-solvent coating, (hence high VOC emissions). Moreover, performance standards, technological limitations, and scientific uncertainty complicated the process.

Over the last few decades the paint industry has established a sensible and effective environmental strategy to meet the public's demands for environmentally friendly products. New product development and reformulation of existing products has removed toxins such as lead and mercury as well as reducing and eliminating VOCs from paints and coatings. The industry involvement in the AIM reg-neg was simply their latest environmental management initiative. Only when this disparate and highly competitive industry tried to coordinate their efforts and product makeup did their environmental strategy become precarious.

NATURE OF THE VOC DISPUTE: WHY THE PAINT INDUSTRY IS REPRESENTATIVE OF THINGS TO COME

Many paints and coatings are traditionally high in solvent content. Solvents function as an aid to application and as a thinner to the product. In the past, high solvent content has been critical to the performance level of coatings demanded by the applicator and end-user. But solvents evaporate VOCs during the manufacturing, application, and curing process. VOCs react photochemically with nitrogen dioxide (emitted by burning petrochemicals) and form harmful ground-level ozone. Ozone (O_3) at ground level exacts a high cost to society's health and economic base. From lung irritation in humans to agricultural damage, effects from VOC emissions take their toll. According to a 1984 report by the congressional Office of Technology Assessment (OAT), "ozone alone is thought to be responsible for about 90 percent of all of the damage that air pollutants cause to agriculture, with a total economic cost that has been estimated at six to seven percent of U.S. agricultural productivity."

Because ozone is a secondary pollutant formed by a chemical reaction, it is difficult to monitor. VOCs, on the other hand, are primary pollutants and are good indicators of the potential of ozone formation. It has been estimated that coatings emissions in the Los Angeles basin make up 21 percent of all VOC emissions (and 41 percent among nontransportation sources).[34] Consequently, in an effort to control smog, guidelines have been devised to control VOC emissions from paints and coatings.

Today the paint and coating industry faces a wide variety of VOC regulations. In 1997, nine states had VOC restrictions specifically targeting AIM coatings (with California, New York, New Jersey, and Texas having the most stringent). In addition, over thirty states had VOC restrictions that could potentially impact paint coatings. The industry had no choice but to reformulate their products. Government, by developing regulation to address the public's concern for clean air, forced technological innovation.

MOBILIZING A RESPONSE:
THE MANUFACTURER'S SURVEY

The paint and coating industry has responded to regulation with research and development to reformulate and substitute for high-VOC-emitting products. Before VOC restrictions, R&D efforts focused on the development of water-base latex interior and exterior paints that provided ease of application and cleanup. To comply with new regulations (and since latex paints inherently emit fewer VOCs) paint manufacturers improved and expanded their existing line of latex paints.

Reformulating high-solvent alkyd paints into high-solid, low-solvent alkyd or oil base paints also helped manufacturers comply with VOC regulations. By reducing solvent content, (i.e., mineral spirits and traditional aliphatic hydrocarbons) and using a lower molecular weight polymer permitting lower viscosity, the industry has been developing paints that emit far fewer VOCs than older, oil-base paints and that conform to local and state regulations.

Manufacturers are exploring more creative technologies. High-performance waterborne materials, such as polyurethanes and epoxies, are becoming more commonplace. Like latex paints, these new coatings are part of a water dispersal rather than a solvent dispersal system. In addition, powder coating and radiation-cured paints hold promise for the future in industrial settings. This new technology, however, is rarely, if ever, used for on-site residential and commercial applications.

Just as they were able to remove lead and mercury from their coatings, the paint and coating industry has developed technologies that have drastically reduced VOC emission. But simply developing technologies to reduce VOCs and ensure regulatory compliance was not enough. If individual paint companies were to continue to satisfy their customers, performance also had to be considered. The result has been a substantial increase in research and development staff and expenditures to maintain and improve the performance characteristics of low-VOC-emitting paints and coatings. Today, 75 percent of the paint industry's R&D expenditures are directed toward lowering VOCs in their paints and coatings.[35]

Individual companies have taken different approaches in response to VOC regulations. Glidden is perhaps striving to be the "greenest" of them all. Glidden has devoted much of its efforts on producing zero-VOC architectural paints. To the rest of the industry, however, the zero-VOC market is still too young to pursue. A spokesperson for Sherwin Williams commented, "The movement from four percent [the VOCs in traditional water-base paints] to zero percent VOC solvents will represent a very small reduction in VOC emissions." The spokesperson also claimed that the new technology risks "significant sacrifices in product performance," a claim undoubtedly discounted by Glidden. Sherwin Williams, like much of the industry, is instead concentrating on improving and expanding their waterborne product line and lowering the VOCs of their alkyd paints.[36]

The performance of waterborne paints and coatings has drastically improved over the years. Many outperform comparable oil-base products. Still, alkyd paints are necessary and preferred for many applications. High-solid low-VOC alkyd paints, then, must reach acceptable performance criteria. Dunn Edwards Corp., a Los Angeles–based company, has tripled its R&D staff to meet the challenge of lowering VOCs and improving the poor performance characteristics of high-solid alkyd paints. Professional painters have criticized the new paint's spread-and-flow characteristics, which result in thicker coats and more paint being used. High-solid paints also tend to yellow very quickly, making them less aesthetically desirable.

The type of technology paint manufacturers have chosen to reduce VOC emissions is largely related to their market share. At the risk of oversimplification, the paint industry can be divided into large and small companies. Larger companies, like Glidden, with their superior financial and R&D resources have focused much of their efforts on waterborne technology and have successfully captured the majority of the waterborne market share.

Smaller and mid-sized locally based companies like Passonno Paints (Albany, New York) and Dunn Edwards have traditionally had the majority of their market share committed to alkyd enamels and specialty coatings. The majority of their (relatively limited) R&D efforts have been devoted to high-solid technology. But ultra-low-VOC-emission restrictions on paints and coatings (below 250 grams per liter) would threaten a large portion of smaller paint manufacturers' market share. The performance characteristics of the current technology would force end-users to look to alternatives like waterborne coatings. Without the resources to take on the waterborne markets, strict VOC emissions are sure to threaten the survival of many small paint and coating manufacturers.

Under the Clean Air Act Amendments of 1990 (CAAA), EPA was charged with studying and regulating VOC emissions from consumer and commercial products to control ground-level ozone. In addition, the EPA could control or prohibit any activity, including the manufacture or sale of paints and coatings that emit VOCs.

In 1989, the EPA estimated in the *National Air Quality and Emissions Trend Report* that more than 66 million people in the United States lived in counties where the ozone standard was exceeded. Because AIM paints and coatings are estimated to account for 20 percent of the total VOC emissions from commercial and consumer products, the EPA considered AIM regulation a priority.[37]

With the decision to study and regulate AIM coatings and paints, the EPA was required by law to formulate regulations with a significant amount of technical, scientific, and economic information on the emissions and the industry to be regulated. Product manufacturers, as well as end-users, had to be given due consideration. In addition, in the spirit of traditional rulemaking (at least since the 1960s) the EPA had to have credible evidence to withstand public comment and scrutiny. But even with hard evidence, traditional rulemaking often ends with judicial review. Litigation is not only costly but delays environmental goals. Delays encourage uncertainty, which creates industry expense. As a result, neither the public good nor the regulated industries are better off.

A NEGOTIATING COMMITTEE TAKES AIM

For more than five years, the NPCA and the paint industry worked with the EPA to craft a national rule on VOC emissions. According to J. Andrew Doyle, executive director of the NPCA, reasonable national standards are in the industry's best interest. Manufacturers "must reformulate for specific regions, inventory products separately, keep different records, and label differently for as many as 45 different product lines."[38]

On October 15, 1992, the 35 member AIM Reg-Neg Committee, comprised of representatives from the EPA, end-users, environmental organizations, industry and industry trade groups, labor, and state agencies, and with the assistance of the Keystone Center (a facilitation contractor retained by the EPA), held its first meeting. Original timetables had negotiations ending May 1, 1993, publication of the proposed rule by late summer 1993, and the final rule by January 15, 1993. In late 1992, it became apparent that the committee would not meet its goals. The EPA, noting progress and signaling a commitment to the reg-neg process, extended the deadline. New timetables were established and again were not met and were subsequently extended.

As early as July 1993, the NPCA and many others on the AIM Reg-Neg Committee agreed, in principal, to phase out approximately 25 percent of the total VOCs from AIM coatings by 1996 (from a base year of 1990) with an additional 10 percent by 2000 and a final 10 percent by 2003. Given this scenario and based on a 1992 AIM survey, over 445.5 million pounds of VOC emission will be eliminated by 2003.[39]

Not all parties on the AIM Reg-Neg Committee agreed with this tentative understanding. Robert Wendoll, director in charge of environmental affairs at

Dunn Edwards and chairman of the Environmental Legislative and Regulatory Advocacy Program of the Southern California Paint and Coating Association, claimed "[the AIM] Reg/Neg could prove to be the single most catastrophic event in the history of the paint and coating industry."[40] His fears stem from the tentative agreement's imposition of a strict national uniform VOC regulation. Wendoll, and others representing small manufacturers, formed the Allied Local and Regional Manufacturers (ALARM) caucus to fight the tentative agreement they perceived as adversely impacting their segment of the industry. To support their position, ALARM argued that strict across-the-board VOC standards would result in poorer-quality products, more frequent recoating, and a consequent increase in VOC emissions. ALARM also questioned the scientific basis for regulating VOCs as a means of reducing low-lying ozone.

In the end, the committee failed to reach a consensus and negotiations were terminated in late 1994. The perceived inequities of a strict uniform VOC standard, questions of performance standards, and scientific uncertainty clouded the negotiations enough to prevent a consensus agreement. The EPA, in the absence of an agreement but armed with two years of knowledge as a result of the negotiations, is currently developing VOC restrictions on its own.

OUTCOMES AND REMAINING BARRIERS

Some of the proposals that addressed the tentative agreement (and will likely be the basis of EPA's rulemaking) established a "table of standards" of VOC limits for specific paints and coatings that will need to be met in 1996, 2000, and 2003. But the restrictions will not affect all manufacturers in the same manner. While some specialty coatings may be exempt, non-flat alkyd coatings will be drastically reduced. As noted above, large paint manufacturers have the majority of their market shares in waterborne systems. Regulations that discourage solvent-based alkyd coatings could increase their market share. Moreover, large manufacturers can draw on their R&D resources to develop new products and/or reduce VOC emissions in existing paints. Smaller, locally based companies, however, do not have extensive R&D resources or the capital to make the adjustments—at least under strict timetables. To be fair, some proposals discussed by the committee included exemptions for small manufacturers with annual sales under $10 million. In addition, smaller firms might be given longer timetables to conform to the proposed restrictions. But without the ability to substitute high-solvent products, even with the exemptions and extensions, it is possible many firms might not survive the proposed rules. Small manufacturers demonstrated during the negotiations that they would not go under without a fight.

The issue is also clouded with scientific and technical uncertainty. Paint manufacturers have argued and have prevailed in legal challenges against regulations in California on the grounds that the technology does not exist to reduce VOCs from many coatings and still get a quality product.[41] Restrictions, they argue, can lead to the substitutions of lower-quality products that have both adverse environmental and economic consequences. High-solid paints, for example, have a thick viscosity with poor flow-and-spread characteristics, often forcing the applicator to add high-VOC-emitting thinners to ease application. Additional priming, topcoating, recoating, touchup, and repair work characteristic of reformulated and substituted paints all presumably lead to added VOC emissions. One has to wonder in the absence of a consensus agreement over a national VOC standard if these judgments would be used as legal precedent against any proposed regulations.

In addition, not all VOCs react the same in the atmosphere, but the differences are poorly understood. William Carter, a member of the Advisory Council, claimed in a technical paper that "emissions of a given amount of one type of VOC might form significantly more ozone than an equal amount of another." Moreover, there are hundreds of different types of VOCs emitted that have not been tested. "This includes particularly almost all the VOCs emitted from water-base coatings."[42] Some manufacturers, then, argue that a push to water-base coatings will result in more reactive VOC emissions.

It seems certain the EPA will move ahead with regulation regardless of these unanswered questions. Public policy is based on known facts, not uncertainty. Still, given the disproportionate effect of a national VOC standard, the proposed rules will be met with resistance. The scientific uncertainty only fuels the regulatory resistance and threatens the overall environmental goals. To better understand the relative effects of VOCs, and to remove the uncertainty as a tool for regulatory delay, the issue demands further research. President Clinton, in his proposed fiscal 1996 budget, demonstrated the need for guidance on scientific questions as one key to effective rulemaking. Clinton called for $77.4 million in federal grants for independent research to answer some of the scientific questions that underlie environmental rulemaking. Some of these funds, if approved by Congress, could be dedicated to study the relative effect of VOC emissions from paints and coatings on ozone emissions.

The paint and coating industry has responded well to the public's environmental concerns. Through ongoing technological innovation resulting in reformulated and new product development, the industry has managed to remove lead and mercury, and has reduced VOC emissions from their paints and coatings. The industry's sound environmental strategy led them to commit to the AIM reg-neg.

Regulatory negotiations ideally end in a consensus agreement to avoid the traditional but sometimes ineffective, delay-ridden, and costly rulemaking process. However, consensus may simply be too difficult to reach for an industry consisting of hundreds of different-sized manufacturers with a wide array of products. Scientific uncertainty and technological limitation—issues that in the absence of the inequities of the restrictions might have been overcome through negotiations—only strengthened the opposition.

The lack of consensus on a national VOC standard and the potential legal challenge to the inevitable rulemaking is an unfortunate precedent. Efforts initiated by the Bush Administration and continued under the Clinton Administration to better incorporate business interests in regulatory rulemaking might be hindered. The outcome of the AIM reg-neg will signal at least a partial failure of regulation negotiations and might cause other industries and regulators to avoid what may otherwise be a potentially promising negotiated rulemaking process. Perhaps a more practical and objective approach for those looking to involve themselves in a reg-neg would be to study and understand the limitations as well as the possibilities of regulation negotiations. The potential still exists.

NOTES

33. Mayfield, Lisa Pritchard, "Reg-Neg Facilitates Agreement on National VOC Rule," *Modern Paint and Coating*, October 1992, p. 110.

34. Lents, James M., "Cleaner Paints Critical to South Coast Air Quality," *Modern Paint and Coating*, October 1991, p. 112.

35. Coeyman, Marjorie, "Fighting to Keep Up Standards of Performance: A Paint-making Technological Revolution," *Chemical Week*, October 13, 1993, p. 30.

36. Kemezis, Paul, "Wait-and-See Stance Taken on Zero VOC Architectural Paints," *Chemical Week*, Vol. 151, October 14, 1992, pp. 52–53.

37. EPA, "Negotiated Rulemaking at the EPA," from Chris Kirtz, director of the Consensus and Dispute Resolution Program at the EPA, November 1, 1993, p. 2.

38. Morris, Gregory D. L., Conrad B. Mackerron, Emma Chynoweth, Catherine Brady, Lisa Tantillo, and David Hunter, "Special Report: Paints and Coatings; Looking for Comfort in Regulations," *Chemical Week*, Vol. 145, October 18, 1989, p. 35.

39. NPCA, "An Interim Report on the Activities of the AIM Reg-Neg Committee," September 1993, p. 1. These figures assume the same production figures in 2003 as in 1990.

40. Anonymous, "What the Industry Is Saying About Reg/Neg, the Regulatory Negotiation Process," *Decorating Retailer*, January 1994, p. 96.

41. Three challenges have gone to final judgment in California (against SCAQMD and Ventura County Air Pollution Control District), and in all three the paint industry has won on environmental grounds. "In sum, there is evidence that the new regulations require lower-quality products. As a result, more product will be used, which leads to a net increase in VOC emissions." Also, *Dunn-Edwards Corp. v. BAAQMD*, 9 C.A. 4th 644 (1992); see ALARM Caucus, "An Analysis of Alternative Systems of Regulating Architectural Coatings Under Section 183 (e) of the CAAA," July 22, 1993, pp. 15, 16.

42. Carter, William P. L., and Arthur M. Winer, "Technical Issues for Regulation of VOC from Architectural Coatings," Atmospheric Sciences Committee, SCAQMD Advisory Council, January 14, 1991, p. 9.

Editors' Note: Business strategy involves panic and resolve. After intelligently assessing key customers and stakeholder concerns, successful corporate environmental strategy boils down to offering senior management a few good options. The paint industry proved unready to accept a VOC initiative. The City of Wichita was ready for innovation that shaped a consensus among conflicting stakeholders. The concluding essay in this chapter is a concise account of how leaders in government and the paper and pulp industry found an answer. This took responsible leadership, a process of building trust, anticipatory issues management, and sheer street smarts.

Successful Voluntary Agreements: The Case of EPA and AFPA

Gail A. Cooper and Amy Schaffer

Gail A. Cooper is an Environmental Protection Specialist in the Hazardous Waste Identification Division, Office of Solid Waste and Emergency Response, EPA. Since joining EPA in 1992 after graduating with an M.S. in Environmental Management and Policy from Rensselaer Polytechnic Institute, Ms. Cooper has also worked as a Special Assistant to the Director of the Office of Solid Waste and as a Project Manager in the Office of Prevention, Pesticides, and Toxic Substances. Ms. Cooper received her B.A. in English from DePaul University in Chicago.

Amy E. Schaffer is the Senior Director of Industrial Waste Programs for the American Forest & Paper Association in Washington D.C., where she is responsible for issues related to hazardous and solid waste management, international environmental affairs, and program coordination within the Regulatory Affairs Department. Ms. Schaffer has a Bachelor's degree from Towson State College and a Master's degree in Public Administration from American University.

After more than a year of negotiation, on April 14, 1994 the EPA and the American Forest & Paper Association (AF&PA)[43] reached an agreement on a voluntary environmental stewardship program for the land application of sludge from kraft and sulfite pulp mills using chlorine or chlorine-derivative bleaching processes. This agreement came to fruition after a 1991 notice of proposed rulemaking published by the EPA, which would limit land application of pulp and paper mill sludge from bleached kraft mills. Choosing to negotiate, rather than proceeding with the rulemaking process, EPA and AF&PA began exploring voluntary alternatives to the proposed regulation.[44]

Although voluntary commitments posed a new set of problems and challenges not associated with the more traditional rulemaking approach, in the end both parties viewed the outcome as a preferable alternative to regulation. Each side agreed that given the circumstances, the benefits of negotiating a voluntary agreement for land application would include a shorter time frame, reducing costs to EPA, industry, and the public, and demonstrate a more positive framework for future efforts which involve voluntary programs. This model for resolution is a good example for environmental strategies juggling the complex realms of public expectation, trade alliance needs, and consumer preferences.

HISTORY OF THE AGREEMENT

In 1984, the Environmental Defense Fund (EDF) and the National Wildlife Federation (NWF) petitioned EPA to regulate certain polyhalogenated dioxins and furans from bleach kraft and sulfite mills, and to initiate research into the prevention of dioxin/furan contamination. EPA granted the petitioners' request to initiate information collection, but denied their request for immediate regulatory action. NWF and EDF filed a lawsuit that was subsequently settled by a consent decree in 1988. As a result EPA was required to revise pulp mill effluent guidelines and to conduct a risk assessment to determine if the management of sludges from bleach mills constituted a risk to human health or the environment.[45] EPA determined that, while the industry's disposal practices were appropriately managed through state regulations, land application practices were not adequately regulated by most of the states and more stringent regulations were necessary.

On May 10, 1991, EPA published proposed rules under section six of the Toxic Substances Control Act (TSCA). The proposed regulations sought to establish a maximum dioxin/furan concentration for soil where sludge has been applied, as well as broader site management practices for the land application of sludge.

The pulp and paper industry, through AF&PA and individual companies, submitted extensive comments to EPA on the proposed rules. The central concern was that the rules controlling dioxin levels in the sludge would be unnecessary once the final effluent guidelines (also required by the 1988 consent decree) were promulgated, because the effluent guidelines would compel process changes to minimize the formulation of dioxin. AF&PA maintained that EPA and the industry would spend significant resources without equivalent benefit. Furthermore, the paper industry argued for incentives as the most efficient way to address the EPA'S concern for reducing the concentration of dioxin/furan in the sludge.

In December 1992, EPA deferred promulgating the proposed sludge land application rule. EPA's decision was based primarily on two factors. First, EPA's Office of Water and Office of Air and Radiation were in the process of developing integrated effluent limitation guidelines and air emission standards for the pulp and paper industry. This integrated (or "cluster") rule was expected to be proposed by the end of October 1993, and promulgated in 1995.[46] EPA recognized that in order for the industry to meet the effluent guidelines, it was likely to make changes to the papermaking process which would have the effect of reducing dioxin and furan levels in sludge, and possibly to levels below concern. It did not make sense to EPA to develop regulations controlling land application of sludge in advance of the implementation of the effluent/air rule requirements.

Second, EPA and AF&PA agreed to enter into negotiations to develop a voluntary environmental stewardship program, serving as an interim step until the effects of the integrated rule could be evaluated between 1995 and 1997. One of the foundations of the negotiation was that EPA and AF&PA agreed that no land application regulations would be issued while these negotiations were ongoing.

ENTERING INTO NEGOTIATIONS

On February 22, 1993, EPA and AF&PA met to begin discussions on the components of the voluntary agreement. The first proposal for a voluntary agreement was submitted by AF&PA on May 10. On May 20, EPA and AF&PA representatives met to negotiate the individual provisions of a memorandum of understanding (MOU), which was the format for the voluntary agreement.

During the summer of 1993, EPA and AF&PA held numerous informal discussions, and met on August 23, 1993, for the second negotiation meeting. During this meeting the parties made major progress toward achieving an agreement. Over the next several months, EPA and AF&PA continued informal communications and exchanged draft proposals for consideration by the respective parties. When EPA and AF&PA met on January 14, 1994, for the last negotiating session, only twelve issues remained, all of which were resolved at that meeting. The next six weeks were spent making minor language changes and reviewing the MOU with EPA management and AF&PA's membership. Finally, on April 14, 1994, after only fourteen months of many draft proposals, and several meetings, EPA and AF&PA signed a final MOU for sludge land application.

THE NEGOTIATION DYNAMIC

Both before and during negotiations, EPA and the AF&PA developed specific strategies and tactics to advance its goals and objectives. While some of these approaches were clearly more effective than others, in the end it was trust, appreciation for the other party's needs and constraints, awareness of the alternatives, and a strong desire to reach a fair agreement that made successful negotiation possible.

Trust as a Lever for Change

Developing and sustaining trust was essential to achieving the voluntary agreement. The ability of both parties to engage in open communication helped bring the negotiations to fruition much more quickly than would otherwise have been the case. Over the course of the fourteen-month negotiation period these discussions became much more relaxed and candid as both parties became willing to reveal their constraints and limitations. The straightforward style was not only adopted during informal telephone communications, but became the norm during the negotiation meetings. These frank discussions led to a greater understanding of the practical, technical, policy, and legal constraints each party faced.

Another sign of the trust that developed was the number of representatives that attended each of the negotiating meetings. The February 1993 negotiation meeting was attended by eighteen people, eleven representing AF&PA's position, and seven representing EPA. By the last negotiating meeting, in January 1994, EPA and AF&PA each were represented by only three people. As trust developed both parties became more comfortable negotiating without a complete complement of specialists, present throughout the early stages of negotiations as a defensive strategy "just in case" an issue in their field arose.

Understanding the Other Party's Constraints and Limitations

Willingness to appreciate each other's needs and constraints helped move the agreement forward. EPA's decision in May of 1993 to accept the industry's invitation to visit two mills engaged in land application of sludge helped EPA representatives better understand the processes and the intricacies involved with papermaking operations, their wastewater treatment systems, and their processes for land-applying sludge.

After the visit, EPA representatives had a better understanding of the practical problems faced by the mills in attempting to control the amount of dioxin in their sludge, as well as the areas where the mills had more leeway in engineering solutions. Having had the opportunity to see the technologies first hand, understand the limitations, and be introduced to the procedures that led up to the land application of sludge, EPA's representatives became more pragmatic and sagacious negotiators.

Similarly, AF&PA's negotiators continually queried the EPA representatives to better understand why EPA would take a particular position on an issue. AF&PA's representatives discovered some of the constraints under which EPA was operating. The association learned that a number of environmental groups were advocating "zero" dioxin in sludge; AF&PA also became more aware of the states' interests in having EPA address land application while providing states with some flexibility. Finally, AF&PA also became sensitized to the dynamics associated with the upcoming release of EPA's draft reassessment of dioxin risk and of the concerns regarding maintaining consistency between the reassessment and any possible voluntary agreement. AF&PA's representatives came to appreciate these problems associated with developing fair, reasonable, and effective environmental policy in an atmosphere of uncertainty and strongly held, but divergent viewpoints.

The appropriate level of dioxin/furan in sludges that were to be applied to lands that might eventually become pasturelands was a final issue to be addressed. EPA's initial proposal prohibited any land application of sludges. AF&PA's members disagreed. AF&PA feared that a total prohibition would result in termination of any land application program, because the mills could not always restrict how farmers would use their lands in the future.

After much discussion, it became clear that EPA was particularly concerned about this pathway of exposure because the Agency's then-unpublished *Dioxin Reassessment* states that the greatest exposure route to humans is through the consumption of dairy and meat products.[47] The draft dioxin reassessment further posits that exposure of cattle and other grazing animals to dioxins/furans was through uptake of soils on grasses. Once the AF&PA negotiators understood the basis for EPA's concern and position, they were able to develop a provision which would ensure that sludges spread on pasturelands would not result in dioxin/furan concentrations greater than the background levels—that is, no additional burdens would be created.

Exploring Alternatives and Options Generated

While both parties maintained a commitment to achieve a voluntary agreement, there were times when each party was doubtful about reaching a satisfactory conclusion. This doubt led to the exploration of other options—which served as another important dynamic to the voluntary agreement negotiations. EPA viewed these actions as exploring other opportunities. AF&PA considered these actions as "threats" to ensure that the negotiations stayed on track.

One option explored by EPA during this time was a joint federal-state cooperative program to limit the practices of land application of sludge. As part of this provisional plan, EPA dedicated a June 1993 Forum on States and Tribal Toxics Actions (FOSTTA) to pulp and paper mill sludge. Representatives from eleven states that allowed land application of pulp and paper mill sludge were invited to Alexandria, Virginia to attend the FOSTTA meeting.

The purpose of the meeting was to provide and update the states on the trends in federal policy on pulp and paper mill sludge management; obtain their input on EPA's objectives and the specifics for the voluntary agreement; and discuss the possibilities for state and federal cooperation in the oversight and management of sludge land-application activities. The response from the state representatives on a joint federal-state sludge land-application management project was overwhelmingly favorable.

AF&PA members were aware of the meeting with the states, and suspicious because they were not invited to participate. Association members were particularly concerned that EPA might decide to work directly with the states and where appropriate compel certain states to make changes in their land application programs. In the long run, the meeting with the states reinforced AF&PA's position that mills in states with advanced programs regulating pulp and paper mill sludge land application should be exempted from the MOU. There were, however, continuing concerns that EPA made commitments to the states regarding the voluntary agreement to which AF&PA was not a party.

EPA explored other options as well—and AF&PA was spurred to continue negotiations by several of those actions—which were designed to show how serious the agency was about managing risks from land application of sludge. While EPA and AF&PA were negotiating, the agency published a notice in the *Federal Register* which implied that if the negotiations were not completed, EPA would issue a test rule under TSCA section four. A section four testing requirement would lead to mandatory testing of all sludges from pulp and paper mills. This type of required testing program would be expensive and quite burdensome on many of the companies. Ultimately, EPA did not act on that notice.

Overcoming Old Paradigms

Finally, the clear desire by both EPA and AF&PA to reach a mutually satisfactory agreement was an essential dynamic for obtaining consensus on the majority of the provisions in the agreement with industry. This win-win attitude carried both parties through a number of rough times during the fourteen-month negotiation period. Without the belief that the other party was submitting proposals it thought were reasonable, negotiations would have broken down, and an agreement would not have been reached. In fact, the few times when it seemed as if an agreement would not be reached were primarily a result of one or both parties reverting to the more traditional win-lose negotiating position. The willingness by both parties to forgo traditional negotiating strategy laid the foundation for an agreement that satisfied all parties concerned.

AF&PA and its members originally looked at the prospect of a voluntary agreement with wary eyes. There was always the sense that EPA had the upper hand in "voluntary" agreements because of its legal authority to bring enforcement actions, to assess penalties, and to issue stringent regulations such as the May 1991 proposed TSCA regulations. However, AF&PA member companies were hoping to establish a more creative and productive relationship with EPA and consequently AF&PA decided to participate in the negotiations. AF&PA and its members believed strongly that the agreement was a major step in the right direction and would help in developing more productive long-term relationships.

THE FINAL AGREEMENTS

EPA and AF&PA negotiated two separate memoranda of understandings. The first MOU was between the EPA and the individual mills that land-apply or distribute pulp and paper mill sludge for land application. It includes limitations for dioxin/furan concentrations in the sludges and in the soils, specific requirements concerning good management practices for spreading sludge, periodic monitoring for dioxin and furan concentrations, and periodic reporting to EPA and AF&PA.

Because the 1984 lawsuit addressed only kraft and sulfite pulp mills using chlorine or chlorine-derivative bleaching methods, the voluntary program outlined in the first MOU applies only to those types of mills. This MOU sets three standards for the concentration of certain dioxin/furans in sludge: (1) a maximum allowable dioxin/furan soil concentration; (2) a concentration limit below which the sludge would be exempt from the majority of the agreement's provisions; and (3) a maximum allowable dioxin/furan concentration limit or "cap" which cannot be exceeded for sludge or sludge products intended to be land applied.

The agreement also set dioxin/furan limitations for soil after application, and in sludge-derived materials which are land applied or distributed in commerce. The MOU was written in such a way as to encourage the continued downward trend of dioxin/furan concentrations through incentives such as reduced monitoring and reporting. The MOU also stipulated specific requirements for testing sludge, taking into account the variability of the testing results. Finally, special management practices were included for sites where sludge has been or will be land applied.

One of the major issues that EPA and AF&PA addressed was the ability to determine if a participating mill was adhering to the provisions of the agreement. The two parties negotiated, and included in the MOU, a record-keeping and reporting system that would determine "compliance" by a mill. In addition, in the spirit of the negotiations, both EPA and AF&PA believed that any potential disputes that might arise over the interpretation of a provision should be resolved through informal discussions between the parties, or if discussions do not resolve the issue, through the use of a neutral panel, rather than litigation.

The second memorandum of understanding between AF&PA and EPA primarily addresses the implementation of the first MOU. AF&PA agreed to collect and compile specific information relating to the testing of sludge from the participating mills and forward the information to EPA annually. In addition, AF&PA publicizes the voluntary agreement and encourages those member mills that are land-applying sludge to sign a MOU with EPA. EPA also agreed to refrain from publishing rules addressing the land application of pulp and paper mill sludges under TSCA section 6 during the period in which the MOU is in effect.

EVALUATION AND POTENTIAL USE FOR FUTURE ENVIRONMENTAL CHALLENGES

Since EPA signed MOUs with the original two pulp and paper mills two and a half years ago, two additional mills have formally adopted the terms of the agreement. This low participation rate, however, belies the qualitative effects that the voluntary agreement has had on the land application of pulp and paper mill sludges across the country. A recent informal survey conducted by the National Council of the Paper Industry for Air and Stream Improvement (NCASI) shows that regardless of the type of pulp and paper mill, the MOU is being used as a template for good management practices for all types of land application of sludges. Land application is one of the many alternative management methods that pulp and paper mills are using to reduce the amount of byproducts being sent to landfills. Mills have used land application of sludges as soil conditioners for silviculture activities, as substitutes for fill dirt in surface mine reclamation, as mulch for landscaping projects, as compost, and as fertilizers in agriculture activities.

Not all of the effects of the voluntary agreement, however, have been positive for the industry. As a result of signing the MOU, one mill received so much scrutiny regarding a sludge product that its market share dropped dramatically and the mill has decided to discontinue the production of the product. On the other hand, due in part to the voluntary agreement and in part to the soon-to-be finalized cluster rule another mill has experienced a decline in its dioxin/furan levels in its sludge which is being land applied.

AF&PA member companies recognize that environmental or human health concerns about the application of sludges must continue to be addressed toward the goal of achieving nonmeasurable dioxins and furans in the land-applied materials. That recognition is manifest in the fact that more than 80 percent of the kraft mills using chlorine or chlorine-derivative bleaching processes produce sludges with dioxin/furan concentrations of less than 10 parts per trillion—the level chosen by EPA and AF&PA at which reporting and monitoring requirements are reduced. The number of mills achieving non-measurable dioxin/furan concentrations will continue to grow as more mills implement new and innovative bleaching technologies in response to the changing marketplace and the implementation of the cluster rule.[48] The MOU with industry helped to establish a benchmark against which mill sludges can be measured.

In addition, establishment of mutually agreed-upon objectives enabled both EPA and AF&PA to find the means to practically meet those objectives. In this case, both parties were sincerely interested in reducing the dioxin/furan contaminant levels in the sludge and each party worked toward developing provisions that would encourage continued reductions. This enabled both parties to jointly promote pollution prevention activities in a meaningful and practical way. During these negotiations, EPA and AF&PA representatives discovered that conducting candid discussions of each party's objectives and needs both furthered the negotiations and resulted in creative solutions to seemingly insurmountable problems. This can serve as an example for the future of nontraditional means for accomplishing agreed-upon goals.

EPA representatives also learned that by sitting down and negotiating with industry, as opposed to going forth with the proposed rulemaking, the scenario was set to continue cooperative agreements in the future. Each party recognized that the other was not a monolithic entity, and that there were areas of consensus, and with continued communications perhaps the number of areas of agreement would increase. At a time when the pulp and paper industry is rapidly changing technologies and processes, it makes good sense for EPA and the industry to maintain a cooperative relationship.

In the end, EPA and AF&PA were pleased with the results of the negotiations, and have continued to discuss both the voluntary agreement and the technological changes being made within the industry. During the most recent annual meeting between EPA and AF&PA, the association requested the voluntary agreement be terminated when the cluster rule is promulgated. EPA and AF&PA believe that the cluster rule will result in adequate reductions of dioxin and furan levels, which will obviate the need to specify the manner in which sludge is land-applied.

This alternative for rulemaking, which considers both the valid and practical interests of industry, as well as EPA's concerns regarding human health and environmental risk, has great consequence for addressing public concerns and expectations on the environment. The agreement's success has not merely encouraged a continuing dialogue between the EPA and AF&PA, but created a precedent for future nontraditional negotiating between EPA and other industries.[49]

NOTES

43. In January 1993, the American Paper Institute (API) merged with the National Forest Products Association and the American Wood Council to become the American Forest & Paper Association (AF&PA).

44. The Office of Pollution Prevention and Toxics was the lead office for EPA during the negotiations, while the American Forest & Paper Association negotiated for their member mills engaged in land-application practices.

45. Sludge produced from the treatment of wastewater effluents of pulp and paper mills has been applied to land for a variety of purposes. Sludge is used as a soil amendment to retain moisture in both agricultural and silvicultural farming, and also for strip mine reclamation. Additionally, sludge is used to make animal bedding, and as a carrier for pesticide delivery. Sludge is also distributed as a soil amendment to landscaping centers, farmers, and other potential users.

46. The Effluent Limitations Guidelines, Pretreatment Standards, and New Source Performance Standards: Pulp, Paper, and Paperboard Category; National Emission Standards for Hazardous Air Pollutants for Source Category: Pulp and Paper Production; Proposed Rules (58 FR 66078) were signed on October 29, 1993 and published in the *Federal Register* on December 17, 1993.

47. In April 1991, EPA announced that it would conduct a scientific reassessment of the health risks of exposure to dioxin and dioxin-like compounds. On September 13, 1994, EPA released a public review draft of its dioxin reassessment for 2,3,7,8-tetrachlorodibenzo-p-dioxin. The document is expected to be complete in 1998 after undergoing a formal peer review by the Agency's Science Advisory Board.

48. The 1993 progress in reducing the TCDD/TCDF content of effluents, pulps, and waste water treatment sludges from the manufacturing of bleached chemical pulp. National Council of the Paper Industry for Air and Stream Improvement (NCASI).

49. For additional information please see Kelly Ferguson and Kirk Finchem, "The 'Cluster Rule' Continues: Industry Asks, 'WhatNow?,' " *Pulp and Paper*, November 1997; Allison Lucas, "Environmental Chlorine-Free Bleaching Grows, While TCF Lags," *Chemical Week*, March 15, 1995; and Ken Patrick, "IP Braced for 'Cluster' Impact, But Optimistic About Alternative Plan," *Pulp and Paper*, September 1994.

QUESTIONS FOR FURTHER THOUGHT

1. What does it mean to "respond to stakeholders?" What systems should a firm implement to respond more effectively to stakeholders?

2. The Guiding Principles of Responsible Care call for a signatory to report health or environmental hazards to the public. Suppose a minor hazardous waste spill occurred at your facility, and was quickly dealt with. As a chemical company executive, how would you handle the incident? (Keep in mind the public relations and financial considerations of disclosure, in the short and long-term.)

3. What performance measures should you use to measure and communicate your firm's environmental performance?

4. Technical professionals often discount public concern for chemical-related health effects by claiming the average citizen does not understand the

scientific and regulatory truth of the matter. How would you approach a meeting with the public on siting a chemical facility in their town?

5. What are some factors that make a dispute more amenable to alternative dispute resolution? What factors might make a dispute more amenable to a litigious framework?

6. How were the parties responding to stakeholders in the Gilbert-Mosley case? Were any stakeholders excluded from the process? How would the exclusion of a stakeholder affect the outcome of an alternative dispute resolution?

CHAPTER

Public Disclosure and Environmental Reporting

GOING BEYOND REQUIRED REPORTING AND FINANCIAL DISCLOSURE

In this concluding chapter, we focus on the "windows" of the corporate mansion—namely, how leaders choose to shape their public disclosures. In the past, environmental communication looked more like a walled-in fortress rather than a mansion, with far fewer windows and many more bricks. Communication was selective and usually provided as a response to a problem. It was difficult to look inside the corporate fortress—and sometimes there wasn't much to see.

Now companies provide a greater degree of transparency by revealing how environmental management systems work from the factory floor or by presenting the environmental mission statement that was penned in the office of the chief executive officer. Benefits from this accessibility begin with increased trust and credibility, and can add competitive advantage. The development of strategic partnerships and stakeholder alliances, including improved relations with regulators and policy makers, must come from a position of mutual trust. In the imperfect world of crisis, contention, and compromise, the establishment of a reliable source of information helps all parties in attempting to negotiate equitable solutions.[1]

An environmental report offers the public a window of corporate performance at one particular moment in time. It can also explain future goals and how policies work to achieve them, and in the end, assist targeted stakeholders in better understanding the challenges and strengths of the disclosing organization. Internally, the demands for credible and useful information require the development of environmental performance metrics to answer public expectations—those that go beyond traditional measures of financial performance and compliance-based data. The company must develop what Peter Senge would call the capabilities of a learning organization.

In this chapter we examine the strategic and functional aspects of environmental reporting: *why* a company would choose to allow the opportunity for additional scrutiny by aggregating information and releasing such a public document; *what* form corporate environmental reports now take and what they will look like in the future; and *how* to get started. These are the fundamentals behind all corporate public disclosure.

Each year, the hurdle for substantive and credible information is raised by the leaders in the field providing the benchmark for others to follow. Not very long ago, corporate environmental reports contained statements that sounded good but consisted of little actual substance. Today there is less tolerance for ambiguous declarations of environmental performance, and instead we see what president and CEO of ARCO Chemical Alan Hirsig calls a "coming of age." Hirsig notes:[2]

> Earning public trust involves a lot more than ad campaigns: it requires performance and openness. The point is that once you establish credibility—that is, that you are honestly trying to do the right thing—you can interact with governments, environmental groups, and community leaders on a more constructive basis.

Environmental concern around the world continues to deepen. An International Environmental Monitor Survey of 30,000 people in twenty-five countries found that the public is looking at the environment as an industrywide responsibility no longer based on individual corporate action. As a market driver, consumer demands will shift from preference of one brand over another to consumer demand for industrywide accountability. This will increase the pressure to move from laggard to leader, to demonstrate a commitment to progress through goal-setting for the future, and to report reliably on past performance.[3]

THE UNCHANGING FOUNDATION OF CORPORATE COMMUNICATION: KNOW YOUR AUDIENCE

In all guises and forms, communication both represents and drives the effectiveness of an organization—and reveals the corporate culture that guides decision making. In order to achieve Hirsig's promise, consistent, reliable forms of communication on the environment must be made available.

Unsolicited analysis may be rigorous and swift, coming from independent reviewers as well as interested stakeholders. Sophisticated scrutiny is well established with public interest groups like the Council on Economic Priorities' Campaign for Cleaner Corporations, through the media exemplified by *Fortune*'s 1993 survey that classified thirty of the nation's top companies as environmental "leaders," "laggards" and "most improved," and socially responsible investor groups such as the Franklin Research and Development Group.[4]

From the corporate policy statement to the material data sheet; from the procedural manual to the employee newsletter; and from the emergency press conference to the corporate home page, a company's actions and attitude toward environmental management will be reflected in the manner and content of the information they communicate.

Even as forms of communication change with new technology, the challenge to be effective—clear and concise—remains the same. The goal of identifying your audience and targeting communications to meet their needs holds true, regardless of whether you are writing a letter to a customer, explaining the planning for a worst-case scenario at a local community meeting, or implementing elements of an environmental management system in an outlying facility.

As we explore voluntary disclosure in corporate environmental reporting, the corporate commitment to environmental leadership must be evident to audiences that include internal customers and employees and the expectations of external stakeholders. A proactive approach to issues management (which is one role that a corporate environmental report can play) includes identifying early concerns and explaining the context of environmental impacts.

Environmental leaders are well-advised to work closely with corporate communications and government relations executives to consider their *emerging audiences* in addition to their traditional ones. Who will be the new customers for deregulated utilities? And who will be the new stakeholders—universities, new public interest groups, and new unions perhaps? What about after a merger or acquisition, when a company has a whole new set of internal customers? The corporate culture will be revealed to new stakeholders, and they will want to know if the environmental commitment is real.

Beyond all legal requirements for a company to disclose its environmental record, the evolution of environmental reports from the green glossy to a substantive profile is being driven by a number of suggestive guidelines. Here we refer readers to the Public Environmental Reporting Initiative (PERI), Coalition of Environmentally Responsible Economics (CERE) Principles, United Nations Conference on Environment and Development (UNCED), and Global Environmental Management Initiative (GEMI).[5] Please also reconsider the principles described by the cases of Macauley and Anderson in Chapter 11 when formatting your disclosures.

As federal right-to-know regulations (e.g., SARA Title III)[6] have been enacted, industries are required to provide information on the risk of the materials they use and produce. Information technology has made it possible for anyone to access this data through EPA databases on the Internet. Therefore, it has become necessary for companies to respond proactively, and get ahead of the information curve. The environmental report can become an internal driver of corporate performance—concurrently developing and refining performance indicators and then self-reporting, rather than becoming the subject of, and having to respond to, another organization's critique.

Most importantly, the report must position its audience to be receptive. A credible environmental report includes setting measurable and improvable environmental targets. Leaders like Du Pont discovered that reporting on their goal setting is a motivator that stretches the company to search for continual improvement toward Goal Zero—zero spills, zero accidents, and zero waste

As the World Business Council on Sustainable Development and the President's Council on Sustainable Development became active in the 1990s, the call for innovation fit nicely into Du Pont's core competency of technological innovation. A new Safety, Health and Environmental (SHE) commitment was developed which clearly stated Du Pont's goals. The goals included eliminating all injuries, illnesses, incidents, waste, and emissions as a critical way to improve business performance. The opportunities associated with improved environmental performance became clear. Not only could Du Pont reduce the cost of operations by eliminating waste and emissions, but revenues increased because yearly improvements gave the company more product to sell. The more visionary businesses also recognized opportunities associated with creating new product and service offerings which helped customers and consumers solve their environmental problems. The key to Du Pont's success is integration of SHE thinking into the business processes.

Figure 12-1 Opportunities Associated with Environmental Performance at Du Pont [7]

(see Figure 12-1). The piece by Mark Brownley on Nortel helps to further clarify the need for linking performance with environmental goals.

MAKING THE PUBLIC REPORT MAKE SENSE

The enterprise that values voluntary disclosure on environmental performance gains multiple advantages at the risk of greater scrutiny. Those that achieve this balance are winning more and more. We have selected and refined three of the best tactical accounts of environmental reporting in this next section.

The chapter continues with an overview of voluntary disclosure, and a brief history of corporate environmental reports written by Erik Meyers, General Counsel for the Environmental Law Institute. Meyers participated in the drafting of the PERI Guidelines, initiated by multinationals in May 1993. (See Figure 12-2 for a list of these companies.) Meyers discusses how the voluntary environmental report came to exist, by placing the history for a voluntary approach in context of more prescriptive legislation and regulation for mandatory disclosure that dates back to the 1970s.

In the essay entitled "What Makes Environmental Reports Effective: Current Trends in Corporate Reporting," Duke University scholar and corporate financial analyst Doug J. Lober discusses the challenges of meeting the needs

Amoco Corporation, BP America, Inc., Dow Chemical Company, Du Pont, IBM Corporation, Northern Telecom, Phillips Petroleum, Polaroid Corporation, Rockwell International Corporation, United Technologies, and European participants: Amoco Exploration Company, London, British Petroleum Company, DOW Europe, Du Pont de Nemours International S.A., IBM-Europe, S.A. Northern Telecom Europe Limited, Phillips Petroleum, U.K., Polaroid (Europa) B.V., Rockwell International Limited.

Figure 12-2 Companies Involved in Developing PERI Guidelines

of multiple stakeholders through report format and content, dissemination strategies, and uniform reporting standards. The chapter proceeds with discussion from Laurence Mach, who applies his experience in consulting on environmental reports for companies like Merck and AT&T, in discussing practical considerations for a company ready to author its first environmental report.

In the final essay, Timothy Herbst examines how the public can now see into the windows of the corporate mansion through the internet, as the web is becoming a key source of corporate environmental performance information.

Linking Environmental Reporting and Performance Measures—Nortel[8]

Mark Brownley

Mark Brownley is communications chief of Nortel Corporation.

Nortel's first corporate environmental report was published in July 1993, squarely aimed at engaging our employees, and communicating to them the "big picture"—the overall approach being taken to improve environmental protection at Nortel. Primarily a narrative description of program plans and successes, the only figures it contained related to CFC elimination and the results of a few projects undertaken at individual locations; while preparing that first report we realized that we had very little quantitative data to report. Moreover, we knew that the report did not have enough relevant information to be of interest to our external stakeholders—customers, suppliers, shareholders, and community members. Grappling with how to meaningfully communicate our environmental activities, we decided to co-develop the PERI Guidelines with nine other multinational companies. At roughly the same time as the publication of the PERI Guidelines in 1994, we released our second annual environmental report—our first to follow the PERI Guidelines. From our perspective, one of the most important aspects of the thinking that emerged from PERI is putting raw data into a context that is meaningful for all the various groups that have some stake in the information. While there is still a great deal to learn about how to put this principle into practice, our understanding has grown and developed over the past four years.

In 1994, we chose our new Environmental Management System (EMS) Standard as a report organizing theme. Our organizing themes for 1995 and 1996 were the business case for environmental management and fulfilling commitments to stakeholders, respectively. In all three reports we ensured that the components listed in the PERI Guidelines were addressed—not necessarily in the same order or to the same depth as described in the Guidelines.

Whereas a theme provides the skeleton for the report, the PERI components have become the report's organs. The PERI Guidelines have spurred us on to develop better metrics, to consider more closely areas that we were previously weak in (e.g., stakeholder involvement), and to ensure that we disclose more data than we might originally have been comfortable with, and do all of this candidly. We do not look to the PERI Guidelines as the last words in report content, but we do use them as a table-stakes benchmark.

The PERI Guidelines have had a significant impact on the development of environmental performance indicators at Nortel. As we prepared our first report according to the PERI Guidelines, we realized that we had very little accurate, quantitative data to report. Given the amount of environmental reporting that some governments and regulatory bodies require of our operations, discovering how little data we could actually report on a companywide basis was something of a surprise. The development of tools and systems that improve our ability to measure environmental performance has been a major thrust of our work over the past four years—driven both by Nortel's commitment to public reporting and to environmental improvement.

CHALLENGES TO IMPLEMENTATION

As discussed above, the 1993 report was the first prepared in accordance with the PERI Guidelines. The exercise as a whole turned out to be much more difficult than we had expected. It made us pause and reflect on our environmental activities from a macroperspective, something that tends not to happen often enough in the day-to-day scramble of projects and deadlines. That period of examination brought us face-to-face with the following issues:

- *Audience.* We needed to give more thought to what audiences we should be addressing in an environmental report, as well as to what a good environmental report should contain.
- *Measurement tools.* We needed to develop better tools and processes for measuring year-to-year progress according to specific indicators and for communicating this information in a meaningful way.
- *Degree of disclosure.* We needed to decide to what extent we were willing to expose ourselves to public scrutiny. We had not widely publicized our internal "free in three" target (CFC elimination) until we had met it. If we went public with the environmental targets we were considering establishing for the year 2000, we would have to be prepared to report on lack of progress if that was what the figures indicated.
- *Tracking environmental progress throughout the organization.* We need to put in place a better process for tracking what was going on related to environmental management throughout the corporation all year round, instead of scrambling to find this information when it came time to write the report.

Our initial foray into reporting using the PERI Guidelines was informative. Reporting according to the Guidelines indirectly drove us to develop improved measuring systems and better relationships throughout the company.

NOTES

1. See Peter Senge's *The Fifth Discipline: The Art and Practice of the Learning Organization,* Doubleday, New York, 1990, for a detailed and effective explanation.

2. Hirsig, Alan R., "Environmentalism Comes of Age: A More Rational Approach for the Twenty-First Century," *Corporate Environmental Strategy: The Journal of Environmental Leadership,* Vol. 4, No. 4, p. 87.

3. Judge, William Q., Alex Miller, and Dorn M. Fowler, "What Causes Corporate Environmental Responsiveness?," *CES Journal,* Spring 1996, Vol. 3, No. 3, p.43.

4. Geffen, Charlette A., "Public Expectations and Corporate Strategy," *CES Journal,* Spring 1996, Vol. 3, No. .3, pp. 33–41.

5. Lober, Douglas J., David Bynum, Elizabeth Campbell, and Mary Jacques, "The 100 + Corporate Environmental Report Study," Duke University Center for Business and the Environment, Duke University, Nicholas School of the Environment.

6. Superfund Ammendments and Reauthorization Act of 1986.

7. Tebo, Paul V., and Dawn G. Rittenhouse, "Sustainable Development: Creating Business Opportunities at Du Pont," *CES Journal,* Spring 1997, Vol. 4, No. 3, pp. 4–12.

8. Brownley, Mark, communications chief of Nortel Corporation, May 30, 1997. Responses to questions on how PERI has impacted corporate performance. Article assembled by Frank Mendelson from an interview with Mark Brownley, November 1997.

Corporate Accountability: The Evolution of Voluntary Environmental Reporting

Erik Meyers

Erik Meyers is General Counsel of the Environmental Law Institute, Washington, D.C. The Environmental Law Institute is a not-for-profit organization created over 25 years ago as an independent research and education center on environmental law and management.

American democracy is based on access to information. Since the earliest days of the Republic and the creation of *The Federalist Papers,* government in the United States has become increasingly open, both institutionally and procedurally. The drive that has made public institutions more open and accountable has spread to private institutions as well. Increasingly, lawmakers turn to information and disclosure requirements to carry out public policy. As an example, the Food Quality Act of 1996 and the Safe Drinking Water Act of 1996 follow the path blazed by the 1986 Emergency Planning and Community Right-to-Know Act by mandating the compilation and public disclosure of information in specified categories on releases to various environmental media by corporate facilities.

Voters and lawmakers are not the only drivers for greater accountability. The U.S. market economy attracts an unprecedented level of participation by both individuals and institutions in the stock markets. Massive amounts of invested capital are managed by mutual funds, pension funds, and other large institutional investors. As a price of investment, these institutional interests demand better quality information about the production and management practices of the public stock companies in which they invest.

The reason for seeking such information is, in part, driven by a sense of social responsibility. However, these investors are increasingly motivated by the belief, backed by some recent studies, that well-managed companies, including their environmental aspects, are those companies producing the best bottom-line results. An increasingly significant source of these data is corporate (voluntary) environmental reports.

The notion of issuing a separate annual corporate report on environmental performance is just a decade old. The first report was issued by the Polaroid Corporation in 1989. A relatively modest effort, Polaroid's report focused on the company's efforts to reduce the use of toxic substances in manufacturing. By 1993 KPMG Peat Marwick noted at least 105 companies worldwide which had published a standalone report.[9] While the number continues to rise, the NatWest Group recently commented that it counted only "a little over 200, out of approximately 36,000 multinational corporations, [which] have publicly reported their environmental performance to their stakeholders."[10]

Corporate environmental reports have also evolved in content and level of detail on performance, and with novel features such as attestation. The corporate environmental report has become the hallmark of a more open, accountable style of business's approach to managing environmental aspects of facilities, manufacturing processes, and products. Companies in industrial and service sectors with significant environmental aspects see performance accountability as key to their global competitiveness. The public reporting function also has an important internal consequence, namely transforming environmental considerations from a peripheral, compliance-driven function to a core strategic element in business management.

This piece examines the voluntary corporate environmental reporting phenomenon from origin to intended audiences, to content and form, and finally to recent influences or drivers that are accelerating the trend to report. The purpose is to inform current leaders on this important trend, as we suggest how the next generation of managers might improve public reporting.

ORIGINS—THE TREND TOWARD ACCESS TO INFORMATION

American public policy reflects an enduring trend in expanding public access to information. We see this expansion taking place in numerous areas of modern life, and through various means, not all of them driven by statutory compulsion. We can see the pattern in areas as diverse as securities, tax, political activity, official records, federal advisory committee activity, and, of course, the environment. While the threat of governmental compulsion is often in the background, increasingly market forces are pushing information disclosure. For example, the clout of institutional investors (e.g., pension funds, mutual funds) is substantial. These investor institutions exercise powerful influence over the actions of companies in which they invest or disinvest. The perception of a company's environmental impact through its products, practices, or processes and the drag of its environmental liabilities influence the value of its stock by affecting its current and future competitiveness.

The National Environmental Policy Act (NEPA), enacted at the beginning of the modern environmental era, instituted a requirement that federal agencies needed to conduct and disclose a thorough environmental impact assessment before taking any major action affecting the environment.[11] The power of this mandated study and public disclosure rule was soon obvious. It spawned similar requirements at the state and local government levels and spurred new information requirements to be enacted into federal law.

The basic building blocks of federal environmental law—Clean Air and Clean Water Acts, Toxic Substances Control Act, 1976 (TSCA), Federal Insecticide, Fungicide and Rodenticide Act of 1972 (FIFRA), Resource Conservation and Recovery Act (RCRA), Safe Drinking Water Act—culminated with the 1980 passage of Superfund, the Comprehensive Environmental Response, Compensation, and Liability Act (CERCLA). Despite an increasingly heated debate over policy alternatives (regulatory or "command-and-control" versus market incentives and other approaches), remarkably constant, broad, and bipartisan support remained for information disclosure laws.

New Jersey's Community and Worker Right-to-Know Act inspired Congress to pass and President Reagan to sign the Superfund Amendments and Reauthorization Act (SARA) package in 1986, which included Title III's Community Right-to-Know requirement and established the annual toxic release inventory for certain key industry sectors. The sobering amount of toxic and hazardous chemical material that companies realized were being releasing to air, water, and land caused many companies to permanently change their philosophy and take action to reduce or eliminate these toxic releases. The first federal Toxic Release Inventory (TRI) in 1988, the well-publicized Exxon Valdez grounding in Prince William Sound, Alaska, and the growing international recognition of the serious challenge of atmospheric ozone depletion and climate change were powerful influences for change. The public perceived substantial environmental risk due to the activities or products of large, multinational businesses. The challenge to the business world was clear: Reduce or eliminate these environmental impacts and be more publicly accountable or risk drastic governmental controls or loss of business.

This sense of urgency spurred hundreds of businesses to draft and adopt the International Chamber of Commerce's Business Charter for Sustainable Development at the World Industry Conference on Environmental Management II (WICEM II) in 1991. The Business Charter contained sixteen principles, which included a commitment to external reporting on environmental matters. The ICC Business Charter and the initiative in the United States by the Coalition for Environmentally Responsible Economies (CERES) with the Valdez Principles (later renamed the CERES Principles), sought to establish new behavioral norms for business organizations. These principles applied to environmental aspects of operations, products, and services. Figure 12-3 describes the key factors driving voluntary environments disclosure and Figure 12-4 illustrates the stages of corporate environmental reporting.

The United Nations Conference on Environment and Development (UNCED or the Earth Summit) drew the heads of state from an unprecedented number of nations to Rio de Janeiro, Brazil during June 1992 to express their common commitment to the protection of the world's environment and human development. The Business Council for Sustainable Development, headed by Swiss industrialist Stephan Schmidheiny, declared at Rio that private business should lead, not wait for government to act, to redefine more sustainable ways of creating the world's goods and services. The road from Rio then led back to Geneva and the International Organization for Standardization (ISO). ISO's Strategic Advisory Group on the Environment soon recommended the establishment of a formal technical committee to initiate the task of developing new, globally applicable standards for environmental management systems, leading to the 1996 adoption of the ISO 14001 environmental management systems standard.

Mere declarations of environmental commitment were not enough. Business customers, governments, communities, and even fellow companies demanded an accounting, a report, on how corporate performance was measuring up to these commitments. In other words, an increasing diversity and number of stakeholders demanded some form of reporting by those declaring allegiance to a higher standard of environmental practice.

Thus, three fundamental factors have emerged as the key drivers of the voluntary corporate environmental reporting movement:

- Current and anticipated governmental mandatory reporting requirements;
- Risk minimization strategy, for risks which include future community expectations, customer demands, and the availability of corporate environmental performance reporting from various third-party sources; and
- Marketing strategy, which includes the desire to seize a competitive advantage, enter a particular market, or project a positive corporate image for innovation, quality, or social responsibility.

It is interesting to observe the steady, upward draw of this combination of factors. What was once innovative is soon commonplace or widely initiated. Creation of temporary competitive advantage draws new competitors and imitators, as others in the same market niche race to be second once the leader has shown the advantage. To lead requires continual innovation. The result in the corporate environmental reporting field is obvious: a rapid expansion in the level of detail; more comprehensive coverage; improvement on metrics; and use of third-party verification or some reference to an industry baseline.

Figure 12-3 Three Factors Driving Voluntary Environmental Disclosure

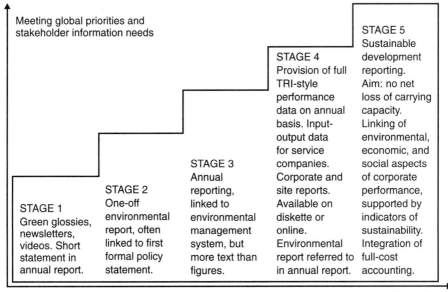

Figure 12-4 Stages in Corporate Environmental Reporting

Source: What the Corporate Environmental Strategy

WHAT THE AUDIENCE WANTS TO KNOW

A threshold decision for would-be corporate environmental reporting drafters involves selection of the intended audience or audiences to address.[12] Information about a company's environmental commitment, impact, and performance record is highly sought after or needed by some, potentially interesting to others, and potentially off-putting to still others. Deciding to which group of audiences to tailor the report is a crucial first step.

As the corporate environmental reporting trend has developed, certain key areas of policy, procedure or management, and performance results have appeared in most current corporate reports. Specific content will depend upon the target audience(s), but generally most companies tend to provide similar categories of information at differing levels of detail.

It is interesting, however, to note that many companies have avoided discussing the environmental impact of their key products or services and instead highlight their environmental policy statements, pollution reductions in the manufacturing process, office recycling, and covering their legal and regulatory compliance records. Philip Morris Companies Inc.'s mid-1996 report states, "Most of our products are made from processed agricultural and dairy materials, and we do not dispose of large quantities of hazardous substances. We do, however, recognize the need to track and carefully manage . . . waste water discharges, air emissions, and solid waste from our operations." No mention is made of EPA's indoor air pollution studies on "second-hand" tobacco smoke, a byproduct of the company's most profitable product line, cigarettes.[13] Other businesses have, however, been more candid. The NatWest Group's 1995/96 report acknowledges that "the foremost environmental impact of a bank lies in the . . . impact of its core activities such as lending" but then notes the lack of meaningful metrics to measure and report on its performance,[14] and Noranda, Inc., a Canadian-based mining concern, states disarmingly on the cover of its 1995 summary environmental report that "Noranda's activities, by their very nature, are intrusive on the environment. We operate mines and smelters. We are major users of forested lands. We explore for oil and gas."[15] Candor and coverage of the full environmental impact of a company's products and services remain a new frontier for the corporate environmental reporting movement.

The chart in Figure 12-5 compares the components of three different reporting frameworks, namely the U.S. corporate-initiated Public Environmental Reporting Initiative (PERI), a UNEP format, CERES report, and Global Environmental Management Initiative (GEMI)/IRRC focus group of companies.[16]

While efforts such as the new U.S. Environmental Protection Agency's Environmental Leadership Program, Project XL,[17] the ISO 14001 standards combined with the ICC Business Charter on Sustainable Development, various industry codes of practice, and others are influencing the content of future reports, at present the PERI framework appears to be one of the more inclusive models widely employed. For that reason, the discussion on content will focus on the PERI model.

The PERI drafters made a disclaimer about their guidelines: "Not . . . everyone will be able to provide all the information called for" given the variety of stages of data collection and environmental management. Even large, well-staffed business enterprises are at different levels in their ability to collect data and measure environmental performance. The latest surveys of corporate environmental reports show great variability in the style, detail, and content of recent editions.[18] PERI is an attempt to create a "roadmap" for those companies interested in issuing an environmental report. PERI reporting guidelines are intended to make the job of reading and analyzing reports easier.

The PERI Guidelines present a set of "core components" for environmental reporting and suggest individual companies or other reporting entities consider adding to these core elements as they progress.[19] Thus, the Guidelines, while recognizing the increasing reporting imperative, permit significant flexibility in actual report content. The core elements are based on the total quality principle of continuous improvement and the maxim of "what gets measured gets done." In this sense, PERI resembles the GEMI Environmental Self-Assessment Program. The GEMI ESAP is a tool for measuring progress

One reporting format worth examining is that of the Coalition for Environmentally Responsible Economies or CERES organization. CERES was established by several socially responsible investment and environmental groups in the wake of the 1988 Exxon Valdez oil spill. CERES emphasized both a corporate commitment to a set of high standards on business practices with respect to the environment and worker health and safety, and also a commitment to report regularly on progress in meeting those commitments. The CERES reporting framework has evolved since its origins with the 1988 CERES Principles. The 1995 CERES Report format (both short and standard forms) includes the following elements:

- Executive summary
- Company profile
- Environmental policies, organization, and management
- Materials policy
- Releases to the environment
- Waste management
- Use of energy
- Workplace health and safety
- Emergency response and public disclosure
- Product stewardship
- Supplier relationships
- Health, safety, and environmental audits
- Compliance

In contrast to the very general frameworks of the industry- and government-sponsored formats (e.g., PERI and EMAS), CERES seeks answers to specific questions in each category. Over thirty pages of detailed questions are contained in the standard CERES report form. The 1995 CERES Report announces the decision of the group to "move forward on the issue of materials accounting"; thus, it asks each endorsing company to initiate a pilot project during 1996 and to be prepared to report back its results beginning with its 1996 report. Preliminarily, the 1995 form asks a number of questions on the topic.

Figure 12-5   The CERES Format

Source: CERES Report, 1995, standard form, Coalition for Environmentally Responsible Economies, Boston, 1996.

toward achieving the ICC Business Charter commitments and is based on a total quality approach of continuous improvement. The Guidelines also recognize and integrate the existing reporting commitments of the Chemical Manufacturers Association's Responsible Care Program, American Petroleum Institute's Strategies for Today's Environmental Partnership (STEP), and EPA's 33/50 program.

Guideline Components

Each reporting organization may decide how, when, and to what extent to present the PERI reporting components listed below. No specific order of presentation is mandatory or encouraged. The recommended content to be included is as follows:

Environmental Management

Summarize the level of organizational accountability for environmental policies and programs and the environmental management structure (e.g., corporate environmental staff and/or organizational relationships). Indicate how policies are implemented throughout the organization and comment on such items as:

- Board involvement and commitment to environmental matters.
- Accountability of other functional units of the organization.
- Environmental management systems in place (if desired, include references or registration under—or consistency with—any relevant national or international standards).
- Total Quality Management (TQM), Continuous Improvement, or other organizationwide programs that may embrace environmental performance.
- Identify and quantify the resources committed to environmental activity (e.g., management, compliance, performance, operations, auditing).
- Describe any educational/training programs in place that keep environmental staff and management current n their professions and responsibilities.
- Summarize overall environmental objectives, targets, and goals, covering the entire environmental management program.

Figure 12-6   Excerpt from PERI Guidelines—Suggested Format on Reporting

THE PUBLIC ENVIRONMENTAL REPORTING INITIATIVE STRATEGY AND ITS EXECUTION

PERI organizes environmental report content into ten major categories: company profile, environmental policy, environmental management system, releases to the environment, environmental risk management, environmental compliance, product stewardship/life cycle management, employee recognition, stakeholder involvement, and resource conservation. Some of these core components involve a significant number of subcomponents.

The company profile and environmental policy components are fairly straightforward. PERI Guidelines suggest describing the size of the company, number and location of facilities, employees, major lines of business, and the general nature of environmental impacts. Corporate environmental policy statements should include relevant scope, applicability, content, goals, and dates of implementation and revision.

Information on employee recognition and stakeholder involvement are also simple to handle. On the former, what is suggested is information on programs for employee reward, education, and information which encourages environmental excellence. On the latter, support for work undertaken by government, academic, public interest, and industry associations on environmental issues, a general description of the company's efforts to involve other stakeholders, and community-based activities are recommended items for report inclusion. While these are bona fide aspects of good corporate environmental management, few external stakeholders place much stock in them.

ENVIRONMENTAL MANAGEMENT SYSTEMS AND ENVIRONMENTAL RELEASES

More complex are PERI components on the company's environmental management system and its environmental releases. The EMS section suggests information on staff organization and lines of authority, EHS relationship to the Board and other parts of the company, discussion of policy implementation, and formal education programs for maintaining currency in professionalism and management, including financial resources for management and compliance functions. Additional suggested elements are references to total quality or other companywide programs which include environmental performance and descriptions of overall environmental objectives and goals.

The environmental release data can be dealt with in several ways. PERI suggests a minimum of three years' data against defined baselines for the following releases:

- Air emissions, including toxic air pollutants
- "Greenhouse" gases and ozone-depleting substances
- Water discharges
- Hazardous and solid waste (including data on how the waste was handled, e.g., recycled, incinerated, treated, injected into deep wells, and whether on- or off-site)

PERI Guidelines also suggest that company targets for waste and emission reductions be identified. Participation (and performance) against voluntary government or trade association programs such as EPA's 33/50 and Green Lights should be included. Du Pont's 1993 report prepared in accord with the PERI guidelines places substantial emission information into trend-graph form, supplemented by detailed charts and additional graphs on its performance.[20] Monsanto includes an extensive at-a-glance chart summarizing major elements of its environmental performance together with a thumbnail description of the company and a profile of its operations worldwide. These informational summaries are backed with more extensive reporting tables in the latter portion of the publication.[21]

The most problematic aspects called for by the PERI guidelines deal with environmental compliance, risk management, and product stewardship or life-cycle management. The variation among companies on compliance data is striking. For example, United Technologies presents a descriptive table plus additional text to identify all state and federal violations by corporate unit, location, type of violation, and amount of fine for items from a low of $195 to a high of $5.3 million. UTC's report also presents hazardous waste site cleanup liability estimates and its health and safety record.[22] Merck discusses its violations candidly but sets a threshold of significance at fines of $25,000 or more.[23]

Amoco uses a performance measure, "citations per inspection based on external inspections," to describe its compliance record. Noting that citations do not necessarily reflect legal violations (since some are withdrawn after follow-up with the issuing agency), Amoco uses its metric to trace an improvement trend in environmental compliance.

Dow uses summary tables to present its compliance information worldwide on a quarterly basis for a three-year period and total fines paid over the same three-year period.[24] IBM presents compliance data in narrative fashion in its opening introduction to its 1992 report,[25] and Du Pont summarizes in the Chairman's letter its total environmental violations and provides additional summary data on remediation expenses. Among non-PERI reports, WMX Technologies provides comprehensive detail on compliance matters, the most extensive of any report.

PERI calls for coverage of environmental risk management matters, including environmental audit programs, remediation programs, current and planned, and emergency response programs. The Guidelines also call for information on product stewardship activities and life-cycle management. Under this heading PERI currently includes such matters as: technical research and design, packaging, materials conservation, energy efficiency and conservation, pollution prevention and waste reduction programs, product take-back or similar postconsumer programs, customer "partnership" programs, and relationships with suppliers. Materials conservation and energy efficiency conservation are now a tenth PERI reporting component.

PRESENTATION OF ENVIRONMENTAL REPORTS

The printed annual report publication is currently the most prevalent form of voluntary corporate environmental report. Increasingly, however, companies are evolving a suite of printed and electronic products to respond more precisely to the needs of particular audiences. WMX Technologies, one of the preeminent corporate innovators in the corporate environmental reporting field, pioneered the publication of a short- and long-form version of its report in 1991. Noranda's 1995 report is similarly printed in both long- and summary-form versions.[26] While CERES publishes standard and short-form versions of its reporting format, according to *CERES Help Guide: Instructions for Companies*, the short form is intended for only smaller (i.e., $25 million or less annual revenues) and generally nonmanufacturing companies and in no case for a company required to report under the Toxic Release Inventory requirements of SARA Title III.[27] What will influence corporate environmental reports in the future?

Let's examine the three major forces, in addition to information technology changes, which will influence the future of corporate environmental reporting:

- Expanded use of information disclosure mandates over traditional command-and-control regulation
- Requirements for increased public accountability in exchange for preferential regulatory treatment (e.g., "alternative compliance" or "Green Track" proposals)
- Expanding private market demands for EHS performance data

INFORMATION LAWS

Reference has already been made to the pivotal role that U.S. information-forcing laws such as NEPA and SARA Title III have played in pushing business organizations to assess, account for, and reduce their environmental impacts. Commitment to Europe's voluntary Eco-Management and Audit Scheme (EMAS) is viewed by some knowledgeable observers as becoming a precondition for doing business within the European Union. EMAS is designed to be implemented on a facility (site-by-site) basis and requires a third-party, verified audit and report on the environmental impact of the subscribing company's facility.[28] While many Europeans see EMAS requirements as adding substantially to the information base, U.S.-based EHS managers consider U.S. domestic mandates far more demanding. For example, the EPA recently announced their expansion of the Toxic Release Inventory of SARA Title III to include additional industry groups and chemical compounds.[29] Nothing comparable is in place in Europe.

The United States and other industrialized nations have pursued a voluntary approach to date for reducing the "greenhouse" gases implicated in global warming and climate change. Recently, however, the U.S. State Department has indicated that it may seek mandatory targets if greater progress cannot be made through voluntary reductions. The threat of more regulation or mandatory reporting requirements on baseline emissions may encourage some companies with significant "greenhouse" emissions to establish voluntary performance metrics to forestall such action. Likewise, EPA's recent *Federal Register* notice called for comment on several alternative approaches to a standardized facility data reporting system.[30] Should EPA and the states eventually create a unified national environmental information database, more companies might be encouraged to publish their environmental priorities and performance record.

These developments are a few of the potential information-forcing rules that may emerge in the United States and abroad. Their potential alone may drive additional corporate environmental reporting activity. Companies listed as a top five or ten TRI emitter in a given area do not care for the negative publicity and most move vigorously to change that status and explain how they are reducing or eliminating adverse environmental impacts.

PRIVATE MARKET DEMANDS

Beyond the information disclosure requirements and the public sector incentives for increased reporting are other private forces which drive the corporate environmental reporting movement. Increasingly, industry groups are collecting and presenting information on their sector's environmental performance. Trade groups see the need to demonstrate accountability and progress to check any demand for increased regulatory pressure. One case in point is the petroleum industry. The American Petroleum Institute (API) has since 1992 published the Petroleum Industry Environmental Performance Report (PIEP Report) which aggregates data from government sources and member companies in eight categories. API's industrywide standardizing format presents a more focused way to compare performance and benchmark best practices within the sector.[31] This industry is banking on its performance reports to help educate the public about its progress. It also creates internal competition among members to match or surpass the industry average.

Another major force is institutional investors of all types and motivations, not only groups like CERES and IRRC representing the socially responsibility investment movement, but also other investors interested in the environmental performance of a company from a purely financial perspective. While studies are mixed, increasingly investment advisers and other business experts are concluding that managing key environmental performance indicators well is part of what makes a company well managed and profitable.[32] A common desire is more standardization in the way environmental performance data are presented.

A final influence to cite in the further dispersion of the corporate environmental reporting impulse is the voluntary environmental management systems standard of the International Organization for Standardization (ISO), adopted in 1996. Although ISO 14001 does not specifically require external reporting, it does require that the adopting company address external communications with relevant stakeholders and demonstrate how it is meeting its "legal and other requirements" commitments, pollution prevention, and continuing system improvement. ISO 14001 may sweep across the global community as ISO 9000, the quality management standard, did. Regardless, there are a number of forces pushing ISO 14001. ISO 14001's guidance explains that an organization's commitment to the ICC Business Charter is part of the "other requirements" that, by subscribing to ISO 14001, the organization declares it is committed to meeting. With ISO 14001 adoption, ICC Business Charter Principle 16 may get new momentum. Leaving aside the ICC Charter, ISO 14001 itself requires a company to set measurable targets and objectives, continually evaluate its progress in meeting them, and let relevant parties know how it has done, elements that strongly support a corporate environmental reporting.

A STANDARD FOR THE FUTURE

The corporate environmental reporting phenomenon is of relatively recent origin. Its history and current trends suggest both staying power and further expansion. New information technologies are important as is the growing awareness of the relationship between effective environmental management and overall business performance. Users of reports want both more standardization and more tailored information which bears on their informational needs. External reporting is a key aspect of an effective and integrated environmental management system. Together these factors suggest that the next century should be full of active years for corporate communications, senior management, and the EHS management team.

NOTES

9. *KPMG International Survey of Environmental Reporting,* KPMG, New York, 1993.

10. *Environmental Report 1995/96,* NatWest Group, London, 1996, p. 9.

11. Please see Lynton Caldwell, "Constitutional Law for the Environment: Twenty Years with NEPA," *Environment,* Vol. 31, No. 10, 1992, or Richard Liroff's *A National Policy for the Environment: NEPA and Its Aftermath,* IU Press, Bloomington, IN, 1976.

12. Lober, Douglas J., "Current Trends in Corporate Reporting," *Corporate Environmental Strategy,* Vol. 4, No. 2, Winter 1997; Erik J. Meyers, "True Confessions: The New Corporate Romance with Environmental Reporting," and Lawrence Mach, "Practitioner Insight on Environmental Reporting," *Corporate Environmental Strategy,* Vol. 2, No. 1, Summer 1994; *Environmental Reporting in a Total Quality Management Framework: A Primer,* Global Environmental Management Initiative, Washington, DC, 1994; *Reporting on Environmental Performance,* Canadian Institute of Chartered Accountants, Toronto, 1993.

13. *Environmental Principles in Progress,* Philip Morris Companies, Inc., New York, 1996, p. 5.

14. *Environment Report 1995/96,* NatWest Group, London, 1996, p. 8.

15. *Summary Environment, Health and Safety Report, 1995,* Noranda, Inc., Canada (undated).

16. "Environmental Reporting Guidelines of Various Organizations," *Environmental Reporting in a Total Quality Management Framework: A Primer,* Global Environmental Management Initiative, Washington, D.C., 1994.

17. Information about EPA's Project XL can be accessed at http://www.epa.gov/rgytgrnj/specinit/p2/volpog/xl.htm.

18. Please see Doug Lober, "Current Trends in Corporate Reporting," *Corporate Environmental Strategy,* Vol. 4, No. 2, Winter 1997.

19. For detailed information on the PERI Guidelines please see www.nortel.com/cool/habitat/commsol/peri.html
20. Please see Du Pont's *Annual Environmental Report, 1993*.
21. Monsanto's environmental information is accessible at .
22. UTC's *Annual Environmental Report, 1993*.
23. Merck's environmental information is available at www.merck.com
24. Dow's environmental information is accessible at www.com.com/cgi.bin/frameop.cgi?/environment/ens.html
25. IBM's environmental information is accessible at www.ibm.com.
26. See *Commitment: Noranda 1995 Environment, Health and Safety Report*, Noranda, Inc., Canada, 1995, and *Summary Environment, Health and Safety Report, 1995*, Noranda, Inc., Canada, 1995.
27. *Help Guide: Instructions for Companies*, CERES, Boston, 1996, p.4.
28. Sustainability Ltd., *Engaging Stakeholders*, London, 1996.
29. Investor Responsibility Research Center, Environmental Information Service, 1350 Connecticut Avenue, NW, Suite 700 Washington, D.C. 20036, *Environmental Reporting and Third-Party Statements*, for the Global Environmental Management Initiative, Washington, D.C., March 1996.
30. Investor Responsibility Research Center, Environmental Information Service, *Environmental Reporting and Third-Party Statements*, for the Global Environmental Management Initiative, Washington D.C., March 1996, p. 22.
31. Investor Responsibility Research Center, *Institutional Investor Needs for Corporate Environmental Information*, Washington, D.C., 1992.
32. Global Environmental Management Initiative, *Conference Proceedings*, Washington, D.C., 1993.

THOUGHTS ON THE ENVIRONMENTAL REPORT

The corporate environmental report is a primary but not exclusive means of providing meaningful information and messages to target audiences. As noted in the earlier essays by Macauley and Anderson, corporations can use trade associations to shape their industry and publics, as well as a rich array of iterative techniques known as issues management. Of course, no single report can do it completely, since public expectations always change or evolve. Nonetheless, what Meyers and Lober give us here is a glimpse at a dominant tool of disclosure—the environmental report.

What Makes Environmental Reports Effective: Current Trends in Corporate Reporting

Douglas J. Lober

Mr. Lober is a Duke University scholar and financial analyst.

Selecting the audience for the environmental report is one of the most important decisions in proceeding with the report for it determines what type of information is necessary and how it should be presented. Employees, local communities, shareholders, customers, the general public, environmental groups, the media, schools and government agencies, and regulators are among the many potential audiences for a corporate environmental report.

Figure 12-7 represents the results of a survey of ninety-seven companies producing reports as to their intended audiences. Employees were the most frequently cited target group, indicated by 82 percent of the companies reporting, followed by shareholders targeted by 74 percent of the reports. Customers and government agencies were cited by over one-half of the report issuers as key audiences. Environmental groups and the local communities were targeted by over 40 percent of the reports. The general public was a target of 35 percent of the reports.

Each of these groups can have unique information needs and might require a particular style of communication. For example, shareholders might be concerned with environmental spending and potential liabilities and would need this information in a timely manner; customers might care about product attributes and packaging and whether an environmental management system is in place; and a local community might want information on plant emissions, emergency responsiveness plans, and community advisory panels.

So far, the reports have had limited success in meeting all these shareholder needs. For example, despite shareholders being cited as a key audience by almost all reports, an institutional investor would discover little of value in the reports from a mainstream investment standpoint. In fact, environmental reports usually exclude such environmental liability data as can be found

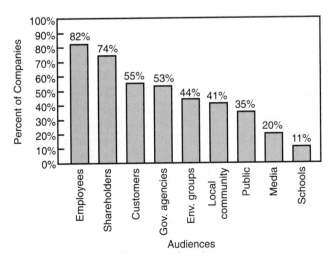

Figure 12-7 Results of Environmental Report Survey

simply by reading the footnotes in annual or 10K reports. One exception is Polaroid, which reprints the environmental notes and other environmental references found in its annual report.

Many corporations have chosen to follow the "smorgasbord approach" by targeting most of these different groups. Procter & Gamble, for example, states that their report "is designed with a diverse audience in mind, ranging from senior scientists in academia and environmental organizations to legislators, regulators, and consumers." Kimberly Clark organizes its report, in order of headings, by employees, customers, stockholders, and society.

Several research efforts are trying to determine just what audience needs are. The United Nations Environment Program and SustainAbility Ltd. has conducted a large study of needs of a broad group of stakeholders,[33] and the Investor Responsibility Research Center (IRRC) has researched the value to stakeholders of third-party statements and other topics in reports.[34] They conclude that the Achilles heel of corporate environmental reports is their credibility, despite the progress in content they have shown in a relatively brief amount of time. "Two keys to providing credibility," according to the IRRC, "are providing a balanced presentation, including negative information, and providing environmental performance indicators." They go on to state that third-party attestation by itself does not address the problem of credibility, without national, international, or industry reporting standards.[35]

Companies are also taking steps to help resolve the audience question. Monsanto and WMX Technologies, for example, conduct their own stakeholder studies. However, even when the needs of the audiences are known, space limitations may prevent these needs from being met. One survey of those using the reports indicated that the preferred page length for corporate environmental reports is one page![36] Furthermore, shorter length may not produce another frequently desired characteristic, credibility. A veteran report writer from Monsanto, Steve Archer, remarked, "A short readable document is less credible but a long credible document is less readable."[37]

One approach which can help companies meet the multi-audience challenge is to direct the report toward only a few audiences. 3M's Environmental Progress Report identifies employees as its key audience, placing the words "recognizing employee contributions" on its cover, and including a letter addressed "Dear 3M employee." Another solution is to produce more specialized reports, such as those covering a business unit, a site, a resource use, or a geographic region, in addition to the corporate environmental report. Another new type of report is one that focuses on the use of specific resources or energy or concentrates on a particular management practice. Gillette, for example, produces an Energy and Water Status Report in addition to its corporate level report. A third solution to the audience challenge is to make additional information available to those who request it. Monsanto and WMX Technologies have chosen to make a more detailed report, including additional examples of environmental practices, available on a separate diskette, which reduces the space needs in the corporate environmental report.

NOTES

33. Please see Richard Welford, *Corporate Environmental Management: Systems and Strategies*, Earthscan Publishers, London, 1996.

34. 61 *Federal Register* 33588, June 27, 1996.

35. 61 *Federal Register* 33671, October 7, 1996.

36. "Petroleum Industry Annual Report Represents How Oils See Themselves," *EHS Management*, June 17, 1996.

37. Cohen, Mark, et al., *Environmental and Financial Performance: Are They Related?*, IRRC, Washington, D.C., 1995; Stephan Schmidheiny and the World Business Council for Sustainable Development, *Financing Change*, MIT Press, 1997; and Darryl Ditz, et al., *Green Ledgers: Case Studies in Corporate Environmental Accounting*, World Resources Institute, Washington, D.C., 1995.

Practitioner Insight on Environmental Reporting

Laurence Mach

Laurence Mach is a partner at Laurence and Susan Mach Creative services, Inc., in Kearney, NJ. He is a creative consultant specializing in public policy, marketing, sales, and corporate communications in all media. He has written, produced, and consulted on environmental annual reports for AT&T, Consolidated Edison, Lucent Technologies, and Merck & Co., Inc.

The following examination of both strategic and practical issues in EH&S annual reports separates what's possible from what's needed by suggesting what the best options are for corporate executives, and by providing additional resources to support environmental and safety communication goals.

STRATEGIC ISSUES

The key strategic issue is: Should a company produce an Environmental and Safety report if it isn't doing so already? In their article, "Demystifying the Trend in Environmental Reports," Stephen Poltorzycki and Gilbert Hedstrom argue that "the issue is no longer *whether* to communicate corporate environmental, health, and safety performance externally, but instead *how* best to do it, and *what* specific measures of performance to report."[38]

There are many reasons for reporting, but each company must decide if these reasons are valid. The reasons include:

- Stakeholder pressure including media, shareholders, employees, and consumers
- Public relations requirements
- Competitive advantage
- Future legal requirements
- Duty to the environment

One approach to begin a report is to answer the following question: "Who is the audience? What stakeholder group or groups are we trying to reach?" Such audiences or stakeholder groups might include community members, customers, employees, legislators, regulators, and shareowners, among others.

Once you define your target audience you have a clearer idea of whether to report and what kind of report to produce. For example, in 1990, when AT&T's Environmental and Safety Engineering Center contemplated producing a report on activities, it first drew up a list of stakeholders to be targeted. The primary target proved to be officers of the corporation. But, as former Environmental and Safety Engineering Affairs Director Thomas S. Davis explains, "Although we wanted to raise the level of awareness among company executives and higher-level managers about our Environmental and Safety corporate goals and activities, we wouldn't have done a printed annual report for this group alone. However, managers—fifth level and above—formed a second key group. And regulators, legislators, and environmental activist groups were also stakeholders we wanted to reach. So we went forward."[39]

To begin, AT&T invested in a small staff of public relations professionals assigned full time to environmental issues. These professionals view the company's environmental reports as a valuable communications link with employees at all levels of the company. To bring the environmental reports' messages to employees, scaled-down versions of two of AT&T's Environmental and Safety reports were inserted into companywide magazines sent to each employee. In addition, freestanding 8×10-foot displays featuring key elements of each year's report have been produced for the annual shareowner's meeting. After the initial use, the displays travel to each AT&T domestic facility for viewing by employees.

Many companies use Environmental and Safety reports as part of larger communications efforts. At Merck and Co., Inc., for example, the reports are valuable to local Merck facilities for use in their community programs, open houses, and dedication ceremonies. Says Bowers, "They like the fact that the Environmental and Safety reports show communities that site Environmental and Safety activity is part of a corporate commitment."[40] Merck's reports are also used at local Emergency Planning Committee meetings by company committee members.

PRACTICAL ISSUES: WHAT FUTURE LEADERS NEED TO KNOW

Once a company identifies stakeholders it wants to communicate with, and once it decides to publish an Environmental and Safety report, it now faces a host of practical considerations. Important considerations include content, format, preproduction, production, and costs.

Content

A major challenge for many companies is making environmental disclosures accessible to the layman: Too much information is useless. But those reports that don't provide enough data are criticized by some stakeholders as "PR-ish" rather than informative. Reports are often criticized as being too complex for the general public to understand, yet too simplistic for scientists to endorse as thorough. That's why content is an issue that keeps many Environmental and Safety people awake at night. What kind of a report should they produce? Should it be like the company's financial annual report? Should it emphasize data? Should it tell people stories? How much data should be included? Should environmental and safety liabilities be included? Does a company earn credibility by including less-than-stellar information, or does such information invite backlash? You don't need to know all the answers before you begin, but you'll need to find answers before long—the sooner the better.

A proverb says, "In a multitude of counselors there is wisdom." How true when it comes to annual reports. If you've never done one, talk to people who have. Counselors are everywhere. Begin by seeking input from the stakeholders you've targeted. Ask them what kind of report they need. For example, Dow Chemical surveyed key members from its target audiences by phone. Talk with consulting firms and services who specialize in environmental reporting. It's worth paying a consultation fee to save time and money in production.

Even after seeking wisdom from a multitude of counselors, you may still find you haven't been able to decide whether you should do a "people" book, or a "data" book. Some stakeholders, notably employees, while interested in the company's environmental and safety goals and progress toward those goals, tend to focus more on what their facility is doing. They react well to "hero" stories of other employees who have excelled in environmental and safety performance. They know that it's people who make or break a company's environmental and safety program. If your primary audience is your company's employees, you might choose a format that emphasizes people and facility success stories. On the other hand, many stakeholders want data—all the data they can get. Many are looking for information on which to base buying decisions. They want to know significant liabilities facing your company. They want to know about fines and penalties levied against your company, about problematic emissions They want to know about your company's obligations for site remediation. If your primary audience consists of such stakeholders, your report will be heavy on data. And the more specificity of data is provided, the more use it is to these important stakeholders.

The issue remains: "What is relevant to the targeted audience? What has value to the readership? A growing consensus is that totally descriptive reports are unacceptable. But as *Coming Clean: Corporate Environmental Reporting* puts it, "Don't let that put you off producing lively, entertaining and informative brochures or publications in this area. There are lots of people out there who . . . will never read a statistical tract."[41] Dorothy Bowers, Vice President of Environmental and Safety Policy for Merck & Co, Inc., explains her company's philosophy on the issue: "We're trying to find a way to have something in it for everybody like we do in our financial annual reports. In those reports," she says, "the financial community looks at the detailed numbers.

Shareholders interested in knowing what they own a piece of, read about our program, our research, and our new products."[42]

People and project stories—"good-deed stories"—*are* important because they give people an opportunity to learn more about your company. People make quality happen, after all. But it won't do to have *only* people studies and case studies. Says Bowers: "Stakeholders need something they can use to measure our progress from year to year. Something to allow them to evaluate our attainment of goals we have set. We need to provide them with enough information so that they can understand how and why we made the progress so that they can begin to gain a perspective on what industry is able to do and is doing."[43]

The content issue becomes thornier as you confront dealing with your company's environmental and safety liabilities, operational problems, fines, penalties, and the like. Should you present "warts and all" and let the chips fall where they might? Should you try to explain or rationalize problems? Should you use the report to polemicize against state or federal regulations? As far as many stakeholders are concerned, your report should lay out the facts that surround a noncompliance problem, an environmental accident, or penalty without arguing the case. If you need to explain your company's point of view, you might include a Policy section in your report for that purpose.

Another thorny issue is meeting the needs of those stakeholders who aren't satisfied with the U.S. Toxic Release Inventory (TRI) data reported under the 1986 Emergency Planning and Community Right-to-Know Act (EPCRA), Title III of the Superfund Amendments and Reauthorization Act (SARA). They aren't satisfied with data reported under the Pollution Prevention Act of 1990 either. These stakeholders want a company's operating data: How many chemicals did a company bring in—and not just the 300 TRI toxic chemicals, but 1,000 or 10,000 different chemicals? Where are the chemicals stored? How much is used? How much circulates around the plant? Much of this data is necessarily proprietary.

Merck's Bowers opposes these kinds of requests. She says, "It's unrealistic to expect companies to release that kind of very economically sensitive information. Particularly when a stakeholder group misuses data the way some stakeholder groups have done with TRI data. For example, Citizen's Action published a report card in New Jersey that evaluated companies on how many of the toxic chemicals released had had pollution prevention projects applied to them. So if you had 21 chemicals on your site, and you did pollution prevention on 20 of them, then you would get an 'A.' If you did pollution prevention on five of them, or four of them, then you would get a 'D,' an 'E,' or an 'F.' It doesn't matter if the four of them were 99 percent of the volume of what reached the environment. That indicates that either they don't understand and aren't interested in learning enough to make a distinction between the *numbers* of chemicals and the *amounts* of chemicals, or they were simply looking for something to make a story. Before we start backing up into more detailed reporting and more detailed data we'd like to see a better appreciation of the data that we're already giving and a better understanding of what it means."[44]

Format Questions and Choices

Consider a format for your report that meets another need of data-hungry stakeholders. They want comparable data from report-to-report so they can make comparative analyses of your reports from year-to-year and so they can make comparisons from company-to-company. Investigate guidelines such as those developed by the Public Environmental Reporting Initiative (PERI). Standardized guidelines help meet stakeholder need for comparative data. Standardized guidelines also serve as a useful means to organize content, especially for companies new to Environmental and Safety reports. Voluntary guidelines such as these may eventually harden into legal requirements describing content and form for environmental reporting, so it may be wise to become familiar with them now.

If your company has established Quality Environmental and Safety goals, you might want to structure your report around those goals. That's what AT&T did. For five years, AT&T reported activity against these goals. Each goal had its own section. But the context of the activity varied according to the theme of that year's report. The report on 1990 activities raised the flag by presenting the company's goals, demonstrating the company chairman's public support of them, and establishing preliminary progress. The report on 1991 activities showed continuing successful progress but did so by demonstrating how principles of Total Quality Management used at AT&T are enabling company Business Units to meet the corporate goals. The report on 1992 activities continued the story but used Business Unit successes to demonstrate how the company's proactive environmental and safety behavior benefits both the environment and the bottom line. Subsequent reports continued this approach.

In September 1995, AT&T announced it would split up into three companies—AT&T Corporation, Lucent Technologies, and NCR Corporation. AT&T gave up its worldwide manufacturing facilities to become a leading telecommunications service company. Its environment, health, and safety organization had to reorganize to accommodate new priorities. Nevertheless, AT&T continues to integrate environment and safety practices into everyday operations and to engage employees and stakeholders by actively communicating about these issues.

In April 1996, Lucent Technologies was introduced as a publicly traded company on the New York Stock Exchange. Its Global Environmental, Health, and Safety Center continues to provide EH&S program guidelines, present best current practices and tools to the Lucent community, and monitor EH&S performance worldwide. Environmental, Health, and Safety Officers are EH&S advocates in the operating units, corporate centers, and regions. Public relations specialists continue to communicate the company's EH&S policy, goals, and activities with internal and external stakeholders.

Preproduction Concerns and Choices

Start early, because it takes time to decide on audience. It takes time to find out what they think and what they want. It takes time to decide on content and to focus your message. It takes time to decide on the best format to convey your message to your primary audience. It takes time to decide the specifications (length, size, appearance, etc.). It takes time to decide distribution plans.

Start early, because in the world of production, time equals money! Either you allow enough time for research, design, writing, production, and printing, or you spend money (sometimes lots of money) in order to meet deadlines. It's important to allow adequate time for each stage of production. Plan your production schedule by counting back from the date you want to release your report. In so far as timing goes, according to Eastman Kodak's Maria Bober Rasmussen, there are several possibilities for releasing an Environmental and Safety Annual Report:[45]

- In conjunction with (or as part of) your company's financial annual report
- At shareowners' meeting
- As soon as possible after the TRI data is available
- To coincide with annual plant tour
- To coincide with Earth Day
- To coincide with Quality Week

Once you have your release date, you can lay out your schedule. Counting backward—very roughly—allow a month for printing, a month and a half for writing and review, a month or more for research, and one to two months for making the up-front decisions such as audience, format, size, and so on. If you're planning on outside help with the project, now is the time to solicit bids. If the project is relatively simple, the bidding process may be equally simple. However, if your report is complex—or if you're counting on the outside help to develop the project with you—bidding is more complex. Don't forget that a low bid may look great to the people in accounting, but if you want the added value that experts bring, weigh all factors, not just price. And a rule of thumb is, if it's clear the vendor is in it for the bucks, forget it.

Production and Anticipated Delays

When the appropriate people have decided on the targeted audience and the basic specifications of the book, you gather information that the writer(s) will need. You may already have a network in place throughout the company to help supply this data; if not, start developing one. Top management support and your cross-functional skills are important in building a network of contributors. The more you can do up front, the more money you save in production, especially if you're using outside writers and designers. Even if your report is done entirely in-house, a tremendous amount of human capital must be spent developing points to be covered in the book.

No matter whether you are experienced in producing annual reports or not, it makes good sense and can save much frustration and wasted money to include as many "players" as possible in your first production meeting. Such a meeting might include key corporate players, writer/consultant, designer, and printer. Experienced consultants—writers and designers—can suggest cost-effective ways to achieve your communications goals. If you're working with outside consultants, bring examples of company publications targeted at the audiences you've chosen for your Environmental and Safety report. Bring copies of your company's latest financial annual report.

At a first meeting you share the parameters and specifications of the project. Hopefully, the budget won't be dictated in advance, but it often is. If you don't have a big budget, be prepared to spend company time instead of money, and be prepared to cut back your expectations. Remember Murphy's Law. Together the attendees of the meeting reach consensus on what is to be accomplished, and approximately how. The creative team—writer, designer, and so on—then go away and create a proposal which they present at another meeting. The writer and/or researcher may need your help in contacting a few people within your company to help round out his or her understanding of your environmental and safety operations.

At an approval meeting, the designer usually presents a layout showing how key spreads in the report will look. The writer presents a treatment of how the report might be organized, how content might flow, what its theme ought to be, and so on. An estimated production schedule and budget based on the specifications is included. Remember, the operative word is "estimate." Reality always intrudes and so does Murphy's Law. The key decision makers should attend this approval meeting. If they can't, someone will have to present the draft to them. If changes are needed in boards or treatment, a second approval meeting may be needed, cascading urgency into the process.

Once approval is granted, production begins. Each company's production schedule will vary according to size of the book, budget, corporate structure, and approval procedures, but the following covers steps common to most:

1. Research.
2. Begin photography and/or artwork (if needed).
3. Begin graphs, charts, etc.
4. Prepare first draft.
5. Review first draft.
6. Prepare second draft.
7. Review second draft.
8. Compile comments and prepare third draft.
9. Review and revise third draft.
10. Review fourth draft (management and legal review).
11. Compile comments.
12. Prepare final draft.
13. Finalize data/graphs/charts.

14. Proofread.
15. Prepare and approve mechanicals.
16. Prepare and approve final proofs.
17. Print.
18. Distribute.

The Big Question: What's the Cost?

If you've engaged outside professionals, don't ask for layouts or proposals for free. You get what you pay for. If you change specifications in the middle of production, be prepared to pay for those changes. If company management is too busy to meet approval deadlines agreed upon in the production schedule, it may cost you money, especially if your release date is a hard one, and you're late going to the printer. Sometimes, when that happens, printers can do miracles and it doesn't cost you. Sometimes it costs a lot.

If you're planning on photography in your report and you or your designer engage a freelance photographer, be advised that, unless you specify otherwise up-front, the photographer retains all rights to the negatives of the images he or she shoots. Your payment only gives you a onetime use of the images. If you make any other use of the images, you must pay the photographer again for those usages. The solution is to negotiate a "buyout" rate up-front. Don't buy advertising rights, however, unless you know that you'll use the images for such purposes. The same rules apply to artwork created for your book by freelance artists.

While on the subject of costs, remember that internal costs are adding up at every stage. Even if your entire report is produced in-house you might wind up spending far more than if you bid the job out or if, like many companies, you make judicious use of outside consultants and other talent. Printing costs are additional to production costs. Many factors affect printing costs:

- Quantity to be printed: Usually the more you print, the cheaper the price per individual book
- Paper: Recycled paper is mandatory and it varies widely in cost and quality. Your designers and printer can advise
- Number of pages
- Color(s): Curiously, many believe color is more expensive to print than black-and-white. It often is. However, if your report includes quality black-and-white photographic images, you may find that printing the full range of tones in the images may mean using four-color printing, netting little difference in cost. On the other hand, your audience will think you spent less, and if that perception is important, go for black-and-white.
- Photography/artwork
- Extras like special cuts or folds

KEEPING YOUR AUDIENCE IN MIND

Keep in mind that if you are embarking on your first report you are entering an evolutionary process, or in quality terms, a process of "continuous improvement." You do not need to know all the answers in order to begin. And there is lots of help out there, from experienced consultants to other corporate practitioners who are usually happy to share their knowledge. You can also benchmark directly with the company leaders.

Evolution is common to environmental and safety activity at companies, and the same is true of the environmental reports. Says Erik J. Meyers, General Counsel and Director of the Environmental Law Institute, "There's been a rapid pull-up in Environmental and Safety reports over the past few years. The recent reports are so much better because standards are rapidly rising. The way to stand out in a crowd of reports is by having better information."[46]

NOTES

Much of the information for this piece the author has collected over the years of producing environmental communications materials and environmental reports for companies. The remaining quotations have been collected through both formal presentation and informational discussions with professionals.

38. Hedstrom, Gilbert and Stephen Poltorzycki, "Demystifying the Trend in Environmental Reports," *Corporate Environmental Strategy Journal*, Vol. 1(3), 1993, p.35.

39. Davis, Thomas, Vice President EH&S, AT&T, quoted from 1994 GEMI conference.

40. Bower, Dorothy, Merck & Co, Inc., quoted from 1994 GEMI conference.

41. *Coming Clean: Corporate Environmental Reporting*, Deloitte Touche Tohmatsu International, London, England, 1993.

42. Bower, Dorothy, Merck & Co, Inc., quoted from 1994 GEMI conference.

43. Bower, Dorothy, Merck & Co, Inc., quoted from 1994 GEMI conference.

44. Bower, Dorothy, Merck & Co, Inc., quoted from 1994 GEMI conference.

45. Bober, Maria, Vice President, Environmental Affairs, Kodak Company, from 1994 GEMI Conference.

46. Meyers, Erik, General Counsel, Environmental Law Institute, comments from 1994 GEMI Conference.

EH&S Information and the World Wide Web[47]

Timothy D. Herbst

Mr Herbst is an Environmental Councilor at E. Bruce Harrison a division of Ruder Finn. Please see p. 254 for a full bio on the author.

INTRODUCTION

The World Wide Web is fast becoming the primary source for EH&S information. Many companies now use the web to disseminate EH&S information, such as EH&S reports. In addition, advocacy groups rely on the web and Internet technology to relay EH&S information to members and other grassroots organizations to support their activist causes, and government entities, such as the EPA, are making EH&S-related databases and mapping tools available on the web. In effect, these organizations are harnessing web technology to make corporate EH&S performance information increasingly public. While still a nascent communication tool, the web has become accessible to a wide audience. Recent surveys have shown that over 37 million people, or 17 percent of the population in the United States and Canada (ages 16 and up), use the Web. This represents an eight percent increase from 1995. Although not a mass media tool, it is clear the web is quickly becoming a primary source for a wide variety of information.

To better understand how and what EH&S information companies are communicating on the Web, and to examine their ability to use the Web to achieve specific organizational and EH&S communication objectives, Ruder-Finn examined Web sites from six organizations. Benchmark companies include: British Telecommunications (BT); Du Pont; IBM; Intel; and Royal Dutch Shell. To examine how advocacy groups use the Internet, Ruder-Finn also included Rainforest Action Network (RAN) in the study.

CONCLUSIONS

1. *Companies and advocacy groups are increasingly using the web to disseminate EH&S information.* Over the last 18 months, companies have moved from posting their EH&S progress report on the web to posting site and facility reports, updated EH&S-related news stories, product and customer focus material with EH&S messages, and issue and position papers. Companies like Royal Dutch Shell and BT have also designed specific feedback tools to solicit stakeholder responses regarding EH&S messages. Advocacy groups also recognize the value of the Web. RAN, for example, uses the web to network with other grassroots organizations thereby creating virtual organizations organized around specific advocacy issues. This same network feeds information to RAN for web dissemination. RAN's use of the web can make local EH&S information globally significant.

2. *While web-based EH&S information is reaching a wider stakeholder audience, this information is not always accurate or balanced.* RAN and other advocacy organizations use the web to disseminate EH&S information to mobilize grassroots organizations and individuals to achieve advocacy objectives. Many companies, however, are only now realizing the potential to reach a larger audience with their EH&S messages

via the Internet. The web offers any person, anywhere, access to company-related EH&S performance messages. One person interviewed claimed that "we are reaching stakeholders we never would have reached before." In many cases, however, EH&S information on the web is posted solely by advocacy groups—sometimes inaccurately. In fact, EH&S related advocacy information still predominates the web. To be sure, users can find multiple and diverse sources as well as a balanced perspective on a given issue. But more often than not, companies are in a catch-up mode to communicate EH&S messages on the web.

3. *Most companies have undefined Web site strategies and are achieving a low return on their web-related investments.* Perhaps as a result of evolving stakeholder expectations regarding disclosure of environmental information or because of the new nature and dynamics of the web, few companies have developed clear EH&S Web-based communication strategies. In general terms, the Web is simply used to widen the distribution of EH&S messages. IBM, for example, primarily uses the web to post existing information housed in its EH&S report. Some de facto web strategies have emerged. For example, Royal Dutch Shell is using the Web to solicit stakeholder feedback regarding its new EH&S and human rights policy. Also, Du Pont uses its site to integrate EH&S messages with business objectives such as product promotion. These examples, however, are not the result of a strategic process; rather they represent an ad hoc response to external pressures or opportunities.

4. *Few companies have adequately analyzed the effectiveness of placing EH&S information on the web.* Of the companies interviewed, there has been little web site usage or user performance evaluation. Companies' lack of evaluation stems from at least two reasons. First, corporate-sponsored EH&S information is still new to the web. Second, they do not consider their web site a strategic communications tool and have not seen an urgent need to rigorously evaluate usage patterns.

5. *Web technology has not significantly changed the way EH&S information is presented.* Most benchmarked companies have minimally repackaged (if at all) EH&S information for their web sites. Often, the print version of the company's EH&S report is simply posted on the web. But web copy is not print copy. To be effective, web copy must make use of headlines, graphics, and layered information. Detailed information should be layered and linked behind summary information to satisfy diverse audience information preferences. Web pages should also have multiple links to view related information. Finally, companies are not taking advantage of the web's ability to link and layer referenced information and links to other sites.

6. *The growing accessibility of the web coupled with greater release of EH&S information is raising stakeholder expectations for additional disclosure.*

Toxic Release Inventory data placement on the web has stimulated interest in making facility Risk Management Plans (including worst-case scenarios) similarly available. Moreover, organizations such as RAN that continue to collect and disseminate advocacy-related EH&S information will drive companies to disclose more about their operations and practices. The implications of these trends dictate strategically focused, preemptive management of EH&S disclosures to meet stakeholder expectations and to counter Web-based misinformation.

7. *The current trends of EH&S information on the web will lead to a reevaluation of corporate communication strategies for EH&S issues.* Given the current trends toward increasing accessibility, more disclosure of EH&S-related information, and raising stakeholder expectations, companies will face both opportunities and vulnerabilities. Opportunities stem from a company's ability to offer graphically enhanced and effective EH&S information, thereby better controlling or influencing the EH&S messages users find on the web. On the other hand, companies will continue to face the threat of damaging EH&S-related messages that can be communicated instantaneously to a global community via the web. To effectively deal with the fast-paced evolution of EH&S information on the Internet, companies will benefit from a managed process that is both proactive and responsive. Tools such as active web monitoring, web site usage evaluation, and preemptive EH&S web-based communications can be incorporated into this management framework.

NOTE

47. Herbst, Tim, "Environmental Reporting and the Internet," *Corporate Environmental Strategy Journal,* Vol. 5, No. 2., 1998.

Editors' Note—Competence, Potency, and Effectiveness are three of the most reliable attributes of praise for an environmental professional, or for any professional for that matter. Leaders need all three attributes.

Competence is the two-foot hurdle, which many can and do jump all week long. In environmental management, the discourse of competence depends on legal, technical, and managerial details. If you fail to fulfill any of these relatively demanding and ever-changing competencies, you will be unable to lift yourself or your firm over the first hurtle toward success. You won't get past Part I of this book without the basic competencies.

These basic competencies are not enough, yet most of the texts in the field only present technical or managerial competence. That is why we've chosen to include lessons valuable for recognizing business opportunities and keeping public expectations in mind—this will allow professional potency. By going beyond mere compliance, you can run the race of environmental excellence with the potency of a strategist, and the effectiveness of a leader.

So, how high are these hurdles, and what might surpassing them yield? The answer is elaborate but heartfelt: If you master all three parts of this text, you might become a leader.

The great American writer E. B. White once noted: "If the world were merely challenging, that would be easy. If it were merely seductive, that would be no problem. But I arise each morning, torn between the desire to enjoy the world and to improve it. This makes it hard to plan the day." You should feel like E. B. White in looking over the domain of this text.

This brings us to the last hurtle, that six-foot demon, effectiveness. Effectiveness can only be measured by calculating the uses of the professional in question. Thus, the truly effective environmental professional would have users in government, industry, and the public interest groups. He or she would be embraced by that full and often competing spectrum of users. They would achieve the effectiveness of commonsense and be employed by many.

Remember, don't just become technically competent. Develop your abilities to recognize business opportunity—that is a potent skill. And, of course, answer your public's expectations. For such is an effective route to leadership and responsibility.

QUESTIONS FOR FURTHER THOUGHT

1. Environmental reporting and communications shape the way in which stakeholders view a corporation. Given the trends discussed on environmental disclosure, what may be the appropriate strategic responses for the next century (i.e., what may be different)?

2. What creates the difference between empty environmental communications, often termed "greenwash," and more legitimate forms of environmental communications? Can you think of an example for each type?

3. What are the risks and the rewards in voluntarily disclosing negative environmental information (i.e., emission rates, spills)?

4. Considering the legitimate skepticism of environmental groups, consumers, and advocates over corporate environmental claims, how would you communicate the benefits of a product launch with positive environmental attributes? Are there risks?

5. Is the communication of environmental news by companies any different from the communication of technical claims of a product, managing stakeholders after a nonenvironmental negative press release, or other types of image-damaging information?

6. How would you, as an environmental "champion" in your organization, convince senior management of the value of crafting strategically appropriate environmental communication strategies?

INTEGRATIVE CASE III

Environmental Commitment at the Southern Company

Dr. Robert Woodall and Thomas Butler

Dr. Robert Woodall is Vice President of Environmental Policy at Southern Company. See the "Executive Spotlight" for a complete biography.

Thomas A. Butler is pursuing a Ph.D. from the Lally School of Management and Technology at Rensselaer Polytechnic Institute. He has ten years of work experience in environmental consulting, and holds an M.S. from the University of Oklahoma and a B.A. from Colgate University.

INTRODUCTION

The electric utility industry is facing its greatest competitive challenge as the twenty-first century approaches—an open marketplace where consumers can choose who provides their electric power. The standard practices of electric utilities will have to be revamped as firms vie for market share in formerly protected service territories. Within this context, environmental management at electric utilities will face new pressures as firms streamline their operations while still striving to maintain their high service quality and environmental performance levels.

Southern Company is the nation's largest electric producer, and it is also the "most respected" in the electric utilities category according to *Fortune* magazine's 1997 "Corporate Reputations" survey.[1] Realizing that environmental performance plays an important part in creating a firm's public perception, Southern Company has been redefining its strategic environmental concerns and initiatives since 1990. These changes have been initiated by both external and internal forces in an effort to strengthen Southern Company's reputation and increase shareholder value through efficiency gains and cost-reduction strategies. With the fast approach of open competition, Southern's environmental strategy has gained even greater importance.

To date, most major U.S. corporations have considered environmental management an essential, but separate, facet of business. Historically, the environmental management function has been responsible for ensuring that regulations are addressed properly, that necessary permits are obtained, and that the company does its best to remain in compliance within permit limits to avoid fines and public scrutiny. However, a new paradigm has emerged at a few firms that are cognizant of how environmental strategy can assist in meeting business challenges.

At Southern Company, this new business paradigm is being methodically embraced. The traditional environmental management function is undergoing a profound and basic transformation. This change is part of a strategic initiative by Southern Company to alter its corporate culture by viewing environmental initiatives and requirements as a cornerstone of competitive advantage.

David M. Ratcliffe, senior vice president for external affairs states, "There has always been a focus in our industry about safety. It is almost second nature to people; they never ask themselves whether we will do the right safety procedures . . . . We want to get to the point where people have this same mindset, that environmental responsiveness, stewardship, and responsibility are second nature, just like safety."[2] Through the integration of an environmental strategy Southern Company hopes to achieve improved environmental performance, as well as competitive advantage through efficiency gains, cost reduction, and brand identification. Under deregulation, the new benchmark is to be the lowest electricity cost producer while minimizing the environmental footprint.

THE ENVIRONMENTAL IMPACTS OF ELECTRICITY PRODUCTION

Southern Company sprang from James Mitchell and Thomas Martin's original vision of an electrical system spread throughout many states. This early vision began with the creation of the Alabama Power Company in 1912. Throughout the early 1900s the organization grew, and its name was changed to Commonwealth and Southern to reflect the power generating capacity it now held in other southern states, namely Georgia, Florida, and Mississippi. In 1933, the creation of the Tennessee Valley Authority created encroachment on their service area with electricity that was made less expensive through government subsidy. This early brush with competition led Southern's then-CEO, Wendell Willkie, to run against President Roosevelt in the 1940 presidential election. It wasn't until 1947, however, that the Southern Company, as it is known today, was established to assume ownership of the common stock among the various subsidiaries.[4]

Currently, as the nation's largest producer of electricity (see Figure III-A for more details), Southern Company generates substantial environmental impacts in an attempt to meet its customer's power demands. The primary contributing factor rests in Southern's reliance on a generation capacity that is primarily coal-based. Its power mix is

---

Southern Company is the nation's largest producer of electricity generating 154 billion kilowatt-hours at its U.S. facilities in 1996. Total 1996 revenues exceeded $10.4 billion with a net income of $1.13 billion.

Southern Company is the holding company for five electric utilities: Alabama Power, Georgia Power, Gulf Power, Mississippi Power and Savannah Electric. Other subsidiaries consist of Southern Nuclear, Southern Communication Services, Southern Development and Investment Group and Southern Company Services.

As have many other utilities, Southern Company has expanded its operations overseas. Southern recently purchased a regional distribution company, South Western Electricity, in Great Britain. Another subsidiary, Southern Energy Inc., provides power in Argentina, England, Chile, the Bahamas, and Trinidad Tobago.

In January 1997, Southern acquired an 80 percent stake in Consolidated Electric Power Asia (CEPA) Ltd.—the world's fifth-largest independent power producer—for $2.1 billion. Additional deals later brought Southern's interest in CEPA to nearly 100 percent. This purchase is part of an overall strategy by Southern to have 30 percent of its earnings come from businesses that are outside of its regulated utility holdings. As many U.S. utilities have realized, the world's burgeoning demand for electricity has created excellent overseas opportunities for increasing revenues in an industry where the domestic demand for electricity has been relatively flat for the past ten years.

Figure III-A Southern Company at a Glance[3]

comprised of 77 percent coal, 17 percent nuclear, 5 percent hydropower, and 1 percent gas and oil. In 1996, Southern announced that it would begin adding gas generation to its fleet, a move that serves to shift its fuel-mix ratio. Due to the current reliance upon coal, Southern's carbon dioxide and sulfur dioxide emissions—based on a standardized measure of lbs/emission per million Btu's generated—are higher than the utility industry average.[5] In 1995 the industry average for CO_2 and SO_2 emissions were 1498.3 and 9.5 lbs./MWh of generation, respectively, while Southern's 1998 emissions projections for each are 1669.8 and 12.4 lbs/MWh of generation. (While these emission rates serve as en existing threat to Southern, the utility projects their emissions to drop below the industry average within ten years as a result of fuel mix changes and new technology.)[6]

This unfavorable comparison to average industry emissions levels of CO_2 and SO_2 brought Southern Company under the scrutiny of the Council on Economic Priorities (CEP), a nonprofit, public interest research organization that evaluates the environmental policies and practices of U.S. corporations. (See the article by Amy Muska at the end of this case for a discussion of groups such as CEP.) In 1994, CEP listed the Southern Company as one of the nation's worst air polluters. Even though Southern had codified an environmental strategy four years earlier, the Council felt that the company was not adequately limiting its impacts on the environment; specifically, its CO_2 and SO_2 emissions. This listing led to a number of negative articles in major news outlets such as the *Los Angeles Times, New York Times, Washington Post,* and the *Atlanta Constitution.* Clearly, this was of no small strategic concern to Southern executives.[7]

Understanding the significance of the CEP listing and the potential for additional damage to their public image, Southern Company engaged in an active dialogue with CEP that included criticism of the methodology used to list them. They presented the CEP with emission projections based on Southern's generation and load forecasts. Based on these projections, which included increased use of natural gas, the company hopes to decrease its future emission rates. In August 1996, CEP delisted Southern, recognizing their efforts to reduce carbon dioxide emissions per megawatt hour by 15 percent by the year 2000, to decrease average peak demand by 11 percent through energy management programs, and its establishment of an effective environmental management system.[8] The dialogue that Southern Company maintained with the Council is representative of a philosophy of openness in environmental management; part of the company's strategic environmental policy is to construct and maintain good working relationships with environmental groups. In this instance, Southern worked directly with CEP, as well as the individual judges, to create an open dialogue on the delisting process, while in some cases firms listed by CEP refused to acknowledge their presence on the list.

This policy of engaging stakeholders fit with the company's overall environmental strategic plan to participate in an open dialogue on their environmental performance, yet this strategy was not always employed at Southern. In *The Choices of Power,* Marc Roberts and Jeremy Bluhm explored a Southern history which contrasts its more recent means of managing stakeholders.[9] Southern had made an effort in the early 1970s to participate actively on regulatory advisory boards while steering clear of more hostile groups. The conclusion of these two Harvard researchers in 1983 was that,

> . . . from Southern's viewpoint, having industry representatives on environmental boards [was] a good way to ensure objective consideration of the facts, as industry experts perceive them, but in areas where there is more hostility to business the emphasis [was] on creating a greater distance between the regulators and

the businesses they regulate . . . . A large and collegial top-management group [had] enabled Southern to respond effectively to most outside demands. A distinct exception [was] Southern's limited capacity to deal with organized citizen groups: having faced much less pressure . . . [the company had] not developed the same kind of sophisticated strategies and structural units.

It's clear that change within Southern required an acknowledgment of these past strategies and ways to surpass the weight of potential historical roadblocks. The experience with CEP serves as an example of successfully addressing stakeholder needs in a new way, and it shows Southern's interest in maintaining relations with the wide array of potential stakeholders. This is echoed by Southern Company's membership in the Global Environmental Management Initiative (GEMI), a nonprofit organization of twenty-one U.S.-based multinational companies. GEMI's mission is to foster the communication and implementation of successful corporate environmental strategies on a global basis, and Rob Minter, manager of environmental policy at Southern Company, is a past GEMI chairman, a position of some visibility in the environmental community.

Below is a list of the current Executive Environmental Policy Council (EEPC) members and their titles. The makeup of the group has changed since its inception, but the current membership does mirror the original spectrum of Southern Company interests.

- C. D. McCrary—Vice President, Southern Company
- W. C. Archer—Executive Vice President, Southern Company
- D. H. Evans—President and CEO, Gulf Power
- L. B. Long—Vice President, Technical Services, Southern Nuclear
- R. E. Leggett—Vice President, International Operations, Southern Energy
- R. G. Moore—Vice President, Power Generation and Transmission, Gulf Power
- C. H. Goodman—Vice President, Research and Environmental Affairs, Southern Company Services
- Steve Spencer —Executive VP, External Affairs, Southern Company
- W. D. Hudson—Vice President, Comptroller, and CFO, Southern Company Services
- J. G. Richardson—Vice President, Governmental Affairs, Southern Company Services
- B. M. Guthrie—President, Fossil/Hydro Group, Southern Company
- G. E. Holland—President and CEO, Savannah Electric
- R. Woodall, Jr.—Vice President, Environmental Policy, Southern Company

In order to effectively reach consensus on decisions through the EEPC, each member's interests are acknowledged and incorporated in decision-making through routine individual meetings apart from the routine group meetings.

Source: Chuck Griffin, external communications, Southern Company, March 1998.

Figure III-B   Southern's EEPC Membership

EMBRACING THE DYNAMICS OF CHANGE

Like so many firms, environmental management at Southern Company has undergone a gradual but steady transformation over the past ten years. In 1990, Southern Company codified its commitment to managing its environmental issues by releasing a statement of environmental principles. This action, initiated by the board of directors, was overseen by Ed Addison, Southern Company's CEO at the time. The statement, incorporated into Southern Company's vision statement, declared:

> We affirm the importance of protecting the environment and making wise use of our natural resources. We will set and achieve environmental goals that are in concert with other goals needed to further the well-being of society.[10]

Although Southern Company is the holding company for all its separate subsidiaries, at that time each subsidiary was establishing its own environmental policy and procedures apart from one another. In 1991, Addison hired a new corporate Vice President of Environmental Policy, Robert Woodall, to address the concern that theirs was no single voice framing the company's environmental direction. Woodall was charged with the responsibility of consolidating and coordinating the company's environmental policy throughout the company and its subsidiaries. One of the first initiatives was to establish the Executive Environmental Policy Council (EEPC), shown in Figure III-B, made up of senior executives from key functions and most subsidiaries.

EXECUTIVE SPOTLIGHT   Robert Woodall, Vice President of Environmental Policy, Southern Company

At Southern Company, we are constantly striving to improve our management of the complex issues that face us. Routinely, we seek feedback from our peers on a number of attributes that we feel good leaders should master. The three attributes that mean the most to me and that have served me well during my twenty-five year career are attitude, vision, and goodwill.

A friend has a prayer that goes like this: "Lord, if you can't change my situation, please change my attitude." We face many daunting, sometimes unpleasant and possibly confrontational situations as environmental representatives of operations consuming large amounts of natural resources. Changing the situation may not be possible and at best comes slowly. But our attitude is something that we alone control and can change instantly.

Vision goes beyond attitude. Vision has been defined as a belief in what can be, even when others don't know it can be, or think it cannot be. Vision is so important. I have been privileged to work my entire career for a parade of managers who had the vision that Southern Company, despite its dependence on fossil fuel, could lead the industry in environmental stewardship. It has often been an uphill struggle, but the vision has not faded.

Laurie Beth Jones, in her book, *Jesus CEO*, discusses "the presumption of goodwill." It reminds me of a favorite verse from the Oxford Bible, Romans 12:10: "Outdo one another in showing honor." In our Southern Company management literature, we suggest at least three ways to achieve this: (1) respect the dignity of each individual, (2) deal fairly with everyone, and (3) support people who are willing to risk failure.

In my job, I have the opportunity to work with many people inside the company and an even greater number outside the company who have some very different views about how the business should be run. Meetings, discussions, and debates have the potential to become heated and at times, contentious. If one can operate under the presumption of goodwill, attempting to outdo one another with honor, it's amazing how productive a meeting can be. It isn't always easy, but it always works.

My career has spanned the most exciting period of environmental activism in the history of the United States. The National Environmental Policy Act was passed while I was in graduate school. I was working part time for the U.S. Water Pollution Control Authority when it became the Environmental Protection Agency. I helped prepare the environmental impact statement for Georgia Power's first nuclear power plant. We discovered totally new species of aquatic life during the course of our work. The company provided me with the opportunity to work with situations I never dreamed of, including testifying before the Nuclear Regulatory Commission, working in foreign countries, and spending a year in Washington as a registered lobbyist. So far, developing Southern Company's Environmental Policy and Environmental Performance Strategy has been the greatest challenge and opportunity.

With this companywide advisory body in place, Woodall looked to develop a strategic environmental plan, and coordinate the company's environmental policies and actions. This was initiated through the creation of a six-point environmental policy. Called a "Statement of Environmental Policy," these principles, shown in Figure III-C, were shaped to guide the company toward recognizing and minimizing the environmental impacts of electrical generation.

These principles were created to inform external stakeholders and Southern employees of the firm's environmental expectations. Prior to this, there were no guidelines for subsidiaries to follow to develop a corporate environmental policy. The EEPC approved, and the board of directors adopted, this new policy in 1992. Southern Company's environmental policy framed the company's strategic commitment for addressing environmental concerns, but it lacked specific goals or measures to gauge the company's environmental progress. To address this problem, Southern created the CARE program.

CARE—DEFINING ENVIRONMENTAL PROGRESS THROUGH GOAL SETTING

Southern Company's Statement of Environmental Policy recognized the need for specific planning and goal setting.[11] In 1993, the company embarked on an environmental planning process called CARE, an acronym which stands for commitment/awareness/responsibility/enhancement, shown in Figure III-D. As Woodall stated, "when we came out with our Environmental Policy Statement, there were very few, if any, electric utilities that had definable measures included in their environmental plans. At the time this was considered a very bold move. We were defining where we wanted to go, and we were establishing measures to see how far we had gone."

It is the policy of Southern Company to conduct its business in a manner that protects the environment by:

- Meeting or surpassing all environmental laws, regulations, and permit requirements, and verifying this commitment through environmental auditing.
- Seeking to ensure that environmental laws, regulations, and permit requirements are based on sound science and cost-effective technology.
- Pursuing opportunities to enhance the quality of the environment.
- Promoting public and employee understanding of environmental issues and the company's environmental activities.
- Establishing company and organizational environmental goals and implementation plans.
- Ensuring that employees are aware of their individual roles and responsibilities in implementation of this environmental policy.

Source: Southern Company, *Environmental Report, 1996.*

Figure III-C   Statement of Environmental Policy

The CARE program was developed by Southern and its subsidiaries at the behest of CEO Addison, to serve as a roadmap for improving environmental performance. CARE was also a means by which the firm could differentiate itself as a premier electric utility company.

Prior to the initiation of CARE, Southern Company had no centralized plan for implementing its environmental strategies. CARE was to take Southern Company beyond the day-to-day activities of environmental management.

CARE was developed at the corporate level, but it included significant input from its subsidiaries. David Ratcliffe, the CEO of Mississippi Power at the time, was not only instrumental in defining the goals and strategies of CARE, but he also promoted the plan at Mississippi Power. Due to his effort and those of his employees, Mississippi Power became a leader among the various Southern Company subsidiary utilities in implementing the initiative. As Ratcliffe stated,

> I thought the document (CARE) was really exciting; I thought it had a lot of good elements to it. It was something our folks put together. It was a no-brainer to endorse it in concert with making it a part of the business. It is not a separate activity that we engage in. It is how we do business every day."[12]

CARE was widely effective since it had clearly defined measures—a first in the utility industry—but the program also had limitations. Its major weakness was that as a standalone document it was not connected to the company's core business strategy. However, CARE did promote a proactive approach: The document defined Southern's environmental management function well beyond typical compliance-based thinking.

Southern's environmental management function was given the role of encouraging subsidiaries to identify new business opportunities for the company as well as define new environmental initiatives that cut costs, improved the firm's public perception, and identified new environmentally based revenue streams.

Commitment—Continuous improvement in commitment to environmental stewardship.

Awareness—Continuous improvement in the level of environmental awareness of customers, employees, and stockholders.

Responsibility—Compliance with all environmental laws, regulations, and permit requirements.

Enhancement—Continuous improvement in voluntary environmental enhancement.

Strategic Objectives

- Be a leading corporate environmental steward in the electric utility industry.
- Be a world leader in providing clean and efficient energy.
- Develop new products and services that provide solutions to environmental and energy needs.

Strategies

- Encourage employee involvement in responsible community programs/ projects that demonstrate the company's commitment to environmental stewardship.
- Demonstrate executive commitment through leadership in environmental programs.
- Promote our core business through helping our customers meet their environmental needs.
- Establish appropriate environmental goals for organizations and employees.
- Increase the understanding of our company's environmental commitment with employees, customers, stockholders, and policy makers.
- Comply with all environmental laws and regulations.
- Perform audits and self-assessments to ensure compliance with environmental regulations.
- Assess and implement cost-effective operation strategies that improve environmental quality.
- Seek opportunities to develop and provide clean energy technologies and expertise to new and existing markets.
- Implement cost-effective pollution prevention and waste minimization programs.
- Implement habitat management programs for appropriate company properties.
- Promote cost-effective energy efficiency management programs.
- Support research and development programs that enable the wise use of our natural and renewable resources.
- Work to protect valuable and vulnerable elements of Earth's environment.
- Work with educators to promote a better understanding of environmental and energy issues.

Figure III-D CARE—Southern Company Environmental Strategic Plan

Source: Southern Company.

Measures

- Improved positive responses on the Employee Vision Progress Survey
- Improved positive responses on customer surveys
- Improved positive responses on Southern Company's Stockholder Survey
- Participation in company/employee-sponsored programs and projects
- Documented performance improvement in meeting compliance goals
- Environmental audit results
- Implementation of cost-effective operational strategies that improve environmental quality
- Development of new environmental products and services
- Amount of pollution prevented and waste material minimized
- Size and quality of habitat enhancement programs
- Emissions avoided by energy efficiency, demand-side management programs, and market penetration of electrotechnologies
- Participation in environmental research and development programs for natural and renewable energy resources
- Participation in classroom teaching and curriculum development

Figure III-D *(continued)*

BEYOND CARE—A BUSINESS-BASED ENVIRONMENTAL STRATEGY

In 1995 Ed Addison retired as Southern's CEO and was succeeded by Bill Dahlberg. Dahlberg envisioned the company becoming America's best-diversified utility. This meant that the firm would not only retain its core business of electric operating companies, but it would also seek to grow through the acquisition and expansion, both domestically and internationally, into other utility services and other noncore businesses.

In a document entitled *Southern Strategies,* Dahlberg articulated in the formidably titled *Bold Aggressive Goal* (BAG) that Southern Company would become the best-diversified utility by increasing shareholder value. Other major goals, or BIGs—Big Intermediate Goals—further guided the company by seeking to achieve leadership in ten areas:[13]

- Have a kilowatt-hour cost that is at or below competitive market price.
- Reduction in overhead costs by 20 percent by 1998.
- Grow revenue while maintaining competitive pricing.
- Generate a positive cash flow above capital reinvestment and dividend requirements.
- Be the number-one power marketer in the Southeast by 1998.
- Generate 30 percent of the company's net income from noncore businesses by 2003, earning a higher ROE than in the core business.
- Grow earnings per share on average of 5 to 6 percent annually.
- Rank in the best quartile of top companies as a "great place to work."

- Rank in the best quartile of top utilities in customer satisfaction.
- Be among the top ten power marketers nationally by 1997 and among the top five nationally by 2003.

To achieve these goals, Southern Company made efforts to reduce costs of electricity production and enter a competitive marketplace as a low-cost producer. While Southern's cost per kilowatt-hour already is one of the lowest in the industry, the company is making plans to cut costs by $780 million by 2003.

There continue to be many challenges in meeting these goals. First, the company is empowering its employees to discover the means to increase efficiency and encourage innovative solutions. Second, costs must be cut without adversely affecting the present quality of service. Finally, Southern must reframe its mindset. New policy initiatives must have either a neutral or an enhancing effect on environmental performance, yet still lead to lower overall company costs.

It became apparent that CARE needed to be revamped to align the company's environmental strategy with his business plan of becoming America's best-diversified utility. The program was inconsistent with Dahlberg's new goals for cost reduction, and there was uncertainty as to how it would be implemented consistently throughout the different system company subsidiaries. Furthermore, there was some confusion between the objectives and strategies outlined in the CARE program.

Nonetheless, CARE had driven change at Southern Company subsidiaries. At Mississippi Power Company, the community enhancement program was important in increasing overall customer satisfaction. CARE was instrumental in helping Mississippi Power evaluate its environmental business risks and liabilities. Employees at Southern Nuclear Operating Company used CARE to help outline an overall strategy for reducing company wastes, minimize the use of chlorine at its plants, and promote participation in EPA's Green Lights and WasteWi$e programs. These and many other CARE-generated efforts have improved environmental performance throughout Southern companies.

Although the CARE process articulated a commitment and direction on the environment, it was too difficult to measure and track. It required greater simplicity and definable measures. In 1995, Ratcliffe became senior vice president of external affairs, directly responsible for the company's environmental policy. Ratcliffe explains,

> if we truly want to be America's best-diversified utility, and are going to create bold aggressive goals, somehow that commitment to that bold aggressive position, or corporate image or corporate presence has to go across the entire organization. Every piece of that has to be picked up at that kind of level. You can't set bold aggressive goals for earnings and then say we want to be second class in environmental systems. That does not work.[14]

In the spring of 1996, Ratcliffe established the Environmental Performance Strategy (EPS) to link closely to the company's new business plan. He engaged assistance from Woodall; Rob Minter, manager of Environmental Policy; corporate public relations personnel; representatives from the various utility subsidiaries; and outside consultants. Since the final product would directly impact the Southern subsidiaries, it was important that the team include the various environmental managers from these firms. This would ensure added insight in developing the product, and more importantly, it ensured unilateral buy-in among the subsidiaries.

To develop this new strategy at Southern Company, several assessments were made, including:[15]

- A critique of the strategies outlined in the CARE document.
- An analysis of environmental costs with specific emphasis on reducing these costs.
- An assessment of the strengths, weaknesses, opportunities, and threats (SWOT) that the business would face between the present and the year 2005. (Current and projected cost impacts of the Clean Air Act were included in the SWOT analysis, as well as an evaluation of core companywide environmental resources and competencies.)

STAKEHOLDER INPUT: A TOOL TO ASSESS AND IMPROVE STRATEGY

The process of developing the EPS was divided into two phases. Phase I was an assessment of existing strategy, while Phase II was a plan development and implementation stage.

The initial effort included an environmental evaluation of the company by selected outside stakeholders and members of Southern Company's Board of Directors. This helped to avoid a common danger: When a strategy is developed in-house, with little or no external review, the final product might not address the concerns of the public and other important stakeholders. The crucial concerns of these stakeholders were incorporated into the development of the environmental business strategy. Stakeholders were interviewed in order to gather their views on the current environmental trends and their expectations of electric utility firms. Input regarding the effect of environmental performance on financial goals was also sought. An assessment of Southern's "Environmental Perception" was measured by using focus groups and surveys of Southern's customers and employees.

In Phase II, a draft of the revised environmental business plan was developed with objectives, strategies, and measurements. The roles and responsibilities of both corporate environmental staff and operating staff were defined.

One of the major outcomes of the effort was to define environmental goals and metrics that were consistent with Dahlberg's *Southern Strategies* initiative. An environmental scorecard tracked programs against the goals and metrics; reviewed research milestones and accomplishments; and assessed voluntary programs and other major Southern Company environmental activities. This scorecard provided a measure by which to evaluate the effectiveness of these initiatives.

Specific environmental issues became a platform for advancing business objectives. For example, the Public Utility Holding Act of 1935 prevents Southern from purchasing a gas energy and distribution firm. The addition of a gas utility to Southern's portfolio of subsidiaries would help the company become more diversified and competitive, and allow Southern to change its fuel mix to reflect market conditions. Since natural gas is the nation's cleanest-burning fuel, the ability to purchase a natural gas company would be in alignment with the environmental goal of reducing environmental impact and increasing efficiency, yet expanding the firm's core business beyond electricity production. For Southern, there is a strong environmental and business argument for the repeal of this law.

MANAGING ENVIRONMENTAL IMPACT INTO
THE TWENTY-FIRST CENTURY

Southern Company's new environmental business plan, *Environmental Performance Strategy: Managing Environmental Impact While Managing the Business,* was approved in March 1997.[16] The plan, shown in Figure III-E, allows Southern Company to reevaluate and realign its environmental strategy relative to the company's business vision. The plan still reflects the CARE approach and sets strategic objectives by which the company can gauge its progress. As stated, "The new companywide strategy—which applies to both all domestic and international operations—seeks to increase revenues and decrease the environmental impact of our business operations." The aim of integrating the environmental business plan into the core business plan of the company is to increase customer loyalty and the favorable perception of the firm while driving down operating costs and increasing shareholder value.

The environmental business plan has been constructed to address a range of issues the company faces in newly entered international markets. The document is cost management–based—it analyzes environmental issues in a business context of cost minimization, while maintaining the commitments of achieving environmental compliance and improving the company's environmental performance.

In differing from CARE, Southern's new environmental business plan defines general strategic objectives to anticipate deregulation. In California, electric utilities must divest themselves of some of their electric generating assets. Since California is considered by many to be the nation's model for deregulation, Southern's management was concerned that setting absolute goals may not be relevant to Southern's future business environment. Southern may also have to divest itself of its generating assets or invest in other types of utilities. If this happens, it would be of little use to establish goals that in the near future may be irrelevant and be perceived as misleading by Southern's stakeholders.

Southern has also defined strategic objectives that its subsidiaries must meet. Subsidiaries will use the business plan as a template by which they can establish specific environmental benchmarks. The consensus of Southern's management was that the subsidiaries have a much better handle on the types of goals that need to be set in their operating areas. Southern's subsidiary companies not only operate in the southern states of Alabama, Florida, Georgia, and Mississippi, but also throughout the United States and internationally—including China, the Philippines, Germany, England, Argentina, Chile, the Bahamas and Trinidad and Tobago.

In Business Planning Objectives, Southern defined six areas to seek improvement and efficiency gains:

- To manage the company's environmental impact while meeting the firm's financial objectives. To support this objective, Southern will establish and track definable environmental performance indicators to determine the effectiveness of its environmental policies.
- Southern will use quantifiable measures to keep a tally of its environmental track record.
- Southern will maintain an open dialogue with its stakeholders by publicly reporting these environmental metrics.
- Southern will establish fuel procurement programs, technology assessment, R&D efforts, and operating strategies that will minimize its environmental footprint while maximizing revenues.
- Southern is committed to grow revenues from environmentally related marketing programs.
- To focus on pollution prevention and waste minimization, with a special emphasis on recycling of ash.

1. Business Environment

Competition and change shape the future of our company and our industry. As competitive forces take hold, public scrutiny of our environmental performance will increase. Consequently, while Southern Company seeks to increase revenues, we will continue to improve the environmental performance of our operations.

Continuing to improve our environmental performance is therefore an important part of our future business success. Southern Company's new environmental performance strategy embodies these business realities and builds on the previous environmental strategy, known as CARE—representing commitment, awareness, responsibility, and enhancement.

The need to integrate our environmental planning and performance with the company's business planning is driven by a number of factors:

- Southern Company is now a global company, and its environmental plan must establish a framework for anticipating and managing a more diverse range of environmental issues at various levels—local, regional, national, and international.

- An environmental plan should follow a business approach by linking the environmental policy to the business strategy.

- Environmental planning must be linked to enhancing revenue, while maintaining a commitment to compliance and improved environmental performance.

- Environmental issues are business issues. Having a strong environmental reputation is one way to differentiate the company in an increasingly competitive marketplace.

- Employees, customers, and other stakeholders continue to expect higher levels of environmental performance.

- A clean and healthy environment is an important economic development asset in the regions where we operate. Improving our environmental performance, and providing technical assistance and other forms of encouragement to other businesses to improve their environmental performance, expands opportunities for economic growth.

2. Business Policy: Environmental Matters

It is the policy of Southern Company to conduct its business in a manner that protects the environment by:

- Meeting or surpassing all the environmental laws, regulations, and permit requirements, and verifying this commitment through environmental auditing.

- Seeking to ensure that environmental laws, regulations, and permit requirements are based on sound science and cost-effective technology.

Figure III-E Southern Company's Environmental Performance Strategy

Source: Southern Company, *Environmental Performance Strategy: Managing Environmental Impact While Managing the Business,* 1996.

- Pursuing opportunities to enhance the quality of the environment.
- Promoting employee and public understanding of environmental issues and the company's environmental activities.
- Establishing company and organizational environmental goals and implementation plans.
- Ensuring that employees are aware of their individual roles and responsibilities in implementation of this environmental policy.

3. Business Planning Objectives

Develop plans and goals for all aspects of our business including power generation, transmission and distribution, marketing, and other services that promote improved environmental performance.

A. Manage our operations to reduce our environmental impact while achieving our financial objectives.

Strategies

- Ensure compliance with all environmental laws and regulations through auditing and continuous improvement for a series of environmental performance indicators—quantifiable measures of key compliance areas.
- Publicly report on our performance in these indicators.
- Aggressively pursue fuel procurement, technology, and operating strategies that are significantly reducing our emissions of SO_2 and Nox. This, along with strategies to meet future generating requirements, is expected to continue to reduce the emissions of pollutants associated with each unit of product (e.g., pounds of SO_2 per megawatt hour), while recognizing that our total emissions will grow as sales grow.

B. Increase shareholder value through managing cost and revenue performance on environmental issues.

Strategies

- Grow revenues from existing environmentally related marketing programs and determine market feasibility for additional environmental products and services.
- Participate with domestic and foreign governments and other organizations to achieve environmental progress and more efficient and flexible implementation of environmental goals.

C. Improve customer satisfaction regarding the environmental performance of Southern Company.

Strategies

- Achieve best quartile environmental performance in the national utility customer benchmark survey regarding how well Southern's residential customers think the company "shows concern for the environment."

D. Demonstrate Southern Company's commitment to activities that enhance the environment.

Figure III-E   *(continued)*

Strategies

While we challenge ourselves to reduce costs, we will:

- Explore and implement incentive program concepts to encourage employees to participate in creating innovative environmental process and business improvement.
- Identify significant water resource issues related to our operations and develop innovative solutions that improve environmental performance.
- Support multiple efforts regarding pollution prevention and waste minimization with particular focus on ash created in the production of electricity.
- Support environmental conservation and education activities in the communities and markets that we serve.
- Demonstrate leadership in the utility industry through aggressively pursuing environmental research and development opportunity.

Figure III-E *(continued)*

Environmental "signature" programs can enhance the perception of a firm and while leading to real additional benefits. For example, Southern Company is planting twenty million trees on company land and other locations in a $4.5 million program designed to offset carbon dioxide emissions from power plants. The tree-planting program, which will continue through the year 2000, is based on the science of carbon sequestration—how trees store carbon. One important factor in carbon sequestration is how trees are used once they have matured and slowed their absorption of carbon dioxide. If dead trees are left to rot, some of the carbon again will be released into the atmosphere in the form of carbon dioxide and methane, meaning the carbon sequestration had lasted only as long as the tree lived.

This is a valued-added program; trees that are planted for the carbon sequestration program can be harvested for lumber when they mature. Southern and private landowners will not only benefit from the revenue produced during the lumber sale, but the carbon that is stored in the wood will be effectively removed from the atmosphere for a greater period of time while used as a building material.

Approximately $800,000 of the $4.5 million will pay for planting trees on company land. The rest will fund tree planting on non-company land throughout Southern's service territory. State forestry officials have assisted Southern in identifying tree-planting sites on non-company land. The company will plant primarily pines since they grow well in the Southeast and can be utilized for lumber.

Source: Southern Company, *Environmental Report, 1996.*

Figure III-F Carbon Sequestration: An Environmental Signature Program

Southern plans to maintain an effective dialogue with government and environmental groups. By entering into the dialogue for pollution reduction and global warming issues, Southern intends to implement programs that are not only good for the environment, but also good for its future business activities.

Furthermore, Southern hopes to expand its business in what Dahlberg refers to as "highly energy efficient and electrically based electrotechnologies."[18] For example, Southern is seeking to promote the implementation of super-efficient electrically based HVAC technologies in its service areas. It is also promoting industrial electrotechnologies that will not only increase the efficiency of some industrial processes, but make them more cost effective. Southern is currently working with Entergy, a worldwide power production and diversified electric service operation in New Orleans funded through EPRI, the Electric Power Research Institute, and Georgia-Pacific on microwave drying of wood to reduce VOCs during the drying process. If this technology proves effective, this would have a positive environmental benefit and a solid business benefit by decreasing drying times and increasing the process energy efficiency.

Southern also looks to increase its customer satisfaction by improving environmental performance and participating in activities such as environmental signature programs, shown in Figure III-F, which enhance their commitment to protecting the environment. Southern continues to participate in organizations such as the Global Environmental Management Initiative, where they have maintained a very active profile, and to identify other organizations where participation would help Southern meet its strategic objectives.

Southern Company plans to integrate its environmental strategies into all of its business activities. By becoming an environmental leader, Southern expects that recognition and "green branding" will help it to compete more effectively in the twenty-first century. It is anticipated that consumers will recognize and choose to do business with electric utilities that not only have a low price, but are also environmentally conscientious.

The Southern Company environmental performance strategy challenges the company to carefully integrate cost reduction, a competitive mindset, and the goal to be exemplary environmental stewards. The goal is to view environmental issues as part of the whole business decision-making process. As stated in Dahlberg's *Southern Strategies* document, "We use change as a competitive advantage." This viewpoint is being established with the integration of environmental strategies into the firm's business plan.

The Challenge of Independent Corporate Environmental Performance Evaluation

Amy Muska

Amy Muska is a research manager at the Council on Economic Priorities (CEP). She earned her Bachelor of Science in Biology from Boston College and received a Master of Science in Environmental Management and Policy from Rensselaer Polytechnic Institute. The views presented in this essay are the author's only, and not those of the Council on Economic Priorities.

WHERE'S THE DEMAND FOR THIRD-PARTY VERIFICATION?

Approximately $1.2 trillion is currently invested in the United States under the affirmation of SRI—socially responsible investing.[19] The concept of integrating personal values, social and environmental concerns with investment decisions originated in the 1960s, as a result of the Vietnam War and companies operating in apartheid South Africa, and it has become a powerful force for social change. Without a doubt, public access to information is a critical driving force for corporate change, including environmental performance, and firms such as the Council on Economic Priorities (CEP), the Investor Responsibility Research Center (IRRC), the Interfaith Center for Corporate Responsibility (ICCR), and Franklin Research and Development Corporation have been formed as a result of the informational demands of investors and other stakeholders.

Independent social and environmental performance evaluators are expected to provide objectivity. Companies regularly issue press releases, conduct press conferences, and publish information about their environmental performance initiatives. Although self-disclosure is an important step, corporate claims on environmental responsibility must be authenticated to a public that requires some independent verification. Groups like CEP, IRRC, and others serve as a legitimizing linchpin between corporate claims and public trust.

UNDERSTANDING THE RATING PROCESS

Corporate evaluations use both primary and secondary source data. Primary source information, obtained by ratings firms through corporate surveys or questionnaires, is obviously an important factor in the evaluation. However, disclosure rates vary among industries and companies, and uniform information cannot be compiled on every company. Industry representatives often express a willingness to disclose environmental performance information but want to know, "How are you going to use this information against me?" Conversely, the environmental community is very eager to assume that corporations "must be hiding something" if they do not respond to requests for performance data. Secondary source information received from federal agencies or other research organizations is also required for the evaluation. The advantage of U.S. Environmental Protection Agency data, for example, is that uniform data sets can be acquired. In addition, secondary sources provide the necessary "check" on the company-provided information.

Historically, ratings have relied heavily on quantitative data, particularly EPA's Toxic Release Inventory (TRI) and other federal databases. Although companies frequently question the data's quality and usefulness, TRI remains one of few sources of comparable information. The downside of using this type of data is that a one- to two-year lag time normally exists between data collection at a facility and publication. The biggest challenge when conducting the evaluations is generating or locating comparable environmental performance data. To account for size differences between companies, researchers employ a process of "normalization."

Although production units would be most appropriate for normalizing, financial information is publicly available and it is often used by rating organizations.

Right-to-Know legislation helped jumpstart voluntary corporate environmental reporting. Yet, these reports suffer from a lack of comparability and quantification. More substantial reporting requires new mechanisms of evaluation and new environmental performance indicators. Although corporate disclosure has increased, the development has been ad-hoc in nature. In addition, the information that is disclosed is primarily qualitative. Environmental performance rating systems have evolved to reflect the expanded information availability. There is a growing trend toward the consumer demand for "extended product responsibility." This emerging concept encourages manufacturers, suppliers, and distributors to accept increased responsibility for all phases of a product's life cycle. Since this information is often presented and obtained in a qualitative fashion as well, its value is debatable.

VERIFYING ENVIRONMENTAL CLAIMS IN THE NEXT CENTURY

Although a great deal of intracompany communication is necessary to capture the value of superior environmental performance, the independent evaluators can contribute in many ways. For example, greater transparency and communication of the rating process can reduce the confusion between factual and rated data for all stakeholders. Delivering consistent and comparable environmental performance information and promoting the use of standardized environmental performance indicators (EPIs) are two fundamental responsibilities of environmental ratings organizations. Fortunately, there is a growing interest in harmonizing and standardizing EPIs within both independent evaluator community and industry. Even companies that are traditionally responsive remark, "We receive different surveys from many nonprofit organizations—we don't have the time to answer them all. Our lives would be made a lot easier if you all used the same one."

The underlying critical task of the independent environmental performance evaluator is to convince skeptics on Wall Street that environmental performance is a good determinant of financial performance and to create greater demand for the evaluations. The process of evaluating corporate environmental performance is continuously evolving. Admittedly imperfect, independently rating corporate environmental performance is an embedded and increasingly significant tool for investors, suppliers, and a wide range of stakeholders. The underlying logic of all firms involved in this field is that economic power can foster environmental protection through consumers, investors, and activists. The concept is simple, but powerful: By avoiding the worst and rewarding the best, individuals can advance corporate environmental progress through careful investment decisions.

Editors' Final Note (on Southern): Readers will discern several important elements that are revealed in this history of the development of Southern Company's environmental policy. First, it takes the power of a leader to convene a "guiding coalition" from throughout the company to develop the vision and goals necessary to move environmental management out of its traditional silo. The leader must know how to (a) facilitate group discussion toward a consensus of diverse positions, (b) develop a set of common interests, and (c) use the power of this credible membership to make the policy a viable and consequential document for the rest of the organization.

Second, the business decisions that ignite a strategic approach to environmental policy are driven by an awareness of competitive advantage, an understanding of how environmental reputation links to business value, and the anticipation of how environmental performance positions the firm in a changing marketplace. Finally, communication skills for internal buy-in and external credibility are a necessity given the long-term approach that defines change in the electric utility industry. Voluntary environmental disclosure may help to develop a dialogue with external stakeholders that includes public interest groups, as well as investors, customers, and shareholders; but those with economic interest must be convinced of the economic value of environmental investment as well as the environmental benefit.

NOTES

1. Robinson, Edward A., "America's Most Admired Companies," *Fortune*, March 3, 1997, pp. 68–76.

2. Interview by Tom Butler with David M. Ratcliffe and W. Robert Woodall, September 25, 1996.

3. Southern Company internal information and *Annual Report, 1996*.

4. Roberts, Marc J., and Jeremy S. Bluhm, *The Choices of Power: Utilities Face the Environmental Challenge*, Harvard University Press, Cambridge, MA, 1981.

5. Council on Economic Priorities Newsletter, Department of Energy, Energy Information Agency, Form 767, 1994 data, December 1996.

6. Industry average based on the 50 largest generating facilities in the U.S., from a 1997 National Resource Defense Council Report on 1995 emission rates. (Southern has mapped out a twenty-year projected emission rate schedule in order to address their higher emission rates.)

7. Quinn, Mathew C., "Southern Co. Ranked Among Nation's Top Polluters," *Atlanta Constitution*, November 29, 1995.

8. Council on Economic Priorities Newsletter, December 1996, p. 2.

9. Roberts, Marc J., and Jeremy S. Bluhm, *The Choices of Power: Utilities Face the Environmental Challenge*, Harvard University Press, Cambridge, MA, 1981.

10. Dahlberg, A. W., *Southern Company 1995 Annual Report—Message to the Shareholders*, p. 2.

11. Southern Company, *Southern Strategies*, internal document describing the company's strategy for the future, January 1996.

12. Interview by Tom Butler with David M. Ratcliffe and W. Robert Woodall, September 25, 1996.

13. Southern Company, *Southern Strategies*, internal document describing the company's strategy for the future, January 1996.

14. Dahlberg, A. W,. *Southern Company 1995 Annual Report—Message to the Shareholders*, p. 2.

15. Interview by Tom Butler with David M. Ratcliffe and W. Robert Woodall, September 25, 1996.

16. Southern Company's *Environmental Performance Strategy: Managing Environmental Impacts While Managing the Business,* 1996.

17. Southern Company, Draft 16, "Stretch—Managing the Environment as Part of Our Business: Increasing Revenues, Decreasing Environmental Impacts," internal company document, Spring 1996.

18. Dahlberg, A. W., *Southern Company 1995 Annual Report—Message to the Shareholders,* p. 2.

19. Social Investment Forum, "1997 Report on Responsible Investing Trends in the United States," December 5, 1997 (report available at www.socialinvest.or/InvSRItrends.htm).

QUESTIONS FOR FURTHER THOUGHT

1. Assess Southern Company's performance measures, based upon the lessons you learned in "Measure for Measure," by Van Epps and Walters. Do they make strategic sense?

2. With impending deregulation of utilities to allow consumer choice, geography will no longer bind consumers to a particular utility. How does a firm like Southern create brand identification? How does environmental commitment improve reputation and sales?

3. Southern Company has expanded its international presence in recent years. How would you manage environmental operations in countries with weak environmental regulations? Would you apply the same standards you follow in the United States? Why?

4. Imagine yourself as vice president of corporate environmental policy at Southern Company. What issues loom on the horizon that you would address through Southern Company's strategic environmental plan, CARE? How does fuel-mix play a part?

5. How do Southern Company's "signature programs" answer public expectations? What would make strategic sense as a signature program for Southern Company? Would certain areas of concentration lend more credibility to Southern Company's efforts?

6. One purpose of the integration of environmental objectives into the core business is to increase customer loyalty. How do you measure customer loyalty?

7. Southern's CARE program defines general strategic objectives, instead of specific tactical goals. Is this wise? How would the use of an information management system facilitate this scenario?

8. What strategic advantage can Southern Company gain through an alliance like the one it formed with Energy? In what areas would it be beneficial for Southern Company to form alliances?

SUGGESTIONS FOR FURTHER READING

- Lippmann, Walter, *Public Opinion*, Free Press Paperbacks, New York, 1997.

  Perhaps the best and most honest text ever written on the complexity of this search is Walter Lippmann's *Public Opinion*. We suggest you reread it each decade of your career. You must read Musashi to know how to battle in the early phase of your career. You must even read Machiavelli to deliver harm swiftly as you mete out slowly the benefits of your new powers. But in the end, it is Lippmann and the strengths of public opinion that will determine if you win or lose. Don't be content with reading only this text. The classes in strategy and in public affairs can, and will, take you further down the road to positions of environmental leadership.

- Tzu, Sun, *The Art of War* (translated by Samuel B. Griffith), Oxford University Press, New York, 1963.

  There are a number of versions of this timeless classic on the art of strategy that you can read. Whichever translation you choose, you will see a classic military strategist, in the Eastern tradition, present his lessons for success in battle—and even discussions of when not to battle. These lessons for war translate well to business strategists. Simply stated, it is often referenced as a "must read" by business strategists.

- Musashi, Miyamoto, *The Book of Five Rings*, Bantum Books, New York, 1983.

  Written in China in 500 B.C., Sun Tzu's work on strategy and warfare has been read and cited by military leaders and corporate leaders alike. With a careful reading, Sun Tzu offers insights that go well beyond military strategy and are as useful for environmental strategists as for soldiers. Like Sun Tzu's text, *The Book of Five Rings* presents the subtle treatment of military strategy that translates easily to understanding the nuance of managing stakeholders in matters of environmental significance.

- Harrison, E. Bruce, *Going Green: How to Communicate Your Company's Environmental Commitment*, Business One Irwin, Homewood, Illinois, 1993.

  Harrison, perhaps one of the first and best professionals on environmental communication issues, brings to the page the perspective of an experienced public relations professional. The text covers broad issues of stakeholder relations external to the firm as well as dealing with internal staff communications. He also gives examples throughout the text that relate to the real world of environmental communications and stakeholder management.

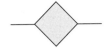

Afterword: Leadership Skills for Sustainable Development

Twenty-five years ago this month, while still an undergraduate candidate at Cornell, I came across a passage that convinced me I could become a writer of books someday. It was written by Marguerite Wildenhain, the Bauhaus potter in her superbly written book *The Invisible Core,* and it reads with a feeling of moral obligation even today:[1]

> There is no reason to be proud of whatever gifts one has . . . . But there is a reason to be deeply thankful for them . . . . The more capacity a person has, the greater and more cogent will be the moral obligation to do something honorable with what he has.

The passage does not end here, with a cliché and the elitist's sense of noble obligations, but instead, returns to a more earthy and sincere point about any craftperson's devotion to his or her way of life:

> Let us look at the implication, man like animals, is by nature lazy, but the creative man would always work. He works not only because he unconsciously acknowledges his ability to do so with the acceptance of deeper human responsibility. He understands that his work-time cannot be what it is for most men, from a certain hour to another definite hour. His work will be his total life, no less. That he feels to be the least he can do to make up for the gift of abilities that he was given.

For those who have seen Wildenhain's pots and have paused before their astounding functional beauty, you know she lived this kind of devoted life. Despite tremendous pressures from the marketplace to increase the output of her work, she resisted these external pressures in a deliberate effort to capture "the invisible core" of each pot. Her passage ends with a point I now find strangely relevant to the current task of reflecting on leadership skills for sustainable development, since so few leaders in history have this kind of artistic restraint she demands of herself:

> Needless to say, there are innumerable temptations along the path of a craftsman to do things badly, to evade responsibility and effort, to look at life flippantly, and one succumbs to these often enough. As a whole, though, this concept of total daily and complete devotion to his work becomes for the nature craftsman not only his moral law, but his deepest concern and his most constant joy . . . this artistic and ethical pressure that permeates his whole life, in work and leisure, in joy and sorrow, will give his work the valid human quality that is the sign of the work of art and out of a technician a creative artist will have developed.

What follows are some final thoughts designed to explain one claim: While most popular management literature can describe how leaders spend their time, staff, and resources on making sure their organizations have a promising future, this same literature is essentially bankrupt regarding the topics of personal restraint and professional devotion evident in the Marguerite Wildenhain passage. Yet deep in our hearts most of us know that sustainable development is not achieved without leaders who can teach the values of such restraint, quality, and devotion on a global scale. Today's leaders in government, business, and NGOs will need to change their usual roles in the next century. As noted by the President's Council on Sustainable Development, it is likely that "more collaborative approaches to making decisions can be arduous and time-consuming (as we have learned over the past nearly three years), and all of the players must change their customary roles. For government, this means using its power to convene and facilitate, shifting gradually from prescribing behavior to supporting responsibility by setting goals, creating incentives, monitoring performance and providing information."[2]

Over the last twenty-five years I have found passages similar to Wildenhain's muses in the admired works of writers as different as William Hazlett, Henry David Thoreau, and George Orwell, and as I got older, I am sure that the "leadership principles of strategic restraint" lie buried in the many diverse works of the world's greatest spiritual literature.

Yet to keep these final thoughts simple and readable, please return to Wildenhain's passage as an example of what is often missing in the post–World War II debates about sustainability. I seldom see any serious examination of restraint in the political, scientific, or corporate claims about sustainable enterprises.

Of course, at this point, many rationalists may ask: Is there any room for restraint in our new paradise of global consumers? Yet what gives us some wiggle room to outsmart the remorseless logic of rampant consumerism is the fact that throughout history leaders can preach about the powers of restraint in credible ways. Here one need only think of Winston Churchill's famous appeal about blood, sweat, and tears, or about Lincoln at Gettsyburg, or Caesar explaining Roman sacrifices. Throughout time, leaders emerge as individuals who discover in us the emotional intelligence it takes to get a job done, even when that set of tasks requires sacrifices and sustained restraint.

Leaders for sustainable development will, across time, define a new business logic. While the dominant language and metrics of that logic must include refinements of the conventional corporate strategic concerns about time, quality, cost reduction, distribution, and critical staffing issues, one can begin to see the emergence of these new leaders in the realm of corporate environmental management. I first sensed this while writing my 1990 book for Simon and Schuster, *In Search of Environmental Excellence: Moving Beyond Blame.* In that book, I assembled a chart to distinguish some new emerging aspects of environmental leadership. Figure A-1 presents an end-of-the-century update of that chart.[3]

I have seen hiring managers select their staff based on the conserving and restraint-based values seen on the chart's right column. Admittedly, this is a rare event. But it does happen more and more, especially because of downsizing.

As we all know, the longing for success built into most business training has little to do with such strategic conservation of resources. Moreover, the

I. ADVERSARIAL POLITICS— BUSINESS AS USUAL	I. BEYOND BLAME STRATEGIES
End-pipe regulations	Solution-oriented public strategies
Legal litigation for problem solving	Building from a common ground of science and law
Enforcement and fines as noted performance measures	Education and development, not just technology and products
II. CONSUMER SOCIETY	II. LESS-IS-MORE APPROACH TO GROWTH
Inability to distinguish between wants and needs	Self-sufficiency and minimalism in organizations and profit centers
Materialism: the American dream held as the key model	Conservation values toward natural resources in day-today actions
Reliance on the superabundance and resilience of nature	Environmental and resource management are part of corporate strategy
III. DOMINANT CULTURE DYNAMICS	III. EMERGENT CULTURE DYNAMICS
Nationalism's inability to act as key to lobbying	Global perspective; grassroots activism—both seen as related
Creator/destroyer attitude dominant	Living as an implicit part of nature, not above nation
Short-term usage valued	Long-term planning valued

Figure A-1 Next Century's Fork in the Road

Source: Updated by Bruce Piasecki for AHC Group; first published in *In Search of Environmental Excellence,* Simon & Schuster, 1990.

supreme machinery of marketing can't directly ask the important key questions about "what is enough." After World War II, most leaders needed to center their efforts along one line of industrial thinking, and this strong, bold line allowed expansive celebration of these kinds, or areas, of innovation:

1. New product development
2. Rights of consumers
3. Transfer of technologies

Government, civil discourse, and corporate policy have, since World War II, essentially centered their agendas along these lines. The result is a well-advertised net increase in the world's rate of consumption, especially in America and other advanced industrial nations.

There have been some significant countervailing developments. Take, for example, our new options of e-mail over express mail, or even France's refusal to follow the American expansionist economic model. Yet despite each small step forward, we sense the rapids of industrial development wherever one looks. As a result, many think of sustainable development as a joke, or at best, as an oxymoron. One significant countervailing development is the noted President's Council on Sustainable Development (PCSD), now led by Marty Spitzer. They note:[4]

> In June 1993, when President Clinton created the President's Council on Sustainable Development, he asked us to find ways "to bring people together to meet the needs of the present without jeopardizing the future." He gave us a task that required us to think about the future and about the consequences of the choices this generation makes on the lives of future generations. It is a task that has caused each of us to think about human needs, economic prosperity, and human interactions with nature differently than we had before.

Nevertheless, many smart people today wonder if the next generation of environmental leaders can apply the rigor and discipline of Wildenhain's art to their corporations. While it is too early to judge how much of this intent is grounded in promotional appeal only, the next section explores this suspicion at length.

WHAT IS ENVIRONMENTAL LEADERSHIP?

As we discussed in Chapter 1, business books abound with cases that explore what creates a leader within a private-sector organization. Environmental books, on the other hand, have emphasized wrongdoing, imminent doom, and identification and solution of technical problems. Seldom do these two traditions meet. Yet with the increasing importance being attached to the qualities of leadership, it is time to look at what distinguishes environmental leadership from other kinds of superior corporate performance.

TOP PERSONAL SKILLS FOR ENVIRONMENTAL LEADERS

- Forget about blame—find out what works.
- Build a broad and deep network of personal friendships, associations, and affiliations.
- Cultivate risk, ambiguity, and uncertainty as sources of powerful change.
- Check your instincts against your clients' needs.
- Replicate success, using lots of small steps to clear the top.
- Make the future of the organization promising to everyone in it.
- Use stories and metaphors to reinforce the goals of the organization and a sense of belonging.
- Select brilliant, reliable deputies.
- Acknowledge the importance of everyone's role.

A look at the skills chain above shows the value that compounds through this skill: Jumping a fifteen-foot hurdle seems impossible, but jumping fifteen feet in three-foot increments gets you to the top of the stairs. The following passage on Lincoln illustrates this point:[5]

> Lincoln had the will and the ability to make tough decisions when necessary. And he did not hesitate once he was convinced that swift action had to take place. However, it is certain that for every crucial decision of his administration Lincoln thought things out well in advance. In fact, he employed a classic decision-making sequence of events that began with an understanding of all the facts that were involved, often obtaining this information himself when venturing into the field. Lincoln would also consider a variety of possible solutions and the consequences of each. Finally, he would assure himself that any action taken would be consistent with his administrative and personal policy objectives. And then he would effectively communicate his decision and implement it.

While few people possess the abilities of Lincoln, one of the greatest presidents in American history, the development of comprehensive, diverse, and personally exacting skills does distinguish today's environmental leader from others in the corporate tribe. As you think about this book keep this ratio in mind: Over 80 percent of your time may be consumed on achieving and keeping compliance, especially in our wild world of rapid mergers and acquisition. Roughly 15 percent of your time will be recognizing business opportunity, especially of you care to escape the corporate dungeon of "mindless functionary." That leaves less than five percent of your time for all the rest on public trust, initial messages, and stakeholder involvement.

Somehow, the environmental leader lives in these often-competing realms of corporate life at once, scaling the hurdles each day. She also is able to survive the adversarial politics of the day, while positioning for the promise of the future.

These nine leadership skills for sustainable development, as discussed in Chapter 1 and echoed once again here, may strike you as naïve, or the excited byproduct of wishful thinking. Yet others are calling for them as well, in less naked and more procedural terms. The President's Council on Sustainable Development, for example, in its lead document entitled Sustainable America, phrases the need in this fashion:[6]

> An economy that creates good jobs and safeguards public health and the environment will be stronger and more resilient than one that does not. A country that protects its ecosystems and manages its natural resources wisely lays a far stronger base for future prosperity than one that carelessly uses its assets and destroys its natural capital . . . . Prosperity, fairness, and a healthy environment are interrelated elements of the human dream for a better future. Sustainable development is a way to pursue that dream through choice and policy.

If Abraham Lincoln were alive today, I could see him saying the above, with emphasis on the pursuit of a different dream. The skills noted with the necessary brevity here boil down to the questions of "choice and policy" which the PCSD pursued in its 186-page document, and its subsequent documents, now available on the Web and cited several times in this section.

In the next few decades, an unprecedented cluster of national leaders must emerge across the globe with these common traits and goals. They must recalibrate existing consumer choices and corporate and governmental polices with such looming questions as greenhouse gases and sustainable yields in mind. The logical and emotional consequences of Rio and Kyoto are the liberation and social support of such a new generation of leaders. What follows attempts to connect this itemization of personal leadership skills to the larger questions of organizational change and personal restraint.

THE CONCEPT OF MOVING BEYOND BLAME

In my earlier book, *In Search of Environmental Excellence*, I stated the following, which still rings true in any discussion of sustainability:[7]

> One of the distinguishing features of the environmental movement is its inclusiveness. Men and women, rich and poor, far and near, are all beginning to ask the same set of questions. As they take off their masks and discover that the battle to save the environment is a journey that cuts across all societal divisions, we discover how universal the concerns for environmental health and safety have become. Throughout the 1990s, the primal issue of mobilizing a response to shared

global challenges will bind generations, races, and nations, and inspire sustained human interest.

Environmental excellence, moreover, is not just stopping mistakes. It is also the search for better answers, an elaborate spiral of greater efficiency, less waste, and saved materials. Sometimes the pursuit involves subtle reversals of institutional trends, reversal which in small ways inspires considerable improvements.

Clearly, the sustainable development debate needs to center itself around the concept of moving beyond blame. Otherwise we will never achieve equity, environmental quality, and economic yields at once, especially if the world obeys the predictions that call for an eightfold increase of economic activity on the path to a sustainable future. But how can we best attach these concepts of moving beyond blame, personal restraint, and leadership skills to a thriving enterprise? In other words, how can we ground these attributes in a reliable set of institutional homes?

HOW CAN WE BEST CULTIVATE LEADERSHIP IN SUSTAINABLE ENTERPRISES?

It has been over 28 years since the birth of American environmentalism, so we all know that the search for environmental excellence is not a straight road. Back in 1990, I warned:[8]

> The road to environmental excellence is not smoothly paved with the certainties of science, nor clearly marked by a legalistic black-and-white view of what's ahead. The desire for an easy ride in the search for answers will often be frustrated by confusion and fears. In response, the technocratic elite may propose to repave the road in order to give the issue the appearance of certainty.

As we enter the next century, I am happy to see that much of my warning was unnecessary. Few expect the debate over sustainable development to be paved over by scientific certainty or legalistic spin doctors, and practically no one expects the issue to take on the appearance of certainty that I had feared in 1990.

Nevertheless, we need more than ever to educate future citizens and leaders for judgments that allow sustainable options. How can this be done? In an effort to answer such an unascertainable question, I will expand my past definitions of environmental excellence by attempting to connect them with stages, or choices, we have within our own careers.

While Maslow's spiral of self-actualization sums up the predicament quite nicely, the following chart (Figure A-2) replaces the question in the commonplace terms of professional success. I do this because I suspect that it is lot easier for successful, "reputation-rich" professionals in the prime of their careers to worry about sustainable development than, say, college freshmen. One reason sustainability seminars fail on most campuses is because the subject requires a maturity of concerns more apt to be found in Elderhostel.

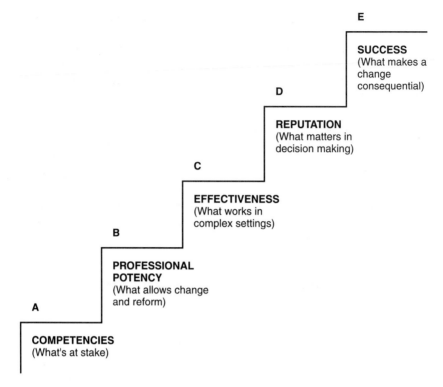

- Note how D and E pull A, B, and C up the chain
- Note how you can't get D and E without A, B, and C

Figure A-2   The Great Chain of Professional Expectations

Source: Assembled by Bruce Piasecki for Environmental Management Seminar at RPI.

LEADERSHIP AND ITS COMPLEXITIES IN REGARD TO SUSTAINABLE DEVELOPMENT

Dante had it right when he said, "He listens well who takes notes." There are musical directives to the great medieval poet's claim that understanding "the act of listening well" takes an effort. Like reading, listening to the leaders is not easy. Yet what a dire necessity for corporate survival each click of a signal, each step of the way, gives us in our work.

Often we are lost on our way, confused at mid-step, because we neglect to listen to the direction given to us by a leader long before we are patient enough to understand.

As discussed in Chapter 8, John Kotter, in his Harvard Business Review text, *Leading Change,* aptly notes eight common modes of failure in attempts to transform complex organizations.[9] Here again, in miniature, are Kotter's eight warnings.

> ### JOHN KOTTER'S COMMON ERRORS IN ORGANIZATIONAL CHANGE
>
> - Allowing too much complacency
> - Failing to create a sufficiently powerful coalition
> - Understanding the power of vision
> - Failure to communicate the vision by a factor of ten
> - Permitting obstacles to block the new vision
> - Failing to create short-term wins
> - Declaring too soon
> - Neglecting to anchor changes firmly in corporate culture
>
> *Source:* John Kotter, *Leading Change*, Harvard University Press, MA, 1995.

In many ways, this book's focus on leadership has been assembled to outsmart these common errors. Clearly, in response to Kotter's "Common Errors," sustainable development advocates must deflate complacency, erase probable obstacles, and reassert his vision, while never prematurely declaring victory. Yet let me spotlight the ways the environmental managers still base leads as a similar productive direction.

Kotter's best chapter is on the importance of generating short-term wins. He notes, "Having a good meeting usually doesn't qualify as the kind of unambiguous win needed in this phase, nor does getting two people to stop fighting, producing a new design that the engineering manager thinks is terrific, or sending 5,000 copies of a new vision statement around the company. Any of these actions may be important, but none is an example of a short-term win." Idealists often pronounce and rely upon such items that Kotter so aptly categorizes as inadequate.

"A good short-term win," Kotter boldly continues, "has at least these three characteristics: (1) It's visible; large numbers of people can see for themselves whether the result is real or just hype. (2) It's unambiguous; there can be little argument over the call. (3) It's clearly related to the change effort."

Sustainable development strategies is only one of a kind of social experiments we need to succeed in liberating twenty-first century environmental management and strategy. What I like about the drive for sustainability is its sophisticated awareness about the needs for limits and long-term planning. The concept refuses to get lost in the morass of its critics. We now know we must learn by doing. We cannot lose time in waiting for a more perfect government, or a more perfect moment for seizing the day's opportunities.

Kotter suggests eight ways to avoid common organizational errors. All eight strike me as remarkably right regarding the strategies we need to adopt before we can achieve sustainability, if even only regionally. The more I reread the other works in this text the more I become convinced that Kotter presents a superb summary of the kinds of hurdles most organizations will need to scale before they can make sustainability real.

While I've tried to simplify my arguments for this text by focusing on an imagined synthesis of attributes in "the leader of tomorrow," Kotter offers a sensible and related set of questions about organizational requirements, resources, and dynamics. Artists like Marguerite Wildenhain never needed to worry themselves with these overwhelming organizational concerns of the next 50 years. But the privileges of such isolated workmanship may be limited by the future because items of survival may strike many as more urgent.

Perhaps, we need to worry as much in the next century about personal restraint as we need to fret about organizational capacity and readiness to change. Both are essential, even inevitable items, unless we allow ourselves to be subsumed by civilization's discontent and technical loathing. Although in this text we have looked to present a sampling of the skills that environmental leaders are using in business, I suspect a blend of Marguerite Wildenhain's personal rigor with Kotter's insights on organizational change will be the only available answer in the near future for organizational change.

NOTES

1. Wildenhain, Marguerite, *The Invisible Core: A Potter's Life and Thoughts,* Pacific Books, Palo Alto, CA, 1973.
2. President's Council on Sustainable Development (PCSD) documents are accessible at www.whitehouse.gov/PCSD/.
3. Piasecki, Bruce and Peter Asmus, *In Search of Environmental Excellence: Moving Beyond Blame,* Simon & Schuster, New York, 1990.
4. President's Council on Sustainable Development (PCSD) documents are accessible at www.whitehouse.gov/PCSD/.
5. Phillips, Donald, *Lincoln on Leadership: Executive Strategies for Tough Times,* Warner Books, New York, 1993.
6. President's Council on Sustainable Development (PCSD) documents are accessible at www.whitehouse.gov/PCSD/.
7. Piasecki, Bruce and Peter Asmus, *In Search of Environmental Excellence: Moving Beyond Blame,* Simon & Schuster, New York, 1990.
8. Piasecki, Bruce and Peter Asmus, *In Search of Environmental Excellence: Moving Beyond Blame,* Simon & Schuster, New York, 1990.
9. Kotter, John, *Leading Change,* Harvard Business School Press, Boston, MA, 1996.

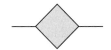

Appendix:
Sources of Environmental
Management Information

INTERNET MATERIALS

With the acknowledgment that addresses and information are dynamic and web sites often move or are discarded, we offer the following sites as samples of the type of information available through the web. Many of the organizations mentioned in this text have sites of there own worthy of a look. Yet, we have decided not to include those company sites, and instead focus on general information and links to environmental information.

Academy of Management (AOM): http://www.aom.pace.edu
AOM's Organizations and the Natural Environment Interest Group: http://web.mit.edu/slrothen/www/ONE.html
Committee for the National Institute for the Environment: http://www.cnie.org
Environmental Careers World Online: http://environmental-jobs.com
Environmental Organization Web Directory: http://www.webdirectory.com
Environmental News Service: http://www.ens-news.com
President's Council for Sustainable Development: http://www1.whitehouse.gov/PCSD
Sustainable Business Network: http://www.envirolink.org
Electronic Network of Environmental Professionals: http://www.envision.net
Tomorrow magazine Website: http://www.tomorrow-web.com
World Resources Institute: http://www.wri.org

JOURNALS/ARTICLES

Below are a few of the journals that publish environmental-business information on a consistent basis. While there are other journals with similar contents, these focus on options for change through case studies and in-depth articles and presentations.

Business and the Environment, Cutter Information Corp., 37 Broadway, Arlington, MA 02174, Phone: (617)641-5125, Fax: (617)648-1950, e-mail: bate@igc.apc.org

Corporate Environmental Strategy: The Journal of Environmental Leadership, c/o AHC Group, Inc., Editorial Offices, 1223 Peoples Avenue, Troy, NY 12180, Phone: (518)276-2669, Fax: (518)276-6380, e-mail: ces@ahcgroup.com. CES is available on Lexis-Nexis at www.Lexis-Nexis.com and published by Elsevier Science.

Environmental Quality Management, John Wiley & Sons, Inc., 605 Third Avenue, New York, 10158, Phone: (212)850-6479, e-mail: SUBINFO@wiley.com

Greener Management International: The Journal of Corporate Environmental Strategy and Prac-tice, Interleaf Productions Limited, Broom Hall, 8–10 Broomhall Road, Sheffield S10 2DR, UK

Organization & Environment, Sage Publications, Inc., 2455 Teller Rd., Thousands Oaks, CA 91320, Phone: (805)499-0721, Fax: (805)499-0871, e-mail: order@sagepub.com

Tomorrow magazine, Tomorrow Publishing, Halsingegatan 9, 113 23 Stockholm, Sweden, Phone: 46-8-33-5290, Fax: 46-8-32-9333, e-mail: info@tomorrow.se

BOOKS ON ENVIRONMENTAL MANAGEMENT

Below are books that are devoted to exploring the intersection of organizational behavior and environmental management. This is, of course, a very short list, and we apologize for all of those fine texts that are not represented here.

Changing Course: A Global Business Perspective on Development and the Environment, by Stephan Schmidheiny, MIT Press, Cambridge, MA, 1992.

Corporate Environmental Strategy: The Avalanche of Change Since Bhopal, by Bruce W. Pi-asecki, John Wiley & Sons, New York, 1995.

Earth in the Balance: Ecology and the Human Spirit, by Vice President Al Gore, Houghton Mifflin, New York, 1992.

Environmental Strategies for Industry: International Perspectives on Research Needs and Policy Implications, edited by Kurt Fischer and Johan Schot, Island Press, Washington, DC, 1993.

From Heresy to Dogma: An Institutional History of Corporate Environmentalism, by Andrew J. Hoffman, New Lexington Press, San Francisco, 1997.

In Search of Environmental Excellence: Moving Beyond Blame, by Bruce W. Piasecki, Simon & Schuster, New York, 1990.

Measuring Corporate Environmental Performance: Best Practices for Costing and Managing an Effective Environmental Strategy, by Marc J. Epstein, Irwin Professional Publishing, Chicago, 1996.

Practical Guide to Environmental Management (7th ed.), by Frank B. Friedman, Environ-mental Law Institute, Washington, DC, 1997.

The Ecology of Commerce: A Declaration of Sustainability, by Paul Hawken, Harper Busi-ness, New York, 1993.

The Greening of Industry Resource Guide and Bibliography, edited by Peter Groenewegen, Kurt Fischer, Edith G. Jenkins, and Johan Schot, Island Press, Washington DC, 1996.

BOOKS ON MANAGEMENT, CHANGE, LEADERSHIP, AND RELATED TOPICS

As we have argued throughout this book, too often the field of environmental management and business strategy is lost in information and dispute without looking

to the research and writing outside of the field for additional guidance on decision making. Below is a selected list of books which may be of value as you build your skill-base and effectiveness as a leader in your organization.

Becoming a Master Manager: A Competency Framework (2nd ed.), by Robert E. Quinn et al., John Wiley & Sons, New York, 1996.

Leading Change, by John Kotter, Harvard Business School Press, Cambridge, MA, 1996.

Lincoln on Leadership: Executive Strategies for Tough Times, by Donald T. Phillips, Warner Books, New York, 1995.

Organizational Culture and Leadership (2nd ed.), by Edgar H. Schein, Jossey-Bass Publishers, San Francisco, 1992.

Organizing Genius, by Warren Bennis and Patricia Ward Biederman, Addison-Wesley Publishing Company, Reading, MA, 1997.

The Art of War (translation), by Sun Tzu, Oxford University Press, New York, 1963.

The Book of Five Rings (translation), by Miyamoto Musashi, Bantam Books, New York, 1982.

The Change Masters: Innovation and Entrepreneurship in the American Corporation, by Rosabeth Moss Kanter, Simon & Schuster, New York, 1983.

The Fifth Discipline: The Art and Practice of the Learning Organization, by Peter Senge, Currency Doubleday, New York, 1994.

The Tao of Personal Leadership, by Diane Dreher, Harper Business, New York, 1996.

The Ultimate Business Library: Fifty Books that Shaped Management Thinking, by Stuart Crainer, Capstone Publishing Limited, Oxford, UK, 1997.

When Corporations Ruled the World, by David Korten, Kumerian Press, San Francisco, 1995.

SELECTED ENVIRONMENTAL READINGS FROM WRI-MEB SURVEY

In 1998, World Resources Institute's (WRI) Management Institute for Environment and Business (MEB) conducted a survey of environmental educators and business faculty to discover the dominant readings and instructional material being presented to business students taking environmental coursework. The list below represents information from this report, titled "Grey Pinstripes with Green Ties: MBA Programs Where the Environment Matters." (The items are listed in order based on the number of votes received.)

The Ecology of Commerce: A Declaration of Sustainability, by Paul Hawken, Harper Collins, New York, 1993.

Changing Course: A Global Business Perspective on Development and the Environment, by Stephan Schmidheiny, MIT Press, Cambridge, MA, 1992.

State of the World, by Lester R. Brown et al., Worldwatch Institute, published annually.

"Green and Competitive," by Michael E. Porter and Claas van der Linde, *Harvard Business Review,* September–October 1995.

"A Natural Resource-Based View of the Firm," by Stuart L. Hart, *Management Review,* October 1995.

"Beyond Greening: Strategies for a Sustainable World," by Stuart L. Hart, *Harvard Business Review,* January–February 1997.

Earth in the Balance: Ecology and the Human Spirit, by Al Gore, Plume Press, New York, 1993.

Costing the Earth, by Frances Cairncross, Harvard Business School Press, Cambridge, MA, 1991.

Silent Spring, by Rachel Carson, Houghton Mifflin, New York, 1994 (re-release).

Measuring Corporate Environmental Performance: Best Practices for Costing and Managing an Effective Environmental Strategy, by Marc J. Epstein, Irwin Press, San Francisco, 1995.

Index

ABB, 11
Absorbent gelling material (AGM), 232
Accounting process, 107–120
Adaptive strategy, 237
Addison, Ed, 312, 316
Adler, Peter, 202
Administrative hearings, 252
ADR, 250–252
Adversarial politics, 331
Adversarial strategy, 236
Agren, Chris, 203
Alestra, 158
Allen, Bob, 152
Allenby, Braden R., 151
Alternative dispute resolution (ADR), 250–252
Amoco, 288
Anderson, Deborah D., 226
Anheuser-Busch Corporation, 180–191
Anticipatory issues management, 226–243
    action plan development/execution, 240, 241
    adaptive strategy, 237
    adversarial strategy, 236
    building stakeholder support, 238–240
    dialogue and mutual solution development, 237

issue change strategy, 236, 237
issue identification/prioritization, 230–235
issue life cycle, 226, 227
issues analysis, 232, 235, 236
opportunity for competitive edge, 228, 229
Apple Computer, 11
AQIRP, 131
Arbitration, 252
Archer, Steve, 294
ARCO, 103, 123–136
Art of War, The (Sun Tzu), 30
Aswald, Kersten, 202
AT&T, 6, 20, 103, 151–160, 296, 299
Atlantic Richfield Company (ARCO), 103, 123–136
Attorney-client privilege, 42
Audit confidentiality, 40–44
Audit privilege laws, 44
Audit privilege with voluntary self-disclosure laws, 44
Audit programs, 29–46
Auto/Oil Air Quality Improvement Research Program (AQIRP), 131

Bailey, Paul, 110
Bamberger, Audrey E., 180

Barton, Emily, 38
Beaton, Eric R., 30
Belanger, Jean, 217
Ben & Jerry's, 103
Bernstein, Carl, 107
Beyond blame strategies, 331
Body Shop, 103
Boethius, Olle, 194
Book of Five Rings, The (Musashi), 30, 214
Bowers, Dorothy, 296–298
Bradley, Bill, 3
Brent Spar incident, 230
Bristol Myers Squibb, 4, 118
British Telecommunications (BT), 304
Browning-Ferris Industries (BFI), 54
Budgetary process, 107–120
Building blocks of federal environmental law, 281
Buntrock, Dean L., 31
Buonicore, Anthony, 165
Burrus, Daniel, 175
Buschmann, Raymond, 43
Butler, Thomas A., 308

Canon Clean Earth Campaign, 122
Carbon sequestration, 322
CARE, 313–315

CARS, 38
Carter, William, 261
Cases. *See* Integrative cases
Cause and effect diagram, 162
CERES format, 285
CERES Help Guide: Instructions for Companies, 289
CERES Principles, 282
Cervin, Richard, 167
Chandler, Alfred D., Jr., 96, 98
Change management, 137–139
Changing language of environmental management, 101
Choices of Power, The (Roberts/Bluhm), 310
Clark, Kim, 142
Cleanup plan, 243–249
Cluster rule, 264, 269
Codes of management practice, 220
Collaborative problem-solving, 251
Coming Clean: Corporate Environmental Reporting, 297
Competence, 306
Compliance Action Reporting System (CARS), 38
Concept of Corporate Strategy (Andrews), 98
Consumer society, 331
Contingent liability costs, 110
Conventional costs, 110
Cook, Lodwrick M., 129
Cooper, Gail A., 263
Corporate environmental performance evaluation, 323–325
Corporate environmental strategy, 9
Corporate Environmental Strategy: The Avalanche of Change Since Bhopal (Piasecki), 9

Corporate Strategy (Ansoff), 98
Cost effectiveness, 59
Cost measures, 53
Costle, Doug, 74
Covey, Steven, 172
Crisis phase, 228
Cross-functional teams, 146
Cushman, John, 253

Dahlberg, Bill, 316, 318, 323
Data mining, 167, 168
Data warehousing, 167
Davis, Thomas S., 296
Deming, W. Edwards, 165
"Demystifying the Trend in Environmental Reports" (Poltorzycki/Hedstrom), 295
DePree, Max, 5
Descano, Linda, 212
Design for environment (DFE) programs, 19, 20, 140, 146, 147, 150–160
DFE programs, 19, 20, 140, 146, 147, 150–160
Dialogue and mutual solution development, 237
Dickerson, Kenneth R., 123, 127, 128, 136
Ditz, Daryl, 61
Dominant culture dynamics, 331
Dow Chemical, 11, 51, 62, 101, 288, 297, 304
Doyle, J. Andrew, 259
Du Pont, 11, 101, 275, 276, 287, 288

Easterbrook, Greg, 131
Eco-management and audit scheme (EMAS), 197, 198, 289
Effectiveness, 307
80/20 rule, 59
Elements of success, 104
EMAS, 197, 198, 289

Emergence, 227, 228
Emergency Preparedness and Community Right to Know Act, 55
Emergent culture dynamics, 331
Environmental accounting, 107–120
Environmental audit privilege law, 44
Environmental audit programs, 29–46
Environmental costs, 110
Environmental information management, 164–192
  Anheuser-Busch, 180–191
  benefits, 27
  change, and, 26
  information management activities, 167, 168
  planning for full cycle of information technology utilization, 179
  reengineering business processes, 174–179
  strategizing for proactive management, 172–174
  upgrading professional skills, 175
Environmental leadership, 329–338
  competence/potency/effectiveness, 306, 307
  decisions of business, and, 26
  great chain of professional expectations, 336
  personal skills, 4–7, 333
  public expectations, and, 213, 214

skills for identifying
business
opportunities, 105
Environmental
management
credibility gap, 13
Environmental
management
programs, 17–19,
137–163
Environmental metrics.
See Performance
measures
Environmental release
data, 287
Environmental reporting,
273–328
audience, 292–295,
303
content, 296–299
costs, 302, 303
evolution of
voluntary
reporting, 279–292
information laws,
289, 290
ISO 14000
standards, 290,
291
Nortel (PERI
guidelines),
277–279
PERI guidelines,
277–279, 284–286
preproduction
concerns/choices,
299, 300
private market
demands, 290,
291
production, 300–302
strategic issues, 295,
296
Environmental signature
programs, 322
Environmentalese, 15, 16
"EPA Final Policy
Statement on
Voluntary Self-Policing
and Self-Disclosure",
44
EPS, 199
Executive leadership
groups, 221

Facilitations, 251
Fair, Thomas, 71, 76
Feasibility studies, 165
Feldman, Stanley J., 212
First Things First
(Covey), 172
Forecasting, 230, 231
Forhman, Alan L., 139
Friedman, Frank, 6, 22,
30
Fukuyama, Francis,
225
Full-cost accounting, 114,
115, 118
*Fundamental Issues in
Strategy* (Rumelt), 95

Gade, Mary, 56
GEMI, 311
GEMI environmental
self-assessment
program, 285
General life cycle, 227
General Motors, 62
Getting to YES
(Fisher/Ury), 251
Gilding, Paul, 102
Gillette, 294
Global Environmental
Management Initiative
(GEMI), 311
Golden rule applied to
EHS management,
217. *See also*
Responsible Care
Good-deed stories, 298
Graham, Ann, 11
Grant, Robert, 96
Great chain of
professional
expectations, 336
Green, Phillip E.J., 162
Green Wall, 10–16
*Grey Pinstripes with Green
Ties: MBA Programs
Where the Environment
Matters*, 341
Guiton, Bonnie, 74
Gyllenhammar, Pehr,
192, 193, 203

Harms, Kimberly A., 32,
33, 35, 36
Harris, Victor, 214

Hart, Stuart, 101
Hellman, Thomas, 118
Henessey, Claudette, 184
Herbst, Timothy D., 254,
303
Hewlett Packard, 20
Hirsig, Alan, 274
Horkeby, Inge, 200, 201

IBM, 288, 304
ICC Business Charter,
281, 282
Image and relationship
costs, 110
*In Search of Environmental
Excellence: Moving
Beyond Blame*
(Piasecki), 331, 334
Informal discussions, 251
Information-forcing
laws, 289, 290
Information
management activities,
167, 168. *See also*
Environmental
information
management
Integrative cases
Niagara Mohawk
Power
Corporation,
71–88
Southern Company,
308–323
Volvo, 192–205
Intel, 140, 304
International Standards
Organization (ISO), 25
Internet, 304–306, 339
*Invisible Core: A Potter's
Life and Thoughts, The*
(Wildenhain), 329, 330
ISO, 25
ISO 14000 standards, 24,
25, 290, 291
Issue characterization,
235

Jansson, Ulf, 195
Jesus CEO (Jones), 312
Johnson & Johnson,
228
Journals/articles, 339,
340

Judicial decisions, 252
Juran, Joseph, 165
Juvenal, 221

Kaosei, 122
Karrberg, Anders S.
    Rison, 201
Kennedy, Keith, 39
Kennedy, Robert, 220
Kimberly Clark, 294
Kloepfer, Robert J., 16
Knapp, Charles, 166
Knowledge acquisition,
    167
Knowledge
    communication, 168
Kolb, David A., 139
Kotter, John, 138,
    336–338

Lagging indicators, 48
Landfill crisis, 230
LCA, 147–149
Leadership. See
    Environmental
    leadership
Leading Change (Kotter),
    138, 336, 337
Leading indicators, 48
Legislation, 100
Less-is-more approach to
    growth, 331
Life cycle assessment
    (LCA), 147–149
Life-cycle costing, 110
Liggett, Walter, 64
Lincoln, Abraham, 6, 7,
    333
Lober, Douglas J., 292
Lockheed-Martin, 140
Lucent Technologies,
    140, 299

Macauley, Dennis, 216,
    218, 219
Mach, Laurence, 295
MacLean, Richard, 109
Makower, Joel, 4
Malone, Tom, 50
Management
    information systems.
    See Environmental
    information
    management

Management systems
    verification, 221
Martin, Thomas, 309
Maxwell, James, 192
McDonalds, 12
Measurements. See
    Performance measures
Mediation, 251, 252
Member self evaluations,
    220
Mendelson, Frank, 211
Merck and Co., Inc., 288,
    296
Metadata, 66
Meyers, Erik J., 279, 303
Migliozzi, Leslie, 191
Minnesota Pollution
    Control Agency
    (MPCA), 52
Minter, Rob, 311, 317
MIS systems. See
    Environmental
    information
    management
Mitchell, James, 309
Mon, Joseph M., 151
Monsanto, 4, 294
Moral advantages, 103
MOTIV, 199, 200
Murdoch, Lynn, 191
Musashi, Miyamoto,
    214
Muska, Amy, 323
Mutual assistance, 222

National Environmental
    Policy Act (NEPA), 281
Negotiated Rulemaking
    Act, 255
Negotiations, 251
Nelson, Robert J., 254
NEPA, 281
New product
    development. See
    Product development
Niagara Mohawk Power
    Corporation, 71–88
Noranda, 288
Nortel, 277–279

OBD systems, 131
Ohmae, Kenichi, 96
Olen Properties, Inc. v.
    Sheldahl, Inc., 42, 43

OnBoard Diagnostic
    (OBD) systems, 131
Opportunity advantages,
    103
Organizational change,
    138, 139, 337

Paint industry (VOC
    standards), 254–262
Paradigm shift, 27
Partnership program,
    221, 222
Patagonia, 6, 103
Paulus, 76
PCSD, 332, 334
People and project
    stories, 298
Performance and
    compliance reporting,
    168
Performance measures,
    47–89
    acceptable risk, 65,
        66
    changing behavior,
        and, 60
    cost effectiveness, 59
    credible
        measurements, 67,
        68
    lagging indicators,
        48
    leading indicators,
        48
    measurement
        attributes, 52, 53
    record of current
        conditions, 66, 67
    selectivity, 67
PERI Guidelines,
    276–278, 284–286
Petroleum industry, 131,
    132, 290
Philip Morris
    Companies, 283
Piasecki, Bruce, 9, 211,
    331
Polaroid Corporation,
    280
Pollution Prevention
    Pays (3P) program, 54,
    55
Porter, Michael, 10, 99
Positioning, 214

Post-audit activities, 34
Potency, 306, 307
Potentially hidden costs, 110
Practical Guide to Environmental Management (Friedman), 30
Pre-audit activities, 34
Preempting the crisis. *See* Anticipatory issues management
President's Council on Sustainable Development (PCSD), 332, 334
Price theory, 97
Principled negotiations, 251
Principles of Scientific Management, The (Taylor), 97
Procter & Gamble, 230–232, 237, 239, 240, 293
Product development
    ARCO (reformulated gas), 123–136
    cross-functional teams, 146
    design for environment, and, 146, 147, 150
    key elements, 144, 145
    life cycle assessment, and, 147–149
    speed, 141, 142
    uncovering potential product alternatives, 150
Proof of concept pilot, 185
Public advisory panel, 220
Public disclosure. *See* Environmental reporting
Public expectations. *See* Environmental reporting, Stakeholder management

Pulp and paper industry (voluntary environmental stewardship program), 262–271

Quality measures, 53
Quinn, James Brian, 96

Raddatz, Alicia K., 40
Rainey, David, 140, 160
Rainforest Action Network (RAN), 304
Ranganathan, Janet, 61
Rappaport, Ann, 109
Rasmussen, Maria Bober, 300
Ratcliffe, David M., 308, 314, 317
Reengineering business processes, 174–179
Reengineering yourself, 175
Rees, Joseph, 221
Reference materials, 339–342
Regulation negotiation (reg-neg), 255
Reichold Chemicals, Inc., v. Textron, Inc., 43
Reporting. *See* Environmental reporting
Resolution phase, 228
Responsible Care, 216–226
    advantages, 222, 223
    codes of management practice, 220
    disadvantages, 224
    elements, 217
    executive leadership groups, 221
    guiding principles, 219, 220
    management systems verification, 221
    measures of performance, 220, 221
    member self evaluations, 220

    mutual assistance, 222
    origin, 217
    partnership program, 221, 222
    public advisory panel, 220
    results/effects, 225
Revolutionizing Product Development (Wheelwright/Clark), 142
Right to know legislation, 253, 275, 281, 325
Roig, Randy A., 37
Rooney, Philip B., 31
Root cause analysis, 37, 38
Rothenberg, Sandra, 192
Royal Dutch Shell, 304
Ruddock, Robert, 40
Rumelt, Richard, 95

SARA, 281
Saving the Earth (Brown/Flavin/Postel, 110
Schaffer, Amy E., 263
Schilling, Joseph, 250
Schmidheiny, Stephen, 99
Schneider, Peter, 37
Scientific management, 97
Self-evaluation privilege, 43
Shell Oil, 230
Shelton, Robert D., 10, 57
Short-term wins, 337
Signature programs, 322
Silent Spring (Carson), 98, 228
Sludge, 271n
Smart, Bruce, 99
Smith, Adam, 97
Smith, Cornelius, 192
Socially responsible investing (SRI), 324
Sokol, David, 71
Sources of environmental management information, 339–342

Southern Company, 308–323
Soyka, Peter A., 212
Spitzer, Marty, 332
SRI, 324
Stakeholder
  management, 216–272
    alternative dispute
      resolution,
      250–252
    anticipatory issues
      management,
      226–243
    paint industry (VOC
      standards),
      254–262
    pulp and paper
      industry
      (voluntary
      environmental
      stewardship
      program), 262–271
    Responsible Care,
      216–226
    Wichita, Kansas
      cleanup plan,
      243–249
Standards, 24, 25
Stein, Jack, 191
Stern, Aliza, 243
Sterner, Kerstin, 201
Strategic advantages, 103
Strategic environmental
  management, 20–22
Strategy/strategic
  thinking, 95–106
Strategy and Structure
  (Chandler), 98
Sugar, J. William, 191
Sun Microsystems, 20

Superfund Amendments
  and Reauthorization
  Act (SARA), 281
Sustainable
  development, 85,
  329–338
System optimization, 85

Taylor, Frederick, 97
Tenneco Gas, 58
Terrain advantages, 103
Tholander, Magnus, 202
3M, 11, 54, 55, 294
Time measures, 53
Total quality
  environmental
  management (TQEM),
  153, 161–163
Total quality
  management (TQM),
  161
Toxic Release Inventory
  (TRI), 55, 281, 324
TQEM, 153, 161–163
TQM, 161
Tree-planting program,
  322
TRI, 55, 281, 324
Triggering event, 228
Trust: The Social Virtues
  and the Creation of
  Prosperity (Fukuyama),
  225
Tylenol crisis, 228

U.S. federal
  mandates/data
  requirements, 168
U.S. laws, 100
United Technologies, 288

Vague audit report
  approach, 41, 42
Valdez Principles, 282
Van Epps, Ronald E., 49
Voluntary environmental
  reporting, 279–292
Voluntary environmental
  stewardship program,
  262–271
Volvo, 192–205

Walters, Susan D., 50
Warner Lambert, 11
Wass, Urban, 199
Wells, Richard, 163
Wendoll, Robert, 259,
  260
Western Electric, 154
Wheel of corporate
  decision making, 165
Wheelwright, Steven,
  142
Whiston, James, 220
White, E.B., 307
Wichita, Kansas cleanup
  plan, 243–249
Wild card events, 231
Wildenhain, Marguerite,
  329, 330, 338
WMX Technologies, Inc.,
  30–40, 52, 288, 294
Woodall, Robert, 308,
  312, 317
Woodward, Bob, 107
Work product doctrine,
  43
World Wide Web
  (WWW), 304–306

Xerox, 20, 101